Gender and Change

Gender and Change

Agency, Chronology and Periodisation

EDITED BY

ALEXANDRA SHEPARD
AND
GARTHINE WALKER

⊛WILEY-BLACKWELL

A John Wiley & Sons, Ltd., Publication

This edition first published 2009
Originally published as Volume 20, Issue 3 of *Gender & History*
Chapters © 2009 The Authors
Book compilation © 2009 Blackwell Publishing Ltd

Blackwell Publishing was acquired by John Wiley & Sons in February 2007. Blackwell's publishing program has been merged with Wiley's global Scientific, Technical, and Medical business to form Wiley-Blackwell.

Registered Office
John Wiley & Sons Ltd, The Atrium, Southern Gate, Chichester, West Sussex, PO19 8SQ, United Kingdom

Editorial Offices
350 Main Street, Malden, MA 02148-5020, USA
9600 Garsington Road, Oxford, OX4 2DQ, UK
The Atrium, Southern Gate, Chichester, West Sussex, PO19 8SQ, UK

For details of our global editorial offices, for customer services, and for information about how to apply for permission to reuse the copyright material in this book please see our website at www.wiley.com/wiley-blackwell.

The right of Alexandra Shepard and Garthine Walker to be identified as the authors of the editorial material in this work has been asserted in accordance with the Copyright, Designs and Patents Act 1988.

Wiley also publishes its books in a variety of electronic formats. Some content that appears in print may not be available in electronic books.

Designations used by companies to distinguish their products are often claimed as trademarks. All brand names and product names used in this book are trade names, service marks, trademarks or registered trademarks of their respective owners. The publisher is not associated with any product or vendor mentioned in this book. This publication is designed to provide accurate and authoritative information in regard to the subject matter covered. It is sold on the understanding that the publisher is not engaged in rendering professional services. If professional advice or other expert assistance is required, the services of a competent professional should be sought.

Library of Congress Cataloging-in-Publication Data

Gender and change: agency, chronology, and periodisation / edited by Alexandra Shepard and Garthine Walker.
    p. cm.
    Originally published as volume 20, issue 3 of Gender & history.
    Includes bibliographical references and index.
    ISBN 978-1-4051-9227-9 (pbk.: alk. paper) 1. Sex role—History. 2. Gender identity—History. 3. Women—History.
4. Women—Social conditions. I. Shepard, Alexandra. II. Walker, Garthine. III. Gender & history.
    HQ1075.G3727 2009
    305.409—dc22

                            2009006561

A catalogue record for this book is available from the British Library.

Set in 10.5/12.5pt Times NR Monotype
by Aptara, India

01   2009

This volume is dedicated to the memory of Jeanne Boydston 1944–2008

Contents

NOTES ON CONTRIBUTORS

Lynn Abrams is Professor of Gender History at the University of Glasgow. She is the author of *The Making of Modern Woman: Europe 1789–1918* (2002) and *Myth and Materiality in a Woman's World: Shetland 1800–2000* (2005) and co-edited *Gender in Scottish History since 1700* (2006). Her current research focuses on Scottish masculinity and theories of oral history.

Padma Anagol is a lecturer in History at Cardiff University. She has written widely on women's agency and resistance during the colonial period of Indian history. She has authored *The Emergence of Feminism in India, 1850–1920* (2006) and *Laxmibai Dravid and the Birth of the Hindu Right* (forthcoming).

Judith M. Bennett teaches medieval history and women's history at the University of Southern California. She has published extensively on peasant women, women's work, female sexuality and 'singlewomen'. Her most recent book, *History Matters: Patriarchy and the Challenge of Feminism* (2006), examines the growing chasm between feminism and history.

Jeanne Boydston was, until 2008, Robinson Edwards Professor of American History at the University of Wisconsin-Madison, where she taught in the graduate programme in the history of gender and women. Her research interests focused on the historical formation of discrete discourses of gender. Her publications include *Home and Work: Housework, Wages, and the Ideology of Labor in the Early Republic* (1990), and the co-authored or co-edited *The Limits of Sisterhood: The Beecher Sisters on Women's Rights and Woman's Sphere* (1988); *Root of Bitterness: Documents in the Social History of American Women* (1996). Tragically, she did not live to see her contribution to this volume in print.

Lynda L. Coon teaches early medieval gender history at the University of Arkansas. Her recent publications include: 'Gender and the Body', in Julia M. H. Smith and Thomas F. X. Noble (eds), *The Cambridge History of Christianity 3: 600–1100* (2008), and 'What is the Word if not Semen? Priestly Bodies in Carolingian Exegesis', in Leslie Brubaker and Julia M. H. Smith (eds), *Gender in the Early Medieval World: East and West, 300–900* (2004).

Monica H. Green is Professor of History at Arizona State University. She has published extensively on the history of women's healthcare, including *Making Women's Medicine Masculine: The Rise of Male Authority in Pre-Modern Gynaecology* (2008). She is currently studying the early history of gynaecological and obstetrical surgery in Europe and the comparative history of women's healthcare.

Martha Howell is the Miriam Champion Professor of History at Columbia University in New York. She is the author of *Women, Production and Patriarchy in Late Medieval Cities* and *The Marriage Exchange: Property, Social Place and Gender in Cities of the Low Countries*. She has also co-authored several books including *From Reliable Sources* and has co-edited several collections concerning society and economy in the late medieval north. At present, she is completing a book called *Commerce Before Capitalism: European Market Culture, 1300–1600*.

Kevin Passmore is Reader in History at Cardiff University. He has edited *Writing History: Theory and Practice* and *Women, Gender and Fascism*, and is the author of *Fascism: A Very Short Introduction*. He is currently completing a history of the right in the French Third Republic.

Alexandra Shepard teaches early modern history at the University of Glasgow. She is the author of *Meanings of Manhood in Early Modern England* (2003) and several articles on the history of masculinity, and is currently researching perceptions of worth and social status in relation to gender and the life course in early modern England.

Dror Wahrman is the Ruth N. Halls Professor of History and Director of the Center for Eighteenth-Century Studies at Indiana University. His publications include *The Making of the Modern Self* (2004) and *Imagining the Middle Class: The Political Representation of Class in Britain* c.1780–1840 (1995). His current book project, with Jonathan Sheehan (Berkeley), is on western notions of order and disorder, randomness and chance, causality and providence from the seventeenth to the nineteenth centuries.

Garthine Walker is Senior Lecturer in History at Cardiff University. Her publications include *Crime, Gender and Social Order in Early Modern England* (2003) and (as editor) *Writing Early Modern History* (2005), and a number of essays on aspects of crime, gender relations and historical theory.

Merry E. Wiesner-Hanks is a Distinguished Professor in the Department of History at the University of Wisconsin-Milwaukee. She is the co-editor of the *Sixteenth Century Journal* and the author or editor of twenty books and many articles that have appeared in English, German, Italian, Spanish and Chinese. These include *Women and Gender in Early Modern Europe* (3rd edn 2008) and *Gender in History* (2001).

1 Gender, Change and Periodisation

Alexandra Shepard and Garthine Walker

This volume marks the twentieth anniversary of *Gender & History* by revisiting and reasserting the potential of women's history and gender history both to complicate and, more fundamentally, to revise received narratives of change. As Ludmilla Jordanova has observed, periodisation hinges on the privileging of particular vantage points and the selection of 'symbolic markers' according to 'the weight given to distinct fields of human activity', and thus constitutes 'a form of classification of the past'.[1] Associated narratives of change are also determined by issues of scale, depending on whether the lens of analysis is focused, to use Fernand Braudel's calibration, on the *longue durée*, the *conjoncture*, or the *événementiel*, and depending on our formulation of the relationship between structure and agency.[2] Despite historians' oft-articulated dissatisfaction with traditional period markers associated with teleological accounts of western civilisation – 'ancient', 'medieval', 'renaissance', 'reformation', 'early modern', 'modern' – their usage persists even if the narratives recounted about them have undergone serious revision as a result of the inclusion of a wider range of historical actors and as the moral or analytical frameworks for the evaluation of change have been dismantled and/or reconfigured. The incorporation of women, and the beginnings of a broader gender analysis that encompasses masculinity, has done much to refine and challenge the characterisation of these epochs but little to question the validity of particular 'periods' as discrete units of study.

Questions of change and periodisation implicitly and explicitly informed women's history and feminist history from the beginning. The women's history that emerged in the 1960s and 1970s was not only inspired by second-wave feminism but also reflected its trajectories and themes. In the UK, for instance, where historians of women frequently had ties to the political Left and the labour movement, women's history was simultaneously informed by and constituted part of developments in social and labour history. Sheila Rowbotham's *Hidden from History* (1973) began with the words: 'This book comes very directly from a political movement'; she was motivated by the desire to 'unravel historically' questions that arose in 'the women's liberation movement and on the Left about the situation of women in contemporary capitalism'.[3] Such concerns had precursors in the work of early twentieth-century scholars, notably Alice Clark (1919) and Ivy Pinchbeck (1930), who investigated the impact on women's work and lives of industrialisation and technological developments. New editions of Clark's book were issued in 1968, 1982 and 1992, and Pinchbeck's in 1969, 1977 and 1981, when feminist interest in these issues was rekindled.[4] In the US, where feminist activism was commonly connected to the civil rights movement, much women's history of the 1960s and 1970s shared liberal concerns about women's claims to citizens' rights.[5] Earlier scholarship here had similarly focused on women's rights and suffrage, the *History of Women's Suffrage* (1881) being perhaps the best known example.[6] By the end of the 1980s, the contributions to a volume marking the state of women's history internationally, which spanned twenty-two countries and all continents, demonstrated the extent to which contemporary feminism not only stimulated women's history but also injected it with a particular flavour according to diverse national and cultural contexts.[7]

Histories of women inspired by feminism sought both to chart the changes over time that brought women to their present circumstances and to create change in the present in order to produce a future for them that was different from their past. The question of where women fitted into conventional accounts of change over time was rapidly reframed to ask, first, *did* women fit into such historical narratives at all, and second, were such changes positive or negative for women? Joan Kelly's 1977 essay on whether women had a Renaissance is perhaps the most-cited example. Indeed, Kelly believed that interrogating accepted schemes of periodisation from women's perspective was one of 'the tasks of women's history'. She argued that, while conventional accounts of the Renaissance presented it as a period of great cultural progress, women's legal, economic and political conditions in the fifteenth and sixteenth centuries deteriorated rather than improved. Kelly's work had implications for the history of the Renaissance as much as for the history of women. The association of the Renaissance as a period of great cultural progress is challenged if conditions declined for some half of the European population.[8] Over the past four decades, historians have applied similar questions to other centuries and regions.[9]

While familiar periodising categories have been declared inappropriate for the history of women, they have not usually been replaced by alternative schemas. Historians have been less diligent in investigating the role of women and gender in *constituting* change.[10] In work on women and gender in history, questions of periodisation and change appear often to have been jettisoned altogether in favour of continuities and stasis. Partly this is a consequence of viewing History as a story of progress and women's emancipation as the standard by which 'progress' for women is evaluated. Hence Gerda Lerner's assertion in 1975 that 'all history as we now know it is, for women, merely pre-history'.[11] This not only applies to textbooks and surveys (where broad brushstrokes are typical and not reserved for women's history) but also constitutes a metanarrative favoured by certain kinds of women's history, especially that informed by radical feminism with its emphasis upon the transhistorical nature of patriarchy and women's oppression by men.[12] Mary Daly's *Gyn/Ecology: The Metaethics of Radical Feminism* (1978), for example, roared across periods and continents, finding and illuminating patriarchy's horrors in Indian sati, Chinese footbinding, African genital mutilation, European witch burning and American gynaecology. In this story of misogyny, women are accorded little agency; or rather, their agency is punished by a society that insists upon their inferiority. For radical feminists, patriarchy, whatever form it takes, always and inevitably insists upon the oppression of women by men. Change over time from this perspective was insignificant as, over the centuries, patriarchy merely shifted to oppress women in new ways. Some forms of women's history did allow for the potential of women's agency and change within existing social, economic and political structures. Liberal feminists, for instance, emphasised the role of education in bringing about change in women's status relative to men, while socialist feminists viewed such change as the desired and possible outcome of a broader restructuring of economic and political life.

From the outset, historians of women lamented the inadequacies, limitations and inapplicability of existing explanatory and theoretical frameworks within academic history.[13] Women's history played a key role in the development of new methods and approaches to historical research in dialogue with practitioners of the then 'new' social history, the Annales School, and feminist scholars in other disciplines. Historians of women were also at the cutting edge of historical research in the 1980s and 1990s. One such development was that of comparative women's histories across nations and continents as well as time. The International Federation for Research in Women's History/Fédération internationale pour la recherche de l'histoire des femmes was founded in 1987 in order to foster such comparisons. Another was the cultural or linguistic turn, as historians of women, sexuality and masculinity were among the first to explore the implications of linguistic theories – especially post-structuralism – for History as a discipline.

The emergence of 'gender' as an analytic category is often associated with this shift as if there was a linear evolution from a focus on feminism (politics) to women (specialised history) to gender (theory). But this is an oversimplification of a far more complex trajectory.[14] However defined, historians continue to explore and publish research categorised as women's and as gender history and, in many instances, the distinction between them is false. The concept of gender was not new in 1986 when Joan Scott first published her essay on gender as a category of historical analysis (nor did she claim it to be). Nor did it 'replace' or sideline women's history. In fact, both *Gender & History* and *The Journal of Women's History* were founded in 1989, and *Women's History Review* followed three years later. Issues of gender – the consequences of being male or female, the meanings ascribed to femininity and masculinity, the manner in which those categories are constructed, the practical repercussions of gendered language and concepts, and the relation of gender to power – were already present in women's history and feminist scholarship in the 1960s and 1970s.[15]

The category of gender was most thoroughly defined and theorised for historians by Joan Scott in 1986, and rapidly became the most popular tool employed to dig deeper below the top soil that earlier women's historians had turned up.[16] Scott's article is one of the most cited historical works of its time, leading to comparisons with E. P. Thompson in terms of its influence on the discipline in general.[17] So great an impact has her definition had that twenty years later, the editors of one volume of gender history describe the concept of gender in Scott's words without acknowledgement in either the text or notes.[18] Scott's achievement was not to invent 'gender' but to define and theorise it as an analytic category in a more nuanced and sophisticated way than historians had done hitherto, and to present a *method* of analysing the concept at work in any historical period. A great strength of this definition and approach lies in its potential to identify and analyse not only gender but also other categories such as class, race, religion, ethnicity, or any other form of difference, and – crucially – the ways in which they operate together discursively to legitimate or undermine historically specific relationships of power. Gender thus offered a lens by which historians could explore not only relations between the sexes, women, or sexuality, but also markets, classes, diplomacy and, indeed, masculinity. An approach that disrupted what seemed to be fixed oppositions such as nature/culture and public/private, and the analysis of how such language and concepts changed over time and in different contexts, did allow for agency and change. However, not everybody has interpreted Scott's argument in this way.

The most heated responses to Scott's work are perhaps from those who made little or no distinction between her debt to post-structuralism and what they believed to be the grave implications for the discipline of History of post-structural linguistic theory in its purest form. In particular, critics suggested that the kind of gender history advocated by Scott locked women into a position of inferiority via binary oppositions in language, which allowed no room for change and, therefore, agency on the part of women and other subaltern groups. A category of analysis that privileged language (and representations) rather than experience (and reality) at its heart was both 'difficult' and 'dangerous' when applied to women's history.[19] Some works of gender history may seem to (re)produce a history of gender that looks very much the same no matter which century or culture is examined. This, however, reflects a broader methodological shift that is not confined to gender historians. The cultural turn has brought with it losses as well as gains. While the influence of post-structuralism, literary and cultural theory, and symbolic anthropology has generated qualitative and textual analyses of particular historical moments, there is little attempt to explain change over time in much historical writing. It is perhaps this, rather than the concept of gender *per se*, that distinguishes much recent gender history from the women's history of the 1970s. Yet change and periodisation were already thorny problems within women's history: the tendency to measure change in terms of either progress or decline, liberation or repression, or alternatively to see these issues as transhistorical; the recognition that the category of 'woman'/'women' itself collapsed in the face of the plurality of women's experiences that defied generalisation about 'the position of women' and therefore its measurement over time. The fact that gender history proved not necessarily to solve all of these problems is not simply a matter of 'gender' leading us astray from what was otherwise a clearly lit path.

Neither have questions of chronology and periodisation been at the forefront of the history of masculinity since its dramatic growth out of the 'new men's studies' of the 1980s. Some of the blame can again be laid at the door of the 'new' cultural history. Emerging alongside the cultural turn, the history of masculinity has emphasised the multiplicity and contingency of male identities, rather than a category that might be traced in a singular way across a linear time scale, and has prioritised representation above the material and subjective realities of men's lives which provide the key to understanding historical agency and the link to questions of causation. As Laura Lee Downs has put it, 'without some way of connecting discursive process to social experience, historians are hard put to *explain* how the meanings of masculine and feminine might shift over time' – let alone how gender has been a constitutive part of wider processes of transition.[20] The most ambitious account of change over time has been undertaken not by a historian, but by the sociologist R. W. Connell, in an attempt to identify the long-term roots of hegemonic forms of contemporary Euro/American masculinity in the Reformation, the rise of individualism, and the relentless engine of imperialism.[21] As Konstantin Dierks has observed, the history of masculinity has tended to work within received metanarratives rather than engage or challenge them.[22]

This general diversion from issues of chronology and periodisation is reflected in the content and coverage of *Gender & History* over the last twenty years. The inaugural volume of the journal included very little discussion of matters of change, with historiographical essays reflecting primarily on the relationship between women's history and gender history, alongside innovatory work in the history of masculinity. While less concerned with challenging established chronologies than with staking out a feminist agenda for the analysis of enduring systems of patriarchal oppression, Judith M. Bennett's landmark essay in that volume implicitly invoked the *longue durée* as the appropriate time-span for gender historians – a point to which she returns in her reflections below.[23] However, subsequent contributors have mostly retained narrower and largely conventional timeframes. One notable exception by Julia M. H. Smith, examining the place of women in the extensive cultural adaptation associated with the transformation of the Roman world, demonstrates the potential of gender history to illuminate key phases of transition without sacrificing complexity or resorting to generalisations about the position of women.[24] Several other essays have similarly sought to integrate gender analysis to enrich existing accounts of change, for example in relation to class formation and its associated modes of capitalist patriarchy, or the reconfiguration of the medieval into the early modern Italian church.[25] Yet the challenges of reshaping established chronologies, while repeatedly lauded as a goal of gender history, have largely been overshadowed by the more urgent imperative of widening coverage in order both to reflect the myriad forms of gender construction and varied experiences of women and men, and to counter the Euro- and US-centrism of gender analysis.[26] *Gender & History* has arguably achieved more success in broadening its geographical than chronological coverage with reference to its stated aims of displacing periodisation based on the dominant narratives associated with the post-Enlightenment west.[27] The only period term to receive any sustained critical engagement within the journal's covers is 'modernity'.[28]

This celebratory volume was envisaged as an opportunity to reflect on the extent to which gender analysis suggests alternative chronologies to conventional periodisation.[29] More fundamentally, the chapters it features explore the ways in which gender functioned as a force of endurance or transition in the past, and the ways in which it might have been constitutive rather than merely reflective of either continuity or change. It seems a fitting tribute to twenty years of *Gender & History* to engage with questions at the heart of the discipline of history as a means of showcasing the contribution gender analysis can make to our characterisation and classification of the past. In the chapters that follow, this has involved not only the rejection of some period markers and the confirmation of others, but also the interrogation of some of the foundational narratives of change associated both with women's history and the shifting construction of gender categories over time. Further, it has generated some theoretical discussion of both how we are to approach women's agency in the past and how we might best deploy the concept of gender as a category of analysis in ways that avoid partiality and anachronism. Obviously, constraints of space mean that we cannot offer exhaustive coverage of these wide-ranging questions and what follows is both geographically and chronologically limited to a few select (albeit as varied as possible) times and places. Sadly, geographical breadth in this instance has given way to chronological depth, despite our many efforts to solicit articles with a non-western and more global range. However the chapters gathered here demonstrate the rich possibilities for rethinking the central tenets of European historiography – including several foundational claims of women's and gender history – even from within the perspectives generated by western scholarship. And the many general reflections on methods for the classification of change and its implications for the interrogation of gender as a category will be of relevance to periods and regions that are not represented here. It is therefore hoped that this collection of chapters will both re-open questions that were of fundamental importance to first- and second-wave feminist scholarship and stimulate further investigation both under and beyond the umbrella of gender history.

With one exception, the contributions that directly interrogate conventional chronologies reject rather than confirm the integrity of period markers in the light of gender analysis. Lynda L. Coon's exploration of early medieval 'somatic styles' challenges both the notion of a 'rupture' between classical antiquity and the so-called 'Dark Age' and the assumption of an alien pre-Enlightenment sexuality based on a 'one-sex' model of the body against which a 'modern' sex/gender system has frequently been juxtaposed, emphasising the eclectic and varied use of classical medical teachings even by the clerical elites whose voices dominate the sources surviving from the seventh to tenth centuries. Investigating the more recent past, Padma Anagol demonstrates how historiographical privileging of the nationalist response to imperialism in modern Indian history has obfuscated women's agency under colonial rule and created a truncated account and inadequate appreciation of feminism in India and the broader formation of Indian subjectivities. Anagol's chapter provides a model of the problems generated by gender-blind scholarship and the legacy of its chronological frameworks that, in this instance, actively inhibit analysis of women's agency. Critical too of discursive approaches to gender for their neglect of female agency and their lack of chronological moorings, Anagol goes on to place gender relationships at the heart of the formation of modern India, stressing its deep roots in the late eighteenth and nineteenth centuries as a corrective to an undue emphasis on the period from 1885 to 1947. Kevin Passmore is similarly critical of the way in which political religions' theorists, explaining the rise of fascism as a feature of the transition between tradition and modernity, have afforded no space for women's agency. Cast as the embodiment of tradition on the basis of femininity's timelessness, women are associated with passivity and superstition in order to draw a distinction between the compliant (feminised) masses and the masculine elite. Passmore traces these assumptions back to the totalitarianism theory of the 1950s and 1960s and, more fundamentally, to the canonical thinkers of the sociological tradition from which political religions theory derives. Moreover, Passmore warns that conventional sociology presents a problematic legacy that also risks being unheeded by gender historians.

The one conventional period marker that receives any defence amongst the chapters below is 'early modernity'. While happy to dispense with the organising principles and disciplinary boundaries associated with the term 'Renaissance', Merry Wiesner-Hanks argues that there certainly was an 'early modern' period for European women and that gender analysis is critical to understanding the key transitions with which it is associated – in particular the Reformation, military revolution, and the dramatic intensification of global interaction. Wiesner-Hanks is concerned not to render women's history 'motionless' over the *longue durée* by contrast to the changes deemed definitive in men's lives, and argues not only that women's as well as men's lives were transformed by the key events associated with early modernity but also that women were key agents and gender played a constitutive role in these changes. These conclusions are given further weight by Martha Howell's chapter on the commercial expansion associated with the early modern west. The commercial revolution, she argues, was accompanied and *enabled* by the creation of a class-specific, normative gender binary that newly afforded honourable masculinity to the merchant by realigning production with the male householder citizen and domesticating (and thereby taming) consumption as the purview of the virtuous wife. Gender was inextricably bound up with, and a dynamic force in, the creation of the class identity of the European bourgeoisie.

Alongside concerns with conventional periodisation, several of the contributors are sceptical about some of the foundational narratives of change and accompanying chronologies produced by women's history and gender history. Monica H. Green takes to task western feminist narratives concerning the history of women's healthcare, and rejects the categorisation of the late medieval period or (more loosely) a pre-modern era as a 'golden age' for European women's medical practices in relation to reproductive health. Such accounts have come about, she argues, from a politically motivated and polarising perspective that has produced a partial story shaped by a moral framework which accords liberating potential to the deeds of women and patriarchal oppression to the activities of men on the basis of distorted evidence and, ultimately, in the face of improving medical outcomes. Lynn Abrams wrestles with the stranglehold that the dominant narrative of 'separate spheres' has placed on the history of women in modern Europe and the paradox created by this model's failure to represent women's sense of their own past within local contexts. Exploring what happens when women's voices are prioritised by historians, Abrams seeks a path through the dissonance created by the relationships between the general and the particular, the mainstream and the margins that leads her to more than a simple confirmation of the heterogeneity of female experience. Rather than a timeless exception to a European rule, Shetland women's accounts of their own agency offer a situational corrective to the narratives told about modern European women and, more importantly, to the methodologies by which they are constructed.

Perhaps one of the most entrenched, albeit widely contested, narratives of change (re)produced by gender history has its roots in Thomas Laqueur's argument that eighteenth-century Europe witnessed a fundamental shift in the construction of the sexed body as a 'pre-modern', 'one-sex' model – based on a male–female hierarchical continuum – was replaced by a 'modern', 'two-sex' system of incommensurable difference.[30] Dror Wahrman revisits these claims, and the counter-arguments they have produced that emphasise either long-term continuities or enduring synchronic diversity (and which are also represented here in the chapters by Lynda Coon and Monica Green). He does so less to adjudicate the merits of each side of the argument than to explore the relationship between gender history and cultural history and the methodological and conceptual limits of the latter's 'uncompromising constructivism' which, he argues, lacks explanatory force when confronted with evidence of long-term continuity. Breaking one of the persistent taboos of feminist history against naturalising the body, Wahrman challenges gender historians to undertake a 'corporeal critique' in order to explore 'where the culturally constructed ends and the ahistorical and extra-cultural begins; and thus, most importantly, how they relate to each other'. This involves widening the lens of analysis to encompass the deep historical perspective afforded by neurohistory – an example of which Wahrman offers to complement other such forays on the basis of psychoanalysis or evolutionary psychology.

Jeanne Boydston's chapter is also concerned with the conceptual limits of gender analysis, but prescribes attending to local particularity above deep historical continuity. Claiming that gender's status as a 'category of analysis' risks ahistoricism by reifying a contemporary, western epistemological order, Boydston argues that we should instead approach gender as 'historical process' and historicise gender as a concept. If gender is the product of social constructionism, then it should behave differently across time and space. The appearance of long-term continuity for Boydston, then, is a chimera that has been produced by the inability of the category of gender to accommodate difference that does not conform to an oppositionally based binary which risks (wrongly) assuming universal status across place and time.

Finally, by way of an epilogue to the volume, Judith M. Bennett contributes some short reflections that once again reiterate the importance of the *longue durée* to feminist history. Concerned that women's history has narrowed its sights to the recent past, Bennett urges historians of women and gender to reinvigorate history's relationship with feminist theory in order to restore its potential to address contemporary agendas for change vested in the long view the distant past affords. We have come, then, full circle to the agenda articulated by the emergent field of women's history in the 1970s. The chapters in this volume have, however, proceeded by way of some approaches and conclusions that are radically at odds with many of the foundational methods and findings of both women's history and gender history. Noting that gender-blind scholarship has not been alone in producing partial accounts of female agency, several contributors confront the uncomfortable reality that women's agency did not only occur in progressive domains, but could sustain and benefit from systems of oppression. Others wrestle with the conceptual constraints inherent in the deployment of gender as a category of analysis, particularly in relation to gender's close association with both the strengths and weaknesses of cultural history. While Boydston advocates detailed attention to the particularities and localities that contradict an assumed oppositional binary pitting male against female, the general consensus is that the long view is one that gender history cannot afford to lose. Nor can the discipline of history afford to be without the perspective this allows, since conventional timeframes are constructively enriched and challenged by gender history and the analysis of women's agency in the past.

Notes

1. Ludmilla Jordanova, *History in Practice* (London: Arnold, 2000), pp. 127, 132.
2. Fernand Braudel, *La Méditerranée et le monde méditerranéen à l'époque de Philippe II* (Paris: Colin, 1949).
3. Sheila Rowbotham, *Hidden from History* (1973; 3rd edn, London: Pluto Press, 1990), pp. ix–x.
4. Alice Clark, *The Working Life of Women in the Seventeenth Century* (London: Routledge, 1919); Ivy Pinchbeck, *Women Workers and the Industrial Revolution, 1750–1850* (London: Routledge, 1930).
5. E.g., Gerda Lerner, 'Women's Rights and American Feminism', *The American Scholar* 40 (1971), pp. 235–48.
6. Susan B. Anthony, Elizabeth Cady Stanton and Matilda Joslyn Gage, *History of Woman Suffrage*, 6 vols (New York: Fowler and Wells, 1881).
7. Karen Offen, Ruth Roach Pierson and Jane Rendall (eds), *Writing Women's History: International Perspectives* (Basingstoke and London: Macmillan, 1991).

8. Joan Kelly-Gadol, 'Did Women Have a Renaissance?', in Renate Blumenthal and Claudia Koonz (eds), *Becoming Visible: Women in European History* (Boston: Houghton Mifflin, 1977), pp. 137–64, here p. 137.

9. E.g., Phyllis Culham, 'Did Roman Women have an Empire?', in Mark Golden and Peter Toohey (eds), *Inventing Ancient Culture: Historicism, Periodization, and the Ancient World* (London and New York: Routledge, 1997), pp. 192–204.

10. For an exception, see Maxine Berg, 'What Difference did Women's Work Make to the Industrial Revolution?', *History Workshop Journal* 35 (1993), pp. 22–44.

11. Gerda Lerner, 'Placing Women in History: A 1975 Perspective', *Feminist Studies* 3 (1975), pp. 5–14, reprinted in Gerda Lerner, *The Majority Finds Its Past* (Oxford: Oxford University Press, 1979), as 'Placing Women in History: Definitions and Challenges', pp. 145–59, here p. 159.

12. This theme is elaborated in Judith Bennett, *History Matters: Patriarchy and the Challenge of Feminism* (Philadelphia: University of Pennsylvania Press, 2006), pp. 54–81, and Merry Wiesner-Hanks, 'The Hubris of Writing Surveys, or a Feminist Confronts the Textbook', in Susan D. Amussen and Adele Seeff (eds), *Attending to Early Modern Women* (Newark and London: University of Delaware Press and Associated University Presses, 1998), pp. 297–310.

14. Noted by Joan Scott, 'Women's History', in Peter Burke (ed.), *New Perspectives on Historical Writing* (Oxford: Polity Press, 1991), pp. 42–66, here p. 43.

15. E.g., Juliet Mitchell, 'Women: the Longest Revolution', *New Left Review* 40 (1966), pp. 11–37, here p. 11; Natalie Zemon Davis, 'Women's History in Transition: the European Case', *Feminist Studies* 3:3/4 (1976), pp. 83–103.

16. Joan Wallach Scott, 'Gender: A Useful Category of Historical Analysis', *American Historical Review* 91 (1986), pp. 1,053–75.

17. Kevin Passmore, review of Joan Wallach Scott, *Feminism and History* (Oxford and New York: Oxford University Press, 1996), *Women's History Review* 7 (1998), pp. 261–5.

18. 'Gender is not only a constitutive element of social relationships based on perceived differences between the sexes, it also is a primary way of signifying relationships of power. It is of crucial importance for the creation of meaning in social and political life far beyond gender [as an object of study] itself': Karen Hagemann and Jean H. Quataert, 'Gendering Modern German History: Comparing Historiographies and Academic Cultures in Germany and the United States through the Lens of Gender', in Karen Hagemann and Jean H. Quataert (eds), *Gendering Modern German History: Rewriting Historiography* (New York: Berghahn, 2007), pp. 1–38, here pp. 3–4. Scott's essay is mentioned later, however: pp. 18–21.

19. Joan Hoff, 'Gender as a Postmodern Category of Analysis', *Women's History Review* 3 (1994), pp. 149–68, here p. 150.

20. Laura Lee Downs, *Writing Gender History* (London: Hodder Arnold, 2004), p. 83.

21. R. W. Connell, 'The Big Picture: Masculinities in Recent World History', *Theory and Society* 22 (1993), pp. 597–623.

22. Konstantin Dierks, 'American Men's History and the Big Picture', *Gender & History* 18 (2006), pp. 160–64. See also the Special Section on periodisation and the history of masculinity, 'What Have Historians Done with Masculinity: Reflections of Five Centuries of British History, circa 1500–1950', ed. Karen Harvey and Alexandra Shepard, *Journal of British Studies* 44 (2005).

23. Judith M. Bennett, 'Feminism and History', *Gender & History* 1 (1989), pp. 251–72.

24. Julia M. H. Smith, 'Did Women have a Transformation of the Roman World?', *Gender & History* 12 (2000), pp. 552–71.

25. Theodore Koditschek, 'The Gendering of the British Working Class', *Gender & History* 9 (1997), pp. 333–63; Sharon T. Strocchia, 'When the Bishop Married the Abbess: Masculinity and Power in Florentine Episcopal Entry Rites, 1300–1600', *Gender & History* 19 (2007), pp. 346–68.

26. See e.g., the introduction to the Special Issue on 'Gender, Nationalisms and National Iden-
    tities', in which the 'need to reconsider existing chronologies in the formation of nations'
    in the wake of gender analysis is acknowledged but deferred as a task for the future. *Gender
    & History* 5 (1993), pp. 159–64.
27. See the editorial to issue 1 of vol. 6 of *Gender & History* (1994), reflecting on the first five
    years' content, pp. 1–6. Similar concerns were echoed in the introduction to the Special
    Issue of vol. 11, on 'Gender and History – Retrospect and Prospect', celebrating ten years
    of publication (1999), pp. 415–18.
28. See e.g., the Special Issue on 'Gender, Citizenship and Subjectivity', *Gender & History*
    13:3 (2001), and the forum on 'Domestic Service since 1750', *Gender & History* 18:2
    (2006).
29. The volume has its origins in a two-day workshop held at Christ's College, Cambridge,
    in April 2007. We are grateful to the Master and Fellows of Christ's College for hosting
    the workshop, and to the participants at the workshop for their contributions. We are also
    indebted to the George Macaulay Trevelyan Fund for financial support for this event.
30. Thomas Laqueur, *Making Sex: Body and Gender from the Greeks to Freud* (Cambridge:
    Harvard University Press, 1990).

2 Somatic Styles of the Early Middle Ages

Lynda L. Coon

The early Middle Ages (*c*.600–900) is an epoch wedged in between two pioneering fields in gender history: late antiquity and the later centuries of the medieval era. In many respects, scholars of late antiquity have set the standard for exploring relationships among gender, sexuality and self-abnegation within the larger theoretical backdrop of the continued influence of classical gender systems on patristic and ascetic cultures.[1] Gender historians have brought the history of the body to the forefront of the understanding of the mystical, heretical and civic communities of high and late medieval Europe.[2] Lodged between famous studies of the dazzling ascetic bodies of the holy women and men of late antiquity and the bloody mysticism of later medieval saints, is the exegetical and philosophical construction of the early medieval body – a corporeal paradigm characterised by massive continuity with classical modes of gender and sexuality embedded in and transformed by biblical, ascetic and Germanic/Celtic readings of the human body and its parts.

There are intriguing varieties of early medieval somatic styles open for a scholarly reading: ascetic bodies, warrior bodies, legal bodies, musical bodies and regal bodies, to name but a few. The early medieval priestly body finds its controlling model in classical discourses on the public spectacle of the virile Roman orator, especially as detailed in the writings of Cicero and Quintilian and often mediated through the patristic corpus of texts.[3] In the non-clerical realm, as Janet Nelson argues, there is an ascetic lay body, which competes with the sacred masculinity of its consecrated counterpart by performing acts of self-denial through compulsive washing after nocturnal emissions or expressing horror at nuptial pleasures.[4] Moreover, there is an aristocratic, warrior body, as Eric Goldberg elucidates, distinguished from its clerical competitor via participation in the hunt, horsemanship and gaming as well as sexual and military prowess.[5]

Karl Morrison details how early medieval musical theorists looked to the human body as 'a little orchestra, with the pulse its rhythm, its deep and high voices tempered to a single consonance of parts'.[6]

In the legal realm, there are, as Katherine O'Brien O'Keeffe proposes, 'forensic bodies', or bodies that announce the crimes they (supposedly) commit by exhibiting mutilations or tattoos, such as the priest–thief who is flogged and has the word *fur* ('robber') branded on his face; or the slanderer, whose excised tongue visibly maps guilt onto her or his body.[7] Julia M. H. Smith shows that there is an early medieval cursing body, whose 'wounding words', such as one man calling another a 'hare' (that is the receptive partner in a male-on-male penetrative sex act), are akin to 'injurious blows' and both have the power to lessen the social standing of their victims.[8] Finally, as Stuart Airlie describes, there is the early medieval regal body, whose purity and defilement speak to larger issues of political boundaries and territorial harmony.[9]

Because of the rich variety of corporeal styles (many of which have only begun to be explored), gender theory and the history of sexuality – the attendant fields to the history of the body – have made recent, significant inroads into the broader discipline of early medieval studies.[10] Yet it is still the case that the early medieval body has not become a major player in the larger narrative history of the body, gender theory, or sexuality studies.[11] Importantly, early medieval bodies offer gender theorists new ways to re-configure old-fashioned textbook periodisations, such as the taken-for-granted 'ruptures' between classical antiquity and the so-called 'Dark Age' (the focus of this chapter) as well the 'conceptual chasm' separating pre-modern sensibilities from modern ones.[12] In terms of the latter 'rupture' – that is, the division between the 'modern' and the 'pre-modern' – a trend in much recent scholarship on sex and gender stresses the invention of a sexual modernity *ex nihilo*, 'out of thin air'. Sexual modernity is contingent on innovations in Enlightenment and post-Enlightenment western societies: consumer culture, print culture and the sexual sciences, to name but a few of the key ingredients of the modern sexual self. In this revised narrative of sex and gender, the pre-modern past becomes an 'alien past', an eccentric backwater to the more germane pursuits of modern historians, who underscore that pre-modern bodies and psyches are at odds with their 'Enlightened' and 'modern' counterparts.[13]

For specialists working in gender and history, the (supposed) estrangement between the pre-modern and modern self has special meaning: modern people have scientifically-driven categories of female versus male; pre-modern people were content with quasi hermaphroditic bodies – bodies conceived within a one-sex model, where female and male existed on the opposite poles of a unified, corporeal structure.[14] To put it in biblical terms, 'moderns' have a view of the sexes more like that presented in

Genesis 1: 27: 'male and female He created them'; 'pre-moderns' inherit the strange, hermaphroditic body of Adam in Genesis 2: 21 *before* God pulls Eve – fashioned from a 'spare part', a rib – out of Adam's flesh.[15] While no historian would make the case that pre-modern bodies and identities were conceptually the same as modern ones, historians of medicine and gender have argued that both ancient and medieval writers understood the sexes – female and male – as distinct biological entities.[16] Modern theorists of 'sex' stress that the radical dimorphism of female versus male, a dimorphism based on chromosomal variation, fails to sustain an immutable, scientifically driven two-sex system.[17] The 'conceptual chasm' allegedly separating the pre-modern from the modern can be breached on either side: pre-modern models of sex and gender do indeed penetrate modern sensibilities and 'modern' sexual identities appear to work their way backwards into the pre-modern world.[18]

The other 'Great Divide' between historical epochs is the one posited between Graeco-Roman antiquity and the so-called 'Dark Ages'. While continuities between antiquity and the early Middle Ages have been the focus of much recent scholarship (and heated debate), there has never been a comprehensive treatment of how classical modes of sex, sexuality and gender made their way into the intellectual, spiritual and spatial traditions of the early medieval west.[19] In spite of this scholarly lacuna, the history of the early medieval body does possess enormous potential to erode the Ancient/Dark Age divide and to wear down the overstated pre-modern/modern rift. This chapter examines how classical modes of gender played significant roles in carving out competitive arenas between clerical and lay elites, *c.*600–900. In order to expedite this goal, the following discussion explores the hermeneutical obstacles standing between the contemporary theorist of gender and the complex nature of the early medieval texts under scrutiny. The analysis then sets out the parameters of classicising techniques of gender deployed by early medieval churchmen and it does so in a way that both challenges the stranglehold of the 'one-sex' model on pre-modern understandings of gender and heals the 'rupture' between the 'Ancient' and the 'Dark Age'. Finally, the chapter maps early medieval somatic and gendered styles onto an architectural space where lay and consecrated bodies met – a ninth-century monastic basilica. The final section uses the spatial and anthropological theories of modernist colleagues to put women back into the historical record, even in spaces where they traditionally have been invisible.

The 'invisibility' versus the 'visibility' of women in the historical record is a major theme in much scholarship on gender and the early Middle Ages. One renowned obstacle to the study of early medieval gender is the fact that males wrote most of the texts from the time period, a fact that is devastating to the study of women's history, *c.*600–900.[20] To make matters more complex, celibate males penned the majority of the extant sources from the era; therefore, using clerical texts to reconstruct early medieval gender paradigms must remain an incomplete endeavour, one beholden to ecclesiastical visions of female and male bodies. Early medieval church-men forged gender systems that routinely sought to feminise lay male bodies through a variety of textual, ritual and spatial means, reflecting the intense competition between these two elite and often kindred groups. The early medieval west did not witness the introduction of a so-called 'third gender' – that is, a liminal category grafted onto the binary opposition of female/male in order to accommodate the virginal styles of early medieval churchmen. Quite the opposite is true. Ascetic intellectuals, from Pope Gregory the Great (*c.*540–604) to Carolingian scholar Hrabanus Maurus (*c.*780–856), fashioned for themselves masculinist models of gender with deep roots in classical Roman, Christian ascetic and biblical prototypes. Such a gender system worked to advertise and sustain the unique and supe-rior qualities of priestly virility and to do so in an open bid for power. The clerical techniques of gender surveyed below do not, of course, represent the reality of the close relations between ascetics and lay elites, who shared family lineages and forged social and political networks. Nor do the classi-cising modes of gender covered in this chapter speak to the somatic styles of all churchmen, especially those of married clerics and cathedral canons, who miss the mark of bodily inviolability. This chapter centres on a very precise reading of sex and gender (but certainly not the *only* one) fash-ioned by an intensely scholarly circle of ascetic men, who exerted massive influence over the philosophical and medical readings of early medieval bodies and their parts, both female and male, and consecrated and lay.[21]

Secular men, this select group of clerical writers consistently under-scored, are prisoners of bodily fluxes and the all-consuming libido – their bodies are like those of women on account of their excessive lust and im-moderate acts. A case in point is when Carolingian Benedictine Hrabanus Maurus cautioned the ruler of the eastern half of the Frankish empire, Louis the German, that a man could not rightly hold on to the title *vir* if he clung to effeminate, secular pleasures.[22] The word Hrabanus chose to characterise this worldly inclination is *mollities*, a classicising term carrying with it meanings of sexual passivity, effeminacy and softness.[23] Hrabanus volleyed *mollities* at Louis within the context of the political conflicts waged between monarchs and holy men in the mid-ninth cen-tury.[24] King Louis had exiled the embattled Hrabanus to a mountain top ascetic retreat in 842 after the abbot – now stripped of his prestigious office – chose the wrong side in the wars fought among the heirs of Louis the Pious. In addition to the body of Louis the German hovering on the brink of secular softness, female bodies comprised an important part of clerical gender studies as well. But like the lay male body, the body of a woman existed – at least in the minds of the male ascetics writing the gendered script – as a static, defiled object against which the purified priestly body was read.[25] At the same time, female bodies haunted ascetic male bodies, and this figurative haunting was at the core of clerical visions of gender.

Although the texts discussed below are decidedly male and clerical, priestly anxieties concerning bodily control and purity were transferred – often in highly competitive modes – to elite lay circles.[26] Indeed, the one solid fact of early medieval gender is that of the anxiety produced in priestly circles concerning the proper gendered balance of the body, the surveillance of ascetic masculinities and the defence of male bodies from the contagion of the feminine. The degree to which these anxieties filtered down to elite lay bodies or even non-elite monastic bodies is, of course, difficult to gauge, though considering the sometimes shrill nature of priestly rhetoric on the 'Dark Age' body and its parts, such as the monk–poet Walahfrid Strabo's (c.808–849) portrait of Charlemagne in hell with demonic beasts mangling his privities, clerics may very well have been losing the battle to dictate gender norms and their attendant power hierarchies with churchmen conveniently positioned on top.[27]

Obviously, there would have been resistance to priestly strictures imposed on female and male bodies covered in this chapter, as it is never simply the case that hegemonic men 'write the cultural script' and that women or non-normative men 'simply and obediently recite their lines'.[28] Early medieval capitularies, penitentials and monastic commentaries suggest that there was a fair amount of defiance of gendered norms at ground level, as both royal and monastic legislation consistently targeted celibate women and men who engaged in mutual masturbation, inserted dildos into the orifices of nuns, enjoyed fellatio, or preferred anal intercourse.[29] The sexuality of married Christians too was subject to legal scrutiny. Emperor Louis the Pious's capitulary of 829 is a case in point: sex in marriage, the edict reads, is solely for producing heirs and never for serving the demon lust.[30] The degree to which these legislative acts represent real sexual practices is obviously debatable and has been debated by specialists in the field.[31] Moreover, the persistence of the legislators intimates the presence of a shadow society of sexual rebels who countered the normative states of the early medieval body: virginity, chastity, or lacklustre male-on-female intercourse aimed solely at producing offspring.[32] Even kissing outside ritual structures could be a problematic activity in the monastery, as monastic kissing was connected with sacred acts – kissing altars, holy men kissing holy men square on the mouths, kissing distinct parts on saintly bodies (feet, hands or shoulders) and giving the kiss of peace as a sign of concord. Kissing women and the excommunicated was out of the question, because such kisses were stained with the carnal and the deceptive – like the insidious kiss of Judas.[33] The inescapable truth is that male ascetics did create the symbolic systems into which the proclivities of female/male or feminine/masculine bodies were situated. In a historical epoch (*c*.600–900) almost entirely devoid of texts written by women or where ethnographic writings penned from the perspectives of lay males are largely absent, scholars must grapple with gender systems stemming from priestly action and belief.[34]

In spite of this rather grim, hermeneutical verdict, it is important to keep in mind the instruction of symbolic interpretative anthropologists who teach that in societies where the boundary between female and male is unambiguously drawn and strictly enforced, massive anxieties concerning gender control, ritual taboos and pollution legislation are typically lacking.[35] In contrast, it is in those cultures where the line between the sexes remains ambiguous or even fuzzy that anthropologists locate a gendered system 'at war with itself' and, through the structures of internal combat, ideals of male hegemony frequently disclose a 'shadow society' of female empowerment or even male defiance of hierarchical notions of sex and gender.[36] In early medieval Europe, with its chaste class of monks, with its anxieties over any sort of sexual contact between humans (even married ones) and with its normative state of female and male bodies dictated to some degree by virginity and impenetrability; fluidity, ambiguity and boundary-crossing were the order of the day. After all, the virginal men of Europe's most powerful same-sex cloisters, who cast themselves as 'weaponless soldiers', were the ones writing the gendered script, and they were doing so at a distance from the high value activities of their powerful lay peers: producing offspring and possessing prowess on the battlefield. Therefore, the early medieval gender system unveiled below is one 'at war with itself' – a metaphorical battle divulged in part by the level of anxiety with which male clerical writers approached the human body, its parts and their functions and qualities.

In order to map out the attributes and hierarchies of early medieval gender systems, it is useful to begin with an evocative and edifying term: labile. The *Oxford English Dictionary* defines labile as 'liable or prone to lapse; prone to fall into error or sin; liable to fall from innocence'. Labile first appeared in the English language in the sixteenth and seventeenth centuries, and the early modern English word betrays its late ancient, gendered origins: 'Apt to slip away, slippery, unstable' (post-classical Latin, *labilis*, 'slipping, gliding, slippery, transient').[37] To be labile then is to be fallen, slippery, unstable . . . *wet*. The polar opposite qualities of this fallen state include being pure, stable, bounded . . . *dry*. The antagonism between being labile and not being labile echoes the major features of western premodern gender systems, where masculinity typically was calculated by the possession of a body that is hot, dry, hard, bounded, airy and closer to spirit in nature. In contrast, the feminine was reckoned by the extent to which one's body is wet, slippery, cold, unbounded, porous, mutable and mate-rial.[38] Unlike male bodies, which could, to a certain degree, safeguard their orifices from leaking, female bodies were subject to periodic 'liquefying assaults'.[39] Therefore, leaky male bodies, such as those suffering nocturnal emissions, moved men closer to the contagious realm of the feminine.[40]

Individual bodies were also battlegrounds for the conflict between the masculine and the feminine, as wetness clung to the left side of the body and dryness to the right; hence the right was associated with the spiritual and masculine, the left with the carnal and feminine.[41] These directional designations were carried over into early medieval intellectual traditions and even the built environment of medieval Christendom, where left/right and the cardinal directions took on gendered meanings. In the case of the four cardinal points, the north was associated with coldness and wetness and the south with dryness and heat, the west with earth and the east with air.[42] Moreover, ancient theorists divided the human body into gendered zones: the upper region with its ruling head and potent mouth was typically rendered as the more masculine region, while the lower body with its wet *pudenda* and insatiable stomach was often reckoned as the more feminine section. The head was perceived as the ruling member of the body and the feet personified its servile class.[43] In all, the gendered attributes of hot/cold, dry/wet, right/left, south/north, upper/lower affected the physical, psychological and even the spiritual status of the human subjects under their domination.

Although the designation 'labile' in English as meaning 'slippery and loose' derives from early modern usage, classical and early medieval writers similarly located the feminine among the unfixed, moist and changeable features of the universe (late Latin, *labilis*). In the ancient and medieval worlds, the conflict between the masculine and the feminine was cast on an elemental stage: the nature of women was closer to that of earth and water. In contrast, men found their natural affinity in the temperaments of fire and air. Thus female bodies were earthbound, whereas male bodies rightfully sought celestial ascent. Ancient medical theorists agreed that the best condition of the human body lies in the state of being dry and stable, but not excessively so, as they considered 'excess' (*luxuria*) to be the paramount feature of the feminine. Pristine bodies were to lean to the right and embrace the masculine side of the gendered temperature register. Somatic dryness segued neatly into the defining traits of manliness (*virtus*) in both classical and early medieval gender paradigms: 'self-mastery' (*constantia*), 'impenetrability' (*pudicitia*)[44] and 'hardness' (*duritia*). Unlike the leaky bodies of women, male bodies were more naturally 'corked up' like bottles. As classicist Anne Carson writes in a definitive work on ancient Greek gender, the body of a woman was more porous than that of a man and therefore had to be artificially 'plugged up' either by veiling, because the head at the top of the body served as a metaphor for the 'head' of the lower-body, the vagina, or by residing in spaces subjected to heavy male surveillance because wetness led to wantonness.[45]

In ancient readings of the body, human beings were suspended between polar opposite corporeal states: wet/slippery on one side of the spectrum and dry/bounded on the other pole. Individual bodies could, in theory, move up and down a sliding, gendered scale dictated by the body's climate. And this mobility suggests that there was a 'gendered' system in play and not a strictly sexed one, as the biological distinctions between male and female break down in the face of the ebb and flow of discrete bodies. Movement along the gender continuum could have material effects. Christian women who were overly hot and fiery in their natures grew beards.[46] Adult male chanters with humid, reedy voices betrayed their inner body's embrace of the wet and slippery gendered zone.[47]

The climate model of early medieval gender gave ascetic males, the ones writing the gendered script, considerable leverage in deciding where the bodies under their sway fell along the hot/dry–cold/wet continuum. Churchmen frequently positioned the male bodies of lay rivals closer to the labile side of the register, that is, the wet and slippery pole. That pole had the power to infect men with feminine traits and to rupture the masculine qualities of *constantia*, *pudicitia* and *duritia*, the very virtues lauded by monastic mandarins, who uniquely claimed to possess them. Similarly, the bodies of cloistered female virgins could approach the masculine side of the register on account of their corporeal inviolability, their Christ-centred constancy and their access to liturgical speech.[48] In contrast, leaky male ascetic bodies – such as those afflicted with nocturnal emissions – ran the risk of emasculating their souls, because soft flesh leads to a womanly afterlife.[49] In the lay world, men who surrendered to the marital state were automatic candidates for the wet and slippery sphere, as intimacy with women *softened* their bodies and made them *like* women, at least from a clerical perspective.

Mandarin scholar of the Carolingian court, Alcuin (*d.* 804), addressed his little treatise on virtues and vices to an elite layman, Count Wido, and he layered Wido's text with the latest in monastic gender pedagogies: the libidinous dangers of the male body and how fornication with women makes manly souls *soft*.[50] Philippe Buc notes how the aristocratic laymen of the ninth and tenth centuries quickly learned that males 'in thrall to women could hardly lead other men'.[51] Married men easily succumbed to the disease of *femineus amor* ('womanly love', 'effeminate love'), an amorous pathology defined by ancient Roman writers and their early medieval counterparts as an immoderate – hence unhealthy – love for the opposite sex.[52] The definition has long legs in western history, for as late as 1923, American dictionaries still identified heterosexuality as a 'morbid sexual passion for one of the opposite sex', a designation echoing classical and early medieval notions of *femineus amor* as an unhealthy and excessive love.[53] In both 1923 America and in classical antiquity, men who loved women too much shared in their wet and slippery natures.

Slippery versus dry plays out on a theological stage as well, because late ancient and early medieval Christian exegetes gendered the path to salvation by taking metaphors from the body's climatic system and applied them to the universal history of the human soul. Here, classical medicine met early medieval exegesis head-on. The most striking example of this gendered strategy is from the controversial corpus of Egyptian exegete and ascetic Origen of Alexandria (*c*.185–254). In his premier philosophical work, *De Principiis* (*c*.230), Origen weaves a complex tale of the soul's descent into the world of the flesh and its heroic return to the celestial heights and he does so in a way fraught with gender trouble.[54] According to Origen, the original state of souls was that of ecstasy – all souls were enraptured in the direct presence of the Godhead and they shared that trance-like state as equal participants in an angelic liturgy.[55] At some point, however, souls who should have remained satisfied with the eternal worship of God suffered the onslaught of inertia and complacency, treacherous spiritual states leading to a precipitous drop in temperature.[56] Once cooled off from an initial state of spiritual fervour, these souls could no longer cling to the awesome heat of the Divine. Hence, the primordial souls slid way down into the slippery material world to varying degrees depending on the intensity of their spiritual lethargy. Only Christ – whose hotness endured – continued to embrace the blaze of the Eternal.[57] Christ's opposites, the wraithlike demons, moved so far down the hierarchy of souls that their 'eerie flesh was as supple as a chill north wind', as Peter Brown expresses it.[58] The gender implications of Origen's primal tale of the soul are obvious. The Godhead and its attendant spirits are characterised by their hot, dry, fiery, stable (that is, masculine) natures; the fallen, the demonic and the fleshly are identified by their cold, slippery, wet, inconstant (feminine) traits. The grand narrative of human salvation lies in the gendered balance, in which masculine souls naturally seek the ethereal heights and feminine souls continue to be enmeshed in the heavy dross of the world.[59]

Pope Gregory the Great's *Pastoral Care* (*c*.591), a 'best-seller' in the Carolingian world – indeed, Alcuin once referred to the book as 'medicine' for the wounds of the soul – also provided priestly audiences with a survey of the spiritual qualities of hot, cold and lukewarm.[60] This last condition, *tepidus* (Latin, 'lukewarm') is not unlike the state of inertia described by Origen, which first prompted primordial souls to cool off. The Pope's pedagogy takes place within the context of an exegetical riff on Revelation (3: 16): 'Because you are lukewarm (*tepidus*), and neither cold nor hot, I am about to spit you out of my mouth', a text with major ramifications for the history of Christian asceticism.[61] Gregory's lesson, with its gendered subtexts, is as follows: a Christian who is 'hot' is one who is constant in good deeds; the individual who is 'cold' is inconstant. The 'lukewarm' person, however, is in a condition laden with spiritual danger. Being *tepidus* means that the soul of a 'hot' Christian has cooled off, thereby bringing that soul closer to the deadly cold register. And yet someone transfixed in a tepid state never completes the act of transitioning from hot to cold, which are perfected states. Similarly, being tepid raises a soul mired in the 'cold' zone of the feminine, but does so only a little. The state of *tepidus*, therefore, is a hybrid one, as the tepid soul never finishes its full metamorphosis to either the hot or the cold registers.

For Gregory, the climatic qualities of the body paralleled the spiritual identities of a true and steady believer (the 'hot'), the unconverted but potentially a target of conversion (the 'cold') and the inert Christian (the 'lukewarm'), who has either lost belief or whose belief is never sufficient enough to ignite the soul's pre-lapsarian passion. Therefore, being 'luke-warm' restricts a Christian body to a liminal state of spiritual progress, betwixt and between the polar-opposite ends of the climatic register and betwixt and between the circumstances of belief and disbelief.[62] The individual who clings to the tepid zone is a climatic hermaphrodite or a heretic, suspended between orthodoxy and paganism, an aberrant creature on account of its mixing of the feminine (cold/inconstant) and the masculine (hot/constant) and its inability to fulfil either gender.

The above survey of the climatic model of the early medieval body is part of a central question currently being debated in gender and sexuality studies (as intimated in the introduction to this chapter): did ancient and medieval medical theorists have a concept of anatomical distinction between female and male, or did their preference for a 'one-sex' model of human biology prevail over discussions of sexual difference? A number of gender scholars have argued that pre-modern thinkers privileged a one-sex model of human anatomy: male and female existed on the opposite poles of a unified, corporeal structure.[63] According to this one-sex model, women's sexual organs were the same as men's, but inverted and hence inferior. In fact, certain classical philosophers viewed female productive parts as dim reflections of their more potent male counterparts. A case in point is the ovaries, deemed in a number of medical circles to be inverted – hence perverted – versions of the male testes. On account of this anatomical inversion, female testes produce weak, womanly seed.[64] The one-sex model offered a paradigm in which the line between female and male is blurred and the possibility of movement among genders – an anxiety-provoking aspect of this corporeal paradigm – is high. As such, the one-sex model represented a female body that performed women's inferior social,

political, spiritual and cultural status by mutedly mirroring a more perfect male body, and a male body that embodied hierarchical privilege and
power precisely because its parts reflect more perfectly the divine ordering
of things.

Historians who emphasise the pre-modern dominance of a one-sex
model stress that only in the eighteenth century did Europeans put forward a new paradigm of biological divergence grounded in the scientific
enterprise of the Enlightenment. Other experts in the field of medical history, most notably medievalist Joan Cadden, argue that classical medical
writers were never so monolithic in their views of the body that they totally ignored a two-sex model based on anatomical difference. Cadden
convincingly asserts that there was no single, overarching scientific model
for understanding the sexed body bequeathed to the Middle Ages by the
star theorists of the Greco-Roman world. Indeed, celebrated medical experts, such as Aristotle, Soranus and Galen, were divided in their opinion as
to the nature of female versus male and they produced conflicting models
of how the process of human conception works or whether or not chastity
creates healthy bodies or debilitated ones.[65] Part of the innovation of the
early medieval era was the eclecticism of its intellectuals and their willingness to blend classical, biblical and even regional folkloric traditions
in the creation of innovative views on human anatomy.[66] As early medieval writers were eclectic in their use of classical medical teachings, it
is not surprising that they freely evoked, as Isidore of Seville does in his
influential textbook of the era, the *Etymologies* (*c*.636), both the one-sex
model, where both sexes generate semen, and the two-sex model, where
only men emit seed, because semen requires a body sufficiently hot to boil
it up right and good. The female body, of course, is too cold to do so, as are
the bodies of certain males, which produce only thin semen. Such semen
is incapable of clinging to female innards and thus feebly slides out of a
woman's body.[67]

In spite of which anatomical paradigm an author such as Isidore
favoured, both the one-sex and the two-sex models place men at the top of
the hierarchy – the one-sex paradigm devalues women through its claim
of female inversion and defection from a masculine norm and the two-
sex model through its privileging of male difference.[68] No matter what
classical medical model they chose to put into play in their writings, medieval writers still routinely blurred the line between sex (biological distinction) and gender (the process of inscribing culture on the body and its
habits).[69] On account of this medical and philosophical mixing, early medieval sex/gender[70] was based simultaneously on anatomy and the social,
economic, cultural, religious and political factors that move a body sexed
with a vagina into the masculine register or a body sexed with a penis into
the feminine register. Therefore, the terms 'sex' (seemingly immutable

biological distinctions) and 'gender' (contingent cultural inscriptions on
the body) work together to create anatomical meaning.[71] Such a sex/gender
system acknowledges that the category of sex can no longer be viewed
simply as 'nature' to gender's 'culture', that is, the one category (sex) is
biological and the other (gender) is mere social construction. The artificial
division between the two terms is misleading as there is no vision or interpretation of 'sex' that is absolutely free from the politics of 'gender', even
in contemporary scientific communities where the language of biology
frequently participates in and promotes a culture of male hegemony.[72]

Like contemporary gender theorists, Isidore and his successors recognised that other contingencies affect the process of making a body sexed
with a penis into the cultural product known as 'man'.[73] Gender theory's chief maven, Judith Butler, once defined gender as 'a repeated
stylization of the body, a set of repeated acts'.[74] Early medieval churchmen, who routinely equated masculinity with physical performance and
corporeal style, would concur: feminine gestures alter a virile coun-
tenance, loose belts emasculate monks and lavish hairstyles transform
men into beguiling creatures.[75] Gender also is, according to its contemporary theorists, a lifelong negotiation, shaped by contingencies of
age, class, sexual orientation, nationality, imperialism, ethnicity and even
the physical location of the body in its environment. Gender is never a
free-floating category that can be deployed in isolation from other vectors,
especially class, age and ethnicity. For medieval intellectuals, religious af-
filiation was the most important component in the gender mix, followed
closely by ethnicity, age, class, kin-group, ritual purity and the positioning of the body in space. Importantly, early medieval sex/gender was not
merely an earthbound category of analysis. Carolingianist Stuart Airlie persuasively argues that 'gender, as constructed in human society, stretched
into heaven itself via the sacred history of the past and through the human
body'.[76]

The above definition of early medieval gender – that is, the interaction of the feminine and the masculine with key vectors of class, ritual
purity, age, ethnicity and the positioning of the body in space – can be
usefully mapped onto an architectural structure where female and male
bodies of various ages and classes met and where consecrated and lay bodies collided: a ninth-century Carolingian monastic basilica. The ensuing
discussion makes the case that the sacred innards of such an edifice are
afflicted with gender trouble.

An illustrative example of such 'troubles' can be found in the virtual
basilica depicted on one of the most famous visual artifacts of the Carolingian era: the so-called Plan of St Gall (*c*.830).[77] The double-apsidal
basilica portrayed on the Plan (see Figures 1–2) was never built – hence the
structure is an excellent example of an architectural typology designed to

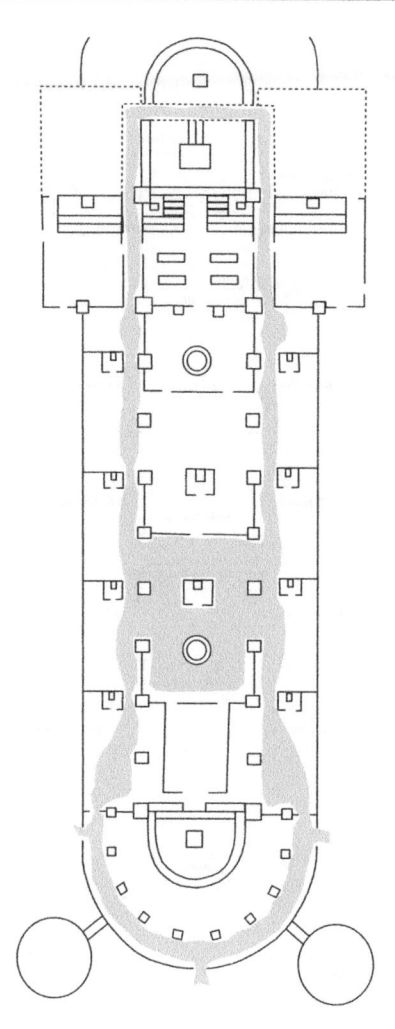

Figure 1: Virtual Basilica, Plan of St Gall (original *c*.830) with spaces open to lay bodies shown in grey. This plan created by Lindsay Turner, 2007 (after Horn & Born).

accommodate 'virtual' ritual practices: pilgrimage, liturgy, baptism, veneration of martyrs' cults. Architectural historian Werner Jacobsen rightly maintains that it is not enough to dismiss the Plan's seemingly idiosyncratic designs (such as its monumental front with towers) as a *Phantasieprodukt*.[78] In fact, the building typology of the virtual basilica resonates with a number of contemporary structures and its liturgical spaces speak to real ninth-century ritual practices. Considering the painstaking work of the scribes who penned the Plan's architectural inscriptions (*tituli*) – labelling,

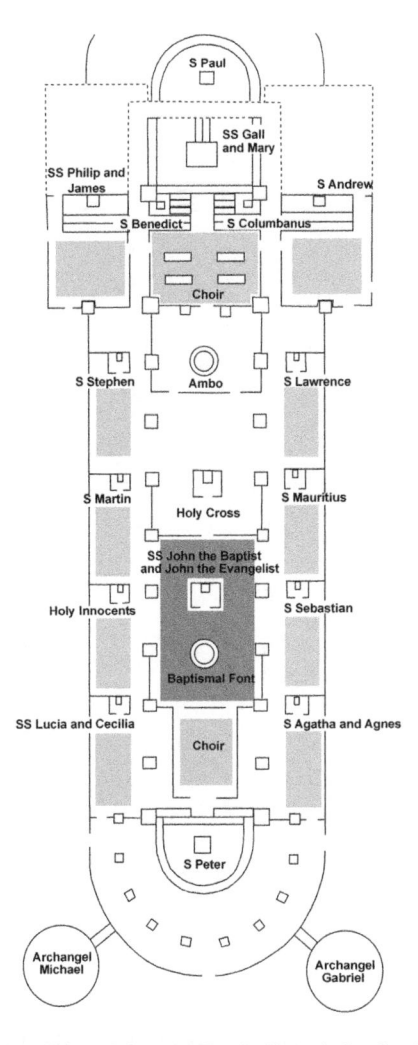

Figure 2: Virtual Basilica, Plan of St Gall (original *c.*830). Altar line-up with lay (darker shading) and monastic (lighter shading) congregational spaces. This plan created by Lindsay Turner, 2007 (after Horn & Born).

defining and even allegorising the buildings displayed on the parchment – it is possible to map out Carolingian ideologies of sacred space in terms of class, ritual status and gender. After all, the artefact under examination here is so meticulous that its creators took the time to record every door or entryway within the complex – some 290 of them in total.[79] The scrupulous rendering of the complex's basilica along with the fact that it is an extraordinary example of a monastic 'meditation machine', that is, a visual mechanism used by monks to 'recollect' heaven and to map out the contours of the faith, make this virtual construction an excellent gauge of monastic mentalities toward numinous edifices as well as potential areas of resistance to those mentalities.[80]

Mapping the somatic styles analysed above (leaky or bounded, labile or constant, cold or hot) onto the virtual basilica exemplifies how gendered paradigms play out within the ritualised structures of an idealised sacred space. This methodology has the added benefit of writing women back into a male space where previously they were thought to be invisible.[81] Figure 1 illustrates the sections of the virtual basilica of St Gall that would be open to the bodies of lay pilgrims. Architectural historians estimate that only one-sixth of the space of the basilica would house lay bodies. The remaining five-sixths would be the exclusive preserve of monastic bodies.[82]

The members of the labile laity (of all ranks) would be squeezed into the two side aisles of the sacred edifice: the north (to the viewer's left) being the exclusive preserve of elite pilgrims; the south (to the viewer's right) is set apart for non-elites.[83] Importantly, aisles in early Christian basilicas (the models for Carolingian abbey churches) were set aside for catechumens, or those receiving instruction in baptism, who were enjoined more to hear the mysteries of the faith rather than to see their enactment.[84] Clearly, the space of the St Gall basilica suggests that lay ears were passive orifices to divine speech.[85] Even the body of an emperor – should he enter the space – would be shunted off passively toward the side aisles of the basilica (like a catechumen), because the architecture and its attendant inscriptions, which draw the spectator's eye to high-status spaces, tell us that the monks did not reserve a special place for him.[86]

Moreover, the laity's view (like that of a catechumen) of the hallowed east end of the basilica would be partially obscured by both the repetition of columns and the series of railings blocking entry to the nave and designed to compartmentalise further the space, a characteristic feature of Carolingian monastic architecture. And the body of a pilgrim attempting to move from the western nave straight up to the sacred east end of the basilica would be blocked at a number of places by partitions. The space of the nave/aisles thus inscribes secondary ritual status onto pilgrim bodies (even that of the virtual emperor). The lay route to the holy east end is circuitous and the laity's ability to gaze directly into the sacred 'head' of the basilica is purposely impeded. In contrast, the monks and the abbot have well-articulated, linear entry points into the sacred east end of the basilica.[87] The space thus flattens the bodies of its lay participants, just as the surveillance towers dedicated to the panoptic archangels Michael and Gabriel (Figures 1–2) at the monumental front of the entire complex were designed to humble pilgrim bodies upon their entry into the hallowed precincts of the abbey.

In the western nave of the basilica, however, there are two central spaces where the laity could penetrate: the area surrounding the baptismal font up to the partition cordoning off the altar dedicated to the Holy Cross (Figures 1–2).[88] In Carolingian basilicas, the altar dedicated to the Holy Cross functioned to mark the barrier between the lay zone (the world) and the monastic zone (the otherworld). This strategy is clearly in play at St Gall, where the liturgical space set aside for lay use is restricted to the western end of the basilica and limited to sectors where universal rites of passage, such as baptism, would be performed. St Peter, whose corporeal remains are housed in the western apse altar, supervises the lay, performative space in the manner of a pastoral shepherd, as an accompanying inscription (*titulus*) specifies.[89] The presence of a baptismal font intimates the participation of both women and men in the space – parents and godparents perhaps of the families who labour for the monks but do so outside the monastic complex or those of elite kin in the region.[90] Although the architectural footprints of Carolingian basilicas do not reveal whether women were absent from or present in male monastic churches, historians have cited ecclesiastical legislation or saints' *vitae* to make the case that most early medieval male monasteries categorically shut their doors to female visitors.

But was there resistance to such strictures on both sides? In an important, revisionist essay, Julia M. H. Smith asks: 'Did women obediently keep away?' and answers: 'Of course not'.[91] Carolingian monastic pedagogue Hildemar of Civate (*d.* 850) concurs: he included queens among the list of invited guests to the ninth-century monastery.[92] The *Rule* itself allowed for the mother of an oblate to be present at her son's binding to the altar of a monastery, a ceremony that took place in the sacred core of an ascetic complex (*RB* 59.1–2). The church synod held at the imperial palace-complex of Aachen in 817 permitted the mothers and fathers of boy oblates to be present at the ritual fastening of their children to the altar.[93] For Smith, there never was a universal or systematic policy banning women from saints' shrines housed in male ascetic complexes. She argues that local practice, or even the tastes of individual abbots, might open the doors to female practitioners of saintly cults. For an anthropologist specialising in ritual, the fact that hegemonic 'doctrine' preaches female exclusion does not rule out the possibility that real 'practice' might teach otherwise. The existence of a building strategy designed to keep the monks apart from visitors – in this case the Plan's segregated lay entry points to the crypt situated to the north and south of the choir versus the monks' direct access from the choir – points to extensive lay use of the structure. Moreover, the corridor-crypt featured on the Plan is a building typology reserved for pilgrimage basilicas.[94] As such, its design intimates the presence of female devotees among the ranks of the pious laity. Yet women remain invisible both within the architectural footprint of these structures and in much of the secondary literature. Scholars who have studied the Plan in detail prefer to use sex neutral terms – 'pilgrims', 'laity', 'visitors' – rather than plunge into a discussion of the possibility of female bodies in male cultic spaces. Richard Sullivan is more precise about the sexed use of the St Gall basilica: males only.[95]

The array of St Gall's virtual altars supports Smith's assertion that certain male monasteries in the Carolingian empire had more permeable, sexed boundaries than one might think. Indeed, the sexed line-up of the St Gall altars is enlightening.[96] The assembly parallels to some degree the altar positions of another well-known Carolingian male-house, St Riquier (*c*.800), but the Plan changes the mix.[97] Whereas St Riquier's altars enshrine only male body parts (save the three dedications to the asomatic, masculine archangels, Raphael, Michael and Gabriel, located in the western lay zone of the basilica, perhaps to mark the area where consecrated and non-consecrated bodies are in closer proximity), St Gall's designer adds female relics. Surrounding the baptismal font in the western zone are the corporeal remains of Roman women martyrs: Saints Lucy and Cecilia to the north and Saints Agatha and Agnes to the south. The female martyrs clearly serve as celestial sponsors of the infants being baptised. In fact, Agnes is the great child-martyr herself for, as the fourth-century pope Damasus (*c*.304–384) writes in a *titulus* he crafted for her, the young girl jumped off the lap of her nurse and straight into the menacing arms of an executioner (martyrdom being a baptism by blood).[98]

Once a pilgrim moves beyond the baptismal space, s/he confronts another altar consecrated to the Holy Innocents (the children slaughtered by Herod the Great; see Matthew 2: 16–18), who, like the helpless baby subjected to salvific waters, were deemed 'will-less martyrs', that is, passive participants in the Christian cult.[99] The Innocents therefore participate in the ritual process being performed on children in the western, lay-orientated nave. Directly in front of the font is an altar consecrated to John the Baptist (the evangelical stand-in for an ascetic priest) and to the immediate right of the spectator is another sacrificial table devoted to the martyr Sebastian, whose early medieval cult was renowned for its apotropaic qualities, including the power to ward off disease. The altars create a theatrical, heavenly ensemble, one framing and directing the events taking place around the baptismal font and aimed at the bodies of innocent infants.

When a lay woman or man crosses the performative space devoted to baptism or the partitioned area to the west of the altar of the Holy Cross (the lay site of receiving the host), s/he is immediately thrust into the side aisles of the basilica and the direction taken (north versus south) depends on social and economic rank. When the pilgrim departs from the lay liturgical space – bounded as it is by numinous children, female martyrs, an evangelical

baptiser and an apotropaic male martyr – the altars metamorphose into
an all-male retinue comprised of monks, martyrs and apostles. Thus, the
closer one gets to the sacred east end, the more militantly masculine the
allegorical reading of the space becomes. The north aisle is flanked by
altars dedicated to ascetic superhero Martin of Tours and Stephen, the
proto-martyr; the south aisle is bordered by the martyrs Mauritius and
Lawrence. In the crossing, there is an altar set aside for Saint Benedict
(north) and another to the Irish ascetic missionary Columbanus (south),
making it clear that this is prime space for the monastic males, as the
body parts of celebrated monks frame the choir area. In the north arm of
the transept, there stands an altar to the Apostles Philip and James; to the
south, another altar is the preserve of the Apostle Andrew. The high altar
is a sex-hybrid: it is dedicated to both Mary (the mother of Jesus) and
the patron and founder of the (virtual) basilica, the hermit Gall. The high
altar is the only one that brings together male and female relics. Indeed,
that altar marks the subterranean space of the crypt located directly below
– with its mucky, dark, chthonic and feminine underworld.[100] The crypt
is a contagious space where virile monks bump into labile pilgrims and
these pilgrims would include both female and male votaries of the cult.
As a place of contagion, the crypt has lesser status (from the monastic
viewpoint) on the Plan than does the western apse dedicated to Peter: a
space off limits to the laity.[101]

In all, the line-up of saints' altars in the basilica provides visual cues as
to the sexed and gendered uses of the space and these numinous prompts
indicate places where male and female, as well as masculine and feminine (that is, consecrated and unconsecrated) collide. The sequence of the
entire structure speaks to the basilica's gender trouble: asomatic angels
(Michael and Gabriel, who are neither male nor female) frame the dangerous threshold space of the monumental entryway, an open orifice to the
outside world. The message sent by the angelic towers may very well be
that the numinous cult of the dead cuts through the sex divide, as Barbara
Rosenwein makes clear.[102] A male apostle, Peter, is the first human saint
encountered in the space (from the perspective of the entering lay woman
or man), but his altar is off limits to the non-consecrated, who take the
annular gallery to enter the basilica on either the north (elite pilgrims) or
south (non-elites) aisles. In so doing, unconsecrated (feminised) bodies are
blocked from penetrating the masculine zone of the western apse. The next
encounter with numinous body parts occurs in the most carnal sector of the
basilica – the western nave's space reserved for a major rite of initiation
for all Christians: baptism. As a universalising rite, the lay participants are
encircled by the apotropaic powers of infants and females as well as male
martyrs and ascetics.

From this limited foray into the sacred centre of the nave, the space ushers the lay body to the side aisles according to class (north/wealthy; south/impoverished). Here we witness the bold re-introduction of earthly hierarchies into the otherworldly space of the basilica. The consecrated patriarchy re-emerges in full vigour as the sides of the nave are lined with the body parts of militant male martyrs and self-abnegators. The female presence in the eastern zone vanishes altogether, save that of the Blessed Virgin in the womb-like space. The bodies of the virile dead thus mirror those of the monks who circulate in the nave, the western apse and the sacred eastern end of the basilica, the spaces devoted to the pure bodies of God's cantors. In contrast, the entire sacred edifice sends a very different sort of message to the lay body (even that of a nobleman or king). Lay bodies are flattened in the space (versus the erect bodies of liturgical impresarios), from the surveillance function of the twin round towers to the horizontal lengthening of the nave area to the sequestering of contaminated pilgrims to the sides and to the segregated entry way into the crypt area. Inferior status within the theatrical space devoted to the Divine Eye, materialised in the basilica by the abbot's panoptic position at the 'head' of the eastern apse, is thus inscribed on the bodies and spatial habits of the laity.

This chapter has taken readers on a 'virtual' pilgrimage to demonstrate where the early medieval somatic styles explored above (clerical/lay, masculine/feminine, bounded/leaky, hot/cold and virginal/married) bump up against one another within the anxiety-ridden contours of sacred space. Although the Plan exists solely in the realm of virtual religious practice, architectural historians no longer view its design as a mere 'product of fantasy', as Jacobsen stresses. Indeed, there is a great deal of resonance between the ritual spaces exhibited on the Plan and those of contemporary edifices (both royal and monastic). When read from the perspective of the monastic elites who etched the design onto the vellum page, the virtual basilica of St Gall visualises how ascetic male bodies trump those of their lay competitors, at least within the confines of an abbey church devised to showcase monastic bodies engaged in numinous and high status activities, such as celestial chant and liturgical action.

At the same time, the basilica betrays the sex/gender systems fashioned by monastic elites by carving out spaces where female practitioners of saintly cults could participate in the liturgy (in the western zone) and carry out cultic practices in and around the altars situated both in the nave and in the treacherous underworld of the crypt. In the corridor-crypt typology featured on the Plan, pilgrims of both sexes and all classes would come into direct contact with the saint or martyr housed there and even touch the 'foot of the coffin through a *fenestella*' or a window-like opening into the tomb – an empowering endeavour for women and men alike.[103] The Plan also produces a ritual theatre where the bodies of virtual monks, who move through the power-space of the choir or the chthonic terrain of the crypt, are dangerously open to the lay gaze. After all, ancient medical theorists bequeathed to their early medieval heirs an understanding of the human gaze as a penetrative process, a 'tactile phenomenon', in which seeing is a form of touching and, like touching, seeing can be a positive act (a warm embrace) or a negative one (the Evil Eye).[104] Therefore, it is possible to read the spatial arrangements on the Plan from the perspective of the potent lay eye and its ability to wound the erect – and hence vulnerable – bodies of virtual monks with ocular power.

Moreover, women's bodies haunt the militantly male space of a Carolingian basilica and its phallic shape (Figure 1) in ways other than as invisible practitioners of saintly cults. Female bodies are embedded in the line-up of martyrs' altars and in even the bodies of the virtual monks, who, by reason of the climatic model of sex/gender, might at any moment slide down the gender register to embrace the wet and slippery end of the spectrum. For monks, reedy, thin chants divulge in a very public manner the slippery and wet – hence feminine and cold – natures of their labile interiors. The stage-like setting of a monastic basilica thus forms a competitive arena where the hot, cold and lukewarm souls of all Christians move up and down the celestial ladder according to the 'constancy' or 'inconstancy' of their belief. The monastic basilica is a witness to the early medieval 'civilization of spectacle', wherein body techniques of ritual (chanting, reading, processing, bowing, circumambulating, venerating relics) are subject to intense scrutiny (and the perils of the Evil Eye) as to their proper virile ('hot') performances.[105] Therefore, it is possible to read the virtual basilica depicted on the Plan from the perspective of the monks who etched the design into the vellum page and promulgated it as a statement of monastic power. More satisfying to the gender theorist, however, is to read against the ascetic vision of the space to recover the agency of women, who may have had more control over the inner workings of basilicas than the historical record allows us to imagine. From an anthropological perspective, it is reasonable to conclude that the sex/gender hierarchy reconstructed here bears witness both to the political acumen of the clerical elites who crafted the narrative and to the tacit authority of those who largely remained 'mute' within its ritual structures, that is, laymen and all women.[106]

***

This early medieval contribution to the present volume has played off the theme of invisibility in a number of ways: the invisibility of women in the architectural footprint of a Carolingian monastic basilica; the invisibility of classical techniques of gender in discussions of early medieval women and men; and the invisibility of the time period, *c.*600–900, in broader works on gender and history.[107] The chapter presents new strategies for writing women back into architectural spaces where traditionally they were thought to be invisible, and does so by employing the spatial and ritual theories of colleagues working in modern fields of sociological and anthropological inquiry. The use of spatial theory here has the added bonus of demonstrating the full complexity of early medieval gender – that is, how the masculine and the feminine interact with key vectors of class, ritual status, age and the positioning of the human body in space (a strategy borrowed both from contemporary philosophers of gender and from classicists). Spatial theory also helps to bridge the gap between women's lived experience in the early medieval era and the gendered politics of the texts penned (largely) by male clerical writers. Finally, 'somatic styles' muddies the waters of chronological division between the pre-modern and the modern. While it is true that early medieval churchmen deployed climatic models of gender – and they did so in ways that empowered their group over lay competitors – it is not the case that these men were unaware of or did not believe in sexual dimorphism. The eclecticism of early medieval approaches to the body and gender reflects an overarching historical reality: 'There is, in truth, no single early Western model of sex and sexual difference'.[108]

Notes

The author wishes to thank symbolic interpretative anthropologist JoAnn D'Alisera, medieval architectural historian Kim Sexton and cultural historian Trish Starks for their pedagogical acumen as well as the two anonymous readers for *Gender & History* who offered excellent critiques of this chapter.

1. Notable examples include Mathew Kuefler, *The Manly Eunuch: Masculinity, Gender Ambiguity, and Christian Ideology in Late Antiquity* (Chicago: University of Chicago Press, 2001); Kate Cooper, *The Virgin and the Bride: Idealized Womanhood in Late Antiquity* (Cambridge: Harvard University Press, 1996); Peter Brown, *Body and Society: Men, Women, and Sexual Renunciation in Early Christianity* (New York: Columbia University Press, 1988).

2. For key works in high and late medieval gender and body history, see Caroline Walker Bynum, *Fragmentation and Redemption: Essays on Gender and the Human Body in Medieval Religion* (New York: Zone, 1991); Bruce Holsinger, *Music, Body, and Desire in Medieval Culture* (Stanford: Stanford University Press, 2001); Dyan Elliott, *Proving Woman: Female Spirituality and Inquisitional Culture in the Later Middle Ages* (Princeton: Princeton University Press, 2004).

3. On classical male bodies, see Shadi Bartsch, *The Mirror of the Self: Sexuality, Self-Knowledge, and the Gaze in the Early Roman Empire* (Chicago: University of Chicago Press, 2006); David Fredrick (ed.), *The Roman Gaze: Vision, Power, and the Body* (Baltimore: Johns Hopkins University Press, 2002); Erik Gunderson, *Staging Masculinity: The Rhetoric of Performance in the Roman World* (Ann Arbor: University of Michigan Press, 2000); Maria Wyke (ed.), *Gender and the Body in the Ancient Mediterranean* (Oxford: Blackwell, 1998); Maud W. Gleason, *Making Men: Sophists and Self-Presentation in Ancient Rome* (Princeton: Princeton University Press, 1995); Catharine Edwards, *The Politics of Immorality in Ancient Rome* (Cambridge: Cambridge University Press, 1993). For the influence of Quintilian on patristic and medieval writers, see John O. Ward,

'Quintilian and the Rhetorical Revolution of the Middle Ages', *Rhetorica* 13 (1995), pp. 231–84.

4. Janet L. Nelson, 'Monks, Secular Men and Masculinity, *c*.900', in Dawn Hadley (ed.), *Masculinity in Medieval Europe* (London: Longman, 1999), pp. 121–42.

5. Eric Goldberg, 'The Carolingian Hunt', paper presented at the 40th Annual International Congress on Medieval Studies, Kalamazoo, Michigan, May 2005.

6. On the human body as a little orchestra, see Karl F. Morrison, '"Know Thyself": Music in the Carolingian Renaissance', in *Committenti e produzione artistico-letteraria nell'alto medioevo occidentale*, Settimane di Studio del Centro Italiano di Studi sull'Alto Medioevo 39, pt. 1 (1991), pp. 369–479, here p. 379. The musical qualities of the human body – especially the body of Christ – are detailed in Holsinger, *Music, Body, and Desire*.

7. Katherine O'Brien O'Keeffe, 'Body and Law in Late Anglo-Saxon England', *Anglo-Saxon England* 27 (1998), pp. 209–32.

8. Julia M. H. Smith, *Europe after Rome: A New Cultural History 500–1000* (Oxford: Oxford University Press, 2005), pp. 100–14, provides a lively discussion of wounding the body with verbal and physical blows. Various early medieval law codes offer wergild penalties for slandering with the term 'hare' (*lepus*) as hares were believed to possess many anuses. See e. g., *Lex Salica* 30.5; text in Karl August Eckhardt (ed.), *Monumenta Germaniae Historica: Leges Nationum Germanicarum* 4 (Hanover: Hahn, 1962), p. 119: 'Si quis alterum leporem clamaverit, C(XX) denarios qui faciunt solidos III culpabilis iudicetur' ('If someone will have called another individual a hare, then let that person be judged guilty to the tune of 120 denars, which equals 3 *solidi*'). For the hare as analogous to a man who allows his anus to be penetrated, see John Boswell, *Christianity, Social Tolerance, and Homosexuality: Gay People in Western Europe from the Beginning of the Christian Era to the Fourteenth Century* (Chicago: University of Chicago Press, 1980), pp. 137–8, 142–3, 356–7; Derrick Sherwin Bailey, *Homosexuality and the Western Christian Tradition* (London: Longman, 1955), p. 84. For the power of the spoken word in early Irish legal cultures, see Robin Chapman Stacey, *Dark Speech: The Performance of Law in Early Ireland* (Philadelphia: University of Pennsylvania Press, 2007), pp. 95–134.

9. Stuart Airlie, 'Private Bodies and the Body Politic in the Divorce Case of Lothar II', *Past & Present* 161 (1998), pp. 3–38.

10. E. g., the essays in Leslie Brubaker and Julia M. H. Smith (eds), *Gender in the Early Medieval World: East and West, 300–900* (Cambridge: Cambridge University Press, 2004).

11. A recent, important foray into the cultural and political realm of the early medieval body and its clerical and lay styles is offered by Janet L. Nelson, 'England and the Continent in the Ninth Century: IV. Bodies and Minds', *Transactions of the Royal Historical Society*, 6th series, 15 (2005), pp. 1–27. For a theoretical overview of early medieval gender, see Julia M. H. Smith, 'Introduction: Gendering the Early Medieval World', in Brubaker and Smith (eds), *Gender in the Early Medieval World*, pp. 1–19.

12. For an in-depth examination of the problems with setting off the 'Dark Age' from its more refined 'Classical' counterpart, see Janet L. Nelson, 'The Dark Ages', *History Workshop* 63 (2007), pp. 191–201. For an innovative and provocative analysis of the 'conceptual chasm' separating pre-modern and modern sexuality and sexual sensibilities, see Thomas Laqueur, *Solitary Sex: A Cultural History of Masturbation* (New York: Zone, 2003).

13. Laqueur, *Solitary Sex*, p. 83, invites his readers to 'skip over' the burdensome details of pre-modern masturbation analysed in Chapter 3 and to jump straight into the more pertinent sections on Enlightenment and post-Enlightenment sexuality. For summaries of the debate between those who see a 'rupture' between the pre-modern and modern sexual past, and those who do not, see Amy Richlin, 'Towards a History of Body History', in Mark Golden and Peter Toohey (eds), *Inventing Ancient Culture: Historicism, Periodization, and the Ancient World* (London: Routledge, 1997), pp. 16–35; Ruth Mazo Karras, 'Active/Passive, Acts/Passions: Greek and Roman Sexualities', *American Historical Review* 105 (2000),

pp. 1,250–65; Marilyn Skinner, 'Zeus and Leda: The Sexuality Wars in Contemporary Classical Scholarship', *Thamyrus* 3 (1996), pp. 103–23. For examples of classicists who work within the 'sexual past as an alien past' paradigm, see David Halperin, *One Hundred Years of Homosexuality: And Other Essays on Greek Love* (New York: Routledge, 1990); John Winkler, *The Constraints of Desire: The Anthropology of Sex and Gender in Ancient Greece* (New York: Routledge, 1990).

14. For the one-sex model of pre-modern bodies, see Thomas Laqueur's groundbreaking and influential book, *Making Sex: Body and Gender from the Greeks to Freud* (Cambridge: Harvard University Press, 1990).

15. For Eve fashioned from a spare part, see Robert Alter, *The Art of Biblical Narrative* (New York: HarperCollins, 1981), p. 141.

16. For the classical world, see Rebecca Flemming, *Medicine and the Making of Roman Women: Gender, Nature, and Authority from Celsus to Galen* (Oxford: Oxford University Press, 2000); for medieval Europe, see Joan Cadden, *The Meanings of Sex Difference in the Middle Ages* (Cambridge: Cambridge University Press, 1993).

17. Judith Butler, *Gender Trouble: Feminism and the Subversion of Identity* (1990; repr. London: Routledge, 1999), pp. 136–41.

18. For scholars who interrogate the pre-modern versus the modern 'sexual divide', see Ruth Mazo Karras, 'Thomas Aquinas's Chastity Belt', in Lisa M. Bitel and Felice Lifshitz (eds), *Gender & Christianity in Medieval Europe: New Perspectives* (Philadelphia: University of Pennsylvania Press, 2008), pp. 52–67; Carolyn Dinshaw, *Getting Medieval: Sexualities and Communities, Pre-and Postmodern* (Durham: Duke University Press, 1999); John R. Clarke, 'The Warren Cup and the Contexts for Representations of Male-to-Male Love-making in Augustan and Early Julio-Claudian Art', *Art Bulletin* 75 (1993), pp. 275–94; John R. Clarke, 'The Décor of the House of Jupiter and Ganymede at Ostia Antica: A Private Residence Turned Gay Hotel?', in Elaine K. Gazda (ed.), *Roman Art in the Private Sphere: New Perspectives on the Architecture and Décor of the Domus, Villa, and Insula* (Ann Arbor: University of Michigan Press, 1991), pp. 89–104; Allen J. Frantzen's discussion of the Anglo-Saxon *baedling* in his *Before the Closet: Same-Sex Love from Beowulf to Angels in America* (Chicago: University of Chicago Press, 1998), pp. 163–7. Mark D. Jordan, *The Invention of Sodomy in Christian Theology* (Chicago: University of Chicago Press, 1997), p. 163, suggests that medieval theologians and theorists of medicine came very close to understanding sexual identity in ways reminiscent of Victorian practitioners in the fields of sexology, psychiatry and medicine.

19. Thomas F. X. Noble stresses that the study of classical vestiges of gender as deployed in early medieval Europe has not been well-served by scholars. See his 'The Transformation of the Roman World: Reflections on Five Years of Work', in Evangelos Chrysos and Ian Wood (eds), *East and West: Modes of Communication*, Transformation of the Roman World 5 (Leiden: Brill, 1999), pp. 259–77.

20. A number of scholars have offered alternative methodologies for writing women back into the historical narrative and have worked hard to reconstruct the corpus of female writings in the early Middle Ages. See e.g., Lisa M. Bitel, *Women in Early Medieval Europe, 400–1100* (Cambridge: Cambridge University Press, 2002); Valerie Garver, *Women and Aristocratic Culture in the Carolingian World* (Ithaca: Cornell University Press, forthcoming); Julia M.H. Smith, 'The Problem of Female Sanctity in Carolingian Europe, *c.*780–920', *Past & Present* 146 (1995), pp. 3–37; Janet L. Nelson, 'Gendering Courts in the Early Medieval West', in Brubaker and Smith (eds), *Gender and the Early Medieval World*, pp. 185–97; Rosamond McKitterick, 'Frauen und Schriftlichkeit im Frümittelalter', in Hans-Werner Goetz and Dagmar Baltrusch-Schneider (eds), *Weibliche Lebengestaltung im frühen Mittelalter* (Cologne: Böhlau, 1991), pp. 65–118; Suzanne Wemple, *Women in Frankish Society: Marriage and the Cloister, 500 to 900* (Philadelphia: University of Pennsylvania Press, 1981).

21. For an alternative vision of how gender played out between churchmen and elite lay circles, see Rachel Stone, 'Bound from Either Side: The Limits of Power in Carolingian Marriage Disputes, 840–870', *Gender & History* 19 (2007), pp. 467–82.

22. Hrabanus Maurus, Epistle 34; text in Ernst Dümmler (ed.), *Monumenta Germaniae Historica: Epistolae Karolini aevi* 3 (Berlin: Weidmann, 1899), p. 469: '...alioquin viri vocabulum non rite teneres, si *mollitiem* voluptatum huius saeculi sequereris'.

23. For *mollities* and its attendant classical vocabularies, see Edwards, *Immorality in Ancient Rome*, pp. 63–97.

24. For Louis's expulsion of abbots, see Eric Goldberg, *Struggle for Empire: Kingship and Conflict under Louis the German, 817–876* (Ithaca: Cornell University Press, 2006), pp. 96–7.

25. Jeffrey Jerome Cohen and Bonnie Wheeler (eds), *Becoming Male in the Middle Ages* (New York: Garland, 1997), p. viii.

26. Nelson, 'Monks, Secular Men', pp. 141–2.

27. For Walahfrid's portrait of Charlemagne in hell, see his *Visio Wettini* 11; text in Ernst Dümmler (ed.), *Monumenta Germaniae Historica: Poetae Latini aevi Carolini* 2 (Berlin: Weidmann, 1884), p. 271: 'Illic etiam quondam principem, qui Italiae et populi Romani sceptra quondam rexerat, vidisse se stantem dixerat, et verenda eius cuisdam animalis morsu laniari, reliquo corpore inmuni ab hac lesione manente' ('And he also related that he had seen him – a one-time prince – standing in that place, he who previously had exerted dominion over Italy and the people of Rome, and that the privities of that very same man were being mangled by the bite of a certain animal, while the rest of his body was remaining immune from this injury'). This text is examined within the larger context of the early medieval body by Nelson, 'Bodies and Minds', pp. 18–19.

28. Thomas Buckley and Alma Gottlieb (eds), 'Introduction' to their *Blood Magic: The Anthropology of Menstruation* (Berkeley: University of California Press, 1988), pp. 1–54, here p. 17. Buckley and Gottlieb's collection provides excellent insight into how theorists can combat cultures in which male hegemony appears to block access to acts of female empowerment or secret women's societies.

29. For the sex legislation in the penitentials, see Pierre J. Payer, *Sex and the Penitentials: The Development of a Sexual Code* (Toronto: University of Toronto Press, 1984); Bailey, *Homosexuality and the Western Christian Tradition*, pp. 91–110, surveys same-sex legislation in the capitularies and penitentials. For nuns' dildos, see Ann Matter, 'My Sister, My Spouse: Woman-Identified Women in Medieval Christianity', *Journal of Feminist Studies in Religion* 2 (1986), pp. 81–93. For Anglo-Saxon sex legislation, consult Frantzen, *Before the Closet*, pp. 138–83.

30. Georg Pertz (ed.), *Monumenta Germaniae Historica: Legum 1* (Hanover: Hahn, 1835), p. 345: 'Et quod commixtio carnalis cum uxoribus gratia fieri debeat prolis, non voluptatis'. This passage is discussed in Ruth Mazo Karras, *Sexuality in Medieval Europe: Doing unto Others* (London: Routledge, 2005), p. 66.

31. For the debate as to whether or not the penitentials provide historians with a 'sociology of sex' for the early medieval era or whether they are a repository of ideology rather than a gauge of actual practice, see Frantzen, *Before the Closet*, pp. 138–83; Rob Meens, 'The Frequency and Nature of Early Medieval Penance', in Peter Biller and A. J. Minnis (eds), *Handling Sin: Confession in the Middle Ages*, York Studies in Medieval Theology 2 (York: University of York Press, 1998), pp. 35–61; Pierre Payer, 'The Humanism of the Penitentials and the Continuity of the Penitential Tradition', *Medieval Studies* 46 (1984), pp. 340–54; Payer, *Sex and the Penitentials*, pp. 3–18. Jordan, *Invention of Sodomy*, p. 41, characterises the penitentials as examples of 'theological speech' about sex acts.

32. For the theory of how such sexual 'shadowing' works, see Frantzen, *Before the Closet*, pp. 13–15.

33. For Judas's kiss, see Matthew 26: 48–9; Mark 14: 44–5; Luke 22: 47–8. Morrison, 'Music in the Carolingian Renaissance', pp. 382–5, surveys the ritual attributes of monastic kissing.

There are a number of Carolingian edicts against monks kissing women on the mouth. See e.g., the legislation of Aachen 816, canon 14; text in Josef Semmler (ed.), *Corpus Consuetudinum Monasticarum* (CCM) 1 (Siegburg: F. Schmitt, 1963), p. 460: 'et nullam quamlibet mulierem osculentur'. For the variety of early medieval kissing styles, see Isidore of Seville, *Liber differentiarum* 1.398; text in J. P. Migne (ed.), *Patrologiae cursus completus: Series Latina* 83 (Paris: Apud Garniere Fratres, 1850), col. 51 (hereafter Migne [ed.], PL).

34. Lay men wrote poetic and literary works, and cloistered and lay women penned a select corpus of hagiographical, poetic, mystical and educational treatises. The bulk of our evidence, however, comes from clerical authors.

35. The use of anthropological theory (specifically, anthropologists who specialise in gender, ritual and religious agency) in this chapter stands in direct contrast to the views of Philippe Buc, *The Dangers of Ritual: Between Early Medieval Texts and Social Scientific Theory* (Princeton: Princeton University Press, 2001). Buc critiques scholars of late ancient and early medieval Christianity who have incorporated structuralist and functionalist models of the anthropological studies of ritual – largely penned prior to the 1980s – into their work on the political 'rituals' of the early centuries of the Middle Ages. The study undertaken here draws from more recent works authored by anthropologists who approach the study of ritual in a way that acknowledges the discursive nature of both the texts and even eyewitness accounts of rituals in contemporary and past societies. Equally, this chapter makes the case that earlier structuralist studies of the body, ritual and gender, such as those pioneered by Mary Douglas (1921–2007), continue to provide important models for scholarship focused on how to write women back into religious systems where their participation is limited (or beyond retrieval) or where the texts describing their cultic activities are authored by men. For notable works in anthropology among the many post-1980 books and articles focusing on gender, ritual, and religious agency, see Janice Boddy, *Wombs and Alien Spirits: Women, Men, and the Zār Cult in Northern Sudan* (Madison: University of Wisconsin Press, 1989); Sherry Ortner, *Making Gender: The Politics and Erotics of Culture* (Boston: Beacon Press, 1996); Fadwa El Guindi, *Veil: Modesty, Privacy, and Resistance* (Oxford: Berg, 1999); JoAnn D'Alisera, 'Mapping Women's Displacement and Difference', in her *An Imagined Geography: Sierra Leonean Muslims in America* (Philadelphia: University of Pennsylvania Press, 2004), pp. 95–123. For a collection of essays exemplifying literary approaches to the study of anthropology, see Edward Bruner (ed.), *Text, Play and Story: The Construction and Reconstruction of Self and Society*, Proceedings, American Ethnological Society (Washington DC: American Anthropological Association, 1983). For the classic structuralist treatment of gender and ritual, see Mary Douglas, *Purity and Danger: An Analysis of Concept of Pollution and Taboo* (1966; repr. London: Routledge, 2002).

36. See Mary Douglas, 'The System at War with Itself', in her *Purity and Danger*, pp. 173–95. See also Buckley and Gottlieb (eds), 'Introduction', *Blood Magic*, pp. 1–54. Buckley and Gottlieb's collection provides excellent insight into how theorists can combat cultures in which male hegemony appears to block access to acts of female empowerment or secret women's societies (as does Boddy's work on the *zār* cult in the Northern Sudan).

37. Citation from the on-line version of the *Oxford English Dictionary* (Oxford, copyright, 2008), entry: labile.

38. The bibliography for the chief features of western pre-modern gender is quite extensive. Key works include Flemming, *Medicine and the Making of Roman Women*; Cadden, *Meanings of Sex Difference*; Leslie Dean-Jones, *Women's Bodies in Classical Greek Science* (Oxford: Oxford University Press, 1994); Dale B. Martin, *The Corinthian Body* (New Haven: Yale University Press, 1995); Danielle Jacquart and Claude Thomasset, *Sexuality and Medicine in the Middle Ages*, tr. Matthew Adamson (Princeton: Princeton University Press, 1988); Aline Rousselle, *Porneia: On Desire and the Body in Antiquity*, tr. Felicia Pheasant (Oxford: Blackwell, 1988).

39. Anne Carson, 'Putting Her in Her Place: Woman, Dirt, and Desire', in David M. Halperin, John J. Winkler and Froma I. Zeitlin (eds), *Before Sexuality: The Construction of Erotic Experience in the Ancient Greek World* (Princeton: Princeton University Press, 1990), pp. 135–69, here p. 138.

40. On nocturnal emissions and the male ascetic body, see Conrad Leyser, 'Masculinity in Flux: Nocturnal Emissions and the Limits of Celibacy', in Hadley (ed.), *Masculinity in Medieval Europe*, pp. 103–20.

41. On the transmission of these gendered physiognomies into the Middle Ages and a survey of the primary sources, see Jacquart and Thomasset, *Sexuality and Medicine*, pp. 48–86.

42. See the diagram provided by Jacquart and Thomasset, *Sexuality and Medicine*, p. 49.

43. Carolingian monastic writer Hildemar of Corbie/Civate, *Expositio regulae S. Benedicti*, in Rupert Mittermüller (ed.), *Vita et regula SS. P. Benedicti: Una cum expositione regulae a Hildemaro tradita* (Regensburg: F. Pustet, 1880), p. 160, analyses the upper and lower regions of the body in terms of their relationship with celestial hierarchies. The upper body, quite naturally, emerges as the superior region while the lower body, especially the feet, is in an inferior position. For Hildemar within the context of Carolingian monasticism, see Mayke de Jong, *In Samuel's Image: Child Oblation in the Early Medieval West* (Leiden: Brill, 1996), pp. 68–73; Mayke de Jong, 'Growing up in a Carolingian Monastery: Magister Hildemar and his Oblates', *Journal of Medieval History* 9 (1983), pp. 99–128. For the manuscript history of the *Expositio*, see Ludwig Traube and Heribert Plenkers, *Textgeschichte der Regula S. Benedicti*, Abhandlungen der Königlich Bayerischen Akademie der Wissenschaften: Philosophisch-philogische und historische Klasse 25 (Munich: Verlag der Königlich Bayerischen Akademei der Wissenchaften, 1910), pp. 40–45. See also M. Alfred Schroll, *Benedictine Monasticism as Reflected in the Warnefrid-Hildemar Commentaries on the Rule* (New York: Columbia University Press, 1941), pp. 23–5.

44. The translation of *pudicitia* as 'impenetrability' is in keeping with important philological and historical work penned by classicists, who argue that *pudicitia* carries with it the meaning of penetration/violation, sexual virtue and the obligation to keep something inviolate that might be violated. See most recently Rebecca Langlands, *Sexuality Morality in Ancient Rome* (Cambridge: Cambridge University Press, 2006). Langlands centres her study of Roman morality on the term *pudicitia*. The classical meanings of *pudicitia* as 'sexual virtue' and 'impenetrability' established by Langlands translate well within the priestly/ascetic contexts of early medieval sex/gender systems.

45. Carson, 'Woman, Dirt, and Desire', pp. 139, 156.

46. Frantzen, *Before the Closet*, pp. 76–7; Jane Tibbets Schulenburg, *Forgetful of Their Sex: Female Sanctity and Society, ca. 500–1100* (Chicago: University of Chicago Press, 1998), pp. 152–3.

47. On the various qualities of male voices, see Isidore of Seville, *Etymologies* 3.20. This passage is cited and analysed by Holsinger, *Music, Body, and Desire*, p. 297. Flemming gives examples of ancient medical theorists who believed that the voices of eunuchs, women and children were 'thinner' and 'weaker' than adult male voices, *Medicine and the Making of Roman Women*, pp. 156, 225.

48. For key studies of early medieval holy women, see Gisela Muschiol, *Famula dei: Zur Liturgie in merowingischen Frauenklöstern* (Münster: Aschendorff, 1994); Jo Ann McNamara, *Sisters in Arms: Catholic Nuns through Two Millennia* (Cambridge: Harvard University Press, 1996); Schulenburg, *Forgetful of Their Sex*; Suzanne F. Wemple, *Women in Frankish Society: Marriage and the Cloister, 500–900* (Philadelphia, University of Pennsylvania Press, 1981).

49. Theodulf of Orléans, *Capitulare ad eosdem* 2.7.11; text in Peter Brommer (ed.), *Monumenta Germaniae Historica: Capitula episcoporum* 1 (Hanover: Hahn, 1984), p. 168; discussed in Laqueur, *Solitary Sex*, pp. 142–4.

50. Alcuin, *Liber de virtutibus et vitiis* 28–9; text in Migne (ed.), PL 101, cols. 633–4.

51. Buc, *Dangers of Ritual*, p. 20.
52. Isidore of Seville, *Etymologies* 11.2.24; text in Lindsay (ed.), *Etymologiarum libri xx*, vol. 2, p. 24. For classical Roman views on *femineus amor*, see Amy Richlin, *The Garden of Priapus: Sexuality & Aggression in Roman Humor* (New York and Oxford: Oxford University Press, 1992), pp. 3–4. For the Greek equivalent to *femineus amor* (Gr., *philogunēs*, the 'woman-lover' or *gunaikomanēs*, the 'woman mad'), see James N. Davidson, *Courtesans and Fishcakes: The Consuming Passions of Classical Athens* (New York: St Martin's, 1998), p. 161.
53. Stephen D. Moore, *God's Beauty Parlor and Other Queer Spaces in and around the Bible* (Stanford: Stanford University Press, 2001), p. 16.
54. For the text of *De Principiis* in 5 volumes, see Henri Crouzel and Manlio Simonetti (eds), *Origène: Traité des principes*, Sources chrétiennes (SC) 252–3, 268–9, 312 (Paris: Éditions du Cerf, 1978–84). For an analysis of Origen's exegesis in terms of its implications for ascetic bodies, see Brown, *Body and Society*, pp. 162–5.
55. *De Principiis* 1.3.8; text in Crouzel and Simonetti (eds), SC, 252, pp. 162–4.
56. *De Principiis* 2.8.3; text in Crouzel and Simonetti (eds), SC 252, pp. 344–6.
57. *De Principiis* 2.6.4–2.6.5; text in Crouzel and Simonetti (eds), SC 252, pp. 318–20.
58. *De Principiis* Preface 8; text in Crouzel and Simonetti (eds), SC 252, pp. 86–8, discussed in Brown, *Body and Society*, p. 165.
59. Origen's exegetical texts were massively influential over the early medieval west, especially among Carolingian intellectual circles; see Henri de Lubac, *Medieval Exegesis: The Four Senses of Scripture*, tr. Mark Sebanc (Grand Rapids, Michigan: Eerdmans, 1998), pp. 161–224.
60. Alcuin, Epistle 116; text in Ernst Dümmler (ed.), *Monumenta Germaniae Historica: Epistolae Karolini aevi* 2 (Berlin: Weidmann, 1895), p. 171: 'et quocumque vadas, liber sancti Gregorii pastoralis tecum pergat . . . Speculum est enim pontificalis vitae et medicina contra singula diabolicae fraudis vulnera' ('And wherever you may go, let holy Gregory's pastoral book accompany you . . . for it is a mirror of the pontifical life and medicine against individual wounds of devilish deceit').
61. See R. A. Markus, *The End of Ancient Christianity* (Cambridge: Cambridge University Press, 1990), pp. 159–60, 166–7. For Gregory's use of hot (*calidus*), cold (*frigidus*) and lukewarm (*tepidus/tepor*) metaphors, see his *Pastoral Care* 3.34; text in Bruno Judic, Floribert Rommel, and Charles Morel (eds), *Règle pastorale*, Sources chrétiennes 382 (Paris: Éditions du Cerf, 1992), p. 510.
62. For liminal status as 'betwixt and between', see the classic essay by Victor Turner, 'Liminality and *Communitas*', in his *The Ritual Process: Structure and Anti-Structure* (Chicago: Aldine Publishing, 1969), pp. 94–113.
63. Most famously and influentially, Laqueur's *Making Sex*. For a critique of Laqueur, see Katharine Park and Robert Nye, 'Destiny is Anatomy', *New Republic*, 18 February 1991, pp. 53–7.
64. Cadden, *Sex Difference*, p. 27; Flemming, *Medicine and the Making of Roman Women*, pp. 199–201.
65. Cadden, *Sex Difference*, p. 3. For Cadden's discussions of Aristotle, Galen and Soranus, see *Sex Difference*, pp. 21–39. Flemming also critiques Laqueur's one-sex model and provides an overview of ancient gynaecology, *Medicine and the Making of Roman Women*, pp. 12–17, 114–22.
66. Cadden, *Sex Difference*, p. 4–5.
67. Isidore of Seville, *Etymologies* 11.1.142; text in Lindsay (ed.), *Etymologiarum libri xx*, vol. 2, p. 20. See also Cadden, *Sex Difference*, pp. 52–3, which explores Isidore's use of the one-seed and two-seed models of human reproduction.
68. Richlin, 'Towards a History of Body History', p. 29; Martin, *Corinthian Body*, p. 32; Lynda Coon, 'Gender and the Body, c.600–1100', in Julia M. H. Smith and Thomas F. X.

Noble (eds), *The Cambridge History of Christianity 3: 600–1100* (Cambridge: Cambridge University Press, 2008), pp. 433–52.

69. For handy medieval definitions of sex/gender and sexuality, see Karras, *Doing unto Others*, pp. 5–9.

70. The use of the term 'sex/gender' here is designed to stress the 'problematic space' between the two categories and *not* to suggest that a 'crisp distinction' exists between them; see Eve Kosofsky Sedgwick, *Epistemology of the Closet* (1990; repr. Berkeley: University of California Press, 2008), p. 29.

71. Butler, *Gender Trouble*, pp. 9–11.

72. Butler, *Gender Trouble*, p. 139; Sedgwick, *Epistemology of the Closet*, pp. 27–8; Flemming, *Medicine and the Making of Roman Women*, pp. 1–28.

73. Cohen and Wheeler (eds), *Becoming Male*, p. xix.

74. Butler, *Gender Trouble*, pp. 43–4.

75. On curtailing flamboyant male ascetic styles, see Benedict of Aniane, *Codex regularum* 62.10–16 (referencing a variety of early medieval monastic precepts against excess and effeminacy); text in Pierre Bonnerue (ed.), *Corpus Christianorum Continuatio mediaevalis* 168A (Turnhout: Brepols, 1999), pp. 530–36. Ardo's *Vita* (38) of Benedict of Aniane expresses anxiety over the length of monastic gowns; text in Georg Pertz (ed.), *Monumenta Germaniae Historica: Scriptores* 15:1 (Hanover: Hahn, 1887), p. 217: 'In abitu quoque dissimiles fecerat multorum consuetudo. Siquidem nonnullis usque ad talos cocullae pendebant. Quam ob rem vir Dei uniformem cunctis tenendum monachis instituit modum, ut non amplius a duobus cubitis excederet mensura vel usque ad genua pertingere posset' ('Moreover, in terms of dress the custom of many [monks] had made them dissimilar to one another. It is even possible that the cowls of some [monks] used to hang down to their ankles. On account of this disparity in dress, the man of God established a uniform style to be binding on all monks, so that the length of their garments should not extend more than two cubits or reach only as far as the knees').

76. Airlie, 'Private Bodies and the Body Politic', p. 23.

77. For a meticulous study of the St Gall 'virtual' basilica, see Werner Jacobsen, *Der Klosterplan von St. Gallen und die karolingische Architektur: Entwicklung und Wandel von Form und Bedeutung im fränkischen Kirchenbau zwischen 751 und 840* (Berlin: Deutscher Verlag für Kunstwissenschaft, 1992). Other key works on the Plan include Charles B. McClendon, *The Origins of Medieval Architecture: Building in Europe, A.D. 600–900* (New Haven: Yale University Press, 2005), pp. 163–72; Peter Ochsenbein and Karl Schmuki (eds), *Studien zum St. Galler Klosterplan II*, Mitteilungen zur vaterländischen Geschichte 52 (St Gall: Historischer Verein des Kantons St Gallen, 2002); Walter Horn and Ernest Born, *The Plan of St. Gall: A Study of the Architecture and Economy of and Life in a Paradigmatic Carolingian Monastery*, University of California Studies in the History of Art 19, 3 vols (Berkeley: University of California Press, 1979); Richard E. Sullivan, 'What was Carolingian Monasticism? The Plan of St. Gall and the History of Monasticism', in Alexander Callander Murray (ed.), *After Rome's Fall: Narrators and Sources of Early Medieval History, Essays Presented to Walter Goffart* (Toronto: University of Toronto Press, 1998), pp. 251–87.

78. Jacobsen, *Klosterplan von St. Gallen*, p. 136.

79. Horn and Born, *Plan of Saint Gall*, vol. 1, p. 68.

80. On the Plan as a meditative *machina*, see Mary Carruthers, *The Craft of Thought: Meditation, Rhetoric, and the Making of Images, 400–1200* (Cambridge: Cambridge University Press, 1998), pp. 228–31.

81. For writing women back into late ancient ritual spaces where they have been invisible, see Aneilya K. Barnes, *Gender and Domestic Space in the First Christian Basilicas* (unpublished doctoral thesis, University of Arkansas, 2007).

82. Horn and Born, *Plan of St. Gall*, vol. 1, p. 127.

83. The *tituli* accompanying the Plan make it clear that elite lay bodies would be ushered into the northern sector of the basilica while lower-class bodies would be moved to the

southern side. For a detailed exploration of the classed dimensions of the virtual basilica, see Lynda Coon, *Dark Age Bodies: Gender and Monastic Practice in the Early Medieval West* (forthcoming University of Pennsylvania Press), ch. 7: 'Gendering the Plan of St Gall'.

84. On the position of catechumens in early Christian basilicas in Rome, see R. Ross Holloway, *Constantine and Rome* (New Haven: Yale University Press, 2004), pp. 61, 72–3.

85. On the esoteric implications of monastic speech, see Conrad Leyser, *Authority and Asceticism from Augustine to Gregory the Great* (Oxford: Oxford University Press, 2000), esp. pp. 120–22.

86. Past architectural historians have argued that the monumental front to the monastic complex with its two soaring round-towers may have been designed to house royal bodies. Recent theorists, however, have moved away from the theory of the western front (or other Carolingian westworks) as a *Kaiserkirche*.

87. The abbot has a private entryway from his *aula* situated in the north-east quadrant of the Plan. From there, he directly accesses the sacred 'head' of the basilica; the monks enter the hallowed east end from the cloister complex located to the south of the choir.

88. Jacobsen takes his reader on a tour where the lay body could penetrate within the hallowed precincts of the St Gall basilica: Werner Jacobsen, 'Der St. Galler Klosterplan – 300 Jahre Forschung', in Ochsenbein and Schmuki (eds), *Studien zum St. Galler Klosterplan II*, pp. 13–56, esp. pp. 47–52. Overall, he argues that the space was 'lay friendly' (*laienfreundliche*) and 'lay open' (*laienoffene*).

89. 'Hic Petrus eclae pastor sortitur honorē' ('Here, the shepherd of the church Peter is choosing [souls] with respect to honour'); text in Horn and Born, *Plan of St. Gall*, vol. 3, p. 23.

90. For the Carolingian liturgy of baptism and the role of godparents in it, see Joseph H. Lynch, *Godparents and Kinship in Early Medieval Europe* (Princeton: Princeton University Press, 1986), pp. 285–304.

91. Julia M.H. Smith, 'Women at the Tomb: Access to Relic Shrines in the Early Middle Ages', in Ian Wood and Kathleen Mitchell (eds), *The World of Gregory of Tours* (Leiden: Brill, 2002), pp. 163–80, here p. 172. See also Janet L. Nelson, 'Les femmes et l'évangelisation au IXe siècle', *Revue du Nord* 269 (1986), pp. 471–85; Jane Tibbetts Schulenburg, 'Gender, Celibacy, and Proscriptions of Sacred Space: Symbol and Practice', in Virginia Chieffo Raguin and Sarah Stanbury (eds), *Women's Space: Patronage, Place, and Gender in the Medieval Church* (Albany: SUNY Press, 2005), pp. 185–205; Schulenburg, 'Women's Monasteries and Sacred Space: The Promotion of Saints' Cults and Miracles', Bitel and Lifshitz (eds), *Gender & Christianity in Medieval Europe*, pp. 68–86.

92. Hildemar, *Expositio*, p. 505.

93. Aachen 817, canon 17; text in Semmler (ed.), CCM 1, p. 477: 'Ut puerum pater et mater altari tempore oblationis offerant et petitionem pro eo coram laicis testibus faciant quam et tempore intelligibili ipse puer confirmet' ('When a father and a mother offer their son to the altar [of a monastery] at the time of his oblation, they should make a petition for him in front of lay witnesses, a petition which the boy himself should confirm at the time when he has the understanding to do so').

94. For a detailed architectural study of the crypt on the Plan, see Jacobsen, *Klosterplan von St. Gallen*, pp. 112–20. Jacobsen identifies the typology as a *Winkelgangkrypta*, 'corridor crypt' or 'rectilinear ring-crypt' not unlike the one built at the abbey of Corvey in the 820s. On the *Winkelgangkrypta*, see also John Crook, *The Architectural Setting of the Cult of Saints in the Early Christian West, c. 300–1200* (Oxford: Clarendon, 2000), pp. 107–20. Crook views the crypt on the Plan as a 'hall-crypt', pp. 136–8.

95. Sullivan, 'What was Carolingian Monasticism?', p. 274.

96. Angelus A. Häussling, 'Liturgie in der Karolingerzeit und der St. Galler Klosterplan', in Ochsenbein and Schmuki (eds), *Studien zum St. Galler Klosterplan II*, pp. 151–83, esp.

pp. 159–63, surveys the altars and their spatial positioning on the Plan as well as the theological/historical subtexts of their arrangement.

97. For the spatial arrangements of St Riquier, see Susan A. Rabe, *Faith, Art, and Politics at Saint-Riquier* (Philadelphia: University of Pennsylvania Press, 1995).

98. 'Nutricis gremium subito liquisse puellam/sponte trucis calcasse minas rabiemque tyranni' ('Immediately, Agnes abandoned the lap of her wet-nurse/Voluntarily she trampled under foot the threats of the savage one and the madness of the tyrant'); text in Antonio Ferrúa (ed.), *Epigrammata Damasiana: recensuit et adnotavit Antonius Ferrua*, Sussidi allo studio delle antichità cristiane 2 (Rome: Pontificio Istituto di Archeologia Cristiana, 1942), p. 176.

99. For the relationship between the Holy Innocents and Christian views on baptism, see Peter Cramer, *Baptism and Change in the Early Middle Ages, c. 200–1150* (Cambridge: Cambridge University Press, 1993), pp. 133–6.

100. For the classic discussion of the feminised cryptic spaces of the pre-Gothic versus the phallic exhibitionism of high medieval architecture, see Henri Lefebvre, *The Production of Space*, tr. Donald Nicholson-Smith (Oxford: Blackwell, 1991), pp. 254–62.

101. I wish to thank Honors Scholar and Classical Studies major Brent Harbaugh (Fulbright College, University of Arkansas) for this point.

102. 'Saints' cults tended to cut the boundaries that separated the laity from the clergy, men from women, rich from poor': Rosenwein, 'Inaccessible Cloisters: Gregory of Tours and Episcopal Exemption', in Wood and Mitchell (eds), *World of Gregory of Tour*, pp. 181–97, here p. 186. For the classic theory of how pilgrimage forces the bodies of its practitioners into a liminal status, see Victor Turner and Edith Turner, *Image and Pilgrimage in Christian Culture* (New York: Columbia University Press, 1978).

103. Crook, *Architectural Setting of the Cult of the Saints*, p. 138.

104. On ancient gaze theory, see Bartsch, *Mirror of the Self*, pp. 138–52. Bartsch notes that the philologist Varro equates the act of seeing with physical violation, p. 150. See also Pamela Gordon, 'Some Unseen Monster: Rereading Lucretius on Sex', in Fredrick (ed.), *Roman Gaze*, pp. 86–109.

105. Bartsch, *Mirror of the Self*, p. 118.

106. Boddy, *Wombs and Alien Spirits*, p. 5, makes the case that the female participants in the *zār* cult in the Northern Sudan both 'tacitly reproduce the dominant system of meanings' imposed by males *and* subvert those meanings by reading rituals 'in light of their own experience'.

107. The play-off of 'visibility' and 'invisibility' is greatly indebted to the pioneering work of classicist David Fredrick; 'Invisible Rome', in his (ed.), *Roman Gaze*, pp. 1–30.

108. Park and Nye, 'Destiny is Anatomy', p. 54.

3 Gendering the History of Women's Healthcare

Monica H. Green

The earliest second-wave historical studies on women in/and medicine, at least in the United States, grew directly out of the women's health movement of the 1960s and 1970s when concerns about birth control and female autonomy in the birth process were high on the political agenda.[1] These, in turn, grew out of earlier work on the history of women's roles in medicine that had been written by participants in the nineteenth- and early twentieth-century fight for women's rights to join the medical professions in North America and Europe. Western historians, both specialists in the history of medicine and historians of women generally, are heirs to this double inheritance. The purpose of the present chapter is to suggest that we have not yet sufficiently examined how the agendas of these two very different groups have affected the questions we ask or, as I will argue here, do not ask. The result is that the central questions of feminist medical history are still dictated, even if only subtly, by the political and intellectual contexts in which that history was born, contexts that no longer define our current objectives as historians. Neither first-wave nor early second-wave feminism articulated the concept of 'gender' – one of several axes along which power is distributed and contested in historical societies, with its implied premise that it is possible to view women's and men's actions as dictated by something beyond their sexed biological being. As this *Gender and Change* book attests, the concept of gender has made enormously productive contributions to historical studies over the past two decades. However, although gender has been incorporated into many aspects of medical history – in the sense, for example, of the creation of gendered identities of individual medical practitioners or gender differentials in the provision of healthcare – certain narratives within the field have remained surprisingly immune to a reconceptualisation that, one would think, should have come from looking at women *and men* in constant interplay over how knowledge of the female body was generated, disseminated and used.[2]

My particular suggestion of 'gendering' the history of the female body and the systems of ideas and practices connected to its medical care might seem at first pointless, or at the very least redundant. Is the female body not, by definition, already feminine? Yet I am proposing no idle semantic games. Rather, I wish to explore how the epistemologies and technologies of the female body are created: who knew what about the female body? And when did they know it? As such, this analysis involves both medicine *for* women and medicine as practised *by* women. My own training is in the traditions of western European medical thought and practice, and it is out of that experience that many of the following questions arise. But, precisely because several years ago I began to read widely in historical and anthropological studies outside the western tradition, I have recognised some limitations of the second-wave framework that I myself grew up with. Chiefly, the central narrative of an eighteenth-century shift to male control of women's healthcare seemed to have its chronology wrong. Attempts to unseat the common assumption that in pre-modern western Europe 'women's health was women's business' have been going on for twenty years, with more and more evidence being brought forward of men's regular involvement in gynaecology, indeed their dominance of the field as it was reflected in learned medicine, from the Middle Ages onwards. Likewise, men's involvement in obstetrics was significant enough to make them, not women, the authoritative figures in certain obstetrical procedures and kinds of knowledge as early as the fourteenth century. Yet, aside from a few specialists in pre-modern medical history, most historians still assume that men were not involved in such aspects of gynaecological care as menstrual dysfunctions or infertility, least of all obstetrical conditions, until the eighteenth century. The tendency to universalise discourse about women's health has, in turn, caused these presumptions about the western tradition to be considered the norm against which claims about the history of women's healthcare in other times and places are then made.

I am proposing more than a simple fine-tuning of chronology, however. If it were merely a question of establishing, for example, that English male practitioners began to involve themselves in obstetrics in the fifteenth century rather than the eighteenth, then all we are doing is pushing a major cultural shift (itself still unquestioned) into an earlier period. This does little to alter our perspective, for surely the eighteenth-century controversies about male midwives' use of forceps or the education of female midwives were no less real for having had precedents in an earlier period. My point is rather to stress the ways the first-wave and second-wave agendas have occluded our peripheral vision by nudging us to think in absolutes that themselves render the historian's pursuit of change over time null and void. In what follows, I propose that it might be worth exploring a *gendered* history of women's healthcare and fertility control, one based on the premise that knowledge about anatomy, physiology or therapeutics does not arise fundamentally out of one's biological nature but from the *experience* of living in a social world where all forms of knowledge are gendered, both in their genesis and in their dissemination. As such, medical knowledge, and the practices that arise out of it, proves to be very much a part of history, continually in flux and contested.

I focus on two topics that have been central to feminist studies of medical history – the history of midwifery and women's knowledge and use of contraceptive devices and abortifacients – and examine more closely where the emphases and oversights in the history of women's medicine have fallen.[3] I argue for the need to set the history of women's healthcare into a larger nexus of analyses: the history of midwifery needs to be part of the history of both medical professionalisation and women's healthcare generally, not treated as an isolated topic, while the history of contraceptives and abortifacients needs to be set into larger questions of demographic history – whatever emotions or motives we would like to see at play in any individual woman's decision to limit or disrupt her fertility, her decisions also had an impact on society as a whole. Precisely because this chapter argues against making universalising claims about women, I will explore how attention to non-western historical narratives and anthropological studies can broaden our awareness of where the western narrative that has thus far dominated medical history has led to historiographical and cultural blind spots. Particularly useful is medical anthropology's focus on ethnographic description – observer participation of, and structured interviews with, members of the society under examination – which allows access not simply to the methods, but to the *motives* behind medical practices that are all too often invisible to the historian relying primarily on written records. By gendering the history of women's healthcare and contraception – questioning our *assumption* that women, and only women, possess some 'natural' knowledge about the female body – we open up conceptual spaces for exploring how that knowledge might have been contested across gender boundaries. My objective is not to 'add men and stir', but rather to call for a fuller, richer history of women's healthcare that shows medical epistemologies as various kinds of situated knowledge.[4] Such a history is of importance not simply to historians of medicine, but to all who hope to explore how persons inhabiting female bodies have navigated their way through history.

The monopoly of midwives: origins of the Ehrenreich–English thesis

Let me begin *in medias res*, with second-wave feminism. Two works by the non-historians Barbara Ehrenreich and Deidre English – *Witches,*

Midwives, and Nurses (1971) and *Complaints and Disorders: The Sexual Politics of Sickness* (1973) – heavily influenced the early articulations of a history of women's medicine among English-speaking scholars (and scholars working in other languages as well).[5] I emphasise that neither Ehrenreich nor English were historians, not to invoke some professional exclusionism (feminist studies would be nothing without its inherent interdisciplinarity), but rather to stress that their theses about the history of women's healthcare were based on uncritical readings of secondary and a limited number of published primary sources and not on the in-depth researches into primary documentation that most of us would consider the gold standard of historical research.[6] The central arguments of the latter book – that women were largely the victims of male medical control and even misogyny in the nineteenth and early twentieth centuries – have effectively been set aside by subsequent, more nuanced work that has shown first, women's agency as patients and (often) their willingness to accept or even seek out the therapies of men; and second, the fact that, when women did become formal medical practitioners, they did not uniformly adopt different perspectives on the practice of women's medicine.[7] In this sense, then, Ehrenreich and English's work on nineteenth-century medicine followed a fairly normal trajectory for the development of a historical question: it put forward a bold thesis that was then tested, questioned and challenged by subsequent study. *Complaints and Disorders* quickly made itself obsolete and it is neither cited by scholars nor does it direct current historiographical agendas.

The influence of their earlier book, however, has been quite different. Put simply, it argued for a 'golden age' in which women practised medicine and shared knowledge about their bodies freely with each other.[8] This non-hierarchical empiricism came to an end when the 'medieval' witch-hunts started targeting learned women for extermination and reduced other forms of women's medical practice to the subordinate and non-authoritative stature of 'nurse'. The reasons for the initial success of this small pamphlet (a mere forty-five pages in its original English edition) in the 1970s should be obvious. It articulated a historical past that conformed to the political present that the women's health movement was attempting to create: one where women could 'once again' control their reproductive processes and be authorities in their own right on matters of their health.

More surprising than the initial success of this book, which did not attempt to hide its polemical intent, is its *continued* popularity. It is still in print in English and has been translated into at least four different languages; only recently it was among the top ten sellers in the category 'Socio-Cultural Anthropology – General & Miscellaneous' at a major online bookseller.[9] It is continually quoted ad infinitum in popular discourse on witchcraft and in historical narratives that female medical practitioners tell themselves and, twenty, thirty years after its initial publication, it was, and still is, cited by professional scholars as 'background' for statements about the history of European midwives and women's other roles in the medical professions.[10]

Moreover, the Ehrenreich and English thesis has maintained a hegemonic hold on the 'grand narrative' of European women's medical history even when it is not directly cited. It posited three central tenets: first, that midwives had an unchallenged monopoly on birth; second, less explicitly (but no less influentially), that they had the same monopoly on *all* of women's health concerns and were the authorities on contraception and abortion as well as other, unspecified aspects of women's medical concerns; and third, that midwives' knowledge and authority, all of which they exercised in the exclusive female realm of the birthing room, elicited the suspicion and then the wrath of male medical practitioners and churchmen, who targeted them for extermination in the witch-hunts.[11] The idea that midwives were the key target of the witch-hunters was soundly demolished by David Harley in 1990, who deconstructed the intertextuality of the *Malleus maleficarum* (*The Hammer of Witches*, a witch-hunter's manual first published in 1496) and other such texts to show that the 'witch-midwife' was a narrow rhetorical trope among inquisitors who cited each other in their works, not a widespread phenomenon that played itself out in regular accusations against midwives. Harley's survey of actual studies of local persecutions finds that midwives were no more of a percentage of the accused than their overall numbers in the population would make likely.[12] The first two tenets of the Ehrenreich and English thesis, however, have remained more or less unchallenged for the past thirty years. Here, I wish to show why these, too, bear rethinking.

Let us step outside historical studies for a moment and consider the following claim:

> Childbirth was the undisputed domain of midwives for well over a thousand years. The midwives of [pre-modern] times were probably folk healers who not only attended births but generally ministered to the health needs of the common people ... Birth was then clearly considered women's business, a definition of the event that was shared, apparently, by all members of society.[13]

This statement comes from a medical anthropologist, Brigitte Jordan, who is regarded as the founder of the comparative study of the anthropology of birth. And as documentation for it, she cites, as her only authority, Ehrenreich and English. Now consider the following:

> During the British eighteenth century, male experts, particularly men-midwives, replaced female midwives, who had enjoyed a *nearly exclusive control* over the world of birth and knowledge about sexuality and reproduction *for centuries*. The

revolutionary nature of this shift cannot be overstated. Female midwives were – and
continue to be – *the almost universal authorities* over human reproduction *in every
region of the world. For millennia*, midwives and other women were the only sex
allowed access to a mother's childbearing body, with men invited into the birth room
only in extreme medical emergencies.[14]

Lisa Forman Cody, the specialist in eighteenth-century British history who
authored this statement, cites Brigitte Jordan's book as one of only two
sources for the history of women's medical care in pre-modern *Europe*. As
these examples show, Ehrenreich and English's narrative appears not only
as the 'core' narrative for histories of midwifery in the west – a source of
truisms that need not be interrogated – but it has then been extrapolated
via anthropologists into a universal truth that is in turn imported back
into European history. The Ehrenreich and English thesis maintains this
power because even works on western history that do not cite it seem
implicitly to support its position since they offer no direct response to it.
In the second work cited by Cody, a superb collection of essays on early
modern European midwives, there is no acknowledgement that, in looking
at midwives, they are only addressing *part* of the cultural investment in
women's health in their given time periods.[15] Gynaecology, infertility,
menstrual problems, not to mention any number of other conditions, make
no appearance here. And nothing is said about the other health practitioners
who provided care to female patients.

There are many ways of assessing who these other practitioners were
and what they were doing, though the most obvious source for the historian
are the texts on women's healthcare that proliferated in Europe throughout
the medieval and early modern periods. In England, for example, traditions of writing on women's medicine go back to at least the thirteenth
century. There is no evidence whatsoever that any texts there – whether in
Latin, Anglo-Norman, or English – were meant specifically for midwives
prior to the sixteenth century.[16] Rather, the audiences of these works were
professional male physicians and surgeons, literate laymen like lawyers,
notaries and landed gentry, and (perhaps the smallest group) laywomen
who may have had no particular medical responsibilities other than care of
themselves and their neighbours and kin. At least ten texts in French circulated in manuscript from the thirteenth to the fifteenth centuries, while
twenty-eight French works on women's medicine and generation were
printed between 1536 and 1627, going through at least sixty-one different
editions by 1670. These works likewise show a considerable range in audiences, including male surgeons and upper-class women.[17] Europe-wide,
in fact, the first text that explicitly addressed midwives since ancient times
was not written until *c*.1460.[18] As for authorship, of some 250 printed
texts on women's medicine in all European languages published prior to
1700, only five were written by female midwives. Yet, as recently as 2007,

Margaret King, in an overview of scholarship on the history of childhood and its attendant concerns, after citing a string of recent editions of fifteenth- and sixteenth-century midwifery texts, states flatly, 'These experts *wrote to advise midwives* . . . they did not presume to usurp the role of midwife, as at this juncture male manipulation of women's bodies in childbirth was inconceivable'.[19] Even though King had already commended a 1990 study that traced the incursion of male practitioners into the birthing room to the fifteenth century, she does not acknowledge that such incursion occurred before the seventeenth century. By keeping the separate 'female monopoly' and 'male incursion' narratives in place – even if shifting the 'transition' to the seventeenth rather than the eighteenth century, as is more commonly posited – King forecloses any possibility of interrogating *why* male authors had so readily been able to produce texts on women's medicine for centuries when their involvement was seemingly 'inconceivable'. King is not an expert on the history of women's medicine and should not bear the burden of having to unpack the problematic blind spots of the narratives she (and her sources) had inherited. But the fact is that the blind spots (and the incongruous analyses they enable) remain.[20] The narrative of midwives' supremacy has remained unchallenged because our paradigm has told us not to look for male involvement in women's medicine before a certain date.

In part, these blind spots are due to a long tradition in the history of medicine of looking from the top down: medical history was the history of practitioners (especially learned physicians who wrote the texts that have served as the primary documentation for such histories) and only secondarily of patients. Male physicians began documenting the genealogy of male expertise in gynaecology in the sixteenth century and, right from the beginning, female expertise was only acknowledged for the long-distant past of Graeco-Roman antiquity.[21] Traditions of writing the history of gynaecology solely as a series of 'firsts' by elite male physicians continue to the present day, with not so much as a nod towards feminist historiography.[22] Histories of midwifery, for their part, have largely been framed as histories of rivalry, either of male midwives against female ones, or one or the other group against male physicians. As Helen King has shown, midwives (both male and female) were debating the history of their discipline in England from at least the seventeenth century.[23] Ethnographic histories of midwifery were being written in Europe and North America from the late nineteenth century, and male physicians like James Hobson Aveling collected an impressive body of historical sources for their reconstructions both of obstetrics and of gynaecology.[24] A common rhetorical trope in histories not written by female midwives or their advocates is to portray female midwives as ignorant. For example, in 1962 the then leading American historian of pre-modern midwives, the Yale professor of anatomy,

Thomas R. Forbes, claimed that, 'The midwife, at that time usually an ignorant and incompetent elderly woman, received meager fees, occupied the lowest level of society, and lived a long and probably unhappy life'. The arrival of medical men, with their anatomical knowledge and obstetrical tools, signalled the salvation of women who had for centuries suffered at the hands of 'ignorant and incompetent elderly wom[e]n'.[25] This battle over historical narratives seems to have been pitched most forcefully in the United States, which witnessed the most extreme suppression of midwives as independent practitioners. Little wonder that American feminists of the 1960s and 1970s reacted against the misogynist master narrative with a 'mistress narrative' that saw pre-modern midwives as learned in empirical wisdom, authoritative and independent. The impact of Ehrenreich and English can be seen most starkly in two works published on opposite sides of the Atlantic in 1978. In that year, Jean Donnison published a revision of her 1974 University of London thesis on the history of midwives in England; this still-valuable study makes no reference at all to allegations of midwives' involvement with fertility disruption and addresses the question of witchcraft as simply symptomatic of a widespread sixteenth-century concern with eliminating various 'superstitious' habits in this time of violent religious reform. In contrast, the American Jane B. Donegan readily incorporated the Ehrenreich and English narrative into her parallel study of American midwives.[26]

The influence of the Ehrenreich and English thesis in feminist histories of medicine is due, then, to the cultural moment in which it appeared. The early second wave women's health movement (especially in the United States) was fighting an uphill battle against the medicalisation of childbirth, the essential outlawing of midwives and the criminalisation of abortion.[27] My critique is not to suggest that the history of midwives or midwifery is without value. Rather, it is to challenge the assumption that, if we have documented the history of midwives, then we have documented the totality of the history of medicine *as experienced by women*. In fact, I would argue that an ironic effect of the Ehrenreich and English thesis has been to obstruct substantive research on the history of midwives in Europe, or at least its early history. There is an important story to be told about women's healthcare and medical practice in Europe up to *c*.1600. But it is neither a story of women's unfettered control over knowledge of their bodies nor of deliberate male attempts to eradicate that control.

Before professionalisation: medieval narratives and male obstetrics

Ehrenreich and English did not make up the myth of medieval women's medical omnipotence out of whole cloth. They were building on work that itself had distilled narratives assembled by first-wave feminist writers of the nineteenth and early twentieth centuries. For these first-wave historians, the European Middle Ages was a golden age for women's medical practice. The female midwife writers of the early modern period – women such as Louise Bourgeois (1563–1636) and Marguerite Du Tertre de La Marche (1638–1706) in France, Jane Sharp (*fl.*1641–1671) and Elizabeth Cellier (*fl.*1668–1688) in England and Justine Siegemund (1636–1705) in Germany – had looked back not to the Middle Ages, but to the biblical or classical past for models of female practitioners. The two women who are now the most famous examples of medieval women's involvement in medicine – Trota of Salerno and Hildegard of Bingen (both of the twelfth century) – had very variable fates in the post-medieval period and were not retrieved for the purposes of a feminist history of medicine until the nineteenth century.[28] At that point, an argument that women of the European past had had extensive responsibilities and options in medical care and practice became an element of a multi-pronged attempt to open up medical schools to women. Assembling random snippets about female practitioners that had been collected by humanists and other scholars since the sixteenth century, the German physician Johann C. F. Harless compiled his *The Service of Women in Science, Health and Healing ...from Earliest Times to the Present Day* in 1830, nearly twenty years before Elizabeth Blackwell was to take the first MD formally awarded to a woman in 1849.[29] Although rather perfunctory, Harless did include some information on medieval women healers. In subsequent years, a sense that the medieval period was a crucial time in European women's history coalesced. At the third National Women's Rights convention in Syracuse, New York, in 1852, Paulina Wright Davis argued that, among the things that had been taken away from American women 'that were ours in the old world', was the practice of surgery, medicine and obstetrics. In the Middle Ages, 'the healing art was ours by prescription. Restore it to us'.[30] The English medical activist Sophia Jex-Blake (1840–1912), made use of medieval evidence in her reconstruction of medical women's history in 1872.[31] By the time the Polish physician Melina Lipinska wrote her still impressive *History of Women Physicians from Antiquity up to Our Own Day* in 1900, a narrative of the range of medieval women's medical practices was solidly in place. Lipinska took advantage of a considerable body of nineteenth-century scholarship on both medieval history and medical history. She employed without question the fiction of women's status as 'professors' at the medical school of Salerno that had originated in the seventeenth century as a local Salernitan tradition and then given more documentary substance by the mid-nineteenth century Salernitan historian, Salvatore De Renzi. Similarly, she made much of the trials of several female practitioners in fourteenth-century Paris that had been published just a few years before her own work appeared.[32]

The narrative of women's medical practice that Jex-Blake and Lipinska put in place, like that repeated in 1938 by their American imitator, Kate Campbell Hurd-Mead (1867–1941), an obstetrician and gynaecologist, was not so much wrong as subject to misinterpretation.[33] For Lipinska and other advocates of women's 'right' to practise medicine, *any* examples from the past that showed women practising medicine were sufficient to make their point: if women had proven their capability to practise medicine before, this automatically invalidated universal claims that women were incapable of doing similar work in the present. No attempts were made to assess quantitatively how significant women's presence was in what historians now call the 'medical marketplace'. Nor was documenting the work of midwives the main objective for nineteenth-century historians or their early twentieth-century followers. They were most concerned to document *learned* female practitioners, such as they themselves wished to be.

The second-wave feminist writers Ehrenreich and English, intriguingly, shifted the focus of the narrative of women in medicine in a subtle but important way. Whereas it had been crucial to the nineteenth- and early twentieth-century advocates of women's right to practise medicine to document the existence of women *doctors*, Ehrenreich and English were intent on rejecting the elitism of the medical profession and focused instead on popular healers. Thus, using a 1940s American elaborator of Lipinska and Hurd-Mead's work as their main source, they omitted any mention of Trota (or 'Trotula' as her name would have been understood then) or of the noble German nun Hildegard of Bingen, who wrote a major piece on natural philosophy and medicine, or of any of the eye doctors or surgeons that Lipinska and Hurd-Mead had documented. Rather, they celebrated Jacoba Felicie, a fourteenth-century Parisian empirical practitioner tried for illicit medical practice, touting her as a veritable martyr to the cause of medical populism.[34] Most importantly, drawing on a thesis originally proposed in the 1920s by Margaret Murray, they latched mightily onto the brief references to 'witch-midwives' in *The Hammer of Witches* and blew these passing references into a whole characterisation of the 'medieval' witch-hunts as persecutions of 'wise women' and their knowledge of medicine and birth control ('midwives' (*obstetrics*) are mentioned explicitly only nine times in a work of several hundred pages, half the number of times as 'archer-sorcerers'). As mentioned earlier, David Harley has pulled apart the whole edifice of these claims, but he raises important questions about why this myth has been so attractive to historians, even when the primary sources contradict it. His focus is on how this mythology had inhibited any real histories of early modern midwives.[35] I suggest that the negative impact on the history of *medieval* women's medicine has been even more profound.

What I and several other researchers have found about the history of women's healthcare in medieval western Europe over the past twenty years is this:[36] the body of documentation for women's involvement in medical practice in medieval western Europe assembled by first-wave feminist historians was sketchy but more or less reliable. This body of data has continued to grow and it supports the general sense that women did practise in a broader range of medical fields and with greater acceptance (or at least less formal obstruction) than they would in the early modern period. However, it has never been documented that women ever constituted a moiety of the medical profession; on the contrary, their numbers have consistently been shown to be minuscule, just 1 or 2 per cent of documentable practitioners. This finding, in turn, fits with growing evidence that medicine was becoming both professionalised and masculinised in the later medieval centuries. Female medical practitioners can be shown to exist, but they were almost always practising alongside or in competition with males. Nunneries can be found employing male practitioners as well as in-house female phlebotomists; queens can be found using female healers to treat themselves or their children, but also having full-time male physicians on their staffs; urban women, even some of quite modest means, can be found calling on male practitioners for any variety of ailments, even (in some emergency situations) childbirth.[37] Midwives made up part of this medical schema but were nowhere near as important a part as the 'second-wave' feminist historians *manquées*, Ehrenreich and English, assumed. To be sure, there is ample evidence that birth assistance was provided in medieval Europe and that it was, by and large, provided by women. It is simply that midwifery does not seem to have been *professionalised* in medieval western Europe prior to the thirteenth century, and even then only sporadically. In most situations, it was a general body of knowledge shared more or less equally among women. This point has been articulated with particular elegance and clarity by the Catalan scholar, Montserrat Cabré, who demonstrates the broad array of medical services performed by women – in their capacities as mothers, neighbours and kin – that never fell under the social categories of 'professional' medical practice.[38]

There was a major contest over medicine in the high Middle Ages, but it was not one between men and women per se but rather between empiricism and book learning. To the extent that this process was gendered, it was because book learning itself was a highly gendered practice, women being excluded not simply from the universities but from the grammar and notarial schools where basic Latin literacy was obtained by men ranging across backgrounds and classes. Women's vernacular literacy increased in this period, but it was not used for *medical* reading with any regularity until after the medieval period had passed. Men (or rather *literate* men) 'took over' many aspects of women's medicine – especially fertility concerns, which very often broadened into concerns with all aspects of the functioning of the reproductive organs – not out of designs to suppress witchcraft or women's contraceptive knowledge, but because they were taking over nearly all aspects of the increasingly professionalised field of medicine. At the same time, male surgeons expanded their involvement in women's particular conditions from treatment of breast disorders to certain aspects of gynaecological surgery and, possibly as early as the late thirteenth century, occasional involvement with difficult births. Women's routine attendance at normal childbirth was not threatened because this was not normally seen as a 'medical' condition that demanded the physician's or surgeon's intervention. Even the one female medical author we have from the Middle Ages who wrote specifically on women's medicine, Trota of Salerno, did not provide detailed instructions on the handling of normal births. Thus, it is in no way surprising to find that, with the exception of Trota, every known author of a medieval text on women's medicine (and there are over 150 such works) was male; that even while some vernacular texts on women's medicine were ostensibly addressed to female audiences, not a single nameable female owner can be found prior to the sixteenth century; or that when gynaecology finally emerged as its own rationally distinct field in the sixteenth century, male writers looked to other male authorities, never to women, to inform and justify their work.[39]

For most readers, my assertion that men were involved in obstetrics will probably come as the biggest surprise. Yet I suspect they were 'hiding in plain sight' more often than we suspect. Let me go back to Brigitte Jordan's anthropological classic, *Birth in Four Cultures*. Jordan devotes her first ethnographic study to a close analysis of the birth practices of a Yucatan midwife. She describes her equipment, explains her methods, analyses the conversations she carries on with the birthing mother, et cetera – all the while insisting, as noted above, that this is a woman's event. But, if we cast our gaze to the periphery of these scenes, we find men: it is the husband who usually goes to call the midwife, the husband who is in fact expected to be present at the birth, taking turns supporting the mother as she bears down. It is a male physician to whom the midwife would refer the repair of any perineal tears and a male physician who would be turned to should other complications arise.[40] If women's health (or rather, women's birthing experiences) were *fully* women's business, then men would not appear even in these peripheral roles.

More work has been done on these questions for the periods bracketing the Middle Ages than for the Middle Ages themselves. Over the last two decades, Ann Hanson, Helen King and Rebecca Flemming, for example, have assembled an extraordinary body of evidence for the gendering of women's medicine in Graeco-Roman antiquity. Hanson studied men's roles in childbirth, finding them functioning as messengers, assistants, emergency surgeons and all around orchestrators of the event. Similarly, King and Flemming have examined the medical writings of the Hippocratics and various Roman writers – nearly all male – to examine the ways males took responsibility to theorise and dictate therapies for women's conditions.[41] For the end of the medieval period, the Renaissance art historian Jacqueline Musacchio has presented a remarkable body of evidence for how childbirth and attendant concerns for fertility directed the sizable material investments of patrician males in northern Italy. Among her findings is that, even though female midwives were clearly employed to attend uncomplicated births, they essentially disappeared once the birth was over. Nearly all other medical concerns were handled by male practitioners, some of whom were clearly stepping beyond the threshold of the birthing room door.[42] Likewise, Ulinka Rublack has shown for sixteenth- and seventeenth-century southern Germany the many ways in which pregnancy was a public concern for communities, but especially the husband, and not something that remained hidden within a closed female group.[43] Most recently, in an extraordinarily rich cultural study, Katharine Park has shown how the development of human anatomical investigations in northern Italy between the thirteenth and sixteenth centuries can be seen as an expanding process of searching for the 'secrets' of women's bodies and generation. That search involved women both as active searchers (one of the first 'autopsies' was the opening of a Benedictine nun by her sister inmates) and as willing participants in the search for anatomical knowledge. But, by establishing the act of anatomising as a masculine endeavour, and by increasing the scope of their gynaecological and obstetrical practice, male medical practitioners could arrogate considerable authority over women's reproduction, to the point of thinking themselves able to instruct the midwife.[44] All these examples of male involvement in obstetrics suggest that we have perhaps focused too much attention on obstetrics as a site of combat between professional rivals ('male control' vs 'female control') and too little on obstetrics from the patient's point of view. What does the patient want in obstetrical care? What kinds of knowledge or authority or power does she look to her attendants for?

As a way of puzzling through the implications of male involvement in obstetrics, examination of a case where men were *not* involved in obstetrical change will be helpful. In her brilliant recent study of the influences of biomedicine on birthing practices in south-east India, the medical anthropologist Cecilia Van Hollen makes the following passing statement in the context of her analysis of European female doctors who established the first obstetrical hospitals (or obstetrical wards) in the late nineteenth and early twentieth centuries: 'Cross-cultural studies in many parts of the world suggest that women *prefer* to be attended by women doctors during childbirth due to *cultural* notions of modesty, regardless of whether or not women are secluded for religious purposes such as in *purdah*'.[45] In India, because of the role of *purdah* (the seclusion of women from direct interactions with men not of their immediate families), upper-caste Hindu and Muslim women refused treatment from male colonial physicians. This refusal was used by American and British female doctors, who were graduating in increasing numbers from medical schools in the United States and Europe with few outlets for professional practice, as an opportunity to establish female-dominated clinical practices in India. Hence, remarkably, there was no masculinisation of women's healthcare in nineteenth- and twentieth-century India.[46] Van Hollen therefore raises a fascinating question: if the problem with women's medicine was not men, what is it about highly technologised biomedicine that has produced such resistance among south-east Indian women in accepting its new paradigms of the body and regimes of bodily submission?

There is much in Van Hollen's analysis that merits discussion. Here I would like simply to focus on her claims about women doctors. Van Hollen locates a presumed nearly universal feminine gendering of obstetrical practice in *women's preference* for childbirth attendants of their own sex, adding only parenthetically (in an unreferenced footnote) that this scenario meets with their husbands' approval. Yet she also locates this preference in *cultural* notions of modesty. One could, conceivably, invoke biopsychological arguments to explain some affinities that women have with other women. Indeed, I do not rule out the possibility that there may be some biological (for example neurodynamic) foundation for women's alleged preference for medical attendants of their own sex. My main objective, however, is to take Van Hollen's emphasis on *the cultural* to heart and ask, if this 'preference' is indeed cultural rather than biological, how can we explain its near universality? Or indeed, *is* it really as universal as has generally been supposed in historical and anthropological studies of childbirth and women's medicine?

Let me first point out a simple – indeed, blindingly obvious – but all too often unarticulated fact: the reproductive organs are also the sexual organs. In a heteronormative context, for a man to engage in any direct physical contact (either ocular inspection or physical touch) of a female's genitalia runs the risk of being seen as a sexual act.[47] Historians of the Anglo-American obstetrical tradition have long honed in on cries of impropriety and sexual scandal in objections to male obstetrical practice in the eighteenth century and later.[48] Yet, perhaps due to the heteronormative biases under which historians have long functioned, it is rarely noted that a woman could feel shame about exposure of her genitalia to another woman or that gynaecological and obstetrical attendance by a woman could also raise the prospect of healing acts veering into sexual acts. One of the duties assigned to European midwives in the pre-modern period was masturbating female patients as a therapy for a condition called 'uterine suffocation'.[49] But the sexual dynamics of cross-sex practice and their implications for social honour and shame could affect men, too. There is, from the Hippocratic Oath onwards, recognition that the male practitioner's reputation could be threatened if he gazed lasciviously on either the male or female servants of the household. As for his treatment of a female patient, any difficulties of communication that arose when the patient was female were attributed to her shame or modesty alone. Yet such a framing of the issues ignored the fact that male access to the sexual organs of 'other men's women' was as much if not more a problem *for men* as it was for women.

I suggest, therefore, that the gendering of obstetrics (and of women's healthcare in general) is, in fact, a *cultural* phenomenon and therefore a historically contingent one. The fact that the birthing body is, by definition, a female body should not blind us to the equally important fact that there is nothing *biological* that demands that the attendant assisting at that birth also be female. By examining the dynamics of how societies have and continue to gender birthing practices, we simultaneously open up space to examine how other historical contingencies (for example the influences of surgical technologies or politically driven population control programmes) contribute to women's level of comfort or discomfort with the range of obstetrical choices on offer to them. Histories of the impact (in some cases, imposition) of European obstetrical practices in colonial contexts are especially enlightening. The increasing masculinisation of obstetrics in the Anglo-American context in the course of the eighteenth to twentieth centuries is generally considered anomalous, never having been paralleled to the same degree in other European contexts.[50] Historical studies of British colonial medicine in fact show an interesting range of cases where the British medical system brought in a concomitant masculinisation of obstetrical practices (for example, Egypt and Jamaica) and where it did not (India, as we have seen, because of the coincidence of *purdah* practices locally combining with the availability of newly-trained female physicians coming from the metropole).[51] Neither in late medieval northern Italy nor in modern America have women uniformly resisted male 'intrusion' into childbirth.[52] By moving away from the universals of 'millennia' and 'throughout time', we can more insightfully examine the multiple factors that contribute to what should be a rich and variegated history of childbirth.

Contraception and abortion, or, what do women (and men) really want?

The other crucial prong of the Ehrenreich and English thesis – that mid-wives had been persecuted for their knowledge of mechanisms to control fertility and that a huge body of 'women's knowledge' about such matters was consequently lost in the early modern period – has been as much a driv-ing force behind modern historiography of women's medicine as has their belief in midwives' pre-modern obstetrical and gynaecological monopoly. A particularly devoted adept of the Ehrenreich and English thesis is the historian of pharmacology, John Riddle. Riddle has put forward the thesis that knowledge of the contraceptive and abortifacient properties of vari-ous plants was widely available in antiquity and the Middle Ages. Such common plants as rue, Queen Anne's lace, savin and wild carrot, Riddle claims, were known to and used by women, who could have simply added extra quantities of these substances to their daily salads to regulate when they would bear children. Particularly important for Riddle's thesis is his suggestion that substances said to 'provoke the menses' are really contra-ceptives and abortifacients in disguise, since causing the uterus to (in our modern terms) shed its endometrial lining would effectively terminate any pregnancy under way or prevent pregnancy from a recent act of sexual in-tercourse. Riddle adopts from Ehrenreich and English the thesis that such female traditions of knowledge transmission were deliberately disrupted by the early modern witch-hunts which, in the course of the nineteenth and twentieth centuries, took the form of legal regulations against the dissem-ination of contraceptive knowledge and the practice of abortion.[53]

Riddle's books were not reviewed in any of the leading journals of fem-inist scholarship (including *Gender & History*) and the isolated criticisms by certain feminist scholars and demographers seem to have had little ef-fect in dampening acceptance of his views.[54] Yet Riddle's claims demand engagement since if, as I and others have argued, there are serious method-ological problems with them, this will have implications for how we un-derstand the history of women's health and healthcare more broadly. There are three questions here, which need to be clearly distinguished. One is whether phytochemicals (the 'active ingredients' in plants used for medic-inal purposes) have the power to disrupt or alter reproductive processes in humans. The second is whether such plants are indeed always *used* to disrupt reproductive processes rather than alter them in other ways; this includes determining whether we can infer the intent of others because of what *we* know about chemical properties. The third question is how know-ledge of such properties is generated, preserved or disseminated, and used, and how gender figures in each of these processes. I will take these three questions in turn.

A quick survey of research published in the last twenty-five years on the topic of gynaecological and obstetrical uses of plants in the *Journal of Ethnopharmacology* shows that all the societies examined – from South America to the South Pacific – had substances in their local pharmacopeias said to affect fertility in some way: enhancing it, disrupting it, helping the menstrual or birth process, etc.[55] This is not the place for a synthetic account of these findings. But even a superficial survey provides persuasive evidence that knowledge of plants that can mimic or disrupt the hormonal and other chemical processes of reproduction has been sought (showing intent to develop a 'technology of the body') and found (showing traditions of empirical observation and maintenance of knowledge) in a variety of human cultures.[56] What these studies also show, however, is a variety of motives for such acquisition of knowledge, a variety of social agents who possess such knowledge and a variety of circumstances in which such knowledge is acquired. In her review of published accounts about native plants used for obstetrical and gynaecological conditions in South Africa, for example, Vanessa Steenkamp argued that, 'the majority of plants are used to *enhance* fertility' (my emphasis). In their study of a community of Mayan women in Guatemala, the medical anthropologists Joanna Michel et al. found both men and women in possession of knowledge about plants affecting reproduction.[57] And in their monographic study of anti-fertility plants used by various Pacific Islanders, R.C. Cambie and Alexandra A. Brewis (now Brewis Slade) found that the development of ethnobotanical knowledge on contraceptives and abortifacients could be pinpointed to the arrival of Christian missionaries in the nineteenth century.[58] Prior to that, Islanders relied primarily on infanticide to keep their population levels within bounds that could be supported by their very limited land space even though, in most cases, the plants they would end up using had long been available to them. In other words, ethnobotanical knowledge itself is historical and its study, *ipso facto*, needs to be historicised.

In returning to look at the evidence for pre-modern Europe, therefore, Riddle's claims about regulation of fertility by phytochemical means are, on the surface, in no way implausible. Granted, there remain important questions about the *efficacy* of these substances, since (in biomedical terms) there are huge differentials depending on the potency of the plant itself (what soil it is grown in, when it is harvested, what part of the plant is used, how it is prepared) and its mode of administration (when in the reproductive cycle it is administered and at what dosages). Importantly, some of these substances are quite toxic; the very real risks of their use should be kept in mind when assessing their actual use historically.[59] Overall, however, it seems that demographers will ignore at their peril consideration of ethnobotanical means of fertility intervention in future studies of fertility patterns and population shifts. But can we comfortably assume that such chemicals – or, more to the point, the *knowledge* of such chemicals and their uses – was sufficiently widespread among communities of European women to justify assertions that women had 'control' over their fertility in the sense that they had the power to choose when and how often they would bear children? The question of intent in use – the second of the problems raised by Riddle's analysis – is crucial here. Alexandra Brewis Slade has suggested the concept of 'flipping technologies'. That is, if a society has developed a medical technology for one purpose, it can sometimes be 'flipped' to produce an opposite result when need arises. If, for example, a society has recognised that a certain substance can be used to bring on the menses in order to 'clean' the uterus so that it is capable of conception or to imitate oxytoxic effects on the uterus to expel a dead foetus that will not otherwise be birthed, it can 'flip' that knowledge to create a different effect: to cleanse the womb not of materials that are impeding conception, but of the conceptus itself.[60] Promoting fertility and impeding it are often two sides of the same coin.

Consider, for example, the following passage, found in the section 'on retention of the menses' in a general medical textbook by a twelfth-century southern Italian male medical writer, Johannes Platearius:

> Likewise, note that those things which are good for provoking the menses also bring out the afterbirth and the dead foetus and the 'brother of the Salernitans'. Note, too, that Salernitan women in the beginning of conception and especially when it begins to move, try to kill the above-mentioned 'little brother', drinking the juice of parsley and leeks.[61]

Here, it seems, is a blanket statement that emmenagogues, ecbolics (foetal expulsives) and expulsives for the afterbirth are all of a piece. Moreover, although Platearius was discussing only Salernitan women's attempts to kill the monstrous growth, the 'brother of the Salernitans', he is clearly identifying the combination of parsley and leeks as an abortifacient. This seems unambiguous evidence, then, that Salernitan women knew of phytochemical means to prevent or disrupt pregnancies.[62] It is all the more significant, therefore, that there is a Salernitan woman's medical writing extant with which we can compare Platearius's statement.[63] In one of her works, Trota of Salerno (active in the early twelfth century) does indeed mention the combination of parsley and leeks as highly effective *for expelling the afterbirth*.[64] These two substances (as well as borage, which she lists as an alternative expulsive) are mentioned nowhere else in her writings; hence, we can consider them 'specifics', drugs that have one particular property only.[65] Trota also provides a recipe employing willow and rue as an emmenagogue, but she introduces this very explicitly as a means *to promote conception*.[66] In other words, in this extraordinarily important document for women's medical practices – important, for our purposes, because this was a moment both when female empiricism was still valued by male practitioners and when there was apparently no systematic suppression of contraceptive knowledge in medical writings – there is no evidence that either emmenagogues or foetal expulsives were used by women for the purpose of *disrupting* normal fertility.[67] On the contrary, Trota's works seem decidedly pronatalist. While there are characteristics in her writings that demonstrate particularly nuanced understandings of the plight of women wishing to employ technologies of the body to enhance their ability to navigate the patriarchal structures in which they lived – 'faking' virginity, dealing with the pain caused by heterosexual intercourse, improving their appearance through cosmetics – disrupting fertility was not part of Trota's agenda. There is, in fact, no substantive difference in perspective between her work and the major Salernitan (male-authored) writing on pharmaceutics, which mentions many more emmenagogic and ecbolic substances – forty-four in all, more than half of the eighty-one said to have gynaecological or obstetrical properties, and fully 17 per cent of the total 258 substances listed.[68] Eight substances (balsam, borax, dittany, galbanum, rue, opoponax, serapinum and red and white bryony (*viticella*)) are said (as Johannes Platearius had noted) to have the triple function of provoking the menses, expelling the dead foetus and bringing out the afterbirth. Parsley is said to be 'harmful to pregnant women because by its power it dissolves the moorings holding the foetus'. Thus, we have evidence from all three of these writers – Johannes Platearius, Trota and the author of this pharmaceutical text – that parsley is a specific 'abortifacient' in our definition. Yet, like Trota, neither Platearius nor the pharmaceutical author shows any indication of eliding parsley with 'cleansing' substances (those that bring on the menstrual flow or rid the uterus of other waste matter – the dead foetus and the afterbirth). On the contrary, as with Trota, the author of the pharmaceutical text believes that substances that 'clean' the womb often also 'aid the conceptus'.[69]

How can we know, at a distance of close to 900 years, whether some aspect of Trota's work was not suppressed or altered by hostile scribes or editors, or even suppressed by Trota herself who preferred not to put certain aspects of her practices down in writing? In fact we can never *prove* that such suppressions did not happen. But we can acknowledge other corroborating evidence that emmenagogues were not always 'code' for abortifacients. In the fifteenth century, Jeanette Camus was put on trial in Dijon for practising medicine illegally. She recounted that, when she was herself suffering from infertility, she learned an effective remedy from a woman in a nearby town. She now gave the same remedy to other women, along with other *bons remèdes pour femmes qui ne peuvent avoir leurs fleurs* ('good remedies for women who cannot have their 'flowers' [menses]').[70]

Interrogated by the medical faculty of Dijon, Jeannette was expelled from town, not for having trafficked in illicit contraceptives (which the medical faculty could have easily discerned), but simply for not having sufficient theoretical knowledge of medicine, the claim commonly used to run empirics (male and female) out of medical practice. As with Trota, in traditional European concepts of humoral medicine, menstruation was vital both to women's health and their fertility. In the sixteenth century, we can find a German noblewoman saying that, 'for the past two years my feminine obligation [that is, menstruation] has appeared only once in a quarter year and still not had a proper color', while Barbara Duden's classic work on the medical narratives of eighteenth-century women shows how important menstrual regularity remained for women's own perceptions of their health.[71] Once again, anthropological work helps us buttress this interpretation since there is already a rich literature on the notion of 'regulating menstruation', which shows that other cultures likewise employ the notion of 'cleansing' the womb in order to regulate health and/or promote fertility.[72] Most importantly, medical anthropological work shows the extreme lengths women in patriarchal contexts will go to seek fertility when their marriages, economic livelihoods and identities depend on being reproductively successful.[73] *Pace* Riddle, not every emmenagogue is *meant* to interrupt fertility and we must therefore be very careful in assuming that we can always infer intent on the basis of what modern western science tells us about chemicals or human physiology.

But surely, one might respond, women could have intuited that whatever 'brings on the menses' also terminates an established pregnancy, that they could 'flip' their knowledge of, say, willow or rue, whenever they wanted. Again, there is no way to *prove* that this did not happen, but it would be well to assess the notion of 'flipping technologies' by tempering it with another concept being developed by cultural anthropologists: the notion of 'persistence of knowledge', that is, how bodies of knowledge – especially in illiterate or marginally literate cultures – are tied to the continuation of *practices* with which the knowledge is linked. If the practice dies out (for example, certain types of hunting), then the knowledge associated with it (say, techniques of tracking) will die out, too.[74] The actual ability to *use* fertility-enhancing or -disrupting herbs depends on close knowledge of soils, harvesting times, preparation methods, administration doses, et cetera. For such knowledge to be sustained in an illiterate society would depend on uninterrupted continuation of the practices that generated the knowledge in the first place. Thus, even if (in raw chemical terms) an emmenagogue can be 'flipped' to become an abortifacient, *effective* use of such a substance in this way would entail the continuation of practices by communities that used the technology often enough to keep the knowledge alive.

Literate societies, on the other hand, can to a certain extent preserve knowledge 'out of context' and retrieve it at will, even when centuries separate the author and the recipient. Which brings us to our third question: whether we can see all this fertility-disrupting knowledge as the exclusive property (and indeed, the exclusive concern) of women, or whether we need to see men as active agents in both its creation and dissemination (as well as suppression). Here, differentials between men's and women's literacy is key. One of the ironic aspects of John Riddle's search for proof that medieval women knew of the contraceptive properties of herbs is his choice of a fourteenth-century French woman, Beatrice de Planisolles, as one of his main female 'witnesses'. In her testimony before the Inquisition, she described one particular contraceptive practice, stating clearly that it was her male lover who brought a contraceptive device to their sexual encounters, very greedily taking it away with him after each encounter lest she take on any other paramours. She made no claims to having contraceptive knowledge of her own.[75] Her lover, however (who never discussed these encounters in his own testimony), would as a priest have been literate to some degree and might have obtained his knowledge of this contraceptive amulet from written sources. Riddle himself relies on male-authored texts – knowledge as embodied *in books* – for his evidence about contraceptive and abortifacient substances. My own research on women's patterns of engagement with medical books in medieval Europe showed that they only rarely possessed medical books, even when it was evident from other data that they owned Books of Hours and other works of devotion or literature.[76] This is equally true of texts on women's medicine which were only rarely addressed to women and which, even when they did have such audience claims, can be shown to have actually been in men's hands. There is, then, very little evidence that medieval women regularly had access to any of the written texts that Riddle cites.

So what did women in fact know about controlling their fertility in the Middle Ages? I do not pretend to have an answer to this question, but the following evidence (all, in this case, coming from England from the period after the mid-fourteenth century Black Death to the late sixteenth century) suggests that we should be looking beyond the midwives that Ehrenreich and English focused on and see knowledge of fertility-disrupting substances as circulating in dispersed loci which themselves may have been shifting historically. In the fourteenth century, scribes from London to York put passages describing abortifacients (and a few other topics) in cipher, though they would have been policing male uses of such information since it is highly unlikely that women ever came near these Latin texts.[77] A late fourteenth- or early fifteenth-century compiler of a Middle English gynaecological text that addressed a female audience refused to translate the description of abortifacients from one of his ancient Latin

sources on the grounds that 'some cursed whore might use it'.[78] Emmenagogues, in contrast, were translated in full with no apparent concern about
their (mis)use. In the fifteenth century, an English translator of Johannes
Platearius's *Practica* altered the passage quoted from the Latin text above
to imply that the women use parsley and leeks to perform abortion outright,
not simply to eliminate the monstrous 'brother of the Salernitans'.[79] Also
in the fifteenth century, another English medical writer, although including
no recipes explicitly labelled contraceptives and abortifacients, nevertheless added to his text significant numbers of emmenagogues as well as
mechanisms to expel the dead foetus, an obstetrical condition he clearly
viewed as presenting grave dangers to the woman. He even stated that it was
preferable to slay a living foetus when it will not come out than to let the
mother die.[80] Claiming that he had composed his text so that women could
use it themselves (in fact, he clearly meant it also for male practitioners like
himself), he expressed no concern about the knowledge of emmenagogues
or foetal expulsives being misused. An ecclesiastical court case from York
in 1509 involved the alleged father seeking to procure an abortion, not
the pregnant woman herself.[81] In 1530, a case was brought before the ecclesiastical court in the diocese of Lincoln involving one Joan Schower,
pregnant out of wedlock. By the time she was examined by midwives,
she was found no longer to be pregnant. She told them that she had been
pregnant but had taken an abortive potion, which was apparently effective.
She had had two previous children out of wedlock, though it is unclear
whether she had tried and failed to terminate those pregnancies or simply
did not try at all.[82] In the same year, also in Lincoln, one John Hunt was
accused of persuading Joan Willys, his live-in domestic servant and now
fiancée, to take 'certayn drynkes to distroy the childe that she is with'.[83]
A licence for English midwives, which dates from 1588, listed as one of
several injunctions that the midwife 'shall not give any counsel or minister
any herb, medicine, potion or any other thing to any woman being with
child whereby she should destroy or cast out that [which] she goes with
[that is, the foetus she is carrying] before her time'.[84]

As in twelfth-century Salerno, there seems to have been no particular
concern about misuse of emmenagogic substances. There was information
on abortifacients in circulation, though such knowledge (or fear of such
knowledge) seems to have been widely dispersed among prostitutes, male
clerics, unmarried women and unmarried men. Only the last item mentions
midwives as a source of such information, and it is the sole proof cited by
Riddle that midwives were a regular repository for such knowledge.[85] I
suspect, however, that this concern arose out some particular historical circumstance rather than a long-standing suspicion. Licensing of midwives
had started on the Continent in the fourteenth century in France and the

fifteenth century in the Low Countries and German territories. Although we have yet to discover the text of any of the early French licences, they are readily available from the other areas that practised licensing. None that I have examined says a word about contraceptives or abortifacients prior to the later sixteenth century, and this despite the fact that moralistic concerns overwhelmingly guide the character of the oaths midwives had to take, first and foremost the requirement that the midwife treat all women in need, whether they be rich or poor.[86] In 1496, Kramer and Sprenger argued in *The Hammer of Witches* that the 'cure' for midwives' superstitious practices was rigorous enforcement of licensing, and David Harley has suggested that it was precisely the assurance of morals provided by licensing that kept midwives relatively immune from witchcraft accusations.[87] Licensing came later to England than elsewhere in northern Europe, being first documented in London near the beginning of the sixteenth century. The widely travelled medical writer Andrew Boorde in his 1547 *Breviary of Health* cites concerns about medical incompetence and immoral or superstitious practices in calling for more systematic emulation of the licensing practices of the Continent. Yet neither in Boorde nor any other evidence we have for licensing prior to 1588 (including the full text of the earliest known English midwife's license, which comes from the diocese of Canterbury in 1567) is there any mention of abortifacients.[88] Apparently, something had happened by 1588 to make provision of abortifacient knowledge by midwives a new concern.[89]

If it is not midwives who were chiefly responsible for dissemination of abortifacient information, was it laymen and -women who were 'flipping' technologies they have encountered through various avenues, including books? I would be hesitant to say that this new concern was tied to women's (including midwives') increased literacy in this period. Women (particularly those of the upper classes) quite suddenly became major collectors of medical recipes in the late fifteenth and sixteenth centuries, though the few studies that have thus far been done on these widespread collections show no particular concern with mechanisms for disrupting fertility.[90] Laywomen may have also been reading newly published midwifery texts by this period, though these, too, did not include abortifacients so labelled.[91] What might the circumstances be that cause shifts in the development and circulation of contraceptive knowledge? Narratives in the history of European and North American contraception have stressed moments of suppression of such knowledge, but I believe we should be looking more closely at where this knowledge on the workings of the female body came from in the first place. In a richly documented study, Cornelia Dayton Hughes showed some years ago how the increasing availability of commercially produced products facilitated Hannah Grosvenor's decision, in mid-eighteenth-century Connecticut, to 'take the trade', an otherwise undescribed commercial abortifacient that her lover pressed upon her. He had obtained this from a male practitioner, who later performed a manual abortion when the product failed to do its work.[92] As Dayton Hughes shows, these botched attempts at abortion (Grosvenor soon died because of the manual intervention) would probably not have happened in an earlier generation when social mores would have made marriage the normal resolution of such a situation. In this new period of social mobility, Grosvenor's lover saw medical technology as a way out.

Slavery is another context in which desperation seems to have led to creative (and perhaps dangerous) experimentation. Londa Schiebinger has studied use of the 'peacock flower' (*Poinciana pulcherimma*) as a contraceptive/abortifacient by enslaved women in the eighteenth-century Caribbean.[93] Equally intriguing is the work of Liese Perrin, who creatively reconstructs the contraceptive practices of slave women in the southern United States through evidence from the Works Progress Administration (WPA) narratives recorded in the 1930s. She found evidence for the use of cotton root as a contraceptive by slave women. Perrin's study is also particularly persuasive because she combines narrative testimony with demographic evidence that shows wider birth spacing than can be explained by documented lactation habits. She notes that men as well as women knew of the contraceptive properties of cotton root.[94] This is an important observation since, in modern ethnobotanical studies, cotton root is also used as a male contraceptive.[95] Perrin's evidence is not persuasive, however, that American slaves brought this contraceptive knowledge over with them from Africa and had been using it systematically for centuries rather than rediscovering it in the American context. Had they done so, one would have expected reduced fertility among slave women throughout the seventeenth to nineteenth centuries rather than just near the end of slavery.

As Perrin's work on American slavery shows, assessment of historical uses of fertility disrupters is best done in the context of demographic analysis, where we can move beyond individual anecdote to look for cumulative evidence for changes in fecundity and proof whether the causes of such changes are deliberate or accidental. My survey of the available literature for medieval Europe shows attempts to disrupt fertility, but undercuts Riddle's assumption that *biochemical* means were most relied on and that this knowledge was primarily the property of women. True, we do find occasional statements about 'womanly arts' of limiting fertility. A later thirteenth-century treatise on generation, for example, the pseudo-Albertus Magnus *Secrets of Women*, mentions that prostitutes and other women are 'learned in this wickedness' of inducing abortions.[96] But, to date, I have found no consistent evidence of the efficacy of herbal preparations. Indeed, infanticide and beatings of a pregnant woman deliberately intended to induce abortion would seem, on the current evidence, to be more common.[97] In the western Alps (modern-day south-east France and north-west Italy) in the fourteenth and fifteenth centuries, Pierre Dubuis counted a total of 2,523 fines levied by the chatelain of the Count (later, Duke) of Savoy, thirty-nine of which had to do with cases of some kind of 'refusal of the child'. Only one case concerned contraception: a woman from Aoste was fined for allowing another woman to 'put on her a certain bone, because of which no woman is able to conceive'. Whether we interpret this as a magical ritual or simply the wearing of some kind of amulet, in neither case does it prove effective knowledge of the chemical properties of plants. Nor is there much evidence for knowledge of abortifacients. In the fifteen cases found (three of which involve two different parties being fined), there was no mention of 'potions of sterility' and only one person was explicitly accused of 'procuring' an abortion. Besides one curious case of a woman being fined for bathing in a certain fountain while pregnant, all the cases involved physical violence against the pregnant woman, usually beatings. Not surprisingly, most seem to have involved violence instigated by a man: a father beat his pregnant daughter, a husband beat his adulterous wife. But one, perhaps two, cases involved beatings by the mother of the pregnant woman. Although the likelihood is that most of these attacks were hostile (and so generated the attention of the court because they were deemed criminal acts by the woman herself), the possibility remains that some of them involved the woman's participation and therefore consent. One woman was fined twice for making what was apparently deemed a false accusation against a priest that he had made her 'take a dangerous jump and made [her] do evil [to her] child'.[98]

In his study of medieval demographic attitudes, Peter Biller found that awareness of and debates about population size became increasingly common among learned (male) commentators from the mid-thirteenth century onwards. Contraceptive practices may have been employed with the deliberate intent of controlling overall population size. Importantly, he suggests not biochemical means of fertility disruption as the major driver in this process, but *coitus interruptus*, a necessarily male-controlled form of contraception.[99] Other evidence shows an increasing awareness of the growth in European populations and a curiosity (and after the Black Death, an anxiety) about generation and reproduction.[100] Nevertheless, the escalating population rates in high medieval Europe were clearly curtailed in the fourteenth century by famine and plague, not by contraception. As Judith Bennett has shown, prior to these Malthusian checks, communities in England had taken into their own hands the policing of sexual activity among poorer women whose offspring, should they be conceived out of wedlock, would add to already straitened communal burdens.[101]

I suspect, therefore, that knowledge of contraceptives and abortifacients, rather than being a readily transmitted body of knowledge among women, was instead a topic on which there was much lore in common circulation, but also much uncertainty, with the result that few people could consistently rely on effective knowledge when they needed it. Medical texts were full of remedies intended to function as emmenagogues or foetal expulsives. And medical men were sometimes consulted, if only surreptitiously, for information that would aid women in terminating unwanted pregnancies.[102] Indeed, it was not unheard of for medical writers to recommend contraceptives – clearly labelled as such and Christian precepts not withstanding – on the argument that some women, incapable (whether for social or economic reasons) of abstaining from sex, nevertheless should not bear children lest a pregnancy kill them.[103] Yet it is not at all clear how consistently effective such knowledge was. The most widely circulating medieval texts on women's medicine, the so-called *Trotula* ensemble, included contraceptives explicitly labelled as such, but these were amulets which, from our perspective, could have had no more than a placebo effect.

Methodological tools to explore the questions raised by Bennett and Biller are still lacking. But let me close with one particularly brilliant and subtly argued study of fertility interventions at the end of the medieval period by the French historian, Christiane Klapisch-Zuber: 'The Last Child: Fecundity and Aging among Florentine Women in the Fourteenth and Fifteenth Centuries'.[104] Using a sample of forty-four upper-class couples who lived at least until the woman reached the natural end to fertility (estimated for her purposes as age forty-five), Klapisch-Zuber found that these women had, on average, eleven children each, a quite high fertility rate abetted both by early marriage (average age at first marriage for women was seventeen) and by use of wet-nurses. Klapisch-Zuber also discovered that most of these women *stopped* having children at least ten years before natural fertility would have ended. Medical conditions resulting from prior births may well have been a factor but, by analysing the sex of the last two children, Klapisch-Zuber found what seems to have been a deliberate tendency to stop childbearing after birth of a male. In other words, couples decided they had 'enough' children when they had a sufficient number of male heirs. Klapisch-Zuber's essay is powerful evidence for interests in alternately promoting or curtailing fertility and, apparently, the existence of effective knowledge of how to effect the latter. Yet frustratingly Klapisch-Zuber hesitates to propose *how* this marked falling off in fertility was achieved – was it by the use of contraceptives? or simply cessation of potentially reproductive heterosexual relations? This is where we need a gendered approach to the epistemology of women's healthcare: if we simply *assume* that it must have been women's knowledge of contraceptive botanicals that produced this effect, then we may be prematurely foreclosing exploration of the demographic effects of male homosexuality, which is now well-documented for Florence in this period, or the practice of coitus interruptus.[105]

Perhaps instances of failed contraception and abortion, or those of women turning to men for contraceptive knowledge or even violent disruption of their pregnancies, are cases where individual women (often young and poor) were not sufficiently connected to female networks that would have given them the knowledge they needed.[106] Even in the context of modern westernised societies where contraceptive knowledge and materials are readily available, unintended pregnancies still occur. In other words, I do not pretend that my few examples questioning medieval women's knowledge of contraceptives or abortifacients constitute conclusive proof that no such knowledge was available prior to the modern period. But I am stressing that we need to weigh *all* pertinent evidence carefully, keeping in mind motives (of men as well as of women) as much as materials or methods. Comparison with the findings of medical anthropology will be crucial in this endeavour. Not only have medical anthropologists already theorised the concept of 'regulating menstruation' – deliberately interfering with menstrual function for both contraceptive and pronatalist ends – but they can also provide us with important data on how botanical substances with fertility-disruptive properties have been discovered in other times and places and how such knowledge is deployed in gendered frameworks.[107] They have also offered us acute analyses of the circumstances in which contraception or abortion is eschewed for infanticide, whether active or passive.[108] Thus, when we turn back to exploring contraceptive or abortifacient knowledge and practices in historical societies, we can do so with better awareness of the range of possible ways gender can inform reproductive possibilities and why, in some circumstances, it seems to be men who have (or are expected to have) greater expertise or responsibility in controlling fertility.[109]

Conclusions

There has been much excellent work in the field of women's medical history – medicine of, for, and by women – in the past three decades, ranging from edited texts to biographies; from studies of the legal repression of abortion in nineteenth- and twentieth-century America to the development (and collapse) of the 'estrogen paradigm' in women's healthcare.[110] As rigorous and insightful as such work is (particularly for the modern period), there has been a surprising lack of coherence to the field. It has been my argument here that there are crucial elements of this history we have overlooked by focusing perhaps too exclusively on *women* and not seeing the ways in which the creation of epistemologies on the female body are not limited to those who inhabit female bodies. Even in such a historically female-dominant area as midwifery, we need to explore how midwives (male or female) contested epistemologies and standards of care among themselves. Already, in 1331 in Marseilles, female midwives on their own initiative called in a male barber-surgeon 'who was experienced in this' when a foetus needed to be extracted from its dead mother. A legal case in 1403, also from Marseilles, hinged on the disputed intervention for a case of retained placenta which escalated – not along a male–female divide, but one of religion – into a fierce accusation of murder.[111] Questions of how obstetrical knowledge is developed and then best transmitted are likewise of great import to the careers of the early modern female midwife-authors, Justine Siegemund in Prussia and Madame du Coudray in France. Contested epistemologies and scientific ways of knowing have animated scholarship in the history of science for many years, and it would be good to bring these same questions of empiricism, experimentation and social worlds of knowledge construction to bear on the development of obstetrical knowledge. Laurel Thatcher Ulrich's study of the Maine and Massachusetts midwife Martha Ballard showed with great nuance how a female practitioner in Revolutionary New England could carve out a medical practice in concert (and occasionally in rivalry) with male practitioners, recognising that she herself could learn from the anatomical skill of a male physician.[112] Just as Katharine Park recounts how the traditional perspective of the history of anatomy as a masculine project (males being both the presumed objects and the subjects of such investigations) blinded her to 'the ubiquity of women's bodies in [her] sources',[113] so I would argue that the historiographical inclinations spawned by the Ehrenreich and English narrative about the history of women's medical practices have had profound effects in stymying a range of questions that, in my opinion, we should be asking. The roles, indeed the very existence, of medieval midwives, the involvement of men in childbirth and women's healthcare more generally, and the history of women's knowledge of, and control over, contraceptive and abortifacient knowledge, have all been neglected because we have been working with a mythology of a golden age that no data has supported.

In Kuhnian terms, are we trying to 'save the system' by ignoring anomalies in a failing paradigm? I would certainly not suggest that the evidence I have presented here proves that we are ready for a paradigm shift. But we are ready, I believe, to interrogate more systematically the creation and dissemination of medical knowledge and practice *as a cultural artefact* rather than a biologically based, and therefore static, set of instincts. In doing so, we can better see where historical change in healthcare lies. Gender then becomes the historical variable itself, one among several elements at play in the formation of technologies of the body. Gendering our analyses of women's healthcare in the west also opens up opportunities for a richer and more productive dialogue with the histories and anthropologies of other places of the world. The medical anthropologist Marcia Inhorn has produced a fruitful synthetic analysis of more than 150 different anthropological ethnographies of women's healthcare and what they can tell us about the varieties of women's experiences with bodily dysfunctions and the range of desired interventions women are willing to pursue. Indeed, she argues that such observation- and interview-based assessment can tell us things about women that have largely been foreclosed by the success of the biomedical paradigm in the west.[114] Even if many of those anthropological studies are grounded on areas that have already felt the imprint of colonialism (which often imposed European concepts of how medicine ought to be gendered), I believe we can still find enough variety in women's differing experiences to inform our historical understanding.

Ironically, then, it might be argued that gender has been *too much* a focus in the history of women's healthcare. There is an important debate beginning now in medical history about what might be called 'the obstetrical transition' – that is, how the radical reduction in maternal and neonatal mortality was achieved in western countries over the course of the nineteenth and twentieth centuries. The Ehrenreich and English thesis that the masculinisation of midwifery was uniformly a bad thing for women (primarily for women as practitioners, but also for women as patients who lost the emotional comfort of an all-female milieu of ritual and support and who were subjected to sometimes cruelly invasive procedures) is a red herring in two respects: it not only exaggerates the English case, as I have already explained, as if it were typical of European traditions generally (female midwives were nowhere else as disenfranchised or circumscribed as they were in England and the United States), but it also occludes attention to how the radical changes in obstetrical outcomes in the modern period have in fact occurred.[115] Several historians have begun to address this question with great nuance and they are finding that much hangs precisely on these questions of education and professionalisation, with gender differentials being perhaps secondary.[116]

It matters that we get these stories right – or at least that we can say with conviction that we have brought all the historian's tools to bear on these questions. Of all the historical traditions, only China rivals the west in the richness and depth of its historical record in the field of women's health.[117] But it is western medicine, in its various manifestations, that is being adopted now as global, intersecting with and sometimes overwhelming indigenous local practices of great age and complexity. Western historical narratives therefore need to be closely scrutinised not only for their own sake, but also for their implications in setting agendas for health policy in the future. The 'safe motherhood' programmes, which have been going on under World Health Organisation sponsorship since the 1980s, take modern western maternal mortality rates (which might well be the lowest rates ever achieved by human populations) as the goal towards which developing nations should strive. Reducing maternal mortality seems an unquestionably noble goal, but there are huge questions whether that goal is to be achieved through relatively straightforward educational programmes like teaching traditional birth attendants the principles of germ theory and asepsis or through massively intrusive and technologically complex surgical interventions that underlie the astronomical rates of Caesarean section seen now in many westernised countries.[118] One could make similar arguments about the contemporary political and economic implications of issues like birth control, bioprospecting for botanicals for their potential clinical uses and other issues addressed in this chapter. The example of HIV/AIDS alone is a chilling reminder of how a worldwide pandemic has developed under the nose of a health infrastructure fully capable, in terms of its science, of understanding and treating (even if not yet curing) the disease, only to lack enough of a basic understanding of gender relations to have foreseen the devastating consequences of the disease for women.[119] For all of these urgent concerns, history matters, gender matters and women's healthcare matters. We have much yet to do.

Notes

My deepest thanks to the participants in the symposium held at Cambridge in March 2007 for their generous comments on a much earlier draft of this chapter, and especially to Garthine Walker and Alex Shepard for their insightful suggestions for revision. A very special *kudos* to Alexandra Brewis Slade for sharing her thoughts on the genesis and circulation of contraceptive knowledge in the context of larger demographic forces.

1. To date, the only attempt at a synthetic history of this period in American women's history is the anthropological study: Sandra Morgen, *Into Our Own Hands: The Women's Health Movement in the United States, 1969–1990* (New Brunswick, NJ: Rutgers University Press, 2002). For references to key primary sources for this period, see the syllabus for the course 'The Women's Health Movement in the 1970s', taught at Yale University by Naomi Rogers, available online at <http:/www.nlm.nih.gov/hmd/collections/digital/syllabi/rogers2.pdf> (accessed 19 June 2005).

2. A comprehensive list of such work would go on for pages. A representative sampling might include Regina Morantz-Sanchez, *'Conduct Unbecoming a Woman': Medicine on Trial in Turn-of-the-Century Brooklyn* (New York: Oxford University Press, 1999); Wendy D. Churchill, 'The Medical Practice of the Sexed Body: Women, Men, and Disease in Britain, circa 1600–1740', *Social History of Medicine* 18 (2005), pp. 3–22; Wendy D. Churchill, 'Bodily Differences? Gender, Race, and Class in Hans Sloane's Jamaican Medical Practice, 1687–1688', *Journal of the History of Medicine and Allied Sciences* 60 (2005), pp. 391–444; Diana Wales, 'Equally Safe for Both Sexes: A Gender Analysis of Medical Advertisements in English Newspapers, 1690–1750', *Vesalius* 11 (2005), pp. 26–32.

3. For the purposes of this chapter, I will be construing 'women's medicine' as referring particularly to aspects of women's health relating to the reproductive organs and their functions. In fact, I and many others are now arguing that 'women's medicine' needs to be viewed as encompassing woman's entire organism, not simply reproductive functioning.

My particular concern here, however, is to reunite the histories of obstetrics (attendance on pregnancy and childbirth) and gynaecology, since much has been lost in focusing solely on attendance at childbirth.

4. On the concept of 'situated knowledge', see most importantly Donna Haraway, 'Situated Knowledges: The Science Question in Feminism and the Privilege of Partial Perspective', *Feminist Studies* 14 (1988), pp. 575–99.

5. Barbara Ehrenreich and Deidre English, *Witches, Midwives, and Nurses: A History of Women Healers* (Oyster Bay, NY: Glass Mountain Pamphlets, 1971–72); Barbara Ehrenreich and Deidre English, *Complaints and Disorders: The Sexual Politics of Sickness* (Old Westbury, NY: Feminist Press, 1973). On the internationalisation of the US women's health movement more generally, see Kathy Davis, *The Making of Our Bodies, Ourselves: How Feminism Travels across Borders* (Durham, NC: Duke University Press, 2007).

6. Ehrenreich took a PhD in biology in 1968. Just before she produced *Witches, Midwives and Nurses*, she published, with John Ehrenreich, *The American Health Empire: Power, Profits, and Politics* (New York: Random House, 1970) and since then has had a highly influential career as a 'public intellectual', publishing on issues of social justice, economics and healthcare. Deirdre English is a journalist.

7. The bibliography on these topics is extensive. Among the most direct challengers of the Ehrenreich and English position have been Regina Morantz-Sanchez, *Sympathy and Science: Women Physicians in American Medicine* (New York: Oxford University Press, 1985); and Nancy M. Theriot, 'Women's Voices in Nineteenth-Century Medical Discourse: A Step toward Deconstructing Science', *Signs* 19 (1993), pp. 1–31. These critiques developed amid transformations in how much history of medicine is done; see Susan M. Reverby and David Rosner, '"Beyond the Great Doctors" Revisited: A Generation of the "New" Social History of Medicine', in Frank Huisman and John Harley Warner (eds), *Locating Medical History: The Stories and Their Meanings* (Baltimore: Johns Hopkins University Press, 2004), pp. 167–93, which includes a useful summary of how women and gender have been addressed in the context of other analyses of difference.

8. Ehrenreich and English, *Witches, Midwives and Nurses*, p. 3.

9. I have identified the following translations: *Hexen, Hebammen und Krankenschuestern* (Munich: Frauenoffensive, 1975); *Le streghe siamo noi: Il ruolo della medicina nella repressione della donna* (Milan: CELUC, 1975); *Sorcières, sages femmes et infirmières: Une histoire des femmes et de la médecine*, tr. Lorraine Brown and Catherine Germain (1976; Montreal: Editions du Remue-Ménage, 1983); *Brujas, comadronas y enfermeras: Historia de las sanadoras; Dolencias y trastornos: Política sexual de la enfermedad* (Barcelona: LaSal, 1981). These all still appear to be in print. For online sales of the American edition, I checked the website of Barnes and Noble on 29 July 2005 (<http://search.barnesandnoble.com/bestsellers/bestsellers.asp?cat= 394783&sort=S>).

10. Although it is not surprising to find it used in such popularising works as Elisabeth Brooke's *Women Healers Through History* (London: Women's Press, 1993), it is stunning to see it cited as a reputable authority in scholarly works such as Renate Blumenfeld-Kosinski, *Not of Woman Born: Representations of Caesarean Birth in Medieval and Renaissance Culture* (Ithaca, NY: Cornell University Press, 1990); Caroline Bicks, *Midwiving Subjects in Shakespeare's England* (Aldershot: Ashgate, 2003); and Carmen Caballero-Navas (ed.), *The 'Book of Women's Love' and Jewish Medieval Medical Literature on Women 'Sefer Ahavat Nashim'*, Kegan Paul Library of Jewish Studies (London and New York: Kegan Paul, 2004). Even when it is not explicitly cited, its influence can be seen in works such as Myriam Greilsammer, 'The Midwife, the Priest, and the Physician: The Subjugation of Midwives in the Low Countries at the End of the Middle Ages', *Journal of Medieval and Renaissance Studies* 22 (1991), pp. 285–329, which argues precisely for a medieval 'golden age' when women had exclusive control over knowledge of reproduction, which was then

suppressed by the combined forces of the Church and the male medical profession. Perhaps most famously, Ehrenreich and English's pamphlet gave rise in 1985 to Gunnar Heinsohn and Otto Steiger's grand thesis of the importance of the witch-hunts for the history of population control: *Die Vernichtung der weisen Frauen* (3rd edn, Erftstadt: Ein März Buch, 2005).

11. Ehrenreich and English deliberately reduced all kinds of women's medical practice to a single plane, using the term 'midwives' in their title as a catch-all phrase rather than a specific referent to birth attendants. On the conceptual confusion this usage has spawned, see the discussion in Monica H. Green, 'Women's Medical Practice and Health Care in Medieval Europe', *Signs* 14 (1988–89), pp. 434–73.

12. David Harley, 'Historians as Demonologists: The Myth of the Midwife-Witch', *Social History of Medicine* 3 (1990), pp. 1–26. It should be noted, too, that some of Ehrenreich and English's evidence was simply fabricated, such as the statement, 'If a woman dare to cure without having studied she is a witch and must die', *Witches, Midwives, and Nurses*, p. 19. They attribute this to the *Malleus maleficarum* but provide no citation. The same quote appears in countless popular regurgitations of *Witches, Midwives, and Nurses*, but also in John M. Riddle's 1997 study, *Eve's Herbs: A History of Contraception and Abortion in the West* (Cambridge: Harvard University Press, 1997), p. 134. The statement appears nowhere in Montague Summers's old translation of the *Malleus* (which elsewhere Ehrenreich and English relied on), and I have had confirmation from Dr Christopher Mackay of the University of Alberta that the citation is bogus (personal communication, 1 April 2008). For a definitive edition and translation, see Henricus Institoris and Jacobus Sprenger, *Malleus Maleficarum*, ed. and tr. Christopher S. Mackay, 2 vols (Cambridge: Cambridge University Press, 2006).

13. Brigitte Jordan, *Birth in Four Cultures: A Crosscultural Investigation of Childbirth in Yucatan, Holland, Sweden, and the United States* (1973; Long Grove, IL: Waveland Press, 1993), p. 50.

14. Lisa Forman Cody, *Birthing the Nation: Sex, Science, and the Conception of Eighteenth-Century Britons* (New York: Oxford University Press, 2005), p. 3. my emphasis.

15. Hilary Marland (ed.), *The Art of Midwifery: Early Modern Midwives in Europe* (London: Routledge, 1993). No essay there asserts what midwives were or were not doing over the course of 'millennia'; rather, all are very closely argued, empirically based studies that restrict their claims to the early modern period.

16. See Monica H. Green, 'Obstetrical and Gynecological Texts in Middle English', *Studies in the Age of Chaucer* 14 (1992), pp. 53–88; Monica H. Green and Linne Mooney, 'The Sickness of Women', in M. Teresa Tavormina (ed.), *Sex, Aging, and Death in a Medieval Medical Compendium: Trinity College Cambridge MS R.14.52, Its Texts, Language, and Scribe*, Medieval & Renaissance Texts and Studies 292, 2 vols (Tempe: Arizona Center for Medieval and Renaissance Studies, 2006), vol. 2, pp. 455–568; Monica H. Green, *Making Women's Medicine Masculine: The Rise of Male Authority in Pre-Modern Gynaecology* (Oxford: Oxford University Press, 2008).

17. Figures for French texts on women's medicine come, respectively, from Green, *Making Women's Medicine Masculine*; and Valérie Worth-Stylianou, *Les Traités d'obstétrique en langue française au seuil de la modernité. Bibliographie critique des 'Divers Travaulx' d'Euchaire Rösslin (1536) à l''Apologie de Louyse Bourgeois sage femme' (1627)* (Geneva: Droz, 2006). On male authorship of texts both medieval and early modern, see Green, *Making Women's Medicine Masculine*; Helen King, *Midwifery, Obstetrics and the Rise of Gynaecology: The Uses of a Sixteenth-Century Compendium* (Aldershot: Ashgate, 2007); Lianne McTavish, *Childbirth and the Display of Authority in Early Modern France* (Aldershot: Ashgate, 2005).

18. Michele Savonarola, *Il trattato ginecologico-pediatrico in volgare 'Ad mulieres ferrarienses de regimine pregnantium et noviter natorum usque ad septennium'*, ed. Luigi Belloni (Milan: Società Italiana di ostetricia e ginecologia, 1952). Compare Green, *Mak-*

ing Women's Medicine Masculine, ch. 3, esp. pp. 145–62, for the limited evidence that midwives were even an aural audience of literature on women's medicine.

19. Margaret L. King, 'Concepts of Childhood: What We Know and Where We Might Go', *Renaissance Quarterly* 60 (2007), pp. 371–407, here pp. 383–4, my emphasis.

20. For example, one of the central arguments of Mary Fissell, *Vernacular Bodies: The Politics of Reproduction in Early Modern England* (Oxford and New York: Oxford University Press, 2004), is that, with the advent of print, male readers for the first time became privy to what had previously been female knowledge. Similarly, the organising principle of Laura Gowing, *Common Bodies: Women, Touch and Power in Seventeenth-Century England* (New Haven: Yale University Press, 2003) is that the female body was governed most of all by other women.

21. Green, *Making Women's Medicine Masculine*, ch. 6, esp. pp. 273–84.

22. See e.g., the similarities in this regard between James V. Ricci, *The Genealogy of Gynaecology: History of the Development of Gynaecology throughout the Ages* (Philadelphia and Toronto: Blakiston, 1950); Michael J. O'Dowd and Elliot E. Philipp, *The History of Obstetrics and Gynaecology* (New York and London: Parthenon, 1994); and Harold Speert, *Obstetric and Gynecologic Milestones Illustrated* (New York and London: Parthenon, 1996).

23. King, *Midwifery, Obstetrics and the Rise of Gynaecology*.

24. James Hobson Aveling, an obstetric physician and founding member of both the Obstetrical Society of London (1859) and of the British Gynaecological Society (1884), wrote his *English Midwives: Their History and Prospects* (London: J. & J. Churchill, 1872) as part of his campaign to improve the education and regulation of midwifery. Anthropological works include George Julius Engelmann's first comparative ethnographic and historical study of childbirth, *Labor among Primitive Peoples, Showing the Development of the Obstetric Science of To-day, From the Natural and Instinctive Customs of all Races, Civilized and Savage, Past and Present* (St Louis, MO: J. H. Chambers, 1882); G.-J. Witkowski's equally ambitious *Histoire des accouchements chez tous les peuples* (Paris: G. Steinheil, 1887), which he followed with his *Accoucheurs et sages-femmes célèbres: Esquisses biographiques* (Paris: G. Steinheil, 1891). One of the few female contributors to these general surveys was Henriette Carrier, *Origines de La Maternité de Paris: Les maîtresses sages-femmes et l'office des accouchées de l'ancien Hôtel-Dieu (1378–1796)* (Paris: G. Steinheil, 1888).

25. Thomas R. Forbes, 'Perrette the Midwife: A Fifteenth-Century Witchcraft Case', *Bulletin of the History of Medicine* 36 (1962), pp. 124–9.

26. Jean Donnison, *Midwives and Medical Men: A History of Inter-Professional Rivalries and Women's Rights* (New York: Schocken, 1977); Jane B. Donegan, *Women and Men Midwives: Medicine, Morality and Misogyny in Early America* (New York: Greenwood, 1978), citing *Witches, Midwives, and Nurses* on pp. 7, 36, 190.

27. Judy Barrett Litoff, *The American Midwife Debate: A Sourcebook on its Modern Origins*, Contributions in Medical Studies 18 (New York: Greenwood Press, 1986).

28. Monica H. Green, 'In Search of an "Authentic" Women's Medicine: The Strange Fates of Trota of Salerno and Hildegard of Bingen', *Dynamis: Acta Hispanica ad Medicinae Scientiarumque Historiam Illustrandam* 19 (1999), pp. 25–54.

29. Johann Christian Friedrich Harless, *Die Verdienste der Frauen um Naturwissenschaft, Gesundheits- und Heilkunde, so wie auch um Länder- Völker- und Menschenjunde, von der ältesten Zeit bis auf die neueste: Ein Beitrag zur Geschichte geistiger Cultur, und der Natur- und Heilkunde, insbesondere* (Göttingen: Vanden-Hoeck-Ruprecht, 1830). On women who took medical degrees through 'irregular' medical study prior to Blackwell, see Gabriella Berti Logan, 'Women and the Practice and Teaching of Medicine in Bologna in the Eighteenth and Early Nineteenth Centuries', *Bulletin of the History of Medicine* 77 (2003), pp. 506–35.

30. Paulina Wright Davis, 'Remarks at the Conventions', *The Una* 1:9 (September 1853), pp. 136–78. I owe this reference to Susan Mosher Stuard, 'History, Medieval Women's',

in Margaret Schaus (ed.), *Medieval Women and Gender: An Encyclopedia* (New York: Routledge, 2006), pp. 368–74.

31. Sophia Jex-Blake, *Medical Women: Two Essays* (Edinburgh: William Oliphant, 1872).

32. Melina Lipinska, *Histoire des femmes médicins depuis l'antiquité jusqu'à nos jours* (Paris: G. Jacques, 1900); and her later summary, *Les femmes et le progrès des sciences médicales* (Paris: Masson & Cie, 1930). Compare Henri Denifle (ed.), *Chartularium Universitatis Parisiensis* (Paris: Delalain, 1891–99), vol. 2, pp. 255–67.

33. Kate Campbell Hurd-Mead, *A History of Women in Medicine* (1938; New York: AMS Press, 1977). Hurd-Mead's work is riddled with scholarly errors of almost every kind and should not be relied on.

34. Their source for this material was Muriel Joy Hughes, *Women Healers in Medieval Life and Literature* (1943; Freeport, NY: Books for Libraries, 1968).

35. Harley, 'Historians as Demonologists'.

36. Work published up to the late 1980s is analysed in Monica H. Green, 'Women's Medical Practice' reprinted with corrigenda and addenda in Monica H. Green, *Women's Health-care in the Medieval West: Texts and Contexts*, Variorum Collected Studies Series CS680 (Aldershot: Ashgate, 2000), Essay I. Subsequent work published until 2004 is sum-marised in Monica H. Green, 'Bodies, Gender, Health, Disease: Recent Work on Medieval Women's Medicine', *Studies in Medieval and Renaissance History*, 3rd series, 2 (2005), pp. 1–46, here p. 15.

37. Katharine Park, *Secrets of Women: Gender, Generation, and the Origins of Human Dis-section* (New York: Zone, 2006); Green, *Making Women's Medicine Masculine*.

38. Montserrat Cabré, 'Women or Healers? Household Practices and the Categories of Health Care in Late Medieval Iberia', *Bulletin of the History of Medicine* 82 (2008), pp. 18–51. See also Green, *Making Women's Medicine Masculine*, ch. 3, pp. 118–62. On the range of women's medical practices in the sixteenth and seventeenth centuries, see the other essays in that same special issue of the *Bulletin*.

39. Green, *Making Women's Medicine Masculine*.

40. Jordan, *Birth in Four Cultures*, ch. 2, pp.11–31.

41. Ann Ellis Hanson, 'A Division of Labor: Roles for Men in Greek and Roman Births', *Thamyris* 1 (1994), pp. 157–202; Helen King, *Hippocrates' Woman: Reading the Fe-male Body in Ancient Greece* (London and New York: Routledge, 1998); Rebecca Flemming, *Medicine and the Making of Roman Women: Gender, Nature, and Author-ity from Celsus to Galen* (Oxford: Oxford University Press, 2001); Rebecca Flemming, 'Women, Writing and Medicine in the Classical World', *Classical Quarterly* 57 (2007), pp. 257–79.

42. Jacqueline Marie Musacchio, *The Art and Ritual of Childbirth in Renaissance Italy* (New Haven: Yale University Press, 1999).

43. Ulinka Rublack, 'Pregnancy, Childbirth and the Female Body in Early Modern Germany', *Past & Present* 150 (1996), pp. 84–100.

44. Park, *Secrets of Women*.

45. Cecilia Van Hollen, *Birth on the Threshold: Childbirth and Modernity in South India* (Berkeley: University of California Press, 2003), p. 43. The term *purdah* is italicised in the original; the other emphases are my own.

46. See Maneesha Lal, 'The Politics of Gender and Medicine in Colonial India: The Countess of Dufferin's Fund, 1885–1888', *Bulletin of the History of Medicine* 68 (1994), pp. 29–66; Maneesha Lal, 'Purdah as Pathology: Gender and the Circulation of Medical Knowledge in Late Colonial India', in Sarah Hodges (ed.), *Reproductive Health in India: History, Politics, Controversies* (New Delhi: Orient Longman, 2006), pp. 85–114; Van Hollen, *Birth on the Threshold*.

47. Terri Kapsalis, *Public Privates: Performing Gynecology from Both Ends of the Speculum* (Durham, NC: Duke University Press, 1997), examines the ways this ambiguity has been exploited as a type of pornography.

48. See e.g, Donnison, *Midwives and Medical Men*; Roy Porter, 'A Touch of Danger: The Man-Midwife as Sexual Predator', in George Sebastian Rousseau and Roy Porter (eds), *Sexual Underworlds of the Enlightenment* (Cambridge: Harvard University Press, 1995).

49. Monica H. Green (ed.), *The 'Trotula': A Medieval Compendium of Women's Medicine* (Philadelphia: University of Pennsylvania Press, 2001), pp. 22–34. In one of the *Trotula* texts, the original author explicitly said that midwives (*obstetrices*) ought not look the parturient in the face lest the latter be ashamed, p. 236, *n*. 48. Through a curious sequence of textual corruption, this reference became an injunction that the *men* assisting ought not look her in the face.

50. See Hilary Marland and Anne Marie Rafferty (eds), *Midwives, Society and Childbirth: Debates and Controversies in the Modern Period* (London and New York: Routledge, 1997).

51. On Egypt, see Hibba Abugideiri, 'The Scientisation of Culture: Colonial Medicine's Construction of Egyptian Womanhood, 1893–1929', *Gender & History* 16 (2004), pp. 83–98; on Jamaica, see Carolyn Sargent and Joan Rawlins, 'Transformations in Maternity Services in Jamaica', *Social Science and Medicine* 35 (1992), pp. 1,225–32. On India, see Lal, 'The Politics of Gender and Medicine'; Van Hollen, *Birth on the Threshold*.

52. Judith Walzer Leavitt, 'What Do Men Have to Do With It? Fathers and Mid-Twentieth-Century Childbirth', *Bulletin of the History of Medicine* 77 (2003), pp. 235-62, and the earlier literature cited therein.

53. John M. Riddle, *Contraception and Abortion from the Ancient World to the Renaissance* (Cambridge: Harvard University Press, 1992); John M. Riddle, *Eve's Herbs: A History of Contraception and Abortion in the West* (Cambridge: Harvard University Press, 1997).

54. Criticism from classical scholars includes Helen King, *Hippocrates' Woman*, ch. 7, pp. 132-56; Walter Scheidel, 'Progress and Problems in Roman Demography', in Walter Scheidel (ed.), *Debating Roman Demography* (Leiden: Brill, 2001), pp. 1–81, who calls Riddle's work 'an embarrassing travesty of scholarship' (p. 39). Critical reviews of *Eve's Herbs* include Lesley A. Hall, *American Historical Review* 103 (1998), pp. 1,211–12; Gigi Santow, *Population and Development Review* 24 (1998), pp. 869–75; Monica H. Green, *Bulletin of the History of Medicine* 73 (1999), pp. 308–11.

55. In all, I found some thirty-two articles published on the topics of gynaecological and obstetrical uses of botanical substances by human populations between 1982 and early 2008. There is also considerable work being done testing natural substances in animal studies.

56. On the concept of 'technologies of the body' as an umbrella term for medical as well as cosmetic interventions, see Green, 'Bodies, Gender, Health, Disease', pp. 3–6.

57. Vanessa Steenkamp, 'Traditional Herbal Remedies Used by South African Women for Gynaecological Complaints', *Journal of Ethnopharmacology* 86 (2003), pp. 97–108, here p. 98; Joanna Michel et al., 'Medical Potential of Plants Used by the Q'eqchi Maya of Livingston, Guatemala for the Treatment of Women's Health Complaints', *Journal of Ethnopharmacology* 114 (2007) pp. 92–101.

58. R. C. Cambie and Alexandra A. Brewis, *Anti-Fertility Plants of the Pacific* (Melbourne: CSIRO Press, 1997).

59. See e.g., Karin E. Netland and Jorge Martinez, 'Abortifacients: Toxidromes, Ancient to Modern – A Case Series and Review of the Literature', *Academic Emergency Medicine* 7 (2000), pp. 824–9.

60. Alexandra Brewis Slade, personal communication with the author, 31 March 2008.

61. Johannes Platearius, *Practica brevis*, my translation. The text has not yet received a modern edition; I cite here from one of the earliest extant copies, Cambridge University Library, Dd.III.51, s. xii.

62. On this idea of 'the brother of the Salernitans', see Mireille Ausécache, 'Une naissance monstrueuse au Moyen Age: Le 'frère de Salerne', *Gesnerus* 64 (2007), pp. 5–23.

63. It is important to understand that the alleged female writer 'Trotula' that Riddle refers to (*Eve's Herbs*, pp. 31–2, 52 and 105), represents not one author but three, whose works

were fused into a single ensemble in the late twelfth century. The passages that Riddle cites as evidence of this 'woman writer's' views in fact come from a text I have identified as male-authored. See Green, *Making Women's Medicine Masculine*, ch. 1, esp. pp. 48–53.

64. Trota of Salerno, *De curis mulierum* (On Treatments for Women), paragraph 146 (Oxford, Bodleian Library, MS Digby 79, s. xiii in.): 'Item sunt quedam quibus remanet secundina post partum, quibus subuenimus ad illius expulsionem sic. Extrahimus succum petrosilini et porri, et distemperamus cum oleo pulegino et oleo nucis, et damus ad potandum. Vel succum borraginis, et cito educetur, tum quia fortassis ueniet et ex conatu uomendi educet, tum quia succus illas uisitat partes que sufficiunt ad expulsionem'. (Likewise there are some women in whom the afterbirth remains after birth; these we aid in the following manner. We extract the juice of parsley and leeks, and we mix them with pennyroyal oil and nut oil, and we give it to drink. Or the juice of borage. And immediately it will come out. Perhaps it comes out from the effort of vomiting, or perhaps because the juice goes to those organs which are needed for expulsion.) The passage reads somewhat differently in the later version of the *Trotula* ensemble, which can be found in Green, *The 'Trotula'*, 146, pp. 122–4.

65. In addition to the previous passage, borage is mentioned in Trota's *Practica* as follows (paragraph 5, Madrid, Biblioteca de la Universidad Complutense, MS 119, *c.* 1200, fol. 140v): 'Ad mulierem que non potest post partum libere purgari, succum de foliis borraginis exprimas, et cum oleo misceas et bibat, et statim purgabitur'. (For a woman who is not able to be freely purged after birth, we express the juice from borage leaves and mix it with oil; let her drink it and immediately she will be purged). Neither borage nor leeks are mentioned as contraceptives or abortifacients by Riddle.

66. Trota, *Practica*, paragraph 1 (Madrid, Complutense, MS 119, f. 140 r–v). 'Secundum Trotam ad menstrua prouocanda, propter quorum retentiones mulier concipere non potest. Si ergo iuuencula fuerit, accipe radicem salicis tenere fluuialis, et bene radas, deinde tritam facias in aqua uel uino bulliri, et accipe frondes rute, et teras, et de succo facias crispellas, et eas comedat, et liquorem in quo radices salicis decoqueris, bibat in mane cum ieiuna fuerit. Quo ter uel quater facto, redduntur eis menstrua'. (According to Trota, [a remedy] to provoke the menses, on account of whose retention *the woman is unable to conceive*. If she is young, take root of river willow and scrape it well. Then, having ground it, boil it in water or wine. And take the leaves of rue and grind them, and make little wafers from its juice. And let her eat them. And in the morning when she is fasting, give her to drink the liquid in which you have cooked the willow root. Done three or four times, the menses will return). A nearly identical recipe appears in Trota's *De curis mulierum* (paragraph 135), though here we find madder being used instead of rue. On the fertility disruptive properties of willow and rue, see Riddle, *Eve's Herbs*, pp. 60–1 and 48–50, respectively.

67. On the tolerance for contraceptive knowledge in medical writings of the period, see Monica H. Green, 'Constantinus Africanus and the Conflict Between Religion and Science', in G. R. Dunstan (ed.), *The Human Embryo: Aristotle and the Arabic and European Traditions* (Exeter: Exeter University Press, 1990), pp. 47–69.

68. Hans Wölfel (ed.), *Das Arzneidrogenbuch 'Circa instans' in einer Fassung des XIII. Jahrhunderts aus der Universitätsbibliothek Erlangen. Text und Kommentar als Beitrag zur Pflanzen- und Drogenkunde des Mittelalters* (Berlin: A. Preilipper, 1939).

69. E.g., under rosemary we find, 'For cleansing the womb and aiding the conceptus, make a fomentation around the pudenda with water decocted with it. The Salernitan women cook its leaves in musk oil and give themselves suppositories with this concoction', Wölfel (ed.), *Das Arzneidrogenbuch*, p. 104.

70. Nicole Gonthier, 'Les médecins et la justice au XVe siècle à travers l'exemple dijonnais', *Le Moyen Age: Revue d'histoire et de philologie* 101 (1995), pp. 277–95, here p. 288.

71. Monica H. Green, 'Flowers, Poisons, and Men: Menstruation in Medieval Western Europe', in *Menstruation: A Cultural History*, ed. Andrew Shail and Gillian Howie (New York: Palgrave, 2005), pp. 51–64; Alisha Rankin, 'Duchess, Heal Thyself: Elisabeth of

Rochlitz and the Patient's Perspective in Early Modern Germany', *Bulletin of the History of Medicine* 82 (2008), pp. 109–44, at p. 134, citing the detailed self-description of symptoms by Lady Anna of Waldeck; and Barbara Duden, *The Woman Beneath the Skin: A Doctor's Patients in Eighteenth-Century Germany*, tr. Thomas Dunlap (Cambridge: Harvard University Press, 1991).

72. Etienne van de Walle and Elisha P. Renne (eds), *Regulating Menstruation: Beliefs, Practices, Interpretations* (Chicago: University of Chicago Press, 2001).

73. Marcia Inhorn, *Quest for Conception: Gender, Infertility, and Egyptian Medical Traditions* (Philadelphia: University of Pennsylvania Press, 1994); Marcia Inhorn, *Infertility and Patriarchy: The Cultural Politics of Gender and Family Life in Egypt* (Philadelphia: University of Pennsylvania Press, 1996).

74. My thanks to Alex Brewis Slade for bringing this concept to my attention, and to Colleen Marie O'Brien for providing a brief bibliography. In her book, *Plants and Empire: Colonial Bioprospecting in the Atlantic World* (Cambridge: Harvard University Press, 2004), Londa Schiebinger employs the concept of 'agnatology', the study of the loss of knowledge, which she sees as deliberate acts of suppression. I prefer 'persistence of knowledge' since it carries no presumption of moral fault, only historical change.

75. Riddle, *Eve's Herbs*, pp. 10–13, 23–4. For a more accurate translation of major portions of this woman's testimony, where the reader can see the full context of her statements on contraception, see Patrick J. Geary, *Readings in Medieval History* (Lewiston, NY: Broadview Press, 1989), pp. 539–40.

76. Monica H. Green, 'The Possibilities of Literacy and the Limits of Reading: Women and the Gendering of Medical Literacy', in Green, *Women's Healthcare in the Medieval West*, Essay VII, pp. 1–76; Monica H. Green, 'Books as a Source of Medical Education for Women in the Middle Ages', *Dynamis: Acta Hispanica ad Medicinae Scientiarumque Historiam Illustrandam* 20 (2000), pp. 331–69.

77. Green, *Making Women's Medicine Masculine*, pp. 110, 159 n. 26.

78. Alexandra Barratt (ed.), *The Knowing of Woman's Kind in Childing: A Middle English Version of Material Derived from the 'Trotula' and Other Sources*, Medieval Women: Texts and Contexts 4 (Turnhout: Brepols, 2001), p. 60, line 311.

79. Cambridge, University Library, MS Dd.10.44, s. xv, fol. 91v.

80. Green and Mooney, 'The *Sickness of Women*', vol. 2, pp. 455–568, lines 679–81.

81. Donnison, *Midwives and Medical Men*, p. 203, n. 7.

82. Alexander Hamilton Thompson (ed.), *Visitations in the Diocese of Lincoln 1517–1531*, 3 vols (Lincoln: Lincoln Record Society, 1944), vol. 2, p. 65, my translation.

83. Thompson, *Visitations*, vol. 2, p. 14. The Middle English passage appears in the original, which is otherwise written in Latin.

84. James Hitchcock, 'A Sixteenth Century Midwife's License', *Bulletin of the History of Medicine* 41 (1967), pp. 75–6, spelling and grammar modernised.

85. Riddle, *Eve's Herbs*, p. 134.

86. I have examined published oaths for the following cities: Brussels (1424), Regensburg (1452), Amberg (1456–64), Württemburg (c.1480), Bern (1540), Heilbronn (undated, but probably sixteenth century). Merry E. Wiesner, 'The Midwives of South Germany and the Public/Private Dichotomy', in Marland, *Art of Midwifery*, pp. 77–94, esp. pp. 87–8, finds new concerns about abortion in Southern Germany in the late sixteenth century. Miriam Greilsammer, 'The Midwife, the Priest, and the Physician: The Subjugation of Midwives in the Low Countries at the End of the Middle Ages', *Journal of Medieval and Renaissance Studies* 22 (1991), pp. 285–329, does not document any such concern in the Low Countries until 1697; see her comments on Bruges on p. 317. I believe she is mistaken to claim on p. 300 that concerns in Bruges in 1551 to prevent midwives from administering medications without physician supervision had anything to do with abortifacients; such prohibitions against administering medicines of any kind was central to later medieval physician control over barbers and midwives.

87. Kramer and Sprenger, *Malleus Maleficarum*, vol. 1, p. 704, vol. 2, pp. 596–7; Harley, 'Historians as Demonologists'.

88. J. Harvey Bloom and R. Rutson James, *Medical Practitioners in the Diocese of London, Licensed under the Act of 3 Henry VIII, c. 11: An Annotated List, 1529–1725* (Cambridge: Cambridge University Press, 1935), pp. 84–85; Andrew Boorde, T*he Breuiary of Helthe* (London: William Middleton, 1547), Extravagantes, fol. xvii; Walter Howard Frere (ed.), *Visitation Articles and Injunctions of the Period of the Reformation*, vol. 2: *1536–1558* (London: Longmans, Green, 1910), pp. 356–7; J. Strype, *Annals of the Reformation and Establishment of Religion, and other Various Occurrences in the Church of England, during the First Twelve Years of Queen Elizabeth's Happy Reign* (London: J. Wyat, 1708–09; Oxford, 1824), pp. 242–3.

89. In her comprehensive study of midwifery legislation in Germany, Sibylla Flügge, *Hebammen und heilkundige Frauen: Recht und Rechtswirklichkeit im 15. und 16. Jahrhundert*, 2nd ed. (Frankfurt am Main: Stroenfeld, 2000), likewise did not find evidence that midwifery ordinances were concerned with abortifacients prior to 1577; see esp. pp. 210, 381, and 401–2. On widespread efforts to criminalise abortion in the sixteenth century, see Wolfgang P. Müller, *Die Abtreibung: Anfänge der Kriminalisierung, 1140–1650* (Cologne: Böhlau, 2000), who also has extensive evidence of abortifacient knowledge coming from a wide variety of actors, male and female.

90. Green, 'Possibilities of Literacy'; Elaine Leong, 'Making Medicines in the Early Modern Household', *Bulletin of the History of Medicine* 82 (2008), pp. 45–168; Rankin, 'Duchess, Heal Thyself'.

91. Green, *Making Women's Medicine Masculine*, ch. 6, pp. 67–71, 301–10.

92. Cornelia Hughes Dayton, 'Taking the Trade: Abortion and Gender Relations in an Eighteenth-Century New England Village', *William and Mary Quarterly*, 3rd series, 48 (1991), pp. 19–49.

93. Schiebinger, *Plants and Empire*.

94. Liese M. Perrin, 'Resisting Reproduction: Reconsidering Slave Contraception in the Old South', *Journal of American Studies* 35 (2001), pp. 255–74. Perrin (p. 256) quotes Deborah Gray White as saying 'These matters were virtually exclusive to the female world of the quarters, and when they arose they were attended to in secret and were intended to remain secret'. My thanks to Calvin Schermerhorn for bringing Perrin's work to my attention and clarifying for me some of the historiographical issues involved.

95. Cambie and Brewis, *Anti-Fertility Plants*, p. 105.

96. See Green, *Making Women's Medicine Masculine*, p. 222.

97. It is critical that in these and other similar cases we distinguish open assault (where miscarriage may have been an accidental result rather than a deliberate goal) from violence specifically meant to terminate a pregnancy. See Sara M. Butler, 'Abortion by Assault: Violence against Pregnant Women in Thirteenth- and Fourteenth-Century England', *Journal of Women's History* 17 (2005), pp. 9–31; Sara M. Butler, *The Language of Abuse: Marital Violence in Later Medieval England* (Leiden: Brill, 2007); and Wolfgang P. Müller, 'Canon Law Versus Common Law: The Case of Abortion in Late Medieval England', in Kenneth Pennington, Stanley Chodorow and Keith Kendall (eds), *Proceedings of the Tenth International Congress of Medieval Canon Law* (Vatican City: Biblioteca Apostolica Vaticana, 2001), pp. 929–41. See also Marianne Elsakkers, 'Inflicting Serious Bodily Harm: the Visigothic *Antiquae* on Violence and Abortion', *Tijdschrift voor Rechtsgeschiedenis – The Legal History Review* 71 (2003), pp. 55–63.

98. Pierre Dubuis, 'Enfants refusés dans les Alpes occidentales (XIVe–XVe siècles)', in Società Italiana di Demografia Storica (ed.), *Enfance abandonnée et société en Europe* (Rome: Ecole française de Rome Palais Farnèse, 1991), pp. 573–90. I discuss here only the cases of contraception and abortion; the remaining ones are either infanticides or abandonments of a child.

99. Peter Biller, *The Measure of Multitude: Population in Medieval Thought* (Oxford: Oxford University Press, 2000).

100. On the rather astounding levels of clerical and lay interest in generation in the later Middle Ages, see Green, *Making Women's Medicine Masculine*, esp. ch. 5, pp. 204–45.

101. Judith Bennett, 'Writing Fornication: Medieval Leyrwite and its Historians', *Transactions of the Royal Historical Society* 6th series, 13 (2003), pp. 131–62.

102. The Bolognese physician, Albert de Zancariis, writing *c*.1325, warns fellow physicians to be wary of women who want to know if they're pregnant so that they can procure an abortion; see Albertus de Zancariis, *De cautelis medicorum habendis*, as cited in Manuel Morris, *Die Schrift des Albertus de Zancariis aus Bologna: De cautelis medicorum habendis* (inaug.-diss., Leipzig, 1914), p. 13. On apothecaries as sources of information on abortifacients, see Flügge, *Hebammen und heilkundige Frauen*, pp. 210 and 280; for a barber, see Müller, *Die Abtreibung*, p. 279, n. 479.

103. E.g., the author (almost certainly male) of the twelfth-century Salernitan treatise called *Book on the Conditions of Women* recommended, on the advice of the Benedictine monk Constantine the African, that 'women who have narrow vaginas and constricted wombs ought not have sexual relations with men lest they conceive and die. But all such women are not able to abstain, and so they need our assistance'. See Green, *The 'Trotula'*, paragraph 83, p. 96, and p. 235, *n*. 43. On the ways in which Muslim precepts about contraception and abortion made their way into Latin (Christian) medical texts, see Green, 'Constantinus Africanus'. See also Nancy G. Siraisi, *Taddeo Alderotti and His Pupils: Two Generations of Italian Medical Learning* (Princeton: Princeton University Press, 1981), pp. 282–3, regarding Mondino de' Liuzzi's (1275–1326) argument that since pregnancy (whether inside or outside marriage) can sometimes be dangerous for women, it is a lesser evil to prevent it than to terminate it once it has begun.

104. Christiane Klapisch-Zuber, 'Le dernier enfant: Fécondité et vieillissement chez les Florentines XIVᵉ–XVᵉ siècles', in Jean-Pierre Barder, François Lebrun and René Le Mée (eds), *Mesurer et comprendre: Mélanges offerts à Jacques Dupaquier* (Paris: Presses Universitaires de France, 1993), pp. 277–90.

105. Michael Rocke, *Forbidden Friendships: Homosexuality and Male Culture in Renaissance Florence* (New York: Oxford University Press, 1996). Rocke argues that, for most men, homosexual activity was never exclusive but rather a prelude or supplement to heterosexual relations within marriage.

106. Gowing, *Common Bodies*.

107. On menstruation, see van de Walle and Renne (eds), *Regulating Menstruation*.

108. Cambie and Brewis, *Anti-Fertility Plants*; David Kertzer, *Sacrificed for Honor: Italian Infant Abandonment and the Politics of Reproductive Control* (Boston: Beacon, 1993).

109. Kate Fisher, '"She Was Quite Satisfied with the Arrangements I Made": Gender and Birth Control in Britain 1920–1950', *Past & Present* 169 (2000), pp. 161–93; Kate Fisher, *Birth Control, Sex and Marriage in Britain, 1918–1960* (Oxford and New York: Oxford University Press, 2006); the essays in the special issue of *Journal of Interdisciplinary History* 34:2 (2003), 'Before the Pill: Preventing Fertility in Western Europe and Quebec'.

110. Out of the dozens of examples that could be cited, several that I have found most useful in my own teaching are Justine Siegemund, *The Court Midwife*, ed. and tr. Lynne Tatlock (Chicago: University of Chicago Press, 2005); Nina Rattner Gelbart, *The King's Midwife: A History and Mystery of Madame du Coudray* (Berkeley: University of California Press, 1998); Leslie J. Reagan, *When Abortion Was a Crime: Women, Medicine, and Law in the United States, 1867–1973* (Berkeley: University of California Press, 1997); Elizabeth Watkins, *The Estrogen Elixir: A History of Hormone Replacement Therapy in America* (Baltimore: Johns Hopkins University Press, 2007).

111. Monica H. Green and Daniel Lord Smail, 'The Trial of Floreta d'Ays (1403): Jews, Christians, and Obstetrics in Later Medieval Marseille', *Journal of Medieval History* 34 (2008), pp. 185–211.

112. Laurel Thatcher Ulrich, *A Midwife's Tale: The Life of Martha Ballard, Based on Her Diary, 1785–1812* (New York: Knopf, 1990).

113. Park, *Secrets of Women*, p. 9.
114. Marcia C. Inhorn, 'Defining Women's Health: A Dozen Messages from More than 150 Ethnographies', *Medical Anthropology Quarterly* 20 (2006), pp. 345–78.
115. For arguments that medicalisation does not always equal masculinisation (or vice versa), see the acute comments of Martin Dinges, 'Social History of Medicine in Germany and France in the Late Twentieth Century: From the History of Medicine toward a History of Health', in Frank Huisman and John Harley Warner (eds), *Locating Medical History: The Stories and Their Meanings* (Baltimore: Johns Hopkins University Press, 2004), pp. 209–36, esp. pp. 222–3.
116. Ilana Löwy, 'The Social History of Medicine: Beyond the Local', *Social History of Medicine* 20 (2007), pp. 465–81; Robert Woods, 'Medical and Demographic History: Inseparable?', *Social History of Medicine* 20 (2007), pp. 483–503; Robert Woods, 'Lying-In and Laying-Out: Fetal Health and the Contribution of Midwifery', *Bulletin of the History of Medicine* 81 (2007), pp. 730–59; Vincent De Brouwere, 'The Comparative Study of Maternal Mortality over Time: The Role of the Professionalisation of Childbirth', *Social History of Medicine* 20 (2007), pp. 541–62. See also Daphne A. Christie and E. M. Tansey (eds), *Maternal Care: A Witness Seminar held at the Wellcome Institute for the History of Medicine, London, on 6 June 2000*, Wellcome Witnesses to Twentieth Century Medicine 12 (London: Wellcome Trust, 2001).
117. Charlotte Furth, *A Flourishing Yin: Gender in China's Medical History 960–1665* (Berkeley: University of California Press, 1999); Yi-Li Wu, 'The Bamboo Grove Monastery and Popular Gynecology in Qing China', *Late Imperial China* 21 (2000), pp. 41–76; Angela Ki Che Leung (ed.), *Medicine for Women in Imperial China* (Leiden: Brill, 2006).
118. United Nations, *The Millennium Development Goals Report, 2007* (United Nations Department of Economic and Social Affairs (DESA), June 2007), downloaded 3 June 2008 from <http://www.un.org/millenniumgoals/docs/UNSD_MDG_Report_2007e.pdf>, recognises that 'no single intervention can address the multiple causes of maternal deaths'.
119. Space does not permit addressing the field of feminist epidemiology; for an overview, see Marcia C. Inhorn and K. Lisa Whittle, 'Feminism Meets the "New" Epidemiologies: An Appraisal of Antifeminist Biases in Epidemiologic Research on Women's Health', *Social Science and Medicine* 53 (2001), pp. 553–67.

4 The Gender of Europe's Commercial Economy, 1200–1700

Martha Howell

During the centuries between 1200 and 1700, commerce was rescued from the margins of Europe's moral economy where it had been confined since classical times. Although suspicion would cling to merchants and their practices for centuries to come (even until today), by the end of the early modern period, commerce had decidedly become the 'business of states' and the merchant could be figured as a cultural hero. The gradual, if incomplete, redemption of commerce has traditionally been told as though it were an ungendered story. Together, the riches brought by traders, the sophisticated technologies of merchants and the economic energy unleashed by the commercialisation of production itself, we have been given to understand, made it impossible to ignore commerce's power and foolish to despise its practitioners.

Although commerce's ability to generate wealth is certainly the *sine qua non* of its ascent, the story of how the merchant became the statesman's partner, if not quite his equal, cannot be told as economic history alone. It was accompanied by a socio-cultural history that operated dialectically with the economic. That history, this chapter argues, had a gender dimension that has not yet been written. Commerce came to be accepted as a socially useful, even honourable, way of life with the help of a gender binary that positioned the sober housewife as partner to the honest and ambitious man of the market.

This is a story about both class and gender, and it thus features one group of Europeans, pre-eminently city dwellers and the precocious market farmers of the day. The lead actors in this story are northerners, for it was in the north that the class took clearest form, but chapters were also written in the south, where the commercial revolution had begun. This social group was not numerically dominant in Europe at the beginning of the period, nor even at its end, when it was not yet a coherent class. Nor were these people the most powerful. Landholding aristocrats still ruled, and would long claim cultural hegemony, only slowly and often reluctantly entering commerce themselves or allowing commercial people to join their ranks. But in the end, this group of people triumphed, making the modern period of western history the age of the bourgeoisie. Early modern historians have thus rightfully made its formation and ascent one of the grand themes of the period.

Although the gender dynamics that fuelled that history have not been fully explored, other parts of this history have been written. In the following pages, I use that scholarship to pull from a much denser tapestry of cultural and social change the particular threads that, I suggest, came together to produce the gender binary that accompanied – and helped enable – the redemption of commerce and commercial people. My sketch is necessarily schematic and provisional for, although it is based on wide reading in economic, legal, social and cultural history of the period, it is not a synthesis of existing research. Instead, it is a call for the research that will more fully expose the links between commerce and gender in this pivotal period. Nor do I claim that the processes I describe occurred everywhere the same way or even that they occurred everywhere. Rather, I argue that by about 1700, a new cultural narrative about gender and newly gendered social practices had taken shape in Europe, which served to contain commerce's dangers and assure commercial classes a place in Europe's moral economy.

***

The story of Europe's 'commercial revolution' usually begins around the turn of the millennium, with the long-distance traders who brought luxury goods to European elites. In most versions of this history, these were men of little account. Jean Favier's *De l'or et des épices: naissance de l'homme d'affaires au moyen âge* [*Gold and Spices: The Rise of Commerce in the Middle Ages*], for instance, offers a standard version of that narrative. The commercial revolution, he explains, began with the 'dusty-footed ped-dler' of the Middle Ages who was only later transformed into the 'homme d'affaires' of early modernity.[1] Specialists focusing more exclusively on southern Europe have uncovered another pattern, in which Genoese nobles learned to trade as a result of their military exploits in the Mediterranean area where Muslim merchants had long been busy.[2] Although the Euro-peans in these histories were male, trade did not grant them honourable masculinity. Favier's peddler was a marginal figure, hardly 'man' at all, and the Genoese nobles who proffered their wares (or plunder) were proud warriors of honourable lineage, not mere merchants.

In those days, commerce was embedded in too toxic a narrative about the evils of wealth to bestow honour on tradesmen. Although the attack on riches that grounded the narrative was very old, as old as European culture itself, the claims about wealth's dangers in the period 1200 to 1700 were explicitly linked to commerce.[3] The vitriolic language circulated in every social arena, even in cities like Bruges or Venice where commerce was queen. Aquinas himself regularly deployed the conventional tropes: 'the foremost tendency of tradesmen is to make money', he wrote in *De Regno*:

> Greed is awakened in the hearts of the citizens through the pursuit of trade. The result is that everything in the city will become venal; good faith will be destroyed and the way opened to all kinds of trickery; each one will work only for his own profit, despising the public good; the cultivation of virtue will fail since honour, virtue's reward, will be bestowed upon the rich.[4]

The same attack was regularly preached by Franciscan and Dominican friars, and was repeated in countless late medieval penitentials: commerce was 'morally hazardous. No one becomes inflamed by greed like the merchant, whose very occupation is centred on wealth and on the daily opportunity to augment his property . . . In order to make a profit, the merchant is tempted to cheat on weights and measures, to hide defects in his wares, to swear falsely about their qualities, etc.'.[5] The church's ban of usury, which was given new force by late medieval scholastics, compounded the opprobrium and made merchants themselves the proximate equivalents of usurers. Some theorists proposed that money was sterile, unable to 'fructify', and that interest charges were thus robbery; others suggested that interest charges were a price extracted for time, and thus a theft from god, who alone 'owned' time. Still others reasoned that usury was a way of taking money without working for it and was thus immoral.[6] Dante, scholars often remind us, put usurers in the seventh circle of hell.[7] Outside the universities and monasteries where scholastics laboured, similar charges were levelled. Writing in the twelfth century, for example, John of Salisbury claimed that church officials themselves had succumbed to commerce's poison: 'they deliver justice not for the sake of truth but for a price . . . The palaces of priests glitter and in their hands the Church of Christ is demeaned'.[8] The venality satires that proliferated in the period continued the assault and the same discourse provided rich material for just about every variety of popular literature.

The attacks did not subside as centuries passed and commerce became ever more a way of life. On the contrary. Sumptuary legislation intended to suppress consumption, which was issued in every corner of Europe, was frequently framed by the same attacks on vanity, greed and the licentiousness that was inevitably linked to commerce. Nowhere was such language more vitriolic than in Europe's commercial cities; let us recall that it was in Florence itself where Savonarola, maddened by what he considered satanic materialism, built 'bonfires of vanities' in which mountains of luxurious clothing, paintings, books and hollowware were destroyed. Nor was it different in the equally commercialised Low Countries; Bruegel, for example, was just one among countless sixteenth-century critics, whose depictions of Avarice or his famous *Everyman* (*Elck*), memorably allegorised the evils of wealth and commerce.[9]

If commerce and commercial people were to be redeemed, commerce had to be freed of the charges that it inevitably bred greed, invited deceit and unleashed wanton desire. Europeans accomplished this feat, I propose, with the help of a narrative about gender that assigned consumption to a female space, on the one hand, and production – or money making – to a male space, on the other. By wisely managing consumption in the service of male-headed households, women defanged consumption. By governing commerce judiciously in the interests of the social whole, men justified their quest for profit.

***

An essential step in this process was to remove women from visible roles in market production itself. This required both socio-political and cultural work, for women had played a by and large unchallenged part in market production and trade since the early days of commercialisation. To be sure, a sexual division of labour prevailed; certain tasks were typically female and others male, but that division was not as rigid as once supposed and, in any case, the line dividing female work from male did not neatly overlap with the murky boundary between work for subsistence and work for the market. Rather, particularly in northern Europe, both men and women produced goods for sale, both worked for wages and as pieceworkers and both ran shops or other commercial establishments.[10]

Some women entered the market simply by producing and selling the kinds of goods that they had traditionally made for domestic use – butter and cheese; beer and ale; cloth and clothing. Many married women crossed into what we might consider male economic space, however, selling the goods the men produced in shops attached to the house or assisting in the workshop itself. Other wives represented husbands who travelled as merchants, keeping their books, storing their merchandise and handling local sales. Propertied widows regularly succeeded husbands as managers of the family workshops, as sole proprietors of market stalls that were sometimes passed from generation to generation, or even as skilled participants in regional and long-distance trade of manufactured goods, raw materials and credit instruments.

These women had obtained entry to the market, however, not with independent rights to control production but as members of households that were production units, a form of what others have labelled 'family economies'.[11] Because women were expected to help provision and manage the household enterprise, it naturally followed that, as the household's work extended into the market, so did theirs.[12] This household was hierarchically structured; its head managed all family property and in some regions had uncontested ownership of it. Systems of community property law (which existed throughout the north in various customary forms and even made appearances in the south, where dotal systems modelled on Roman law were the supposed norm), granted husbands full control over all community goods and in some regions that category included all property in the household. So long as he lived, the husband automatically occupied this managerial position, which gave him authority to 'govern' family members, including the right to discipline his wife, children and employees with beatings.[13] Power in the household was thus gendered and the gender system of the day was to a significant degree constituted by the patriarchal household. Gender was not the only element of this hierarchical structure. Age and property completed the edifice, and both were equated with marital status. Whether kin, employees, or apprentices, all the unpropertied – and thus usually the unmarried – members of the household stood below and took orders from the head of household and his immediate subordinate, his wife.

Hence, this was no 'golden age' of women's work if that is understood to mean that their work made women the approximate equals of men. Rather, it was a moment in European history when the imperatives of the emergent market coincided, however unstably, with the imperatives of the patriarchal household. And that moment passed as the commercial economy grew.[14] Women who worked for wages now answered to employers who organised ever more complex and rationalised putting-out systems. Their work schedules, their wages, even the spaces of their work now became matters of (unequal) negotiation between the women and their employers; husbands and fathers were effectively marginalised. Male dominance could also be challenged when wives took an active part in their husbands' businesses. Anxiety over market conditions, disputes about business decisions taken, a wife's failures as salesperson of her husband's wares, a husband's ineptness in the workshop – such issues easily disturbed marital harmony, giving women reason to complain and to challenge their husbands' authority. As James Collins put it in describing the process in early modern France:

> when women found more [economic] opportunities as individuals, they began to pose more of a threat to patriarchal order... The independent business woman, although still socially part of a household, was economically distinct from it and from her husband... Young, single women came to possess cash resources, the fruits of their labors as servants and *journalières*, that helped to free them from parental tutelage... As the chief producers of cash for their households, rural women may have become more threatening to their husbands in an economy in which cash was increasingly important.[15]

Marital property law could further intensify marital strife, perhaps especially so in north-western Europe where women appear to have been most active in market production. In much of that area, some form of what historians call 'community property law' prevailed. In the classic communal regime, what historians call a 'universal' system, all the assets of both husband and wife were merged into one undifferentiated marital property fund; the wife had claims to some, or occasionally all, of that property during her widowhood and in some versions of the customary law she was treated as co-owner of the assets during marriage. Although in structure a 'partnership' of a kind, this was a partnership of radically unequal people, for during the marriage the husband was the sole and absolute manager of the conjugal fund (even if he was not always considered the sole owner), including all property that his wife might have brought to the marriage or acquired in its course.[16] In some areas, the community property account included all wealth in the household, of whatever kind and however acquired; in most, however, a portion of the goods each spouse had brought to the marriage (almost always 'immovables') was excluded from the community account and reserved for the natal line. Douai, in French-speaking medieval Flanders, is an example of the first 'universal' community system; Paris exemplifies a version of the second.[17] Although typical of the north of Europe, community property systems were not confined to that region; artisanal families in the south also frequently formed community property accounts, presumably because that system best facilitated management of the family economy.[18] In such systems, the wife under coverture was thus denied formal recognition of her economic contribution to the marriage, which surely threatened peaceable relations in the household. These systems could even more directly put the husband at risk. As legal head of household, he was solely responsible for all debts incurred by family members, including those his wife may have generated in her own business. Positioned to act in her husband's name, a wife could ruin him. It was thus that the system of 'feme sole', which separated a wife's assets from her husband's, acquired its logic.[19]

There were added problems in areas of community property law for, when the husband predeceased his wife, his widow assumed the male position as head of household, thereby acquiring a significant portion of marital property (sometimes all of it). The archives from late medieval northern cities confirm that such widows often readily took charge, sometimes even when there were adult sons.[20] Widows in this part of Europe could also serve as guardians of minor children, with no more supervision by his kin than their husbands would have had to endure as widowers.[21] In some places widows who headed households even represented the household in public affairs. In medieval Frankfurt am Main, for example, widows who headed households were required to equip a man for guard duty on the city walls, thus hiring a substitute for the civic duties they were themselves unable to perform (just as incapacitated [or rich] male heads of households did).[22] In medieval France, women sat as *maîtres jurés* of guilds in which they held masterships (they lost these rights in the early modern period).[23]

Such tensions between the economic and cultural gradually drove women to the margins of the market. Guilds began to write regulations explicitly excluding women from trades to which they had once been admitted, or they let regulations lapse that had as a matter of course spoken of widows, wives and daughters as members.[24] As cultural historians and literary scholars have long understood, the process of women's marginalisation from market production was accompanied and helped along by the wide circulation of misogynist images that put 'women on top', with the venerable trope of Phyllis riding Aristotle or the ubiquitous 'woman in breeches' as favourites, or those featuring unruly, dissolute and licentious women.[25] Marriage was at the centre of these stories, for it was usually the married or widowed woman – figures like the dangerous, if also ridiculous, Wife of Bath – who could displace men as heads of household and she who could transfer property from one man to another.

The result was a class-specific sexual division of labour. Women at the bottom of the socio-economic hierarchy necessarily continued to work for wages and took in piecework, but their sexuality, like their work, was increasingly suspect precisely because the women were often not physically confined to the household and were, in any case, not fully under the male head of household's control. Indeed, the 'public' space of the market was increasingly figured as male, or at least as a space dangerous for women. This was true even in cities where women played an important role in the market economy. As Barbara Hanawalt has reminded us, the English poem 'What the Goodwife Taught Her Daughter' admonished that a woman in public acquired 'an yvel name'; to avoid scandal, she was instructed to dress carefully, walk 'modestly' and speak quietly.[26] By the nineteenth century, as Joan Scott has eloquently argued, French polemicists labelled 'l'ouvrière . . . un mot impie, sordide', insisting that the woman's availability to the market was a sign that she was truly a 'public' woman.[27]

During these same centuries, marital property and inheritance law was also enlisted in the effort to limit women's control of property. Men wrote wills, for example, requiring widows to pass family property on to children or return it to the husband's natal kin if the women remarried; sometimes men even passed their property directly to heirs, entirely bypassing the widow. In many regions of community property law, people also began to restrict the size of the communal account, marking more property as lineal so that it would automatically pass to heirs, not to the widow. In areas where no community property fund was created by marriage but where wives brought dowries that were sequestered during the marriage, the marital property regime itself denied women full property rights, because the woman's dowry was not fully hers; she was trustee for her children or for her natal kin and simply creditor to her husband during the marriage. There too widows who remarried could be penalised, for many marriage contracts and many wills were written to deny the widow any 'increase' on her dowry or benefice from a will should she remarry. As the medieval centuries slid into the early modern, these arrangements became ever more popular, particularly among the rising class of urban entrepreneurs and merchants, even in the north where customary law had not known such provisions.[28] In early modern Paris, for example, the bourgeoisie learned to use testamentary, marital property and inheritance law to protect rents and bureaucratic offices for heirs by assigning them to the lineal account (what they called *propres*), in effect depriving widows of those assets.[29]

The attacks on aggressive females were even more frequently embedded in furious diatribes about consumption itself that circulated with new energy in these centuries.[30] Although worries about luxury and wealth itself had long been at the centre of European moral discourse, the luxuries brought by commerce, now available more widely and in ever-mounting quantities, seemed not just a threat to individual morality but also to the entire social order. Throughout the entire late medieval and early modern period, the charges against luxury and consumption flew, and it was not until the eighteenth century that Europeans began to fashion a discourse allowing them simultaneously to celebrate consumption and to put it to work in shoring up power structures.[31] In this context, old tropes figuring women as vain, greedy and endlessly desirous acquired new force.[32] Commerce, it was endlessly repeated, awakened, fed and enabled female lust because it made 'everything' available, to everyone, in a way that seemed uncontrollable. Comic tales levelled the charges by conflating the desire for luxuries with sexual desire – and assigning the desires to women. The wives in the tales from the *Quinze Joies de Mariage* [Fifteen Joys of Marriage], for example, trade their bodies for finery, lie without shame and spend their hours plotting how to accumulate jewels and clothing. The wife in Chaucer's *Shipman's Tale* similarly exchanges sex for elegant clothing. Where everything is for sale, these tales taught, the entire social fabric unravels; desire is unregulated, spiritual vows are discarded, kinship is betrayed, the marital bond distained.

The Italian sumptuary laws of the day, which so obsessively focused on women's dress and ornamentation, articulated the same logic. Often literally repeating misogynist rhetoric of the age, they charged women with relentless pursuit of finery, wanton disregard for their husbands' wallets and shameless preening. The priors of Florence's *Officiale delle donne* [Office for Women], the body that enforced sumptuary laws in the mid-fifteenth century, declared, for example, that

... these officials ... have an honest desire ... to restrain the barbarous and irrepress-
ible bestiality of women who, not mindful of the weakness of their nature, forgetting
that they are subject to their husbands, and transforming their perverse sense into a
reprobate and diabolical nature, force their husbands with their honeyed poison to
submit to them ... These women have forgotten that it is their duty to bear the children sired by their husbands and, like little sacks, to hold the natural seed which their
husbands implant in them, so that children will be born. They have also forgotten that
it is not conformity with nature for them to decorate themselves with such expensive
ornaments.[33]

Giacomo della Marca, a Franciscan polemicist, hinted that women's love
of finery made them loose, for they dressed to display themselves in public,
not to please their husbands. He begged husbands to 'have another look
when they [wives] leave the house. They dress up in anticipation of their
own pleasure, but when they come home they take off their jewels and look
like bakers' wives'.[34]

As several scholars have pointed out, sumptuary legislation and the
rhetoric that accompanied these laws worked to disassociate the male elite
of the city from the luxury they feared was destroying republican values,
even as it provided an excuse for the existence of these same luxuries –
which they provided and which provided them their wealth. Diane Owen
Hughes has argued, for example, that women, along with Jews, were made
to stand for all that was both required and feared: by making women
and Jews the culprits, men freed themselves from the stain of material
desire.[35] Carole Frick has similarly explained the logic of the hypocrisy
that had Florentine men condemning women's love of finery even while
they dressed their wives and daughters in elegant costumes for public
display. The strategy allowed men to reserve for themselves the 'old' more
conservative (if nevertheless costly) dress and simultaneously to flaunt
their riches.[36]

Despite the warnings of moralists, the invective of polemicists, or the
norms established by lawmakers, change came slowly and unevenly, however, for women and their families needed the earnings from market production and the market economy could make good use of their labour. Thus,
wives and widows of small retailers and less prosperous artisans, whose
labour could still be contained by the patriarchal household, would long
participate in management of the household's business, in the retail shop
or the workplace itself. Poorer women would continue to work for wages,
peddle used goods on the street, or set up boutiques where they sold their
hats or ribbons. But the more prosperous wives, widows and daughters of
established artisans and merchants, the women who would come to define proper bourgeois womanhood, were in gradual retreat from business,
quietly and increasingly tentatively submerging any work for the market
or any assets they brought to the marriage under the umbrella of their

husband's business. By the eighteenth century, and long before in some regions, such woman only rarely took a visible role in urban commerce or market production itself.[37]

Instead, they were learning the lessons imparted by the conduct books and housekeeping manuals of the period, which taught that women's job was to manage consumption in their husbands' interests, carefully choosing and wisely using the treasures he brought home. This monotonously repeated lesson not only defanged consumption by domesticating it, but also provided ideological justification for yielding control over productive assets to men: just as wise consumption was woman's duty and the home her space, they taught, wise production was man's and the market his realm.

In 1580, the Italian moralist Torquato Tasso put it this way:

> It is well ordered that . . . the office of acquiring should be attributed to the man and that of preserving to the woman. The man struggles to acquire and carries out farming or operates in commerce in the city . . . but the woman looks after that which has been acquired and her virtues are employed inside the house, just as the man demonstrates his outside.[38]

Juan Luis Vives's 1523 *Institutio foeminae christianae*, which circulated widely in Europe both in Latin and in translations, was the implicit and often explicit model for such texts. Nowhere was its impact better registered than in the Low Countries, where the cosy domestic interior and the industrious housewife would serve as the antidote to what Simon Schama has memorably called 'the embarrassment of riches'.[39] There moralists repeatedly issued *exempla* describing the good housewife as nurturer of family and domesticity, and painters set out literally to illustrate Vives's text. Heemskerck's well-known print series of 1555, *Praise of the Virtuous Wife*, is typical. Although one of the six prints displays the wife selling the cloth she has woven and another has her buying a piece of land, all her buying and selling is for her family; her activities in the market represent her as the good consumer and household manager, not as player in commerce. Another three prints have her spinning, cooking and dressing her family, and the last pictures her bestowing a crown on the husband she serves.[40] Women, such images and texts insisted, had important work in the house and, although that did not preclude contact with the market economy, a wife's place was 'inside', a husband's 'outside'. England was no different; there, for example, an early seventeenth-century text seems almost to repeat the Italian language of a generation earlier:

> The dutie of the Husband is to get goods; and of the Wife to gather them together, and save them. The dutie of the Husband is to travel abroad, to seeke [a] living; and the Wives dutie is to keep the house. The dutie of the Husband is to get money and provision; and of Wives, not vainly to spend it.[41]

It was the same in German-speaking cities, where women were learning to behave as the conduct books instructed. Patrician and upper middle-class women, Heidi Wunder explains, 'began to limit themselves to organisational tasks in the household and devoted more time to decorating the living spaces in a stately manner and enjoying a "homey" life with their children and husbands'. Although the wives of less well-off artisans could not depend on servants as their richer neighbours could, domesticity also 'began to determine their work roles. In the process, a woman's position as mistress of a household with authority over children and domestics became much more important. In this role they were . . . of incalculable value to their husbands'.[42]

Scholars have rightly been cautious about taking the conduct books as literal descriptions of practice. The tracts are, however, useful evidence for historians, for they articulate a vision of womanhood that would serve to demarcate class, and it is perhaps that function that made them so attractive a model for behaviour. Unlike poorer women who roamed the streets selling wares and competing for wage work, the women who populate conduct literature were safely at home, managing the money their husbands earned outside. These 'good housewives' – a group that ideologically included both the rich alderman's wife and the less prosperous shopkeeper's spouse – would never spend wastefully or wantonly; they would leave it to the aristocrats to dress fancifully and to the poor to try to copy that flamboyance with second- and third-hand goods. The narrative of the conduct books thus not only sharply distinguished the home from the market, it created a gender-specific class ethic that freed middle-class women of the sins associated with commerce's wildness. These women were not the voracious, undisciplined – even sexually available – consumers depicted in sumptuary legislation or comic literature; nor were they the public women whose labour was for sale and whose persons were on public display. They were the wise managers of consumption, the people who tamed it by being themselves tamed.

***

During the same centuries, a new narrative that sought to disassociate commerce from fraud was unsteadily emerging, and that too would acquire a gendered dimension by rendering the man of the market the provider for the community and the guarantor of public probity. The discourse did not succeed in entirely cleansing commerce; indeed the vitriolic language linking trade with deceit and moral rot would long survive in European culture, making its way into polemic texts, giving familiar tropes to comic literature and providing convenient justifications for regulatory action.[43] But even as early as the thirteenth century, scholastics were admitting that commerce was necessary and searching for a way to bracket its dangers.

They found it by arguing that commerce's dangers lay not in the wealth it generated but in its ability to go underground. Merchants, their goods and money easily crossed geographic boundaries; commerce moved people and things from place to place, dumping riches here and leaving poverty there, disappearing into far corners of a scarcely mapped continent – and beyond, into an almost uncharted world. Being untraceable themselves, merchants could hide supplies that no accounting system of the day could easily track, awaiting scarcity and the high prices that followed; they could obscure the origins of their goods, lying about their rarity or the difficulties of acquiring them; they could make up stories about the powers of their merchandise, even inventing maladies for which their products were the perfect cure.[44] Producers were just as bad. They masked shoddy workmanship, skimped on materials, used inferior ingredients to reduce costs. Cloth bearing the honoured seal of Ghent or Bruges might in fact be a cheaper copy made in some unknown village with Spanish, not Cotswold, wool. Bread might be made with spelt, not wheat. A silver coin might be clipped or debased with mere copper; a clever artisan might even fake a holy relic.

Commerce also dematerialised wealth itself. As it transformed material objects into money values, trade made goods anonymous, emptying them of specific content that had once clearly bespoke their actual use. Today a prized tapestry, an elegant garment, a barrel of wine, or a gold flagon, commercial goods like these were something else tomorrow – maybe a service, another garment, a coin, or just an IOU. Buyers and sellers themselves lost identity in the same way, for trade could be conducted anywhere, by faceless people, unknown and unknowable except by way of the goods delivered and the money exchanged. Wholesale trade was particularly vulnerable to this charge, for much of it escaped any fixed site, even the periodic fairs. Goods for long-distance markets were often bought sight-unseen, negotiated by letter; payments were made through agents and their bankers and settled by third or fourth parties at the next international fair, typically many months and many miles distant, by means of letters of credit, bills of exchange and other mysterious documents. Even the most powerful bankers of the day were uncomfortable. The Fuggers (Germany's pre-eminent sixteenth-century merchant bankers) are said to have complained that doing business with the Genoese meant playing with pieces of paper (*mit Papier*), whereas they themselves operated with real money (*Baargeld*) – the 'typical reaction', Braudel commented, 'of traditional financiers failing to understand a new technique'.[45]

The solution, however, was not to ban commerce but to bring it into the open. In that way, commercial dealings could be made fair (just), the merchant made honest and commerce made socially useful. Told in different ways, this narrative circulated in popular literature and was depicted in

images of all kinds. In fiction, the lesson was often imparted by negative example. Shoddy merchandise, dishonest traders and sneaky moneylenders
were systematically condemned, ridiculed and exposed. Robert Wilson's
Three Ladies of London, for example, made fraud the signature of commerce. As Lady Lucre (one of his central characters) explains, merchants
lie about the origins of their goods in order to escape import duties:

> I know you Merchants haue many a sleight and subtill cast.
> So that you will by stealth bring ouer great store:
> And say it wa in the Realme a long time before.[46]

The same themes obsessed storytellers and playwrights in the Low Countries.[47] *The Tale of the Grain Merchant* (a Dutch-language *fabliau* or
sproke) attacked merchants who secretly bought up grain in times of plenty
in order to sell it dearly in times of dearth. In Cornelis Everaert's *The Wealth
of Someone Else*, two nasty characters misrepresent their wares and merchants profit from price discrepancies by selling their goods at the highest
prices in certain markets, while neglecting to supply other markets.[48]

Accompanying the stories of fraud and greed, however, were stories of
good commerce; in these tales, the good was inevitably depicted as 'honest', and honesty inevitably rendered commercial wealth socially useful.
The equation was simple: open trade produces plenty and benefits the entire community. In 1561, a competition among chambers of rhetoric in
the county of Brabant, for example, featured fifteen plays, one from each
chamber, written in response to the question: 'How proper are the smart, talented merchants who conduct their business fairly?'[49] All the plays praised
commerce, working to distinguish the 'good' merchant from the bad, and
all took the merchant's honesty not just as the sign of his personal honour
but also as the quality that enabled him to serve the common good. Given
that the competitions were staged and financed by Antwerp's merchants, it
is no wonder that trade was celebrated but, as a recent scholar has pointed
out, the terms of the defence are significant. Merchants were not just to
be tolerated, they were to be praised. They brought goods from afar, they
protected against the uncertainties both of the harvest and of markets, they
paid for defence, they set up schools and they supported civic activities.
The Herethals chamber (one of the fifteen competitors) presented the win-
ning performance. In this play, two allegorical characters, cities (urbanites)
and counties (nobles), join to persuade a third, the village (peasants), of
the benefits brought by trade and merchants.[50]

Similar arguments appeared in sixteenth-century English texts. In the
1525 *Gentleness and Nobility*, for example, the merchant simply assumes
his 'nobility', boasting that the work of merchants saves the country from
'beggary', bringing wealth, profit and pleasure:

... if our commodities be utteryed for nought
In to straunge landis, and no ryches brought
Hydry therefore, we shuld come to beggary,
And all men dryffn to lyf in mysery.
Then we noble marchauntis that in this reame be,
What a grete wealth to thys land do we:
We utter our wayrs and by their good chepe,
And bring them hyder, that grete proffet
And pleasure dayly commyth to this region
Too all maner people that here do won.[51]

The same themes informed religious texts. The mendicant friars, whose sermons otherwise so often excoriated merchants, filled their penitential handbooks with instructions urging honesty, promising that honest trade could redeem the merchant.[52]

Although the clerics intended their lessons about honesty and openness for the spiritual benefit of individual merchants, scholastics offered a more general theory that equated open trade with social justice. It was most explicitly expressed in the theory of the 'just price'.[53] The just price itself was a purely normative concept, informed by what Aristotle had called commutative justice, the equilibrium reached when individuals with different needs were able to satisfy themselves by means of fair trade. While the price agreed upon in such a transaction would necessarily vary because individual needs were different and were differentially affected by supply conditions, it was 'just' if it had been negotiated in an open market. In the minds of scholastic theorists, this was the physical marketplace of face-to-face exchange, what Braudel called the 'normal' market of 'economic life' where 'the transactions necessary for everyday life ... were exchanged for money or vice versa and the deal was resolved on the spot, the moment these things changed hands'.[54] As Cardinal Cajetan, the authoritative sixteenth-century commentator on Aquinas's *Summa*, put it, the just price is 'the one, which at a given time, can be gotten from the buyers, assuming common knowledge and in the absence of all fraud and coercion'.[55]

Lawmakers of the day evidently agreed: commerce required strict supervision if it was to cure 'beggary'. Scholars have long emphasised that this logic informed all late medieval market regulation. Over a century ago, for example, the editors of Paris's first edition of guild ordinances, the thirteenth-century *Livre des métiers*, commented that individuals alone were then thought powerless before commerce:

... no one then would have imagined that the public could defend itself against producers of shoddy goods or against dishonest merchants, whether by denouncing them or refusing to patronize them. This notion of individual responsibility or 'self government' [English in the original], applied to the ordinary business of life, would have been considered an enormity ... the society was based, in effect, on an implicit delegation of individual rights to the collectivity.[56]

Thus, lawmakers everywhere took it upon themselves to assure transparent trade. They punished practices such as hoarding, engrossing and forestalling, the very sins featured in so many literary texts, not just to assure supplies but also in pursuit of a just price.[57] In Paris, residents' access to food supplies was protected by other rules as well, most powerfully by one that allowed citizens to take a portion of the goods traded between merchants in the marketplace at the price negotiated by the merchants themselves (the *droit de partage*). Inhabitants were assured that they could acquire provisions at what lawmakers clearly considered the most just price – that obtained by the most knowledgeable bargainers.[58] In pursuit of similar ends, rulers urged and sometimes forced peasants to deliver their goods to urban markets and forbade them to use middlemen of any kind, all in an effort to assure supplies and affordability. As a 1305 ordinance of Philip the Fair expressed it, 'all products must be delivered to and sold in open markets, and we absolutely prohibit anyone from buying or selling provisions or foodstuffs other than in open markets and from buying wheat or other grains for resell on the same market days'.[59] Commerce, it was obvious to all, had to be disciplined.

Disciplined women, disciplined consumption and now disciplined business practices: the combination produced space for 'good' commerce. Men would inhabit the space with the help of a new honour code that managed to make the pursuit of riches both glorious and civic-minded. The good merchant was thus a hero of a new kind: bold, he was also prudent; clever, he was also honest; ambitious for himself, he was also generous. The model was built, in part, on notions of artisanal honour that had emerged in cities where artisan entrepreneurs had carved out social and political space.[60] In this code, a man of honour was financially and socially independent, he was of good 'credit', reputation and 'fame'; and, as the mark and *sine qua non* of his status, he was married, the provider of a good household. Herman Pleij has argued that the popular literature published in Dutch-speaking cities of the day went even further, not only celebrating these qualities but also asserting that brains and ambition were part of the mix. These plays, poems and stories, he explains, 'show that enterprise, the desire for profit, approval of individual cleverness, moderation and self-control were, between 1300 and 1500, the main guiding principles not only for urban society, but also for efforts to raise oneself above the daily grind in the new environment'.[61]

Simultaneously, the medieval knightly honour code was enlisted to accommodate the merchant adventurer, a code perfectly articulated in Hakluyt's famous collection of travel narratives and similar texts that detail the exploits of English merchants in foreign trade during that nation's tumultuous sixteenth century.[62] Although the hundreds of texts in the collection tell many different stories about the risks, excitement and mystery of foreign trade, they combine to make the merchant a hero. He is not always successful, to be sure, and not always in control of the information he needs. Nor does he enter foreign places as their conqueror; sometimes he stands in awe of the wealth, culture and power of the places he visits. But the man that emerges from these narratives is, nevertheless, a heroic type: he is curious, brave, adventuresome, loyal and clever, a recognisable descent of the medieval knight-errant (not incidentally, he is also Christian and English). He is also, however, unashamedly in search of wealth, eager for profit, calculating in his encounters with others – a bearer of a new, mercantile, conception of honourable manhood.

Hakluyt's compilation is hardly an unmediated record of how trade operated in those days. Having been assembled and edited by Hakluyt himself, the collection was a kind of propaganda piece, but it is exactly its role as propaganda that makes it historically significant. It is a testament to what could be imagined, sold and presumably embraced. And, as Favier's *Gold and Spices* so nicely illustrates, it is evidence of how powerfully this story has inflected historians' understanding of the period. The dusty-footed peddler that begins Favier's narrative is a meek and isolated figure, no hero at all; his *homme d'affaires* that emerges in the course of this book is a powerful figure whose ability to control information, manage markets and create wealth for his and for society's benefit renders him fully masculine and heroic. In this way, his image could converge with the less glamorous figure of the householder citizen, whose more sober pursuit of profit and whose industriousness helped expand the field of honour for all men of the market.

To be sure, cheating and cheaters still lurked on the margins of these images, just as vain and silly women liable to whoredom threatened the industrious housewife, the tasteful consumer and the conjugal household in which such women served. These tropes, so familiar from such texts as the early *Play of the Sacrament*, or the later *Jew of Malta, Merchant of Venice* and the French comedy *La Trésorie*, would long circulate.[63] But alongside them would circulate their antidote – conduct books, plays, stories and poems that featured civic-minded merchants and honest tradesmen whose well-ordered households were graced by women who bought and sold, not to satisfy their vanity but to serve their families. These were fictions, but they did non-fiction work by marking the boundaries of honour and encouraging discipline.

***

Commerce had begun the period able to confer honour on no-one. It was considered a moral danger and it was not just clerics, resentful aristocrats, or the newly dispossessed who worried about its corrosive power. Even in thoroughly mercantile Italian cities, businessmen regularly made deathbed bequests to assuage their guilt about their (possibly fraudulent) gains from trade; Savonarola, as I have mentioned, incited the Florentine population, including many of the rich, to frenzied immolation of luxuries; legislators throughout the continent, as we have also seen, impotently issued sumptuary laws intended to repress display of commercial bounty.[64] And everywhere, north and south, east and west, merchants cleansed their wealth by turning it into land – and themselves, they hoped, into gentry.

Commerce's dangers had not lessened by 1700. Then, just as in 1200 (and just as today), commerce's ability to put things, people and value in constant motion and to make one exchangeable for the other made it dangerous. In fact, it was surely more dangerous because it had become more powerful. Just as it had in 1200, commerce in 1700 awakened greed, invited fraud and diverted people from spiritual pursuits. But by 1700, it had become possible for men of the market not only to claim honour but also to position themselves as the moral equals of traditional elites. In the centuries to come, they would even claim moral superiority, arguing that trade – once almost universally derided as a necessary evil – was the model for a good society.[65]

The difference between 1700 and 1200 owed much to the riches generated by commerce: it had become so powerful that it had to be accommodated. This chapter has argued, however, that the accommodation did not occur automatically or easily. It was achieved with the help of complex socio-cultural processes that created an honour code for the male merchant. That code depended in part upon the 'virtuous wife' beloved of early modern moralists, the woman who dutifully, gladly managed her husband's household. By devoting herself to useful, tasteful consumption for the benefit of his household, she not only escaped the charges of whoredom, profligacy, vanity and greed that so easily were attached to women who dealt in the market, she simultaneously made consumption safe for men. Profits were now 'honourable' because they would be invested in the household that was the foundation of the good society. Supervised by a community that fed on their wealth, men were now freed for vigorous – even heroic – pursuit of gain. The story of the commercial revolution in Europe was not, thus, simply an economic history. It was also a social, legal and cultural history that redefined male and female for a rising class of people, and, in fact, helped define the class itself.

Notes

1. Jean Favier, *De l'or et des épices: Naissance de l'homme d'affaires au moyen âge* (Paris: Fayard, 1987).
2. For recent studies, see Quentin Van Doosselaere, 'From Feudal to Modern: Social Dynamics and Commercial Agreements in Medieval Genoa' (unpublished doctoral thesis,

Columbia University, 2006); Avner Greif, *Institutions and the Path to the Modern Economy: Lessons from Medieval Trade* (Cambridge and New York: Cambridge University Press, 2006); Stéphane Lebecq, *Marchands et navigateurs frisons du haut Moyen Age* (Lille: Presses universitaires de Lille, 1983).

3. For a review of this cultural discourse and its history during the commercial revolution, see Lester Little, *Religious Poverty and the Profit Economy in Medieval Europe* (Ithaca: Cornell University Press, 1983).

4. Aquinas, De Regno, II, 7 (ii, 3), cited and tr. by Odd Langholm, *Economics in the Medieval Schools: Wealth, Exchange, Value, Money and Usury according to the Paris Theological Tradition, 1200–1350* (Leiden: Brill, 1992), p. 222.

5. Langholm, *Economics in the Medieval Schools*, p. 573.

6. Joel Kaye argues that changes in the understanding of money, nature and equality during the commercial revolution forced Aquinas to abandon many of these arguments against usury. Instead, Aquinas based his critique essentially on the point that usury was charging for the use of money that had already been sold. Joel Kaye, 'Changing Definitions of Nature, Money, and Equality *c*.1140–1270, Reflected in Thomas Aquinas' Question of Usury', in Diego Quaglioni, Giacomo Todeschini and Gian Maria Varanini (eds), *Credito e usura fra teologia, diritto e amministrazione: Linguaggi a confronto (sec. XII–XVI)*, Collection de l'Ecole française de Rome 346 (Rome: Ecole française de Rome, 2005), pp. 25–55. While scholastics allowed many exceptions to the rule of 'no interest', arguing that compensation was due lenders for losses that were not mere charges imposed for the use of money and while the prohibition never succeeded in suppressing all credit arrangements, the ban had a profound effect on the structure of such instruments and on the way trade was conducted. An extensive discussion of the ways usury laws affected financial practices is provided by John Munro, 'The Late-Medieval Origins of the Modern Financial Revolution: Overcoming Impediments from Church and State', Working Paper, Archive of the Department of Economics and the Institute for Policy Analysis, Department of Economics, University of Toronto (2001–03).

7. Attacks on usurers are leitmotifs of chronicle literature as well. In his *Chronica Maiora* of the mid-thirteenth century, for example, Matthew Paris complained about 'the snares of the usurers', cited in Joel Kaye, 'Monetary and Market Consciousness in Thirteenth and Fourteenth Century Europe', in S. Todd Lowry and Barry Gordon (eds), *Ancient and Medieval Economic Ideas and Concepts of Social Justice* (Leiden: Brill, 1998), pp. 371–403, here p. 375.

8. John of Salisbury, *Policraticus: Of the Frivolities of Courtiers and the Footprints of Philosophers*, ed. and tr. Cary J. Nederman (Cambridge: Cambridge University Press, 1990), p. 133, cited in Joel Kaye, 'Money and Administrative Calculation as Reflected in Scholastic Natural Philosophy', in David Glimp and Michelle E. Warren (eds), *Arts of Calculation: Quantifying Thought in Early Modern Europe* (New York: Palgrave Macmillan, 2004), pp. 1–18, here p. 2 *n*. 5.

9. On Bruegel, see Bret Rothstein, 'The Problem with Looking at Pieter Bruegel's *Elck*', *Art History* 26 (2003), pp. 143–73; Ethan Matt Kavaler, *Pieter Bruegel: Parables of Order and Enterprise* (Cambridge and New York: Cambridge University Press, 1999). More generally on artists and commerce in the early modern Low Countries, see Keith P. F. Moxey, 'The Criticism of Avarice in Sixteenth-Century Netherlandish Painting', in Görel Cavalli-Björkman (ed.), *Netherlandish Mannerism: Papers Given at a Symposium in Nationalmuseum Stockholm, September 21–22 1984*, Nationalmusei Skriftserie 4 (Stockholm: Nationalmuseum, 1985), pp. 21–34; Elizabeth Alice Honig, *Painting and the Market in Early Modern Antwerp* (New Haven: Yale University Press, 1998).

10. The evidence for these patterns is abundant. For representative empirical studies, see Margaret Wensky, *Die Stellung der Frau in der stadtkölnischen Wirtschaft im Spätmittelalter* (Cologne: Böhlau, 1980); Barbara Hanawalt, 'Women and the Household Economy in the

Preindustrial Period: An Assessment of Women, Work, and Family', *Journal of Women's History* 11:3 (1999), pp. 10–16; Barbara Hanawalt (ed.), *Women and Work in Preindustrial Europe* (Bloomington: Indiana University Press, 1986); Martha Howell, *Women, Production and Patriarchy in Late Medieval Cities* (Chicago: University of Chicago Press, 1986); Myriam Carlier and Tim Soens (eds), *The Household in Late Medieval Cities: Italy and Northwestern Europe Compared: Proceedings of the International Conference, Gent, 21st–22nd January 2000* (Leuven: Garant, 2001); Monica Chojnacka, *Working Women of Early Modern Venice* (Baltimore: Johns Hopkins University Press, 2001); Shennan Hutton, '"On Herself and All Her Property": Women's Economic Activities in Late Medieval Ghent', *Continuity and Change* 20 (2005), pp. 325–49; Heide Wunder, *He is the Sun, She is the Moon: Women in Early Modern Germany* (Cambridge: Harvard University Press, 1998); Merry Wiesner-Hanks, *Working Women in Renaissance Germany* (New Brunswick, NJ: Rutgers University Press, 1986); Ralph A. Houlbrooke, *The English Family 1450–1700* (White Plains, NY: Longman, 1984); Mary Prior, *Women in English Society, 1500–1800* (New York: Methuen, 1985).

11. On the family or household economy in late medieval and early modern Europe, see Louise A. Tilly and Joan W. Scott, *Women, Work, and Family* (New York: Holt, Rinehart and Winston, 1978); Sheilagh Ogilvie, *A Bitter Living: Women, Markets, and Social Capital in Early Modern Germany* (Oxford: Oxford University Press, 2003); Sara Mendelson and Patricia Crawford, *Women in Early Modern England: 1550–1720* (Oxford: Clarendon Press, 1998); Howell, *Women, Production and Patriarchy*. By the late Middle Ages, especially in north-western Europe, these households were nuclear. The nuclear household had been formed by a couple who had first married as adults of about the same age, who had exercised a significant degree of choice in the selection of their spouse and who established their own residence. The households thus formed were populated only by the couple, their minor children, a few servants and the occasional dependent relative. Married couples governed their households, had full possession of the property that financed their marriage and directly participated, through the household's head, in community affairs. On the nuclear household, see in particular John Hajnal, 'European Marriage Patterns in Perspective', in David Victor Glass and David Edward Charles Eversley (eds), *Population in History: Essays in Historical Demography* (London: Arnold, 1965), pp. 101–43; Richard Smith, 'Some Reflections on the Evidence for the Origins of the "European Marriage Pattern" in England', in Christopher Charles Harris and Michael Anderson (eds), *The Sociology of the Family: New Directions for Britain*, Sociological Review Monograph 28 (Keele: University of Keele, 1979), pp. 74–112.

12. See Wunder, *He is the Sun*, which provides a lucid discussion of this social logic. In these households, she notes, 'the bride and groom combined their resources to provide the basis for an independent life as a married couple. This life had to be secured by the work of the spouses, usually throughout their lives: through housekeeping in the narrower sense, but at times and in case of need through every conceivable kind of work', p. 68. See also Martha Howell, *The Marriage Exchange: Property, Social Place, and Gender in Cities of the Low Countries, 1300–1550* (Chicago: University of Chicago Press, 1998).

13. On domestic violence, see Myriam Greilsammer, *L'envers du tableau: Mariage et maternité en Flandre médiévale* (Paris: A. Colin, 1990); Susan D. Amussen, '"Being Stirred to Much Uniqueness": Violence and Domestic Violence in Early Modern England', *Journal of Women's History* 6:2 (1994), pp. 70–89; Susan D. Amussen, 'Punishment, Disciplines and Power: The Social Meanings of Violence in Early Modern England', *Journal of British Studies* 34 (1995), pp. 1–34; Margaret Hunt, 'Wife Beating, Domesticity and Women's Independence in Eighteenth-Century London', *Gender & History* 4 (1992), pp. 10–33; Manon van der Heijden, 'Women as Victims of Sexual and Domestic Violence in Seventeenth-Century Holland: Criminal Cases of Rape, Incest, and Maltreatment in Rotterdam and Delft', *Journal of Social History* 33 (2000), pp. 623–44.

14. For discussion of this tension and its effects in various settings, see James B. Collins, 'The

Economic Role of Women in Seventeenth-Century France', *French Historical Studies* 16 (1989), pp. 436–70; Tine De Moor and Jan Luiten van Zanden, *Vrouwn en de geboorte van het kapitalisme in West-Europa* (Amsterdam: Boom, 2006); Hans Medick, 'Zur strukturellen Funktion von Haushalt und Familie im Übergang von der Traditionellen Agrargesellschaft zum Industriellen Kapitalismus: Die Proto-Industrielle Familienwirtschaft', in Werner Conze (ed.), *Sozialgeschichte der Familie in der Neuzeit Europas: Neue Forschungen*, Industrielle Welt 21 (Stuttgart: Klett, 1976), pp. 254–82.

15. Collins, 'The Economic Role of Women', pp. 467–8. On the new independence given to wage-earning women, see De Moor and van Zanden, *Vrouwen en de geborte van het kapitalisme*.

16. Because these regimes tended to provide women the same succession rights that men enjoyed, some legal historians have considered them 'egalitarian' in spirit. See Jean Gilissen, 'Le statut de la femme dans l'ancien droit belge', in *La femme: Recueils de la société de Jean Bodin pour l'histoire comparative des institutions 11–13* (Brussels: Editions de la librairie encyclopédique, 1959–62). For evidence of the non-egalitarian nature of these regimes, see Martha Howell, 'From Land to Love: Commerce and Marriage in Northern Europe during the Late Middle Ages', in *Jaarboek voor middeleeuwse geschiedenis* (Winter, 2008).

17. For a discussion of northern customs of this type, see Robert Jacob, *Les époux, le seigneur et la cité: Coutume et pratiques matrimoniales des bourgeois et paysans de France du Nord au moyen âge* (Brussels: Facultés universitaires Saint-Louis, 1990); Philippe Godding, *Le droit privé dans les Pays-Bas méridionaux du 12e au 18e siècle*, Mémoires de la Classe des Letttres, Collection in 4o, 2nd sér., pt 1 (Brussels: Academie Royale de Belgique, 1987).

18. See Jean Hilaire, *Le régime des biens entre époux dans la région de Montpellier du début du XIIIe siècle à la fin du XVIe siècle: Contribution aux études d'histoire du droit écrit* (Montpellier: Causse, Graille and Castelnau, 1957); Diane Owen Hughes, 'Urban Growth and Family Structure in Medieval Genoa', *Past & Present* 66 (1975), pp. 3–28; Jutta Sperling, 'Marriage at the Time of the Council of Trent (1560–70): Clandestine Marriages, Kinship Prohibitions, and Dowry Exchange in European Comparison', *Journal of Early Modern European History* 8 (2004), pp. 67–108; Allan A. Tulchin, 'Same-Sex Couples Creating Households in Old Regime France: The Uses of the Affrèrement', *Journal of Modern History* 79 (2007), pp. 613–47.

19. 'Feme sole' is the English term; the convention existed throughout the north, as *kopvrouw* (*coopwijf* and various) in Dutch, *femme marchande publique* in standard French, *Kauffrau* in standard German. For a recent study of the practice in England, see Marjorie K. McIntosh, 'The Benefits and Drawbacks of Femme Sole Status in England, 1300–1630', *Journal of British Studies* 44 (2005), pp. 410–38. The same logic informed the German convention of *Schlüsselrecht*, which, by granting the wife a fixed credit line with local retailers and service providers, limited the obligations she could incur in the course of provisioning the household.

20. For examples of these patterns, see Margaret Wensky, *Die Stellung der Frau in der stadtkölnischen Wirtschaft im Spätmittelalter*; Hanawalt, 'Women and the Household Economy'; Hanawalt (ed.), *Women and Work in Preindustrial Europe*; Howell, *Women, Production and Patriarchy*.

21. For a close study of these practices in late medieval Ghent, see Marianne Danneel, *Weduwen en wezen in het laat-middeleeuwse Gent* (Leuven: Garant, 1995).

22. Karl Bücher and Benno Schmidt (eds), *Veröffentlichungen der historischen Kommission der Stadt Frankfurt a.M.*, VI: *Frankfurter Amts- und Zunfturdunken bis zum Jahre 1612*, I.1 and I.2 (Frankfurt am Main, 1914) I, p. 4, no. 10.

23. Collins, 'The Economic Role of Women', p. 458.

24. For representative studies of this process, see Hanawalt, 'Women and the Household Economy'; Wiesner-Hanks, *Working Women in Renaissance Germany*; Howell, *Women,*

Production and Patriarchy in Late Medieval Cities; Collins, 'The Economic Role of Women'; Jean H. Quataert, 'The Shaping of Women's Work in Manufacturing: Guilds, Households, and the State in Central Europe, 1648–1870', *American Historical Review* 90 (1985), pp. 1,122–48.

25. The 'woman on top' trope was famously described by Natalie Zemon Davis, 'Women on Top: Symbolic Sexual Inversion and Political Disorder in Early Modern Europe', reprinted in Barbara A. Babcock (ed.), *The Reversible World: Symbolic Inversion in Art and Society* (Ithaca: Cornell University Press, 1978), pp. 147–90. For examples of such images, see Keith P. F. Moxey, *Peasants, Warriors, and Wives: Popular Imagery in the Reformation* (Chicago: University of Chicago Press, 1989).

26. Barbara A. Hanawalt, 'Medieval English Women in Rural and Urban Domestic Space', *Dumbarton Oaks Papers* 52 (1998), pp. 19–26, here p. 22.

27. 'worker . . . a wicked, sordid word'. Joan W. Scott, '"L'ouvrière! Mot impie, sordide . . .": Women Workers in the Discourse of French Political Economy, 1840–1860', in Joan W. Scott (ed.), *Gender and the Politics of History* (1988; rev. edn, New York: Columbia University Press, 1999), pp. 139–66.

28. See e.g., Christiane Klapisch-Zuber and David Herlihy, *Les Toscans et leurs familles: Une étude du Castado Florentin de 1427* (Paris: Presses de la Fondation Nationale des Sciences Politiques, Èditions de l'Ècole des Hautes Ètudes en Sciences Sociales, 1978). More generally on Florentine women from merchant families and the patriarchal system of that culture, see Christiane Klapisch-Zuber, *Women, Family and Ritual in Renaissance Italy*, tr. Lydia Cochrane (Chicago: University of Chicago Press, 1985); Isabelle Chabot, 'La loi du lignage: Notes sur le système successoral florentin (XIVe/XVe – XVIIe siècles)', *Femmes, dots et patrimoines, Clio – Histoire, Femmes et Sociétés* 7 (1998), pp. 51–72. Stanley Chojnacki, 'The Power of Love: Wives and Husbands in Late Medieval Venice', in Mary Erler and Maryanne Kowaleski (eds), *Women and Power in the Middle Ages* (Athens: University of Georgia Press, 1988) suggests, however, that relations between husband and wife in merchant families of Venice during the same period acquired a more egalitarian aspect. For evidence about the spread of more lineal arrangements in northern areas of community property law, see Jacob, *Les époux.*

29. Ralph E. Giesey, 'Rules of Inheritance and Strategies of Mobility in Prerevolutionary France', *American Historical Review* 82 (1977), pp. 271–89. Giesey builds on previous work by French scholars, especially Charles Lefebvre, *Les fortunes anciennes au point de vue juridique: Leçons d'ouverture, cours de 1911–1912* (Paris: Sirey, 1912). See Giesey, 'Rules of Inheritance', p. 272, *n.* 2, for further references. Philippe Godding, *Le droit privé dans les Pays-Bas méridionaux*, p. 143; and Jacob, *Les époux*, are among the scholars of the Low Countries who have also called attention to this tendency in the history of private law. See also Barbara B. Diefendorf, *Paris City Councillors in the Sixteenth Century: The Politics of Patrimony* (Princeton: Princeton University Press, 1983).

30. During most of the Middle Ages, the luxuries accumulated by elites were thought essential to social order and were thus implicitly, if not always explicitly, excused; the display of riches not only demonstrated and thus constituted power, they did social good in the form of the 'largesse', 'liberalité' and 'charity' that was expected of both secular and ecclesiastical elites. In effect, gift-giving served to expiate the sin of surplus. As the commercial revolution progressed, however, this story no longer worked.

31. In the discourse that then developed, consumption, although motivated by selfish desire, also sped social intercourse and could be useful if governed. The trick, then, was to consume wisely. 'Good taste' became the tool, serving both to provide a justification for consumption and to separate the worthy from the unworthy consumer. For a general discussion of the history of ideas about luxury's dangers (and benefits), see Maxine Berg and Elizabeth Eger, 'The Rise and Fall of the Luxury Debates', in Maxine Berg and Elizabeth Eger (eds), *Luxury in the Eighteenth Century: Debates, Desires and Delectable Goods* (Basingstoke: Palgrave Macmillan, 2003). On 'taste', see Pierre Bourdieu, *Distinction: A*

Social Critique of the Judgement of Taste, tr. Richard Nice (Cambridge: Harvard University Press, 1984).

32. For this argument, see Howard R. Bloch, *Medieval Misogyny and the Invention of Western Romantic Love* (Chicago: University of Chicago Press, 1991).

33. Ronald Rainey, 'Dressing Down the Dressed-Up: Reproving Feminine Attire in Renaissance Florence', in John Monfasani and Ronald G. Musto (eds), *Renaissance Society and Culture: Essays in Honor of Eugene F. Rice, Jr* (New York: Italica Press, 1991), pp. 217–37, here p. 232. See also Ronald Rainey, 'Sumptuary Legislation in Renaissance Florence' (unpublished doctoral thesis, Columbia University, 1985).

34. S. Jacobus, *Sermones Dominicales*, vol. 1, p. 112; cited in Diane Owen Hughes, 'Distinguishing Signs: Ear-Rings, Jews and Franciscan Rhetoric in the Italian Renaissance City', *Past & Present* 112 (1986), pp. 3–59, here p. 25.

35. Hughes, 'Distinguishing Signs', pp. 37–8.

36. Carole Collier Frick, *Dressing Renaissance Florence: Families, Fortunes, and Fine Clothing*, Johns Hopkins University Studies in Historical and Political Science (Baltimore: Johns Hopkins University Press, 2002).

37. Although, as Davidoff and Hall have shown, they played a key role in financing the household enterprise. Leonore Davidoff and Catherine Hall, *Family Fortunes: Men and Women of the English Middle Class, 1780–1850* (Chicago: Chicago University Press, 1987). Bourgeois women also continued to work actively in market production in some places beyond this period, as Bonnie Smith has documented; there too, however, they gradually retreated. Bonnie G. Smith, *Ladies of the Leisure Class: The Bourgeoises of Northern France in the Nineteenth Century* (Princeton: Princeton University Press, 1981). According to Steven Kaplan, Parisian married and widowed women also remained active in grain brokerage into the eighteenth century. Steven Kaplan, *Provisioning Paris* (Ithaca: Cornell University Press, 1984), here p. 501. For an argument based on such evidence – that women's exit from market production and the associated social model of 'separate spheres' was more an ideological construct than a social reality – see Amanda Vickery, 'Golden Age to Separate Spheres? A Review of the Categories and Chronology of English Women's History', *Historical Journal* 36 (1993), pp. 383–414. Be that as it may, this ideological construct had material bases and material consequences. Women may still have participated in market production – not just poor women or the wives of small shopkeepers, but richer women as well – but there is no doubt that the latter were in steady retreat from active participation. For an attempt to reconcile the apparently contradictory evidence that women were being driven from (or were voluntarily exiting) market production even while many continued to run shops, help in their husbands' businesses and take part in household financial management, see Collins, 'The Economic Role of Women'.

38. Torquato Tasso, *Discorso della virtù feminile e donnesca*, ed. Maria Luisa Doglio (Palermo: Sellerio, 1997), pp. 56–7, quoted in Evelyn Welch, *Shopping in the Renaissance: Consumer Cultures in Italy 1400–1600* (New Haven: Yale University Press, 2005), pp. 221–2 [her translation].

39. Simon Schama, *The Embarrassment of Riches: An Interpretation of Dutch Culture in the Golden Age* (London: Collins, 1987).

40. These images are reproduced and described in Ilja M. Veldman, 'Lessons for Ladies: A Selection of Sixteteenth and Seventeenth-Century Dutch Prints', *Simiolus: Netherlands Quarterly for the History of Art* 16 (1986), pp. 113–27.

41. John Dod and Robert Cleaver, *A Godlie Forme of Householde Government: For the Ordering of Private Families, According to the Direction of Gods Word* (London, 1612), pp. 167–8, quoted in Alexandra Shepard, 'Manhood, Credit and Patriarchy in Early Modern England, c.1580–1640', *Past & Present* 167 (2000), pp. 75–106. For the way these tropes were endlessly reproduced in drama, see Natasha Korda, *Shakespeare's Domestic Economies: Gender and Property in Early Modern England* (Philadelphia: University of Pennsylvania Press, 2002); and for an exploration of the relationship between male

and female honour in this ideology, Faramerz Dabhoiwala, 'The Construction of Honour, Reputation and Status in Late Seventeenth- and Early Eighteenth-Century England', *Transactions of the Royal Historical Society*, 6th series, 6 (1996), pp. 201–13.

42. Wunder, *He is the Sun*, p. 81. For examples of German conduct books of the period, see Paul Münch (ed.), *Ordnung, Fleiss, und Sparsamkeit: Texte und Dokumente zur Entstehung der 'bürgerlichen Tugenden'* (Munich: Deutscher Taschenbuch Verlag, 1984); Helmut Puff, 'Die Ehre der Ehe – Beobachtungen zum Konzept der Ehre in der Frühen Neuzeit an Johann Fischarts Philosophisch Ehzuchtbüchline' (1578) und anderen Ehelehren des 16. Jahrhunderts', in Sibylle Backmann, Hans-Jörg Künast, Sabine Ullmann and B. Ann Tlusty (eds), *Ehrkonzepte in der Frühen Neuzeit: Identitäten und Abgrenzungen* (Berlin: Akademie Verlag, 1998), pp. 99–119; Steven Ozment, *When Fathers Ruled: Family Life in Reformation Europe* (Cambridge: Harvard University Press, 1983).

43. It was deployed, for example, in a jurisdictional dispute between two courts in eighteenth-century Paris. As Amalia D. Kessler has summarised it: 'commercial pursuits – by focusing attention on the achievement of base, material ends – were thought necessarily to detract from virtue and thus to be harmful to both self and community'. In her view, commerce was, even at this late date, still 'regarded with disdain and suspicion'; if it was 'a necessary evil', it was nevertheless 'a public hazard', Amalia D. Kessler, 'From Public Hazard to Social Good: The Parisian Merchant Court and the Rise of a New Conception of Commerce', paper delivered at the Columbia University Legal History Seminar, November 2005, pp. 2–3.

44. For a recent study of such narratives of scarcity and exoticism, see Paul Freedman, 'Spices and Late-Medieval European Ideas of Scarcity and Value', *Speculum* 80 (2005), pp. 1209–28.

45. Fernand Braudel, *The Wheels of Commerce*, vol. 2: *Civilization and Capitalism, 15th–18th Century*, tr. Siân Reynolds (Berkeley: University of California Press, 1992), p. 394. For a general discussion of these issues, see Sharon Collingwood, *Market Pledge and Gender Bargain: Commercial Relations in French Farce, 1450–1550*, Studies in the Humanities 23 (New York: Peter Lang, 1996); Jean-Christophe Agnew, *Worlds Apart: The Market and the Theater in Anglo-American Thought, 1550–1750* (Cambridge and New York: Cambridge University Press, 1986).

46. Lines 441–5, cited in Derrick Higgenbotham, 'Peddling Promises: Merchants, the Art of Exchange, and the Culture of Credit in Late Medieval and Early Modern Theatre', p. 24. My thanks to the author for allowing me to cite this unpublished paper.

47. Peter Stabel, 'Negotiating Value: Market Behaviour and Price Formation in the Towns of 14th and 15th Century Flanders', in Marc Boone and Martha Howell (eds), *In But Not Of the Market: Movable Goods in the Late Medieval and Early Modern Economy* (Brussels: Koninklijke Vlaamse Academie van Belgie voor Wetenschappen en Kunsten, 2007), pp. 53–71.

48. His plays are published in Cornelis Everaert, *Spelen*, ed. Jacob Wijbrand Muller and Lodewijk Scharpé (Leiden: Brill, 1920).

49. The competition, known as the *Landjuweel* in Antwerp, was theoretically held every three years, travelling from major city to major city in the county. For a detailed analysis of this competition and the themes on display in the various performances, see Alexandra Kirkman Onuf, 'Local Terrains: The "Small Landscape" Prints and the Depiction of the Countryside in Early Modern Antwerp' (unpublished doctoral thesis, Columbia University, 2005). Similar competitions were held throughout the southern Low Countries in this period. For studies of the *rederrijkers* in this region, see the work of Anne-Laure van Bruaene, including '"A Wonderfull Tryumfe, for the Wynnyng of a Pryse": Gilds, Ritual, Theater and the Urban Network in the Southern Low Countries, *c*.1450–1650', *Renaissance Quarterly* 59 (2006), pp. 374–406; Anne-Laure van Bruaene, 'Sociabiliteit en competitie: De sociaal-institutionele ontwikkeling van de rederijkerskamers in de Zuidelijke Nederlanden (1400–1650)', in Bart Ramakers (ed.), *Conformisten en rebellen:*

Rederijkerscultuur in de Nederlanden (1400–1650) (Amsterdam: Amsterdam University Press, 2003); Anne-Laure van Bruaene, 'De contouren van een nieuw cultuurmodel: Rederijkers in Vlaanderen en Brabant in de zeventiende eeuw', Handelingen der Koninklijke Zuid-Nederlandse Maatschappij voor Taal- en Letterkunde en Geschiedeni 58 (2005), pp. 221–37; Peter Arnade, Realms of Ritual: Burgundian Ceremony and Civic Life in Late Medieval Ghent (Ithaca: Cornell University Press, 1996).

50.   Spelen van sinne, vol scone moralisacien, uutleggingen ende bediedenissen op alle loeflijcke consten (Antwerp: M. Willem Siluius, 1562). See Onuf, 'Local Terrains', pp. 140–50 for a detailed analysis.

51.   Lines 246–55, John Rastell, 'Gentleness and Nobility', in Richard Axton (ed.), Three Rastell Plays: Four Elements, Calisto and Melebea, Gentleness and Nobility (Cambridge: D. S. Brewer, 1979), cited in Derrick Higginbotham, 'Peddling Promises', p. 1.

52.   Odd Langholm, Merchant in the Confessional: Trade and Price in the Pre-Reformation Penitential Handbooks (Leiden: Brill, 2003), esp. chapter 14, pp. 233–43. Goods should be traded in the open and supplies brought to market promptly, without any attempts to corner the market or create monopoly. Prices should be negotiated fairly – i.e., negotiated in a situation where everyone had the same information.

53.   Joel Kaye has influentially exposed the link between commercial practices and their logics on the one hand and scholastic theory more generally on the other. See in particular, Joel Kaye, Economy and Nature in the Fourteenth Century: Money, Market Exchange and the Emergence of Scientific Thought, Cambridge Studies in Medieval Life and Thought, 4th series, 35 (Cambridge and New York: Cambridge University Press, 1998); Kaye, 'Monetary and Market Consciousness'. For scholastic theories of the just price, see Raymond de Roover, 'The Concept of the Just Price: Theory and Economic Policy', Journal of Economic History 18 (1958), pp. 418–34; Raymond de Roover, 'Scholastic Economics: Survival and Lasting Influence from the Sixteenth Century to Adam Smith', Quarterly Journal of Economics 69 (1955), pp. 161–90; Raymond de Roover, La pensee économique des scolastiques: Doctrines et méthodes (Montreal and Paris: Institute d'études médiévales, 1971); and more recently, Langholm, The Merchant in the Confessional, esp. chapter 15, pp. 244–56. There were differences of opinion about the precise definition of the just price, but the Aristotelian schematic formed the basis of all theory. On the just price, see de Roover, 'The Concept of the Just Price'; de Roover, La pensée économique des scolastiques; Langholm, Economics in the Medieval Schools; Langholm, The Legacy of Scholasticism in Economic Thought: Antecedents of Choice and Power, Historical Perspectives in Modern Economics (Cambridge and New York: Cambridge University Press, 1998); Langholm, The Merchant in the Confessional; Kaye, Economy and Nature in the Fourteenth Century.

54.   Braudel, Wheels of Commerce, p. 455.

55.   Comments on the Summa theologica, II, ii, qu. 77, art. I (Leonine edition, VI, p. 149), cited in de Roover, 'The Concept of the Just Price', p. 423.

56.   René de Lespinasse and Francois Bonnardot (eds), Les métiers et corporations de la ville de Paris: XIII siècle: Le livre des métiers d'Etienne Boileau, Histoire Générale de Paris (Paris: Imprimerie nationale, 1879), p. xi [my translation].

57.   De Roover, 'The Concept of the Just Price', pp. 428–34. See also Hans van Werveke, 'Les villes belges: Histoire des institutions économiques et sociales', in La ville, Recueils de la Societé Jean Bodin 7, vol. 2: Institutions économiques et sociales (Brussels: Editions de la Librairie encyclopédique, 1955). See also Peter Stabel, 'Markets in the Cities of the Late Medieval Low Countries: Retail, Commercial Exchange and Socio-cultural Display', in Simonetta Cavaciocchi (ed.), Fiere e mercati nella integrazione delle economie europee, secc. XIII-XVII: Atti della 'Trentaduesima settimana di studie', 8–12 maggio 2000 (Florence: Le Monnier, 2001), pp. 797–817; Peter Stabel, 'From the Market to the Shop: Retail and Urban Space in Late Medieval Bruges', in Bruno Blondé, Peter Stabel, Jon Stobart and Ilja Van Damme (eds), Buyers and Sellers: Retail Circuits and Practices in Medieval

and Early Modern Europe, Studies in Urban History 9 (1100–1800) (Turnhout: Brepols, 2006), pp. 79–109.

58. Similar objectives governed, to cite one more example, in sixteenth-century Lille, where residents were permitted to buy first in grain markets; bakers came next, and only then were merchants of milled grain allowed to deal. Paul Delsalles, 'Façons de vendre, façons d'acheter, sur les marchés au coeur de l'Europe (XVIe siècle et première moitié du XVIIe siècle)', in Cavaciocchi (ed.), *Fiere e mercati*, pp. 335–59.

59. The provision was intended to prevent regraters from buying up supplies and reselling at higher prices. Although the *Livre des Métiers* of *c.*1268, ostensibly an edition of the regulations adopted by the guilds of Paris themselves, had permitted regraters to sell bread; later ordinances either omitted mention of bread as one of the products they handled or explicitly prohibited the practice. A letter from the provost from 1367, for example, stated that 'nul ne soit si hardi de revendre ne regrater pain en laditte ville, sur paine de perdre ledit pain ou sa valeur'. René de Lespinasse (ed.), *Les métiers et corporations de la ville de Paris*, I: *XIVe–XVIIIe siècle, ordonnances générales, métiers de l'alimentation, deuxième partie (Boulangers)*, III (1367, 14 avril), no. 3 (Paris: Imprimerie Nationale, 1886–97), p. 200.

60. On honour generally, see classic statements by Julian Pitt-Rivers, 'Honor and Social Status', in John George Peristiany (ed.), *Honour and Shame: The Values of Mediterranean Society* (Chicago: University of Chicago Press, 1966); Julian Pitt-Rivers, 'Honor', in David Sills (ed.), *International Encyclopedia of the Social Sciences*, 18 vols (New York: Macmillan, 1968), vol. 6, pp. 503–11; Julian Pitt-Rivers, 'The Anthropology of Honour', in Julian Pitt-Rivers (ed.), *The Fate of Shechem, or, the Politics of Sex: Essays in the Anthropology of the Mediterranean* (Cambridge: Cambridge University Press, 1977), pp. 1–17; Friedrich Zunkel, 'Ehre', in Werner Conze, Otto Brunner and Reinhard Koselleck (eds), *Geschichtliche Grundbegriffe: Historisches Lexikon zur politisch-sozialen Sprache in Deutschland*, 8 vols (Stuttgart: Klett, 1972–97), vol. 2, pp. 1–63. More recent work includes Martin Dinges, 'Die Ehre als Thema der Stadtgeschichte: Eine Semantik im Übergang vom Ancien Régime zur Moderne', in *Zeitschrift für Historische Forschung* 16 (1989), pp. 409–40. On the particularly gendered/sexed nature of honour in the late medieval and early modern period, see Martin Dinges, 'Ehre und Geschlecht in der Frühen Neuzeit', in Backmann, Künast, Ullmann and Tlusty (eds), *Ehrkonzepte in der Frühen Neuzeit*, pp. 123–48; Puff, 'Die Ehre der Ehe'. On masculinity and honour in artisanal society, see Merry E. Wiesner, 'Wandervögels and Women: Journeymen's Concepts of Masculinity in Early Modern Germany', *Journal of Social History* 24 (1991), pp. 767–82; Ruth Mazo Karras, *From Boys to Men: Formations of Masculinity in Late Medieval Europe* (Philadelphia: University of Pennsylvania Press, 2003), esp. chapter 4, pp. 109–50. Most scholars take it for granted that honour is always gendered because honour is an attribute of a social self, and the self is by definition gendered, but gender, as Garthine Walker has pointed out, cannot be reduced to sexuality; nor can gendered honour be seen in terms of static binaries in which men 'do' and women 'are' (my terms): Garthine Walker, 'Expanding the Boundaries of Female Honour in Early Modern England', *Transaction of the Royal Historical Society*, 6th series, 6 (1996), pp. 235–45.

61. Herman Pleij, 'Restyling "Wisdom", Remodeling the Nobility, and Caricaturing the Peasant: Urban Literature in the Late Medieval Low Countries', *Journal of Interdisciplinary History* 32 (2002), pp. 689–704. See also Herman Pleij, *Het Gilde van de Blauwe Schuit: Literatuur, volksfeest en burgermoraal in de late Middeleeuwen* (Amsterdam: Meulenhoff, 1979), esp. pp. 248–50.

62. Richard Hakluyt, *Voyages and Discoveries: The Principal Navigations, Voyages, Traffiques and Discoveries of the English Nation*, ed. Jack Beeching (Harmondsworth: Penguin Books, 1972).

63. For a reading of *La Trésorie*, a relatively obscure Renaissance comedy, that emphasises the problem of money and commerce in sixteenth-century France, see Jotham Parsons,

'Money and Merit in French Renaissance Comedy', *Renaissance Quarterly* 60 (2007), pp. 852–82.

64. For examples of merchants who sought to redeem their 'usurious' activities by making lavish bequests at death, see Benjamin Nelson, 'The Usurer and the Merchant Prince: Italian Businessmen and the Ecclesiastical Law of Restitution', *Journal of Economic History* 7 (Supplement) (1947), pp. 104–22; Francesco L. Galassi, 'Buying a Passport to Heaven: Usury, Restitution and the Merchants of Medieval Genoa', *Religion* 22 (1992), pp. 313–26; Lawrin D. Armstrong, 'Usury, Conscience, and Public Debt: Angelo Corbinelli's Testament of 1419', in John A. Marino and Thomas Kuehn (eds), *A Renaissance of Conflicts: Visions and Revisions of Law and Society in Italy and Spain* (Toronto: Center for Renaissance and Reformation Studies, 2004), pp. 173–240.

65. In addition to the literature cited in note 31, see Albert O. Hirschman's classic, *The Passions and the Interests: Political Arguments for Capitalism Before its Triumph* (Princeton, NJ: Princeton University Press, 1977).

5 Do Women Need the Renaissance?

Merry E. Wiesner-Hanks

Joan Kelly's path-breaking article, 'Did Women have a Renaissance?' first published in 1977 in the collection *Becoming Visible: Women in European History*, led historians of women in many fields to question the applicability of chronological categories derived from male experience.[1] Thirty years later, the questioning continues, augmented by doubts about whether chronological categories derived from the experience of *some* women can be applied to women's history as a whole, or whether change that is generally seen as only tangential to gender relations should qualify as a major turning point. Such doubts arise in part from questions about 'women' as an ontological category, and the close attention paid to multiple axes of difference in women's and gender history. But what is lost if feminist historians, in their sensitivity to difference, refuse to apply structures of periodisation? If a primary (some would say *the* primary) contribution of historians to the scholarly and larger worlds is the analysis of change over time, what happens if women's and gender historians step back from this task? Does this make women's and gender history 'motionless', a word used by Le Roy Ladurie to describe European history over the *longue durée*, in an article that appeared the same year that Kelly's did? I will argue that it does, both for the era of the Renaissance and for broader swaths of time. 'Renaissance' may ultimately not be a useful category when exploring women's and gender history globally, but 'early modern', a term developed more recently, is. This chapter will explore ways in which women's and gender historians, and scholars in other fields, have challenged both of these chronological categories and make suggestions about new questions that historians might ask to keep gender central to future research on this era.

At the time Kelly asked her now-famous question, the term 'Renaissance' was already being contested. In his 1978 presidential address to the American Historical Association, William Bouwsma surveyed historians' reservations about the term, seeing these as part of a larger 'collapse of the traditional dramatic organization of Western history'.[2] Bouwsma was writing only a year after Kelly's essay appeared, and the critique of the term coming from women's history is not part of his considerations. His justification for resurrecting the Renaissance, however, points to what has inspired feminist historical and literary critiques of the label. Bouwsma advocated a return to the dramatic organisation of history, with the Renaissance as a key pivotal event, important because it created an 'anthropological vision . . . that culture is a product of the creative adjustment of the human race to its varying historical circumstances rather than a function of universal and changeless nature, and the perception that culture accordingly differs from time to time and group to group'. That nicely captures the spirit of what we now oddly call the '*new* cultural history', as well as the opening of every world history textbook these days. In a rewording of his idea later in the same article, however, Bouwsma inadvertently also captures the feminist critique of the Renaissance. He notes, 'as the creator of language, man also shapes through language the only world he can know directly, including even himself . . . the notion of man as the creator of himself and the world was heady stuff'. I do not think Bouwsma was insensitively using gendered language here; he was simply being accurate. As countless discussions of 'self-fashioning' since have pointed out, in the opinion of the men who created Renaissance culture and of most subsequent scholars, it was *man* who was to be the creator of *himself*, *man* who was the measure of all things.[3]

The highly gendered nature of the Renaissance's 'anthropological vision' has been a steady theme in the work of Margaret King on women humanists, Constance Jordan on Renaissance feminism and the huge number of studies of English women writers.[4] Although it appeared originally that most of this feminist analysis of the Renaissance would be a further move away from the 'drama of history' (Bouwsma's words), dethroning the Renaissance yet again, in many ways it has not done so. The drama is still there, but the outcome is tragedy rather than triumph. The Renaissance is still the beginning of a trajectory, but that trajectory leads to Rousseau, the banning of women's clubs in the French Revolution, the restrictions of the Napoleonic Code and separate spheres. Though women's history of the nineteenth century rarely searches for roots in the Renaissance, that of the eighteenth century, as in works by Christine Fauré, Joan Landes, Olwen Hufton and Lieselotte Steinbrügge, who trace the development of 'democracy without women' and 'the limits of citizenship', certainly does.[5]

Some very recent feminist scholarship, especially that of Diana Robin, has moved away from this position somewhat. Instead of concentrating on men's ideas and the political developments that resulted from them, Robin and others explore ways in which a few women in Italy and France in the fifteenth and sixteenth centuries boldly claimed the humanist education that was the centre of the 'Renaissance' strictly defined (that is, the rebirth of classical culture).[6] Women such as Isotta Nogarola, Cassandra Fedele, Laura Cereta, Louise Labé and Madeleine and Catherine des Roches argued in letters and then in published writings that learning was compatible with virtue and that women could indeed be both eloquent and chaste.[7] Several put this assertion into practice, writing and reciting public orations in Latin and Greek, and circulating their letters, both common practices for male humanists. In the 1530s, women in several Italian cities established informal groups for the presentation and discussion of written work – what would later be termed 'salons'. The poet Vittoria Colonna was the centre of several such groups and published a book of poetry under her own name in 1538, the first solo edition of a woman's poetry to appear in print in Europe; later in the century Labé and the Mesdames des Roches (who were mother and daughter) published their work as well. Such scholarship has answered Joan Kelly's question with a definite 'yes', noting that female humanists clearly regarded the new learning as liberatory and understood themselves to be engaged in self-fashioning. This emphasis on women's own ideas and words is welcome, though the glacial pace at which these arguments in favour of women's abilities and education were translated into institutional opportunities for learning provides another rather depressing trajectory. Such scholarship suggests, however, that there is value in exploring ideas in their own times rather than always placing them within long-term historical processes.

Scholars who focus on female humanists are not the only ones who stress the continued value of considering the Renaissance as a distinct period. In a recent essay, Leah Marcus surveys debates about the term 'Renaissance' in literary studies and notes that literary scholars are more loath to give up the Renaissance than historians because it allows them to preserve literature as a separate discipline in these days of ever-increasing interdisciplinarity.[8] I was intrigued by this comment and it led me to investigate a quite prominent recent example of the rejection of the 'Renaissance'; the renaming and redefinition of the *Journal of Medieval and Renaissance Studies* as the *Journal of Medieval and Early Modern Studies*. The 'Statement of Purpose' for the renamed journal provides good evidence for Marcus's point. In two paragraphs that use the words 'history' and 'theory' or variations of them many times, the words 'literature' and 'literary' never appear (though the word 'texts' does appear, in a phrase downplaying their centrality). I was so struck by this that I wrote to Michael Cornett, the managing editor, who answered with his reflections about both the journal and periodisation in general. He confirmed my initial impression, commenting that 'there has been a conscious attempt to keep literary study from dominating the journal because of its great success in opening up all these questions of a conscious engagement with the past and the artifice of historical study'.[9] There are two ways to view this, of course. One is to see it as confirming the fears of Marcus's colleagues in Literature, that if you dump the Renaissance you dump literary studies as a separate field. The other is the way some of my colleagues in History will no doubt see it, as representing not the abandonment of literature but its total triumph, a point of view which might find further support in Cornett's later comment that 'if literary work seems to lead the way, that's because literary scholars have led the way in rethinking historical study and it will take time for other disciplines to catch up'.[10] Harrumph, we historians might say, perhaps we do not *want* to catch up. If scholars of literature wanted to rethink historical study, why didn't they become historians in the first place? If they want to tell us about the 'artifice of historical study' and assert that all history is text, wouldn't it be nice if they could read all texts in their original? (We social historians who work with handwritten sources can generally feel superior with that question.)

In fact, the term that replaced 'Renaissance' in the journal's title, 'early modern', was originally devised not by literary scholars, but by historians rethinking quite different issues. In 1926, the medieval historian Lynn Thorndike used the term in a survey of European history, explicitly rejecting the idea that the 'so-called Italian Renaissance' (his terminology) by itself had brought anything new.[11] In 1941, several articles used the term to discuss economic issues related to early British colonisation and the English civil war. By the late 1950s, 'early modern' was being used more widely in textbook titles and, in 1970, Cambridge University Press began publishing the series Cambridge Studies in Early Modern History.[12] Most of the earliest works in that series focused on economic history, but by the late 1970s the term was being used in political and social history as well. Even a few scholars of religion, particularly those who examined popular religion in parts of Europe other than Germany (topics that at the time would not have been understood as 'the Reformation') began to use the term.[13] In the 1970s and 1980s, using the term 'early modern' in scholarly writing generally signalled an interest in theory derived from the social sciences, particularly from the *Annales* school, though the *Annalistes* themselves did not use the term, but stayed with *histoire moderne*. In terms of self-understanding, being an 'early modernist' was thus distinguished from being a Renaissance or Reformation historian (or one who combined these, as a 'Ren-and-Ref' historian) by one's theoretical perspective as well as subject matter.

In the 1990s, however, the broad understanding first used in textbooks spread into scholarly research and publishing. In 1995, scholars in Canada started an online journal, *Early Modern Literary Studies* and Germanists in the United States started the group Frühe Neuzeit Interdisziplinär, which sponsors roughly triennial conferences and conference volumes; in 1997, historians at the University of Minnesota launched the *Journal of Early Modern History: Contacts, Comparisons, Contrasts*; in 1998, the *Sixteenth Century Journal* adopted the subtitle 'The Journal of Early Modern Studies'; and in 2000, the Group for Early Modern Cultural Studies (which was started in 1993) began publishing the *Journal for Early Modern Cultural Studies*.

Though there were some debates about the issue, 'early modern' generally became the label of choice for scholarship on women and gender as well.[14] The first book by literary scholars to use the term was actually *Rewriting the Renaissance: The Discourses of Sexual Difference in Early Modern Europe*, published in 1986.[15] In 1994, as an outgrowth of the Folger Library colloquium on 'Women in the Renaissance', a group of scholars from many disciplines formed the Society for the Study of Early Modern Women, which now sponsors book prizes, travel scholarships, sessions at various meetings, a listserv and triennial conferences at the University of Maryland, called some variation on 'Attending to Women'.[16] These conferences have resulted in conference volumes and, in 2006, the group began publishing a journal, *Early Modern Women*. Its website does not comment on periodisation, but says simply that it 'welcomes scholars and teachers from any discipline who study women and their contributions to the cultural, political, economic, or social spheres of the early modern period and whose interest in it includes attention to gender and representations of women'.[17] In 1996, the University of Chicago Press began publishing a series of translations of works by (and a few about) women, The Other Voice in Early Modern Europe, edited by Margaret King and Albert Rabil, Jr. This series has published almost forty books and many more are on the way.[18] In 2001, with the sponsorship of Erika Gaffney, Ashgate Press began publishing the series Women and Gender in the Early Modern World, edited by Allyson Poska and Abby Zanger, which now has more than forty titles.[19]

Each of these journals, groups and book series defines the period slightly differently: *The Sixteenth Century Journal* as roughly 1450 to 1660, *Early Modern Literary Studies* as 1500 to 1700, *Early Modern Women* as 1400 to 1700, the Other Voice as 1300 to 1700, the *Journal for Early Modern Cultural Studies* as roughly 1550 to 1850 and the *Journal of Early Modern History* as even longer, roughly 1300 to 1800. The varying definitions of the period reflect the perspectives and aims of editors and publishers, but also reconceptualisations of the field. The break between medieval and early modern was originally set at 1500, with Columbus and Luther the most important figures. In most recent research and teaching materials, it has moved backwards at least to 1450 to take into account the invention of printing with movable metal type, the effective use of gun-powder weaponry, the conquest of Constantinople by the Ottomans and the earliest European voyages down the African coast. In a few cases it has moved still further backwards, fully encompassing the Renaissance in Europe and the end of the Mongol Empire in Eurasia. The end of the early modern era tends to vary by discipline. In Literature, especially in the English literature that dominates the field, it is generally set at around 1700. In history, it is almost always 1789 or 1800. The former date privileges the political history of western Europe, of course, though there were other significant changes in the decade: Edmund Cartwright invented the steam-powered loom and opened the first cloth-making factory using his new machines, and the first fleet of convicts set sail from Britain to Australia, carrying about a thousand people. Thus the 1780s saw new processes in in-dustrialisation and colonisation, two related developments that are markers in most literature of the break between 'early modern' and 'modern'. The year 1800 works just as well to mark this break, however, and is widely used.

But if 'Renaissance' carries intellectual baggage, what about 'early mod-ern'? This is a question that is also at least thirty years old, for Bouwsma and many other analysts have pointed to some general problems with the term – its assumption that there is something that can unambiguously be called 'modernity', its retaining of a notion of linear trajectory with a final act, whether that final act is termed the Second Coming, the dictatorship of the proletariat or, more recently, 'the end of history'.[20] In an article in *Speculum*, Lee Patterson sharply critiques this 'crude binarism that locates modernity ('us') on one side and premodernity ('them') on the other'.[21] Randolph Starn comments that the term is 'saddled with a teleological modernizing directory', and 'formed by the backfill from the debris of the collapsed breakthroughs to modernity that had not (quite) come about'.[22]

In the early 1990s, historians of Asia began to use the term, but they also debated its applicability.[23] Reflecting sentiments that are widely shared, Leonard and Barbara Andaya comment, 'especially in light of subaltern writings that reject the notion of modernity as a universal . . . the very invo-cation of the word implicitly sets a "modern Europe" against a "yet-to-be modernized" non-Europe'. Thus the world beyond Europe joins the Mid-dle Ages as a 'them' as compared to 'us', both of them orientalised, a linkage that David Wallace judges extremely harshly in 'Carving Up Time and the World'. He charges, 'Renaissance critics today continue to imitate the temporal and territorial expansionism of their Renaissance forbears' whose 'restless and destructive individualism' led to 'the erasure of pre-Columbian America'.[24]

Both Wallace and Marcus caution that 'early modern' might be even more expansionary than 'Renaissance'; Wallace warns of the

'Renaissance/early modern Behemoth', and the medieval historian Nancy Partner agrees, noting that 'even the Renaissance is rapidly losing its metaphorical romantic substance and is being engulfed in the rapacious maw of the Early Modern academic machine'.[25] The expanding scope of 'early modern' in the newer journals suggests that such concerns might be warranted. I'm not sure if five centuries – the longest definition of the period – qualifies as 'temporal expansionism' with a 'rapacious maw', for this is still only half the size of the medieval or classical millennium, but it still is a big bite of history. All of this criticism has made many of us who use the term more self-conscious about doing so. Newer textbooks and surveys include discussion of the origins, presuppositions and limitations of the term in their introductions, as does one of the newer journals in its prospectus.[26]

If 'early modern' is problematic for history in general, what about its particular problems for the history of women and gender? Though learned societies, journals and book series focusing on women and gender have accepted it, developments that have traditionally marked 1450 or 1500 as the beginning of a new era – the European voyages of discovery, the printing press, gunpowder weaponry, the development of nation-states, the expansion of pre-industrial capitalism, the conquest of Constantinople by the Ottoman Turks and the Protestant Reformation – have been told as a story of men, though rarely explicitly so: men in ships, male printers, male merchants and investors, male soldiers and generals, male officials and a very male Luther. Several periodisation structures have been developed that focus on issues related to gender, including Lawrence Stone's idea about the change from 'open lineage' to a 'restricted patriarchal nuclear family' to a 'closed domestic nuclear family' and Thomas Laqueur's notion of a change from a 'one sex' to a 'two sex' model of gender differentiation.[27] Stone's idea has been demolished as a general model, however, and discarded as overly simplistic even for the English gentry on which it is based.[28] Laqueur's remains influential, though more so among non-specialists than among historians of science and medicine, who have rejected it as far too dichotomous and teleological.[29] Thus does 'early modern' leave us in the same dilemma that 'Renaissance' does, that is, using a periodisation for women's history drawn rather unreflectively from men's?

One of the most powerful voices arguing that 'early modern' has just as many problems as 'Renaissance' has been Judith Bennett, who in a number of publications uses examples from women's work experiences and other areas of life to challenge what she terms the 'assumption of a dramatic change in women's lives between 1300 and 1700'. She notes that historians who focus on issues other than women are questioning the 'master narrative of a great transformation' and asserts that 'women's history should ally itself with those who are questioning the master narrative' because 'the paradigm of a great divide in women's history is undermined by many factual anomalies'.[30] Bennett has recently broadened her focus and called for an emphasis on continuities in women's history and on what she terms the 'patriarchal equilibrium' across all periods, not simply across 'the great divide' of 1500.[31]

In emphasising continuity in this period, historians of women and gender would be putting themselves in august company. Though American followers of the Annales school generally called themselves 'early modernists', *Annalistes* themselves saw no dramatic break, but posited a *longue durée* stretching from the eleventh century to the nineteenth, the period Le Roy Ladurie termed 'motionless'.[32] In fact, as Susan Stuard has pointed out, women already appear in some Annales school works – a historical school Natalie Davis termed a 'sodality of French brothers' – as the perfect example of motionless history, primarily part of a household, serving as a means of exchange between families.[33] This approach was adopted at least in part by Bonnie Anderson and Judith Zinsser in their survey of European women's history, for they discuss peasant women from the ninth century to the twentieth in a single section, going beyond the timeframe of even Le Roy Ladurie.[34] Motionless indeed.

Such wholesale rejection of periodisation makes me, and a number of other women's historians, uneasy. In reviewing Anderson and Zinsser's textbook, Gianna Pomata comments, 'I perceive here the shade of essentialism, the idea of an unchanging female nature'.[35] In discussing women in Annales school works, Stuard notes: 'By such formulations gender for women, if not for men, was assumed to be a historical constant, not a dynamic category that changed in Europe's formative centuries and changed again with the transition into modern times'.[36] With this critique, Stuard hints at both essentialism and ahistoricism, but here we are back to a medieval/modern transition again!

I think this is fine, for three reasons. First, on at least one of the traditional markers of the division between medieval and early modern, the Reformation, we now have a large body of scholarship that suggests that change outweighs continuity. That scholarship has not simply gone looking for change, but has considered both change and continuity in structures and processes.[37] Second, on some of what have been seen as the key elements marking a transition, including changes in military technology, we still have surprisingly little scholarship that takes gender into account. Before we can decide if these do or do not mark significant changes for women or for gender, we need far more research, but, in my opinion, the existing analysis suggests that they do. Third, though some historians of areas outside of Europe have harshly criticised the term and its assumptions, others have decided that the era was marked by processes that made it distinctly different from what came before and after. The processes they identify as key characteristics of the period are all gendered, and scholarship is beginning to analyse this. Thus, as scholarship on women and gender takes a more global perspective, change outweighs continuity across the medieval/modern divide.

First to the Protestant and Catholic Reformations. Over the last thirty years, studies have looked at women active in iconoclastic riots and religious wars, women defending convent life in word and deed, women preaching in the early years of the Protestant Reformation, pastors' wives creating a new ideal for women, women defying their husbands in the name of their faith, women converting their husbands or other household members, women writing and translating religious literature.[38] Other work has focused on the ideas of the reformers and the effects of the Reformations on notions of gender, including ideas about masculinity, patterns of sexuality and the family. This work has emphasised the differences between the ideas and ideals of the reformers and the institutions that were established and ended, highlighted women's agency and the actions of men supporting and restricting that agency, discussed the great differences between northern and southern Europe, rural and urban, rich and poor on nearly every issue related to the Reformations.

Research on women in the Reformations (my own included) originally tended to take a definite stance on a question similar to Joan Kelly's: not whether women *had* a Reformation, but whether Protestantism was good or bad for women. (A colleague calls this the Glinda-test, from the good witch in the *Wizard of Oz* who asks Dorothy whether she is a good witch or a bad witch.) This question has generally fallen out of favour, in part because of the stress on difference and diversity – which women? Where? When? Married or single? Old or young? Urban or rural? Mothers or childless? It has also fallen out of favour as more research explicitly focuses on gender and includes men in its purview.

People have also quit applying the Glinda test because they are de-emphasising the role of the Protestant Reformation *alone* in changing women's lives or gender structures. Heide Wunder, for example, points to a 'familialization of work and life' before the sixteenth century, in which the marital pair became the basic production and consumption unit. Thus Reformation ideas about the family did not create the bourgeois family, but resulted from it, which was one of the reasons that Protestant arguments in favour of marriage as the 'natural' vocation of women and an acceptable life for men were accepted so readily by Catholics.[39] Beate Schuster similarly sees praise of the male-headed bourgeois household as part of a new 'morality of settledness' that emerged out of an urban context before the Reformation and I have argued that gendered ideas about men as workers and women as 'helpmeets' emerged in craft and journeymen's guilds before they become part of Reformation ideology.[40]

While some scholars have stressed the role of social and economic factors as causative agents, others have followed the path recommended by Bennett and emphasised continuities. Protestant ideas about marriage, spousal relations and proper family life do not sound much different than those of pre-Reformation Christian humanists.[41] Women's patterns of piety centring on Christ showed relatively little change from the fifteenth to the seventeenth centuries.[42] Convents were increasingly cloistered after the Council of Trent, but the papal bull *Periculoso* calling for the cloistering of all women was actually issued in 1298, and post-Tridentine convents had more permeable walls than we once thought.[43] In theory, convents were closed in Protestant lands, but in practice in some areas they remained open as schools or secular endowments for women and 'spinster clusters' gathered in city neighbourhoods, sometimes in the very same building that had once housed a Beguinage or similar establishment.[44] Perhaps we have enough evidence, then, to suggest that the Reformations did not mean much real change for women, or for structures of gender?

We actually have more evidence that suggests that they did, particularly in studies of the ways in which after the Reformations, Protestant and Catholic religious authorities worked with rulers and other secular political officials to make people's behaviour more orderly and 'moral'. This process, generally termed 'social discipline' or 'the reform of popular culture', has been studied intensively over the last several decades in many parts of Europe. Scholarship on social discipline recognises the medieval roots of such processes as the restriction of sexuality to marriage, the encouragement of moral discipline and sexual decorum, the glorification of heterosexual married love and the establishing of institutions for regulating and regularising behaviour, but it also emphasises that all of these processes were strengthened in the sixteenth century. The enormous body of scholarship on marriage, divorce, the family and sexuality in the context of the Reformations makes clear that the roots of this heightened attention to social discipline are complex and include much more than theology.[45] Though most studies are not directly comparative, as a whole they make it clear that these changes occurred in Catholic areas as well as Protestant and that they involved church bodies, such as the Inquisition, as well as secular courts and other institutions.

The intensification of social discipline brought changes in men's lives as men. For craft masters, merchants and other middle-class men, the qualities of an ideal man increasingly centred on their role as heads of household: permanence, honesty, thrift, control of family members and servants. Manhood was linked to marriage, a connection that in Protestant areas even included the clergy. This notion of masculinity became increasingly hegemonic and was enforced by law as well as custom. Men whose class and age would have normally conferred political power but who remained unmarried did not participate to the same level as their married brothers; in some cities they were barred from being members of city councils. Unmarried men were viewed as increasingly suspect, for they were also not living up to what society viewed as their proper place in a gendered social order.[46]

The enforcement of social discipline had an even greater impact on women's lives. Laws regarding such issues as adultery, divorce, 'lascivious carriage' (flirting), enclosure of members of religious orders, interdenominational and interracial marriage were rarely gender neutral. The enforcement of such laws was even more discriminatory, of course, for though undisciplined sexuality and immoral behaviour of both women and men were portrayed from the pulpit or press as a threat to Christian order, it was women's lack of discipline that was most often punished.

The complexity of the process of social discipline leads to an unwillingness to draw up grand schema and timetables – no one is currently setting specific dates for developments like the 'rise of the restricted patriarchal nuclear family', as Lawrence Stone once did – but this scholarship does suggest that there was enough of a break with a pre-1500 past to retain this date as significant in the history of gender. Scholarship on social discipline is thus re-emphasising the role of the Reformations in shaping women's and men's lives, and may finally lead to gender being viewed as both an integral part and causative agent of the Reformations, just as social class became – for most people – in the 1970s.[47] It also makes clear that changes in gender ideology and structures are processes that take many decades or even centuries, and that religious concerns on these issues are interwoven with political ones.[48]

From a topic in early modern history on which there has been an enormous amount of work involving gender; the Reformations, to one on which there has been surprisingly little: military organisation and technology. Newer scholarship on the dramatic changes in weaponry, tactics and the size of armies that led Michael Roberts to dub this a 'military revolution' is just as empty of women as it was fifty years ago when Roberts coined the term, and in only a few studies are military developments linked to masculinity.[49] Barton Hacker's 1981 article remains, to my knowledge, the most complete discussion of the fact that soldiers in the sixteenth and seventeenth centuries often brought their wives, girlfriends, or other family members along on campaigns to cook for them and do their laundry, for armies did not provide such services.[50] As Hacker notes, such individuals might well outnumber the actual troops and at times included soldiers' mothers, so they do not fit our preconceptions of 'camp followers' very well.

A few studies are beginning to suggest ways in which notions of masculinity might have influenced military developments. These include Treva

Tucker's article about the impact of considerations of social status and ideals of noble masculinity on men's choice of weapons and tactics.[51] The most deadly and also most prestigious type of fighter in the fifteenth century was the cavalryman, wearing full plate armour and carrying a lance and sword; he rode a large warhorse which also wore plate armour. Such men-at-arms were almost always members of the nobility. During the fifteenth and sixteenth centuries, foot-soldiers armed with longbows, cross-bows, pikes, arquebuses and eventually muskets were increasingly effective against heavily-armoured knights and their horses; a nobleman had to figure he would lose his horse every time he went into battle. Infantry, who were usually commoners, became the heart of early modern armies, which grew in size exponentially; in 1500, for example, Spain's army was about 25,000 troops and a century later over 200,000. Foot soldiers were usually commoners, however, and the loss of their unique status as fighters was not lost on nobles. Pistols appeared to offer them a way out of their dilemma, a way both to use gunpowder and yet stay above the infantry – both figuratively and in actual combat. Mounted pistoliers, termed *reiters*, became an increasingly important group in battle, but they still favoured tactics that would allow them to display their individual prowess, however, which were not the most effective militarily.

Both the issue analysed by Hacker – the role large numbers of women played in supplying and supporting armies – and that analysed by Tucker – the role considerations of masculine honour played in shaping actual battles and other aspects of military life – are key factors in the 'military revolution' (and military history in any era, one might add). They need far more attention and other issues involving military developments call for gendered analysis as well. War and its financing were central to the growth of the nation-state, that core 'early modern' development, for nations came to rely on ever-larger standing armies. Military campaigns had traditionally been fought from March to October when food was available for men and animals, and the soldiers were simply sent home for winter. This was no longer advisable with a standing army – going home meant a high likelihood of desertion – but governments could not afford to build barracks for the troops. Some troops lived in tent camps (with their female supporters), while others were housed with civilian families, with the family expected to provide a place for a certain number of soldiers to sleep and keep warm. In theory, the soldiers were supposed to pay for their food but, as their pay itself often remained theoretical, they simply took what they needed by force. The economic, political, social and ideological effects of the growth of standing armies were enormous. It was surely different for men and women (and by area, social class, ethnic group, etc.), but so far this has received relatively little attention from either military or gender historians. Historians of early modern masculinity have emphasised that men in this era appeared to be 'anxious' about their masculinity, uncertain as to what was expected of them, worried about contradictions that seem to have emerged in codes of manhood, and eager to assert and demonstrate their masculinity in a variety of ways.[52] Changes in military technology are generally not discussed as one of the factors creating this anxiety, however, though they certainly played a role, just as military battlefields were an important arena for working out anxieties about masculinity. Thus my hunch is that, like the Reformations, the military revolution will eventually be judged a significant development in the history of gender, though at this point the limited amount of research makes it too soon to tell.

The first rulers to build a standing army were actually the Ottoman sultans, whose conquest of Constantinople is another key marker of the divide between medieval and early modern. The nucleus of the Ottoman army was the Janissary Corps – from the Turkish *yeni cheri* ('new troops') – a group of professional soldiers recruited originally from non-Muslim war captives from newly conquered areas and later primarily from the sultan's Christian subjects in Greece and the Balkans. Boys who became Janissaries were taken away from their families at a young age, raised in Turkish foster homes and sent to schools for military and other training. They were legally slaves of the sultan, but they could gain power and prestige through their service; the most capable became senior officials and ambassadors as well as admirals and generals. The highest Janissary often held the office of grand vizier, second only to the sultan. What did this system mean to the women whose sons were taken away? What did it mean to the Muslim women who raised them? What did it do to marriage patterns in the villages that they left? How did the system shape Ottoman notions of masculinity? Leslie Peirce has done some wonderful work on various aspects of gender in the Ottoman Empire, but clearly the state that ruled one-third of Europe could use more.[53]

Consideration of Ottoman developments points to the third of my defences of 'early modern'. All of the religious, social, military and political changes I have talked about so far pale in comparison to (but are intimately connected with) the most significant development in the era: new contacts between peoples brought about primarily – though not only – by European voyages. As the *Journal of Early Modern History* puts it: '"Early modern" is a convenient description for the age that was marked by a quantum leap in the level of global interaction'.[54] Sanjay Subrahmanyam expands on this, noting that the period 'defines a new sense of the limits of the inhabited world, in good measure because it is in a fundamental way an age of travel and discovery, of geographical redefinition'.[55] He sees the effects of these interactions in 'complex changes in political theology' and 'new and intensified forms of hierarchy, domination, and separation'.[56] Evelyn Rawski agrees, noting that 'elites, ideas, and religions moved across regions with greater frequency than ever before, significantly influencing intellectual and cultural life'.[57] World history scholarship has stressed the origins of this transformation in the immediately preceding period, a time of increased interregional contact and cross-cultural interaction involving Turkic migrations, the Mongol, Inca and Aztec Empires, and the Indian Ocean trading network.[58] It has also highlighted the disastrous results of these new contacts, particularly for peoples of the western hemisphere and noted the roles played by Asians and Africans in shaping these encounters; it is no longer just a story of intrepid Europeans in ships.[59] Intensified interaction remains at the heart of the story, however. Indeed, in some of the newest conceptualisations of world history, interaction itself is the key driving agent in all of history.[60]

Every one of these global interactions was gendered, as new scholarship is beginning to make clear. The contacts between cultures in the era before 1400 that had worked to change gender structures had often been carried out through the transmission of ideas and construction of institutions by individuals or small groups of people; the spread of neo-Confucianism and Islam are both examples of this. Beginning in the late fifteenth century, however, international contacts often involved the movement of large numbers of people over vast distances. In all of these movements, the gender balance between men and women was never equal, so that traditional patterns of marriage and family life were disrupted and new patterns were formed. The vast majority of merchants, conquerors, slaves and settlers who travelled great distances were men. Though there were attempts to keep groups apart, this proved impossible and in many parts of the world a *mestizo* culture emerged in which not only ethnicity, but religions, family patterns, cultural traditions and languages blended. Women acted as intermediaries between local and foreign cultures, sometimes gaining great advantages for themselves and their children though their contact with dominant foreigners, though also sometimes suffering greatly as their contact with foreigners began when they were sold or given as gifts by their families, or taken forcibly.[61] The migration of large numbers of men also had an influence on gender structures in the areas they left. Two thirds of the slaves carried across the Atlantic from Africa were male, with female slaves more likely to become part of the trans-Saharan trade or stay in west Africa. This reinforced polygyny, because slave women could join households as secondary wives, thus increasing the wealth and power of their owner/husbands through their work and children.[62] (They were often favoured as wives over free women as they were far from their birth families who could thus not interfere in a husband's decisions.) In parts of Europe, male migration also contributed to a gender imbalance among certain social groups. Because Christianity and Judaism did not allow polygyny, solutions were more difficult than in Africa. This may have contributed to the entry of more women into convents in Catholic areas, or to dowries reaching the stratospheric heights they did for wealthy families in Italian cities, which itself led to more women being sent to convents. In Protestant areas, male migration reinforced an existing pattern of late marriage and large numbers of women who remained single.

The goods that were carried in international trading networks also shaped gender, which in turn influenced that trade. Consumer goods such as sugar and coffee required vast amounts of heavy labour, leading to the development of plantation economies in tropical areas with largely male slave workforces. These slaves wore clothing made from cloth that was often produced in European households, where traditional gender divisions of labour were broken down because of the demands of the international marketplace, so that men, women and children all spun and wove. The new consumer goods –foodstuffs, clothing, household furnishings – were purchased by middle- and upper-class Europeans and their descendents in North America and Australia, with women's role in such households gradually becoming more oriented toward consumption rather than production. Class status was signified by the amount and quality of goods in one's home, all of which required purchase, cleaning, care and upkeep, which became the work – though unpaid – of the women of a household, aided perhaps by a servant or two.[63]

European colonisation in all parts of the world brought peoples who had long been separate from one another together, but this was generally perceived as a problem, not an opportunity. Not surprisingly, colonial authorities all regulated sexual encounters with indigenous people and among groups of immigrants.[64] In this, they adapted the structures of social discipline begun in Europe to the colonial context. Laws regarding intermarriage were usually framed in gender-neutral language, but what lawmakers were most worried about was, as the preamble to a Virginia law of 1691 states: 'negroes, mulattoes, and Indians intermarrying with English, or other white women' and the resultant 'abominable mixture and spurious issue'.[65] The concern about 'issue' was picked up by Thomas Jefferson, who commented, 'Were our state a pure democracy . . . there would still be excluded from our deliberations . . . women, who to prevent deprivation of morals and ambiguity of issue, should not mix promiscuously in the public meetings of men'.[66]

Attitudes towards sexual relations between certain types of individuals and the policies and practices that resulted from those attitudes, were shaped by notions of difference that were increasingly described as 'race', a category that came to be regarded as inherited through the blood, so that the children of parents from different cultures were regarded as 'mixedblood'. As many studies (and the quotations above) have made clear, 'race' is a gendered category, and so is 'mixed-blood'. In eighteenth-century

Saint Domingue, for example, mixed-race men were thought to be foppish and beardless while mixed-race women, according to one European visitor, 'combine the explosiveness of saltpeter with an exuberance of desire, which, scorning all, drives them to pursue, acquire and devour pleasure'.[67] Critiques of the masculinity of men in other parts of the world were common features in European colonial discourse, but this view was also shaped by the fact that the mixed-race men of Saint Domingue were generally half-French. In the eighteenth century, men in other parts of Europe, especially Britain, worried about the effects of French culture on the masculinity of their own area, particularly among well-to-do gentlemen. In Britain, such concerns led to the creation of a distinctly British version of the gentleman, who dressed in a more subdued way, rarely showed his emotions and spoke little. Such constructions of national masculinities were accompanied by a disparagement of the masculinity of other nations; in this case, French men were increasingly described as effeminate and knowledge of the French language viewed as appropriate only for women (an idea that has been remarkably long-lived, judging by the gender balance in secondary school French classes in the US).

The construction of national masculinities was intimately tied to the construction of nationalism itself, a topic that has been central to explorations of the development of modernity. Scholarship on gender and nationalism has primarily focused on the nineteenth century, but work that examines gender and nationalism in the early modern era is beginning to appear.[68] As they were in the nineteenth century, women were agents in the initial creation of nationalism, as Margaret Ferguson's work on women writers in England and France has made clear.[69] The women whose 'fantasies of empire' she examines in detail – Christine de Pizan, Marguerite de Navarre, Elizabeth Cary and Aphra Behn – are canonical Renaissance women writers, so her research suggests one way in which the histories of the few women who participated in Renaissance culture as it has traditionally been understood link to more global processes of change. There are, no doubt, many others.[70]

Just as sixteenth-century voyages built on earlier trading connections, so these gendered and sexualised encounters built on earlier ones. The first laws prohibiting the marriage of two 'races' were the 1366 Statutes of Kilkenney, designed in part to keep the Irish and English populations in Ireland separate.[71] Trade shaped the gender division of labour in many cultures since at least the agricultural revolution, if not before, and women were intermediaries in many ancient and medieval encounters. There are thus strong continuities in every process I have just mentioned. Only in 1492, however, did these encounters begin to encompass the world. This date clearly marked a great divide in the history of the women of the Americas, but also (though more slowly) shaped the lives of the German women whose work was the focus of my first book. Though I did not think about it at the time, I cannot think about them now without considering where the linen cloth they were weaving was going, where the diseases they were treating might have come from and what the guns they were helping to make were doing. Women in Europe who were far from an ocean and never left their village or town were increasingly enmeshed in the global economy.

Though the concept was already suspect, that book used the word 'Renaissance' in the title, because at that point I was not sure that 'early modern' worked for a study that included the fifteenth century. Now I am. 'Renaissance' may ultimately not be a useful category when exploring women's history globally, although it could become one of many 'efflorescences', to borrow Jack Goldstone's term for periods of marked expansion.[72] Thus, do women need the Renaissance? Perhaps not. Do they need early modern? Absolutely. Every development of the era brought change to the lives of many women and stunning transformation to the lives of others, including their lives as women. The history of gender needs 'early modern' as well, for the Reformations, the military revolution, the 'quantum leap' in global interactions, and many other changes of the era also brought significant change to the lives of men as men.

Even more so, however, 'early modern' needs women. The story of 'modernity', including its early and its post- phases, needs our continued assertion that women were important agents in its creation and that gender is central.[73] How could it not be, in an era that began in 1405, when Christine de Pizan wrote the *City of Ladies*, and ended in 1792, when Mary Wollstonecraft published *The Vindication of the Rights of Women*?

Notes

1. Joan Kelly, 'Did Women Have a Renaissance?', in Renate Bridenthal and Claudia Koonz (eds), *Becoming Visible: Women in European History* (Boston: Houghton-Mifflin, 1977), pp. 137–64.
2. William J. Bouwsma, 'The Renaissance and the Drama of Western History', *American Historical Review* 84 (1979), pp. 1–15.
3. Stephen J. Greenblatt, *Renaissance Self-Fashioning: From More to Shakespeare* (Chicago: University of Chicago Press, 1980).
4. Margaret King, *Women of the Renaissance* (Chicago: University of Chicago Press, 1993) and many of the essays collected in her *Humanism, Venice, and Women: Essays on the Italian Renaissance*, Variorum Collected Studies Series (Aldershot: Ashgate, 2005); Constance Jordan, *Renaissance Feminism: Literary Texts and Political Models* (Chicago: University of Chicago Press, 1990); Margaret Hannay, *Silent But for the Word: Tudor Women as Patrons, Translators, and Writers of Religious Works* (Kent, OH: Kent State University Press, 1985); Elaine Beilin, *Redeeming Eve: Women Writers of the Renaissance* (Princeton: Princeton University Press, 1987); Elaine Hobby, *Virtue of Necessity: English Women's Writing 1649– 1688* (Ann Arbor: University of Michigan Press, 1988); Wendy Wall, *The Imprint of Gender: Authorship and Publication in the English Renaissance* (Ithaca: Cornell University Press, 1993); Kate Chedgzoy et al. (eds), *Voicing Women: Gender and Sexuality in Early Modern*

Writing (Keele: Keele University Press, 1996); Maureen Quilligan, *Incest and Agency in Elizabeth's England* (Philadelphia: University of Pennsylvania Press, 2005).

5. Joan Landes, *Women and the Public Sphere in the Age of the French Revolution* (Ithaca: Cornell University Press, 1988); Carole Pateman, *The Disorder of Women: Democracy, Feminism and Political Theory* (Stanford: Stanford University Press, 1990); Christine Fauré, *Democracy Without Women: Feminism and the Rise of Liberalism in France* (Indianapolis: Indiana University Press, 1991); Olwen Hufton, *Women and the Limits of Citizenship in the French Revolution* (Toronto: University of Toronto Press, 1992); Lieselotte Steinbrügge, *The Moral Sex: Woman's Nature in the French Enlightenment*, tr. Pamela E. Selwyn (New York: Oxford University Press, 1995). See also many of the essays in Hans Erich Böedeker and Lieselotte Steinbrügge (eds), *Conceptualizing Woman in Enlightenment Thought* (Berlin: Berlin Verlag Arno Spitz, 2001).

6. Diana Robin, *Publishing Women: Salons, the Presses, and the Counter-Reformation in Sixteenth-Century Italy* (Chicago: University of Chicago Press, 2007).

7. The writings of these women and many others have been translated and published in the University of Chicago Press series, *The Other Voice in Early Modern Europe*, edited by Margaret King and Albert Rabil.

8. Leah Marcus, 'Renaissance/Early Modern Studies', in Stephen Greenblatt and Giles Gunn (eds), *Redrawing the Boundaries: The Transformation of English and American Literary Studies* (New York: Modern Language Association, 1992), pp. 41–63.

9. Michael Cornett, personal communication. My thanks to Professor Cornett for his very long and thoughtful comments.

10. Michael Cornett, personal communication.

11. Lynn Thorndike, *A Short History of Civilization* (New York: Crofts, 1926). His phrase regarding the Renaissance appears on pp. 186, 295, 386 and 434.

12. This process has been traced in Randolph Starn, 'The Early Modern Muddle', *Journal of Early Modern History* 6 (2002), pp. 296–307.

13. The most influential of these was Natalie Zemon Davis, *Society and Culture in Early Modern France* (Stanford: Stanford University Press, 1975).

14. Debates about periodisation among feminists in the 1990s included a session at the Berkshire Women's History Conference in 1996 entitled 'Complicating Categories, Crossing Chronologies: Periodization in the History of Women from Medieval to Modern', and a session at a 1996 interdisciplinary conference 'Gender in Perspective in the Early Modern Period', sponsored by the Zentrum zur Erforschung der Frühen Neuzeit at the University of Frankfurt entitled 'Defining Moments: Feminist Stakes in the Late Medieval/Renaissance/Early Modern Conundrum'. In 1997, the Istituto Storico Italo-Germanico in Trent also sponsored a conference entitled 'Tempi e spazi di vita femminile tra medioevo ed età moderna' at which the issue was discussed.

15. Margaret Ferguson, Maureeen Quilligan and Nancy Vickers (eds), *Rewriting the Renaissance: The Discourses of Sexual Difference in Early Modern Europe* (Chicago: University of Chicago Press, 1986). This volume resulted from a 1982 conference held at Yale that had a slightly different title, 'Renaissance Woman/Renaissance Man: Studies in the Creation of Culture and Society'. The conference was the first one, to my knowledge, to focus on the feminist critique of the Renaissance. Changes in standard language between 1982 and 1986 can be seen not only in the use of 'early modern' by the time the conference volume was published, but also by the use of 'gender', which was just entering scholarly discourse in the early 1980s. In the interests of full disclosure, I presented a paper at the conference and have a chapter in the volume.

16. Again in the interests of full disclosure, I was on the organising committee of EMW and served as its second president in 1995–96.

17. Society for the Study of Early Modern Women, <http://www.ssemw.org/emwindex.html>.

18. The complete list of titles can be found at: <http://www.press.uchicago.edu/Complete/Series/OVIEME.html>.

19. The complete list of titles can be found at: <https://www.ashgate.com/ shopping/search results.asp?seriesid=2046&seriesdesc=Women%20and%20Gender%20in %20the%20Early%20Modern%20World&location=series>.

20. 'The end of history' is the title of Francis Fukayama's philosophical reflections, *The End of History and the Last Man* (New York: Free Press, 1992).

21. Lee Patterson, 'On the Margin: Postmodernism, Ironic History, and Medieval Studies', *Speculum* 65 (1990), pp. 87–108.

22. Starn, 'Early Modern Muddle', p. 299.

23. Anthony Reid, 'Introduction: A Time and a Place', in his *Southeast Asia in the Early Modern Era: Trade, Power and Belief* (Ithaca: Cornell University Press, 1993); Leonard Blussé and Harriet T. Zurndorfer (eds), *Conflict and Accomodation in Early Modern Asia: Essays in Honour of Erik Zürcher* (Leiden: Brill, 1993); Leonard Y. Andaya and Barbara Watson Andaya, 'Southeast Asia in the Early Modern Period: Twenty Five Years On', *Journal of Southeast Asian Studies* 26 (1995), pp. 92–8; Jack A. Goldstone, 'The Problem of the "Early Modern World"', *Journal of the Economic and Social History of the Orient* 41 (1998), pp. 249–84, with replies by Peter van der Veer and David Washbrook; 'Early Modernities', special issue of *Daedalus: Journal of the American Academy of Arts and Sciences* 127 (1998). Lynn A. Struve provides an excellent survey of this discussion among Asian historians in the introduction to *The Qing Formation in World-Historical Time* (Cambridge: Harvard University Asia Center, 2004) and several of the essays in that volume explicitly consider the question.

24. David Wallace, 'Carving Up Time and the World. Medieval-Renaissance Turf Wars; Historiography and Personal History', University of Wisconsin-Milwaukee, Center for Twentieth Century Studies, Working Paper No. 11, 1990–91, pp. 6, 7. More recently Wallace seems to have settled on 'premodern' as an acceptable term, however, and called for an expansion of his own: of the canon of premodern English women writers to include Mary Ward, the seventeenth-century Catholic religious reformer who sought to create female apostolic congregations with a mission beyond convent walls: 'Periodizing Women: Mary Ward (1585–1645) and the Premodern Canon', *Journal of Medieval and Early Modern Studies* 36 (2006), pp. 397–453. Wallace may be right that Mary Ward is unknown in English literature; she is very well known in discussions of the reforming activities of Catholic women, however, which have been a key part of the scholarship on gender and the Reformations I trace below. See especially Anne Conrad, *Zwischen Kloster und Welt: Ursulinen und Jesuitinnen in der Katholischen Reformbewegung des 16./17. Jahrhunderts* (Mainz: Zabern, 1991); Ulrike Strasser, *State of Virginity: Gender, Religion, and Politics in an Early Modern Catholic State* (Ann Arbor: University of Michigan Press, 2003); Laurence Lux-Sterritt, *Redefining Female Religious Life: French Ursulines and English Ladies in Seventeenth-Century Catholicism* (Aldershot: Ashgate, 2005).

25. Nancy F. Partner, 'Did Mystics Have Sex?', in Jacqueline Murray and Konrad Eisenbichler (eds), *Desire and Discipline: Sex and Sexuality in the Premodern West* (Toronto: University of Toronto Press, 1996), pp. 296–311, here p. 297.

26. Jonathan Dewald, 'Intoduction', in *Europe 1450 to 1789: Encyclopedia of the Early Modern World*, vol. 1 (New York: Charles Scribner's Sons, 2004) pp. xxix–xxx; Merry E. Wiesner-Hanks, *Early Modern Europe, 1450–1789*, Cambridge History of Europe (Cambridge: Cambridge University Press, 2006), pp. 1, 6–7; *Journal of Early Modern History*, prospectus <http://www.hist.umn.edu/~jemh/prospect.html>.

27. Lawrence Stone, *The Family, Sex, and Marriage in England, 1500–1800* (New York: Harper and Row 1977); Thomas Laqueur, *Making Sex: Body and Gender from the Greeks to Freud* (Cambridge: Harvard University Press, 1990). To these theories we could add Foucault's model of the birth of 'sexuality' in the late eighteenth century, when sexual acts and desires began to be a matter of concern for various types of authorities, who wished to know, describe and control them. Michel Foucault, *L'Histoire de la sexualité*, vol 1: *La Volonté de savoir* (Paris: Gallimard, 1976). Most scholarship since Foucault has

moved the beginning of 'modern' sexuality to the late nineteenth century, however. See Roy Porter, 'Is Foucault Useful for Understanding Eighteenth and Nineteenth Century Sexuality?', in Nikki R. Keddie (ed.), *Debating Gender, Debating Sexuality* (New York: New York University Press, 1996); Robert A. Nye (ed.), *Sexuality* (New York: Oxford University Press, 1999). Feminist critique of Foucault has also pointed out that gender, to say nothing of women, is not part of his ideas. See Caroline Ramazanoglu (ed.), *Up Against Foucault: Explorations of Some Tensions Between Foucault and Feminism* (New York: Routledge, 1993); Susan Hekman (ed.), *Feminist Interpretations of Michel Foucault* (University Park: Penn State University Press, 1996).

28. Margaret Hunt, *The Middling Sort: Commerce, Gender, and the Family in England, 1680–1780* (Berkeley: University of California Press, 1996). For an overview of research on the family in this era, see Merry E. Wiesner-Hanks, 'Family, Household and Community', in Thomas A. Brady Jr., Heiko A. Oberman and James Tracy (eds), *Handbook of European History in the Later Middle Ages, Renaissance and Reformation, 1400–1600* (Leiden: E.J. Brill, 1994), pp. 51–78.

29. Joan Cadden, *Meanings of Sex Difference in the Middle Ages: Medicine, Science, and Culture* (Cambridge: Cambridge University Press, 1993). Ulinka Rublack also notes that Laqueur looks only at 'sexual intercourse in the reproductive process, ignoring gestation and parturition as part of female reproductive labour' and finds that sexual difference was indeed an 'ontological category' well before the eighteenth century. 'Pregnancy, Childbirth and the Female Body in Early Modern Germany', *Past & Present* 150 (1996), pp. 84–100.

30. Judith Bennett, 'Medieval Women, Modern Women: Across the Great Divide', in David Aers (ed.), *Culture and History 1350–1600: Essays on English Communities, Identities and Writing* (London: Harvester Wheatsheaf, 1992), pp. 147–75. An abridged version of this appears in Ann-Louise Shapiro, *Feminists Revision History* (New Brunswick: Rutgers University Press, 1994), pp. 47–72. See also Judith Bennett, *Ale, Beer, and Brewsters: Women's Work in a Changing World* (New York: Oxford University Press, 1996).

31. Judith Bennett, 'Confronting Continuities', *Journal of Women's History* 9 (1997), pp. 73–94, with responses by Sandra E. Greene, Karen Offen and Gerda Lerner, pp. 95–118; Judith Bennett, *History Matters: Patriarchy and the Challenge of Feminism* (Philadelphia: University of Pennsylvania Press, 2006), chapter 4, pp. 54–81.

32. Emmanuel Le Roy Ladurie, 'Motionless History', *Social Science History* 1 (1977), pp. 115–36.

33. Susan Mosher Stuard, 'The *Annales* School and Feminist History: Opening Dialogue with the American Stepchild', *Signs* 7 (1981), pp. 135–43; Susan Mosher Stuard, 'Fashion's Captives: Medieval Women in French Historiography', in Susan Mosher Stuard (ed.), *Women in Medieval History and Historiography* (Philadelphia: University of Pennsylvania Press, 1987), pp. 59–80. Davis's comment is from her address as president of the American Historical Association, 'History's Two Bodies', *American Historical Review* 93 (1988), p. 23. She later explores the work of women in the Annales school, where they served as assistants and researchers, in 'Women and the World of Annales', *History Workshop Journal* 33 (1992), pp. 121–37.

34. Bonnie S. Anderson and Judith P. Zinsser, *A History of Their Own*, 2 vols (New York: Harper and Row, 1988).

35. Gianna Pomata, 'History, Particular and Universal: On Reading Some Recent Women's History Textbooks', *Feminist Studies* 19 (1993), pp. 7–50. Pomata softens her review by seeing only the 'shade' of essentialism, a softness not found in the critique of subaltern studies coming from Indian feminists, who point out that women sometimes emerge only as a type of 'eternal feminine', victimised and abject. This point was made explicitly by Tanika Sarkar in her paper at the plenary session entitled 'Gendering Historiography', at the 1996 Berkshire Conference on Women's History, and is made tangentially in her 'Rhetoric Against the Age of Consent: Resisting Colonial Reason and Death of a Child-Wife', *Economic and Political Weekly*, 4 September 1993, pp. 1,869–78. See also

Kamala Visweswaran, 'Small Speeches, Subaltern Gender: Nationalist Ideology and Its Historiography', in Shahid Amin and Dipesh Chakrabarty (eds), *Subaltern Studies IX: Writings on South Asian History and Society* (Delhi: Oxford University Press, 1996), pp. 83–125.

36. Stuard, *Fashion's Captives*, p. 71. Elsewhere Stuard and JoAnn McNamara have pointed to the twelfth century as a particularly important period of change in ideas about gender and gender relations. See JoAnn McNamara, 'The *Herrenfrage*: The Restructuring of the Gender System, 1050–1150', in Clare Lees (ed.), *Medieval Masculinities: Regarding Men in the Middle Ages* (Minneapolis: University of Minnesota Press, 1994), pp. 3–30; Susan Mosher Stuard, 'The Dominion of Gender: Women's Fortunes in the High Middle Ages', in Renate Bridenthal et al. (eds), *Becoming Visible: Women in European History* (Boston: Houghton Mifflin, 1997), pp. 153–74.

37. Elsewhere I have considered issues of change and continuity in economic developments in this era. See e.g., my *Working Women in Renaissance Germany* (New Brunswick: Rutgers University Press, 1986) and the two chapters on economics and technology in *Early Modern Europe*.

38. For an overview of this scholarship, see the historiographical 'focal point' in the *Archiv für Reformationsgeschichte* 92 (2001), pp. 274–320, with articles by Lyndal Roper, Heide Wunder and Susanna Peyronel Rambaldi and my 'Women, Gender, and Sexuality', in Alec Ryrie (ed.), *Palgrave Advances: The European Reformations* (Aldershot: Palgrave, 2006), pp. 253–72. For an extensive bibliography, see the companion website <http://www.cambridge.org/womenandgender> of the forthcoming third edition of my *Women and Gender in Early Modern Europe* (Cambridge: Cambridge University Press, 2008).

39. Heide Wunder, '*Er ist die Sonn, sie ist der Mond': Frauen in der frühen Neuzeit* (Munich, 1992). English edition, *He is the Sun, She is the Moon: Women in Early Modern Germany*, tr. Thomas Dunlap (Cambridge: Harvard University Press, 1998).

40. Beate Schuster, *Die freie Frauen: Dirnen und Frauenhäuser in 15. und 16. Jahrhundert* (Frankfurt: Campus, 1995); Merry Wiesner-Hanks, 'Guilds, Male Bonding and Women's Work in Early Modern Germany', *Gender & History* 1 (1989), pp. 125–37; Merry Wiesner-Hanks, 'The Religious Dimensions of Guild Notions of Honor in Reformation Germany', in Sibylle Backmann, Hans-Jörg Künast, Sabine Ullman and B. Ann Tlusty (eds), *Ehrkonzepte in der frühen Neuzeit: Identitäten und Abgrenzungen*, Colloquia Augustana 8 (Berlin: Akademie Verlag, 1998), pp. 223–33.

41. See John K. Yost, 'Changing Attitudes towards Married Life in Civic and Christian Humanists', *American Society for Reformation Research, Occasional Papers* 1 (1977), pp. 151–66; Margo Todd, 'Humanists, Puritans and the Spiritualized Household', *Church History* 49 (1980), pp. 18–34; Margo Todd, *Christian Humanism and the Puritan Social Order* (Cambridge: Cambridge University Press, 1987); Diane Willen, 'Godly Women in Early Modern England: Puritanism and Gender', *Journal of Ecclesiastical History* 43 (1992), pp. 561–80.

42. Christine Peters, *Patterns of Piety: Women, Gender, and Religion in Late Medieval and Reformation England* (Cambridge: Cambridge University Press, 2003).

43. On the former point, see Elizabeth M. Makowski, *Canon Law and Cloistered Women: Periculoso and its Commentators, 1298–1545* (Washington, DC: Catholic University of America Press, 1997). On the latter, see P. Renée Baernstein, *A Convent Tale: A Century of Sisterhood in Spanish Milan* (New York: Routledge, 2002); Elizabeth A. Lehfeldt, *Religious Women in Golden Age Spain: The Permeable Cloister* (Burlington, VT: Ashgate, 2005); Strasser, *State of Virginity*.

44. Merry Wiesner-Hanks and Joan Skocir (eds), *Convents Confront the Reformation: Catholic and Protestant Nuns in Germany* (Milwaukee: Marquette University Press, 1996); Amy Leonard, *Nails in the Wall: Catholic Nuns in Reformation Germany* (Chicago: University of Chicago Press, 2005).

45. The scholarship on social discipline and the Reformations is huge. For a recent theoretical discussion, see the 'Focal Point: Confessionalization and Social Discipline in France, Italy, and Spain', with articles by James R. Farr, Wietse de Boer and Allyson Poska, in *Archiv für Reformationsgechichte* 94 (2003), pp. 276–319. Representative monographs include: Martin Ingram, *Church Courts, Sex and Marriage in England 1570–1640* (Cambridge: Cambridge University Press, 1987); Jeffrey R. Watt, *The Making of Modern Marriage: Matrimonial Control and the Rise of Sentiment in Neuchâtel, 1550–1800* (Ithaca: Cornell University Press, 1992); Michael F. Graham, *The Uses of Reform: 'Godly Discipline' and Popular Behavior in Scotland and Beyond 1560–1610* (Leiden: Brill, 1996); Georgina Dopico Black, *Perfect Wives, Other Women: Adultery and Inquisition in Early Modern Spain* (Durham: Duke University Press, 2001).

46. Analysis of masculinity in the Reformation is only beginning. See Scott Hendrix and Susan Karant-Nunn (eds), *Masculinity in the Reformation Era* (Kirksville, MO: Truman State University Press, 2008).

47. I won't hold my breath on this, however. Some of the textbooks, handbooks and companions that survey the Reformations include ample discussion of gender, while others barely mention it; there are usually a few pages on women and marriage, but only in the section on Luther's own marriage and the debate over clerical celibacy. Euan Cameron's magisterial textbook, *The European Reformation* (Oxford: Clarendon Press, 1991) gives women and the family (linked, of course) four pages out of 500 and ideas about sexual morality, one; Mark Greengrass, *Longman Companion to the European Reformation, c.1500–1618* (London: Longman, 1998), which describes itself as covering 'every aspect of the careers and writings of Luther and Calvin' has one page on marriage and two on church discipline, including some sexual issues; Carter Lindberg, *The European Reformations* (London: Blackwell, 1996) has a solid six-page section on ideas and practices regarding celibacy and clerical marriage; Jonathan W. Zophy, *A Short History of Renaissance and Reformation Europe: Dances over Fire and Water* (Upper Saddle River, NJ: Prentice Hall, 1999) integrates material on women, gender and sexuality better than any other survey.

48. For scholarship that examines connections among gender, religion, and the nation-state, see Ulrike Strasser, *State of Virginity*, and her 'Embodying the Middle Ages, Advancing Modernity: Religious Women in Sixteenth- and Seventeenth-Century Europe and Beyond', in Charles H. Parker and Jerry H. Bentley (eds), *Between the Middle Ages and Modernity: Individual and Community in the Early Modern World* (London: Rowman and Littlefield, 2007), pp. 231–51; Luisa Accati, 'L'importanza della diversità nella definizione de sé e nella definizione dello stato moderno: Appunti sulla controriforma', *Archiv für Reformationsgechichte* 92 (2001), pp. 264–73; Anne Mclaren, 'Gender, Religion, and Early Modern Nationalism: Elizabeth I, Mary Queen of Scots, and the Genesis of English Anti-Catholicism', *American Historical Review* 107 (2002), pp. 739–67. There is also a steadily increasing body of literature that looks at gender and the nation-state without emphasising the role of religion, including Sarah Hanley, 'Engendering the State: Family Formation and State Building in Early Modern France', *French Historical Studies* 18 (1989), pp. 4–27; Isabel Hull, *Sexuality, State, and Civil Society in Germany, 1700–1815* (Ithaca: Cornell University Press, 1996); Mihoko Suzuki, *Subordinate Subjects: Gender, the Political Nation, and Literary Form in England, 1588–1688* (Aldershot: Ashgate, 2003).

49. The original 1955 Roberts essay positing a 'military revolution' is included in Clifford J. Rogers (ed.), *The Military Revolution Debate: Readings on the Military Transformation of Early Modern Europe* (Boulder, CO: Westview Press, 1995). Newer scholarship includes Geoffrey Parker, *The Military Revolution: Military Innovation and the Rise of the West, 1500–1800* (Cambridge: Cambridge University Press, 1996).

50. Barton C. Hacker, 'Women and Military Institutions in Early Modern Europe: A Reconnaissance', *Signs* 6 (1981), pp. 643–71.

51. Treva J. Tucker, 'Eminence over Efficacy: Social Status and Cavalry Service in Sixteenth-Century France', *Sixteenth Century Journal* 32 (2001), pp. 1,057–95.

52. There are now at least ten books on early modern masculinity (most of them on England) and countless articles. These include Mark Breitenberg, *Anxious Masculinity in Early Modern England* (Cambridge: Cambridge University Press, 1996); Kathleen Long (ed.), *High Anxiety: Masculinity in Crisis in Early Modern France* (Kirksville, MO: Truman State University Press, 2002); David Kuchta, *The Three-Piece Suit and Modern Masculinity: England, 1550–1850* (Berkeley: University of California Press, 2002); Alexandra Shepard, *Meanings of Manhood in Early Modern England* (Oxford: Oxford University Press, 2003); Allison Levy, *Re-membering Masculinity in Early Modern Florence* (Burlington, VT: Ashgate, 2006).

53. Leslie Peirce, *Morality Tales: Law and Gender in the Ottoman Court of Aintab* (Berkeley: University of California Press, 2003); Leslie Peirce, *The Imperial Harem: Women and Sovereignty in the Ottoman Empire* (New York: Oxford University Press, 1993).

54. *Journal of Early Modern History*, prospectus <http://www.hist.umn.edu/~jemh/prospect.html>.

55. Sanjay Subrahmanyam, 'Connected Histories: Notes toward a Reconfiguration of Early Modern Eurasia', *Modern Asian Studies* 31 (1997), pp. 735–62, here p. 737. For a particularly forceful articulation of this view, see Jerry Bentley, 'Early Modern Europe and the Early Modern World', in Parker and Bentley (eds), *Between the Middle Ages and Modernity*, pp. 13–32. World history textbooks also emphasise connections. One popular textbook labels the era the 'origins of global interdependence': Jerry H. Bentley and Herbert F. Ziegler, *Traditions and Encounters: A Global Perspective on the Past* (Boston: McGraw Hill, 2000) and another 'the globe encompassed': Richard W. Bulliet, *The Earth and Its Peoples: A Global History* (Boston: Houghton Mifflin, 2004).

56. Subrahmanyam, 'Connected Histories', p. 739. Along with increasing interaction, Joseph Fletcher and Victor Lieberman have also identified common developments in many societies that, in Lieberman's words, 'distinguished all or part of the period *c*.1400–1800 from antecedent and succeeding eras'. Victor Lieberman, 'Introduction', *Modern Asian Studies* 31 (1997), p. 452. Joseph F. Fletcher, Jr, 'Integrative History: Parallels and Interconnections in the Early Modern Period, 1500–1800', in his *Studies on Chinese and Islamic Inner Asia* (Aldershot: Variorum, 1995), item X.

57. Evelyn S. Rawski, 'The Qing Formation and the Early-Modern Period', in Struve (ed.), *Qing Formation*, p. 211.

58. See especially Janet L. Abu-Lughod, *Before European Hegemony: The World System A.D. 1250–1350* (New York: Oxford University Press, 1991).

59. On the latter point, see especially Andre Gunder Frank, *ReOrient: Global Economy in the Asian Age* (Berkeley: University of California Press, 1998); Victor Lieberman, *Beyond Binary Histories: Reimagining Eurasia to c.1830* (Ann Arbor: University of Michigan Press, 1999).

60. David Christian, *Maps of Time: An Introduction to Big History* (Berkeley: University of California Press, 2005). Christian identifies 'acceleration in the pace of collective learning' as the most important force driving both change itself and the pace of change.

61. See the essays by Verena Stolcke on the Atlantic World, Barbara Andaya on Southeast Asia and Marcia Wright on Africa in Teresa A. Meade and Merry E. Wiesner-Hanks (eds), *A Companion to Gender History* (Malden, MA: Blackwell, 2004). For North America, see Susan Sleeper-Smith, *Indian Women and French Men: Rethinking Cultural Encounter in the Western Great Lakes* (Amherst: University of Massachusetts, 2001).

62. Jennifer Morgan, *Laboring Women: Reproduction and Gender in New World Slavery* (Philadelphia: University of Pennsylvania Press, 2004).

63. The fullest discussion of this is Maxine Berg, *Luxury and Pleasure in Eighteenth-Century Britain* (New York: Oxford University Press, 2005).

64. See my *Christianity and Sexuality in the Early Modern World: Regulating Desire, Reforming Practice* (London: Routledge, 2000).

65. William Waller Hening (ed.), *The Statutes at Large; Being a Collection of All the Laws of Virginia, from the First Session of the Legislature*, vol. 3 (1823; facsimile reprint Charlottesville, VA: University of Virginia Press, 1969), p. 86.

66. Thomas Jefferson, Letter to Samuel Kerchival (1816), in Paul Leicester Ford (ed.), *The Works of Thomas Jefferson*, vol. 10 (New York: G. P. Putnam's Sons, 1904), p. 46.

67. Baron de Wimpffen, quoted and translated in John D. Garrigus, 'Tropical Temptress to Republican Wife: Gender, Virtue, and Haitian Independence, 1763–1803', unpublished paper.

68. A good survey of the scholarship on this issue is provided in Mrinalini Sinha, 'Gender and Nation', in Bonnie G. Smith (ed.), *Women's History in Global Perspective*, vol. 1 (Urbana: University of Illinois Press, 2004), pp. 229–74.

69. Margaret W. Ferguson, *Dido's Daughters: Literacy, Gender, and Empire in Early Modern England and France* (Chicago: University of Chicago Press, 2003).

70. Two new books that examine women's reflections on the more globally-connected early modern world, and their role as cultural agents in creating this world, are Nora E. Jaffary (ed.), *Gender, Race, and Religion in the Colonization of the Americas* (Burlington, VT: Ashgate, 2007) and Kate Chedgzoy, *Women's Writing in the British Atlantic World: Memory, Place and History, 1550–1700* (Cambridge: Cambridge University Press, 2007).

71. I discuss changing notions of 'race' in *Early Modern Europe*, p. 466–73. See also the special issue on race and ethnicity of the *Journal of Medieval & Early Modern Studies* 31 (2001), with contributions by Hahn Thomas, John Dagenais and William Chester Jordan.

72. Jack A. Goldstone, 'Efflorescenses and Economic Growth in World History: Rethinking the "Rise of the West" and the British Industrial Revolution', *Journal of World History* 13 (2002), pp. 3,238–9.

73. For suggestions about how to make gender the central theme when *teaching* about the period, see Ulrike Strasser and Heidi Tinsman, 'Engendering World History', *Radical History Review* 91 (2005), pp. 151–64, which describes their course at the University of California, Irvine, 'World History: Gender and Politics, 1400–1870'. There is a revised and updated version in *World History Connected* <http://worldhistoryconnected.press.uiuc.edu>.

6 Gender as a Question of Historical Analysis

Jeanne Boydston

Almost twenty years ago, in a little-noticed paper for an American Council of Learned Societies conference, historian of American slavery Barbara Jeanne Fields went on record as an abiding sceptic of 'categories of analysis'. 'The phrase itself – categories of analysis – has a dry, ugly sound to my ears', she confided. 'When I encounter the phrase . . . in the opening pages of a book that I am not professionally obligated to read, I put the book down immediately'. 'If not kept strictly in their place', she cautioned, 'they get above themselves and go masquerading as persons, mingling on equal terms with human beings and sometimes crowding them out altogether'.[1]

Of course Fields wrote partly (not entirely) tongue-in-cheek. Nevertheless, when I first came across the piece in the early 1990s, I was dismayed. At the time, the project of consciously and carefully delineating categories of historical analysis – race, class, nation, identity and, in my field, gender – promised an ever more nuanced history of power and resistance, one in which subjects that had been rendered unseen or unintelligible by the terms of older frameworks would become visible in dramatically new and significant ways. Like many others, I thought that not only the future of my field but its very vindication *as* a field lay in that project. I was disappointed to find a historian I admired as much as Fields demurring at the prospect.

Now, twenty years later, my enthusiasm for categories of analysis has cooled considerably, and particularly for the reigning category of analysis of my own field, *gender*. Given the lingering controversy over the naming of the field, I want to be clear that it is not the substitution of 'gender' for 'women' that concerns me. My complaint is not that 'gender' history has distracted us from the important work of recovering 'women's' history. Much of that project does remain undone, but I am not convinced that focusing on 'gender' (as opposed to 'women') impedes us from doing it. Neither am I unhappy about including males in what we once called 'women's history' or about investigating the histories of manhood/ masculinities as well as womanhood/femininities.[2] The worlds of females – at their most communal and institutional and at their most intimate, at their most fragile and at their most potent – have included males. The cultural processes that have produced 'women' have also produced 'men'. Gender is the concept in our current practice that encompasses this relational dynamic. It seems useful to shift the name of the field, from women's history to gender history, to reflect this. And as I hope is clear both from this chapter and my larger work, in expressing my present concerns, I in no way suggest that we should cease examining the ways in which the construction of gender has occurred and been important in the history of human societies.

What I do worry about – what gives Fields's essay its present salience for me – is that, as a category of analysis, gender may be functioning in our work in just the sorts of ways she deplored. There is a difference between a concept – theorised but uninstitutionalised, advanced but still in motion – and a more fixed and furnished category of analysis. Even as a concept, 'gender' has been the subject of almost continuous debate in the field of women's and gender history (although this discussion has become less welcome, it seems to me, since we began to deploy gender as a category of analysis). Over the years, we have struggled with limited success to problematise the relation of 'gender' as a social construction to designated 'male' and 'female' bodies; too often, we assume that whatever female people do *is* 'femininity' and whatever male people do *is* 'masculinity'. We have argued without much resolution over the possibilities for theorising gender in other than binary and oppositional terms (or in terms of a continuum on which the poles remain 'male' and 'female'). Perhaps of greatest concern to me, although we have argued for 'gender' as a historical process, we have frequently treated that process as non-historically-contingent – that is, as unfolding in much the same way and in much the same terms in all societies. We have largely disregarded the very local and particular character of the concept as most of us have come to understand and use it – *local* to the cultures of the twentieth-century United States and western Europe and particular to the nature and struggles for power within those cultures. These, I think, remain critical points of interrogation for the *concept* itself.

In claiming that same concept as a broad category of analysis, we have done nothing to resolve those issues. If anything, by our inattention we have further secured them as silent biases in our work, accepting a flattening of complex historical processes and meanings, and fostering a uniformity in the history whose resistances and irregularities we seek to understand. Everywhere invoked, almost regardless of the time, place or culture under investigation, as a category of analysis gender seems almost nowhere critically reassessed with respect to time, place and culture. In a sense, relying on gender as a *category of historical analysis* has stymied our efforts to write a history – or many histories – of gender *as historical process*. In Fields's words, as a category of analysis gender now goes rather haughtily 'masquerading' as historical subjects, 'mingling on equal terms' with historical actors and processes 'and sometimes crowding them out altogether'.

In the chapter that follows, I explore these reservations in greater conceptual and historical detail. I ask what it means to name a particular concept a 'category of analysis' and revisit the process through which particularly American feminist historians came to understand 'gender' in that way. I note some of the broad areas of historical research that have been stymied by this practice – including the study of gender in twentieth-century western Europe and the United States, the very places and times where, if anywhere, such a category should work best. In a more extended examination of my own field of expertise, early American history, I seek both to comment on the interpretative limitations imposed by the current widespread understanding of gender as a category of analysis and to suggest alternative ways of understanding the history of gender in this place and period. Finally, I speculate on new conceptual approaches to gender history, asking for a praxis that refuses gender as a set of more or less universalised assumptions and, instead, always interrogates it anew as a set of relatively open questions applied to a discrete time and place of inquiry.

***

It is useful, I think, to begin that discussion by asking just what a category of analysis *is*. How is it constituted, and what work do we expect it to do?

Categories of analysis are *subjective*, fashioned in the critical minds of historians to help us identify, organise and assess certain kinds of evidence of particular interest to us. Thus, although they may carry an urgency for us that makes them appear both natural and inevitable, categories of analysis are always contemporary, constituted in and marked by the present – our present as historians. (Obviously, we perceive evidence of our categories in our sources, but that perception is itself at least in part an act of constitution.) This temporality is by no means a fatal flaw in the usefulness of categories for historians. Quite the contrary, to suggest that categories of analysis exist *a priori* in the sources and have merely to be revealed (like a Michelangelo sculpture imprisoned in the marble) is to misunderstand the character of history as a discipline and to misrepresent the role of the historian as a maker of meaning.

Nevertheless, the fact of particularity should give us pause. Categories of analysis are not analytically neutral. They are not mere frameworks for organising ideas. They are frameworks that reflect and replicate our own understandings of the world. The moment we cease to acknowledge that aspect of their work and invest any particular category of analysis with the authority of permanence and universality, we cease to be historians and become propagandists of a particular epistemological order.

And yet the very process of categorisation – the naming of an abstracted class – is inherently a simplifying, consolidating and universalising process. These qualities, too, are a part of the usefulness of categories, the whole purpose of which is to bring order and meaning to an otherwise unruly tangle of data and permit us to hold steady the otherwise constant flurry of difference and change. On the other hand, these qualities remove categories from 'real' time and space and locate them in a type of critical utopia. They tend to reduce the mess and variability of lived experience to a few elements that are allowed to stand, falsely, as a substitute for that experience, and to collapse complicated and distinct historical processes into stable, materialised representations. When we use a category of analysis we authorise that process of reduction, with all of its numerous and inevitable concealments and misrepresentations. Of course, merely using the category does not absolutely preclude us from noticing anomalies in our field of analysis but, as the episteme of the analysis, the reason-imbuing framework, a category of analysis can mark whatever is beyond it as irrational and nonsensical, an annoyance to be either fitted into the category or purged as irrelevant.

But the anomalies are just what ought to interest us as historians – not so we can figure a way to force them to conform to the framework, but because they disrupt the common sense of the framework and may signal that something is being missed or suppressed within it. For historians, that 'something' is likely to be local practice, the ground of particular, historical time and space that marks the insufficiency of the category's truth-claims. The anomalies may be quite small (an unexpected combination of symbols) or more glaring (a dramatic exception to the category's rule). They may turn out to be constitutive of the category, in the sense that the plausibility of any category of analysis resides in part on its capacity to exclude. Often, however, irregularities point to more fundamental problems in the category itself.

Identifying the practices that are incomprehensible within our framework is hard work – harder the more deeply a category has become ingrained in the practice of the field. A particular category of gender has become the common sense for our work as gender historians. And yet the rewards can be considerable. To paraphrase Pierre Bourdieu, only by a break with the categorical vision, 'which is experienced as a break with ordinary vision', can we begin to bring the anomalies into clearer view.[3]

***

The current 'ordinary' understanding of gender as a category of historical analysis stems from late twentieth-century feminist political mobilisation in Europe and the United States, within which the field of women's history developed as both product and practice.[4] Although early women's historians were far more likely to employ the category 'woman' ('woman's roles' or 'perceptions of woman' or 'myths about woman') than the analytical language of 'gender',[5] most embraced an idea of gender roughly akin to Gayle Rubin's classic early formulation: that 'in every society' there is 'a set of arrangements by which the biological raw material of human sex and procreation (*sex*) is shaped by human, social intervention (*gender*)'.[6] It was the work of feminism to expose those gender systems and redress their injustices to women (later, to men as well as women). In this context, it was the work of *women's historians* to discover and reveal such patterns in the past (including in the ways historians had written about the past), to return women and women's activities to the historical record and to illuminate the ways in which women in the past had attempted to resist sexual oppression in the societies within which they lived.

The distinction between 'sex' and 'gender' remained common in feminist organising and history, but the framework was not without its critics, especially among theorists who questioned whether even physical bodies were not bearers of purely socially constructed meanings. However, in part because the field of women's history originated in the methods of social history, in part because early women's history did not seriously interrogate bodies as a historical subject, most early women's historians did not directly confront the dilemmas of the sex/gender distinction, which continued to inform the assumptions of their work. The period from the late 1960s to the mid-1980s certainly saw a lot of theorising about 'gender' among women's historians, but the emphasis was not on problematising the term 'gender' itself so much as it was on problematising the relation of gender to other categories, particularly class and patriarchy.[7] In many ways potentially very useful, most efforts of this sort continued to conceptual gender, class and other social processes as conceptually distinct, making it difficult to capture the complexity and particularity of their unified processes in a given historical circumstance. In the absence of a constitutively 'raced' concept of gender, for example, gender always reflected the racial systems of western European culture and reverted to the implicitly white position.

By the 1980s, it was becoming more difficult for women's historians to avoid re-evaluating the way they used the concept 'gender'. Although the fuller investigation of these points would follow in theorising 'intersectionality' and in the studies of gender and colonialism of the 1990s, scholars of

race and slavery in Europe and the Americas were vigorous in pointing out
that the bodies of women of colour had been socially constructed to meet
the interests of Europeans since the first colonial contacts.[8] 'Stand point'
theory, which questioned the adequacy of generalised and abstracted categories for capturing the distinctive processes of forms of oppression and
privilege in a woman's experience, was one response to these criticisms of
mainstream feminist analysis.[9]

Several additional circumstances specific to the academy in the 1980s
gave urgency to the quest for a more deeply theorised concept of gender
in the field of women's history. The field was thriving. By the 1980s,
it supported influential journals in the United States and Europe, and
works in women's history were beginning to appear on the lists of prominent publishers and in prominent general historical journals. The sheer
volume of production seemed to require some greater consistency of
terms. In the academy, the legitimacy of the field of women's history
and of women's historians was under almost constant attack. In particular, women's history was dismissed as narrow, over-specialised and
immaterial to the truly important matter of history (framed in seemingly neutral terms as politics, war and so forth, but more accurately
defined as the actions of males) and women's historians were accused
of trying to fashion their own personal frustrations into a respected academic field. A more unified concept of gender, detached from the heat
of activism and justified instead as one of the fundamental organising categories of history, might provide legitimacy for the field and its
practitioners.

Here entered the matter of the 'category of analysis'. If gender could be
argued to be a key field of experience for both men and women – for *all*
people – then one might posit gender as a subject of universal relevance.
This was the political context for Joan Wallach Scott's splendid essay,
'Gender: A Useful Category of Historical Analysis', which opened the
December 1986 issue of the *American Historical Review*, a commanding
placement in a flagship journal of the profession. As Scott noted, 'The
proliferation of case studies in women's history seems to call for some
synthesizing perspective' and 'the discrepancy between the high quality
of recent work in women's history and the continuing marginal status of
the field as a whole . . . points up the limits of descriptive approaches that
do not address dominant disciplinary concepts . . . in terms that can shake
their power and perhaps transform them'.[10]

Scott's broad purpose was to examine the implications of feminists'
growing tendency 'to use "gender" as a way of referring to the social organization of the relationship between the sexes', and to offer a 'useable
theoretical formulation' of gender as a category of historical analysis. She
devoted the first half of the essay to an assessment of the main schools of

feminist theorising in the 1960s and 1970s – all of which seemed to her 'limited at best because they tend to contain reductive or overly simple generalizations that undercut not only history's disciplinary sense of the complexity of social causation but also feminist commitments to analyses that will lead to change'.[11] Patriarchal theory claimed universal primacy for gender as an analytical category (with little attention to its relationship to other oppressions) and assumed 'a consistent or inherent meaning' for the physical differences between males and females; it rendered history 'in a sense, epiphenomenal, providing endless variations on the unchanging theme of a fixed gender inequality'.[12] Marxist theories suffered from something of the opposite problem: they had trouble formulating any independent analytical status for gender at all. Everything was 'the by-product of changing economic structures'.[13] Although her specific criticisms of different schools of psychoanalytic theory varied, Scott found in all of them 'the tendency to reify subjectively originating antagonism between males and females' and 'to universalize the categories and relationship of male and female'.[14] The ability of the field to define its own boundaries and at the same time to challenge 'non-feminist historians' depended on 'gender as an analytic category'.[15] The challenge was to formulate a concept of gender that could be used as an independent category of analysis, yet rejected 'the fixing of the binary opposition of male and female as the only possible relationship and as a permanent aspect of the human condition'.[16]

The category Scott herself offered did not resolve these issues, however. Although much of the article was devoted to the inadequacies of specific social scientific methodologies for the historical study of gender, Scott did not reject the social science model per se. Finding that gender theorising 'is often not done precisely or systematically',[17] she fashioned her definition on the model of a scientific claim, with the implications of neutrality and universality implied by that form: gender had two parts and four subparts, identifiable and structurally consistent (although with some operational variation).[18]

Far from dislodging the binary, the first part of the definition restated it: 'gender is a constitutive element of social relationships based on perceived differences between the sexes'.[19] This approach complicated the 'sex/gender distinction' by deflecting analysis from the *naturalised* body to the *perceived* body, but this was a deflection, not a displacement, for perception now became the real subject. If perception is the ground of politics and if people *perceive* male and female bodies as gendered in a binary opposition (which seems to be what Scott meant when she paraphrased Bourdieu to the effect that 'established as an objective set of references, concepts of gender structure perception and the concrete and symbolic organization of all social life'),[20] then we are left once again with a concept of gender as a natural oppositional binary: gender is as much hard-wired in the human psyche as Freud would have had it hard-wired in the human anatomy. Scott did offer a theory of variability. The four subparts to her first proposition (culturally available symbols, normative concepts that interpret those symbols, polities and social institutions, and organisations that structure these normative concepts in daily life and subjective identity) operate simultaneously but with changing and culturally distinct intensities.[21] None of them, however, altered the fundamental binary structure of gender itself. Gender history would be the story of their complex and altering interplay but these would be variations within an enduring oppositional configuration of gender.

Scott's second proposition provided that 'gender is a primary way of signifying relations of power'. As became clear in her discussion of this proposition, Scott's approach was marked by a twentieth-century, western conception of the nature of power, associated especially with the work of Michel Foucault and the Frankfurt school. Power, in this formulation, is by definition a process of creating advantage – the 'differential control over or access to material and symbolic resources' – with the goal of exercising dominion.[22] (What game theorists call a 'Pareto improvement', a deployment of power that benefits one site without disadvantaging others, is largely unthinkable within this framework.) Foucauldian power is also often insinuative in its mechanics, operating through socially dispersed forms of interiorised self-discipline that are fundamentally western European and bourgeois. Within this frame, claims to freedom are illusory and in fact serve to entrench a totalising regime. This approach to power had important implications for Scott's model of gender: it further secured a binary, oppositional framework for thinking about matters of male and female, and it virtually ruled out (as naïve) distinctions between male and female that might not be about this kind of differentialising power. Within this category, it is difficult to imagine distinctions between males and females that are not invidious to one or the other group, and thus correspondingly difficult to conceive of distinctions that do not register as primary axes for allocating authority.

One way of reading this definition of gender as a category of analysis is, of course that, if the perceptions of male and female bodies in a given historical circumstance are *not* perceptions of binary difference and/or do not function as vehicles of domination, then the process under study is *not* gender. I'll return to this later. Let me just note here that such a definition would relegate cultures not characterised by the oppositional binary to a strange negative historical and intellectual space, as *the non-gendered Other* – the absence of a specific western gender formation adding to their strangeness rather than raising questions of the adequacy of the category.

Powerful and timely, 'Gender: A Useful Category of Historical Analysis' was soon being cited everywhere, albeit often without the critical reading the essay deserved. Scott herself returned to these matters in several essays – perhaps most importantly in 'Some More Reflections on Gender and Politics' (1999). Here, Scott recognised the persisting problems in gender historians' theorising of gender as a category, and, indeed, seemed to back away from some of the categorical claims of the first essay. She noted the 'universalizing impulses of both feminism . . . and social science and the tendency to treat "national and/or cultural differences . . . as second-order phenomena" to an assumed "self-evident . . . fundamental difference of 'women' from 'men'"'. Scott explicitly rejected analyses that employ gender to mean 'a set of fixed oppositional categories, male and female'. And yet, in its emphasis on investigating 'how sexual difference is constituted by politics (how, to put it another way, masculinity is secured by attributing its antithesis to femininity and in what terms)', the essay seems to restate just such a configuration of gender. Perhaps for this reason, 'Reflections' seems not to have provoked the 'critical reassessment, if not revision and reconceptualisation, of the terms that have been most used in our analysis', as Scott hoped.[23]

***

Still, that reassessment has been ongoing. A number of non-western historians argue that not all societies have been organised on the basis of gender, at least not 'gender' in the way implied in the work of most western historians. Among the most outspoken scholars on the subject is African historian Oyèrónké Oyewùmí. Oyewùmí argues that western work on gender has been, and continues to be, preoccupied with the oppositionally-sexed body, which – as literal body or as representation – inhabits the category 'gender' and invests it with a rigid corporeal determinism. But this valorisation of the body is not universal. On the contrary, it is historically specific to European cultures and western history. Here Oyewùmí takes the step clearly implied in social constructionist thought, but seldom taken by social constructionists:

> If gender is socially constructed, then gender cannot behave in the same way across time and space. If gender is a social construction, then we must examine the various cultural/architectural sites where it was constructed, and we must acknowledge that variously located actors (aggregates, groups, interested parties) were part of the construction. We must further acknowledge that if gender is a social construction, then there was a specific time (in different cultural/architectural sites) when it was 'constructed' and therefore a time before which it was not. Thus, gender, being a social construction, is also a historical and cultural phenomenon.

'Consequently', she concludes, 'it is logical to assume that in some societies, gender construction need not have existed at all'.[24]

Wonderfully provocative as this conclusion is, it seems to me both to exceed Oyewùmí's evidence and to obscure her most interesting argument, which (to my mind) is *not* that no social distinctions between men and women existed in pre-colonial Yorubaland (they plainly did, in the division of labour as well as in symbols for social roles, for example), but that gender construction *as defined by the current category of analysis in the form employed by so many western historians* did not occur. Systems of distinction other than male/female were also important – at times more important than the male/female dyad – as primary symbol sets for articulating relations of superior and inferior power. Conversely, male/female distinctions did not always function invidiously towards women. What Oyewùmí is refusing is the claim of a western European category to universalism – in a sense, the right of European and north American scholars to define the 'gender' for African women's history. For her, a society in which 'gender' was never constructed means a society in which perceptions of sexual difference are 'not always enlisted as the basis for social classification'. In pre-colonial Yoruba culture, according to Oyewùmí, the *primary* principle of social classification was seniority, which, she emphasises, 'was based on chronological age . . . [and] did not denote gender'.[25] This does not mean that Yoruba speakers were unaware of differences between male and female bodies, or that Yoruban culture did not embrace tropes of male and female bodies, or that pre-colonial Yoruba people lived in a golden age in which power was never deployed brutally and for purposes of domination and never articulated through seemingly natural systems of discourse. It means simply that perceptions and representations of sexual opposition were not presumptively a *primary* field for the articulation of *that* particular power. That is to say, she makes an important case that the category 'gender' as understood by western feminist historians on the basis of their own local histories cannot claim universal relevance.

Oyewùmí was not the first to raise this challenge. In an important article written just as Scott's category was seizing the imaginations of western feminists, Ifi Amadiume criticised the ethnocentricity of early feminist anthropologists (and, by extension, feminists scholars generally) to whom 'the universal social and cultural inferiority of women was a foregone conclusion' as a result of their failure to recognise that 'the domestic/public dichotomy which led them to th[is] conclusion . . . was a feature of their own particular class and culture'. In her own work on Igbo culture in eastern Nigeria, Amadiume did identify a gender system through which numerous mythic, social and culture distinctions were articulated according to a binary of masculine and feminine. But she also found that in this binary, the attributes associated with females did not necessarily lead to the economic or political subordination of the social group women, and that various social institutions, especially those of 'male daughters' and 'female husbands', permitted individual females officially to enter and enjoy the privileges of social positions gendered masculine.[26]

In the early 1990s, Barry S. Hewlett made a similar argument, focusing on misunderstandings of the roles of males as a result of universalising western analytical categories. In his work among the central African Aka, Hewlett found father–infant relations that utterly defied the gender expectations of Western theory – fathers who 'spend 47 per cent of their day holding or within an arm's reach of their infants', who are gentle, soothing to their infants, and 'more likely than [the] mother to hug and kiss the infant'.[27]

More recently, Iranian historian Afsaneh Najmabadi returned to the subject of the ethnocentricity of gender as a category of historical analysis. Like Oyewùmí, Najmabadi worried about the 'largely Anglo-American history of gender as a named category' and about the implications of that history for the use of gender as a category of historical analysis 'beyond the Americas and the modern'. She identified as a particular concern the persistence, in the seemingly neutral category, of a gender binary 'derived from Western psycho-behavioural categories of gender-role determination', noting her own struggle with the concept in writing what became *Women with Mustaches and Men without Beards: Gender and Sexual Anxieties of Iranian Modernity*:

> The project had begun as a project on the work of gender for the formation of Iranian modernity on iconic, narrative, metaphoric, and social levels. But there was another labor of gender that I had overlooked: the production of gender itself as a binary, man/woman – itself an effect of a paradigmatic shift in categories... from a view in which all genders were defined in relation to adult manhood to a view in which woman and man became opposite and complementary, to the exclusion of other categories that would not fit.

Her first 'labor of gender' was to break free of the modern, western category, and of the narrative implicit in that category, in order to tell another story (suppressed within the western model) of gender as it had existed and functioned in non-modern Iran. That task required acknowledging the 'gender binary' as a product of a particular historical moment, not as a universal category. It meant fundamentally 'renegotiat[ing] *meanings* of gender and sexuality as well as their *analytic utility*' outside of the epistemological confines of the west.[28]

***

But the problems of employing an oppositionally binary concept of gender as a category of historical analysis are not confined to the study of non-western cultures and they are not resolved simply by acknowledging differences between those societies and an equally problematic category, 'the west' (or one of its variants). That route tends to reify the current largely Anglo-American category as the normative discourse of 'gender' (from which other cultures are deviations). Equally important, it conceals the contemporaneous variability and historical transformations of gender discourses *within* Europe and the United States, or, at best, subordinates those alternatives within a narrative that assumes the eventual triumph of the binary as we presume it to have existed in the late twentieth century. An overview of the scholarship on the history of women and gender in the United States illustrates the extent and costs of that approach.

The nineteenth century is a useful place to begin since it was here that the field of United States women's history largely began, with classics like Carroll Smith Rosenberg's 'Beauty, the Beast and the Militant Woman', Kathryn Kish Sklar's *Catharine Beecher* and Nancy Cott's *The Bonds of Womanhood*.[29] These scholars were drawn to antebellum America, at least in part, in search of the historical roots of the forms of oppression they identified in their own late twentieth-century world and the origins of 'feminism', the name given to resistance to that particular form of oppression. What they found was the 'cult of domesticity'. As Nancy Cott observed in 1977, 'The ideology of domesticity may seem to be contradicted functionally and abstractly by feminism, but historically – as they emerged in the United States – the latter depended upon the former'.[30] There was nothing unusual about this connection between contemporary life and historical inquiry. Like all historians, early women's historians selected for study subjects that could be associated with matters of current interest. In this case, they focused on elements of social and intellectual life in the early American republic that seemed identifiable in terms of feminist concerns: questions of familial, political, legal and economic subordination of women as a group to men as a group and of the discursive conventions that articulated and justified that subordination. In the process, of course, they defined women's history as the history of subjects identifiable through the lens of the feminist critique, which assumed an oppositional binary of male/female as its primary trope.

This inclination to notice the past through the epistemology of late twentieth-century feminism – that is, to assign importance to evidence and events that could be understood as either oppressive or liberatory within the paradigm of the gender binary – continued to organise the field of women's history as historians reached forward to the late nineteenth and twentieth centuries and back into the revolutionary and then the colonial period. Until recently, scholarship on the late nineteenth and early twentieth centuries has been almost wholly preoccupied with the creation of the conditions that gave rise to late twentieth-century feminism and has pursued two strands in particular: the growing hegemony of the 'ideology of domesticity' even as women's educational opportunities and labour force participation and education expanded; and the responses of women to the constraints (and occasionally the possibilities) of that binary. Key themes included maternalism, reproductive control, aspects of suffrage movement, legal discrimination, sexism in the labour force and heterosexual family life (and the same-sex friendships that defied heterosexual domestic patterns). Understanding their work as 'part of a larger movement to reassess and redefine the position of women in the contemporary world', early American women's and gender historians showed a similar preoccupation with 'domesticity' – in this case, its origins and antecedents. Key themes here included 'patriarchal' household hierarchies, early gender divisions of labour and the exclusion of females from the franchise and public life.[31] Indeed, by the late 1980s, 'separate spheres' had become such a pervasive analytical rubric for writing American women's history that some scholars began to voice concern. In an important essay on 'the rhetoric of women's history', Kerber acknowledged the framework's initial importance as 'a strategy that enabled historians to move the history of women out of the realm of the trivial and anecdotal and into the realm of analytical social history'. But she also cautioned women's historians that 'to continue to use the language of separate spheres is to deny the reciprocity between gender and society, and to impose a static model on dynamic relationships'.[32]

Through the late 1980s and 1990s, in the wake of both Kerber's and Scott's interventions, historians of early American women broadened their attention from merely confirming the existence of the binary to examining the ways in which that structure was marshalled and deployed in specific changing discursive and social environments. The result was a literature that began to articulate the complex interactions of gender with other social formations and cultural discourses – most notably 'class', 'race' and region. These studies (which included, for example, Sarah Deutsch's *No Separate Refuge*, Peggy Pascoe's *Relations of Rescue* and Stephanie McCurry's *Masters of Small Worlds*) introduced a critical geographical and cultural breadth to the field and set a new standard for historical specificity in the changing manifestations of gender in the history of the United States.[33] At the same time, they did not fundamentally question the character of the category of gender itself. Rather, they accepted the oppositional binary as the neutral categorical formation within which specific cultures might impose specific variations. Broadening the array of categories at play was an important revision that allowed for the investigation of more numerous social and cultural discourse variations, but doing this without questioning the categories themselves foreshortened the possibilities for recognising genuinely alternative formations. In terms of the history of women and gender, this enabled a narrative that was at once vastly more nuanced and complex and yet fundamentally unchanged. Manifestations of 'gender' altered over time and space, but 'gender' itself did not.

The very familiar history of the woman suffrage movement offers a striking double-layered case in point of the problems of imposing the separate spheres model on American women's history – double-layered because, as Lisa Tetrault points out, the model was first imposed by the suffragists and then sustained by feminist historians. In *The History of Woman Suffrage*, Susan B. Anthony, along with Elizabeth Cady Stanton and Matilda Gage, constructed a narrative of the movement as a struggle against 'separate spheres' – that is, against a gender binary so rigid and so privileging of men and penalising of women that it far superseded other societal inequities in its pervasiveness and harm. To a striking extent, women's historians of the United States have echoed that view in their own work, criticising women's rights advocates who allied with Republicans in supporting freedmen's rights as either naïve or treacherous and largely isolating the narrative of women's suffrage from the rest of post-Reconstruction United States.[34] Race scholars, most notably Rosalyn Terborg-Penn, have long objected to this approach as concealing the strategic and substantive importance of racial consciousness to the way white suffragists understood both their oppression and its redress.[35] In her recent work, Tetrault argues that this narrative also concealed a much more varied and less rigid gender system in the late nineteenth century, strategically exaggerating both the polarisation of the struggle and the breadth of the opposition. Women had long voted in municipal and some state elections. While many state and national legislators opposed expanding the female suffrage, many common people did not; active supporters and friendly listeners – including quite a few men – flocked to suffragists' lyceum lectures, which furnished some of the suffragists with both celebrity and a fairly nice income.[36] The binary may not have been either so fully invidious or so broadly entrenched as many of us have supposed.

Other turn-of-the-century studies raise similar possibilities, although they have stopped short of explicitly contesting the category. In her study of early twentieth-century female labour activism, Nan Enstad emphasised the importance of breaking up consolidated and rigid categories of identity. She argued instead for an analytical language of 'subjectivity': 'Subjectivity is . . . related to the concepts "self" and "identity", with a crucial distinction: subjectivity emphasizes a process of becoming that is never completed. It is based on the principle that who one is is neither essential nor fixed, but is continually shaped and reshaped in human social exchange'. As she demonstrated, the growth of popular culture at the turn of the century – exactly at the moment when the woman suffrage movement was reaching its broadest appeal – provided labouring young women with both material and social forms for rearticulating 'the female'. The representation of 'the lady' that so inspired labouring women, for example, was not a mere pale and envy-riven reflection of 'the lady' of elite discourse: it was its own gender marker, signally a distinct gendering process. For the same period, George Chauncey identified a varied and complex array of sexualities among urban males, all of which hint at the existence of multiple understandings of gender – including, for example, the 'pansy', the 'Nance', the 'fairie' and the 'buttercup' as well as 'he-men' and 'she-men'. Even professional sexologists of the period analysed the genders into three sexualities: male, female and intermediate. This evidence of non-homonormativity, to use Lisa Duggan's term, points to an absence of clear heteronormativity in both practice and identity at the turn of the century – that is, to the absence of a controlling oppositional binary. Other works, such as Regina Kunzel's *Fallen Women, Problem Girls: Unmarried Mothers and the Professionalization of Social Work, 1890–1945*, have traced this more complex understanding of sexuality deeper into the twentieth century. Although some historians distinguish 'sexuality' from 'gender', identifying a gender binary as foundational and sexual varieties as epiphenomenal, work like Enstad's, Chauncey's and Kunzel's invite us to flip that framework – to take variation as the rule and to understand categories with 'normative' claims as but instances of the epiphenomena of that variation.[37]

The implications of this shift are too numerous to discuss fully here, but one deserves especial note. Understanding the history of gender in late nineteenth- and early twentieth-century America as a far more complex discourse than the binary category recognises also allows us as historians to comprehend the 'feminist' politics of the late twentieth century far more broadly and complexly. As anyone who lived through that period knows, 'feminist' politics were never only about male and female. They were always also about race, about class, about sexuality, about age and region and religion and nationality. Moreover, 'feminism' was about these discourses constitutively, not merely additively. Perhaps abandoning a category of gender that privileges the oppositional male/female binary in the late nineteenth and early twentieth centuries will enable us to write a more nuanced and useful history of late twentieth-century feminism as a complexly consolidated historical moment. Perhaps we will even come to consider that the male/female binary was an epiphenomenon.

∗∗∗

The failure to question the category 'gender' has also continued to shape the way we organise and understand *early* American history. Although a number of recent studies seem to suggest the existence of gender discourses that were not rigidly binary or oppositional, women's and gender historians seldom take up those possibilities in a serious way, viewing them instead as preludes to the coming of the binary or as proto-binaries themselves.

Reflecting the analytical dominance of the category, most studies of seventeenth- and eighteenth-century settler women frame those women's lives in terms of their roles as wives and mothers (in contrast to a man's roles as husband and father) on the assumption that all other arenas of their lives were subsumed to these two. To be sure, 'wife' was a clearly marked legal status with important meanings and implications for colonial white women, but the accumulating studies of settler women suggest far more complex social/economic identities – including those of head of household, family governor, supervisor of servants and slave-owner, agriculturalist, manufacturer and trader, not to mention sometimes business-owner, lawyer, councillor, author and scientist.[38] Although some women's historians acknowledge that the role of deputy husband 'reinforced a certain elasticity in pre-modern notions of gender', most still subordinate these roles under those of 'wife' and 'mother' contained within a 'domestic' arena.[39] If 'domestic' means 'household' (a term I prefer as freer of the discourse of gender spheres), then such a description is probably accurate. But if those 'domestic' boundaries are to include all of a given women's daily possibilities, then they must be drawn so generously as to be virtually meaningless analytically. Mary Beth Norton has suggested that, to make sense of this, we may need to question the assumption that gender was always primary in colonial women's lives. She argues that the role of the 'deputy husband' – or 'fictive widow' – points to the potential primacy of status, not gender, as a discourse of power in the seventeenth century. Especially in elite families, Norton argued, a wife might act aggressively to protect her husband's interests as she saw them, even when he saw them differently. Most records of this practice suggest that a woman might pay dearly for such independence, but such documents – the trials of Ann Hibbens, Anne Eaton and others – condemn the egregiousness of particular cases rather than the practice itself.[40]

A number of recent works have, like Norton's, discovered important variations in the historical meaning of gender – indeed, have concluded that the imposition of a particular category of 'gender' was integral to the process of colonisation. Unlike Norton's analysis, however, most of these have backed away from questioning the category 'gender', instead subordinating those exceptions to an overall trajectory of the coming of the 'modern' trope; they become, literally, exceptions that prove the historical norm of the emerging oppositional binary, rather than possible signs of historically discrete alternatives to that binary. Studies in virtually every area of social and cultural life – law, politics, family life, the economy, religion – have found striking and consistent transgressions of the presumed all-encompassing male/female binary in settler culture.[41]

Some of the most exciting work has been in the relatively new area of early American sexuality, where the concept of the relentlessly oppositional binary among European immigrants is beginning to receive concerted critical attention. At least since Edmund Morgan put the lie to the stereotype of Puritan sexual prudery, early American historians have documented the robust and varied sexual lives (and fantasies) of the Euro-peans who came to the Americas.[42] And what a lot of them there were! Men with vaginas, women with Devil's teats, cross-dressers, sodomites, pas-sionate same-sex lovers, devotees of bestiality, child-sex, sadomasochism and, perhaps least common, celibates.[43] Until recently, historians of Amer-ican sexuality have tended either to discount the rather extravagant sexual practices of the colonists as exotic exceptions or to treat them as discrete acts that did not really measure up to an interiorised 'sexuality' at all and certainly did not challenge the rigid binary that held 'gender' in its iron grip. Even in more recent work, this proliferation of practices is generally marshalled to underscore the later constriction of sexual/gender discourse rather than to point to the historical discreteness of particular formations.

In her study of sexuality in revolutionary-era Philadelphia, for example, Clare Lyons suggested that 'serial non-marital monogamy, self-divorce, and boisterous, bawdy, and public heterosocial sex play' as well as interra-cial sexual relationships constituted continuous identities, acknowledged by both the individuals and the communities within which they lived. This seems very much an argument for a historically discrete polymorphous discourse of gender, later replaced by a binary one – and Lyons made this claim in her introduction:

> Before the eighteenth century gender . . . was one among many ordained and fixed hierarchical relationships that ordered society . . . The Enlightenment undermined the belief in such natural hierarchies and upset the basis for woman's subordination to man. A new conceptual framework would be necessary if the gender hierarchy was to be maintained. The response, developed over the eighteenth century, was to reconceptualize gender by positing radical differences between men and women and fixing them in the anatomical body. The creation of binary opposite gendered sexualities was at the core of this new gender system.[44]

As promising as this analysis is, however, it actually does little to dislodge the binary as a transhistorical formation. The seemingly polymorphous early sexualities are in fact all constituted through the male/female oppo-sitional binary. The new sexual regime only narrows and disciplines their expression as an aspect of 'domesticity'.[45]

A related assumption of the colonial primacy of the twentieth-century Anglo-European category played through Kathleen Brown's path-breaking study of the double helix of race and gender in the historical construction of slavery in *Good Wives, Nasty Wenches, and Anxious Patriarchs*. The book began with a relatively open-ended definition of gender simply as 'his-torically specific discourses, social roles, and identities defining sexual difference and frequently deployed for the purposes of social and political order'. Analytically, Brown left those roles, identities, relationships and purposes unspecified, not presuming (at least, not theorising) that gender would function the same way in different societies. On the contrary, she was at pains to situate the settlers' concept of gender historically in early modern England and to underscore its instability there. 'Contact', she argued, was, among other dynamics, a 'gender frontier' – a struggle articulated through distinct systems of representations associated with male and female bodies. Nevertheless, the study focused on the colonists and the concept of gender they would eventually fashion through contact – a concept that moved relentlessly towards the male/female binary and early forms of southern 'domesticity'. Perhaps as a result, Euro-American perspectives (from the early modern period but also from the late twentieth century) seemed to spill over into assumptions about other cultures: Brown's characterisation of the Powhatan Indian confederacy as 'patriarchal' seemed oddly Euro-centric and she paid little attention to the existence or resilience of discrete system(s) of gender carried to the Americas by enslaved Africans.

African American women and gender historians have long deplored the tendency of the field to understand gender largely in Anglo-European terms. As early as 1971, Joyce Ladner argued that white feminists were ignoring the particularity of African American women's history. She focused particularly on ways in which west African cultures articulated concepts of gender quite different from the concepts that characterised early modern England – distinctions between males and females that did not necessary constitute a subordination either of *female persons* or of all things symbolically 'feminised'.[46] This situation has in some ways improved over the intervening forty years, especially with the publication of Jennifer Morgan's *Laboring Women*, which begins the project of integrating west African gender systems into the history of enslaved African women in America.[47] As Stephanie Camp observed in a celebration of the twentieth anniversary of the publication of Deborah Gray White's *Ar' n't I a Woman*, the idea of 'the entangled nature of race and gender in US history . . . is a commonplace one now'. But as Camp immediately noted, 'we still have a great deal to learn about how exactly that entanglement played out on the ground'.[48] Perhaps the discrepancy arises from the limitations of our category. Perhaps the 'entanglement . . . on the ground', messy and changing and offering up a variety of understandings of both race and gender, simply defies the singular category through which we insist on trying to analyse it. The work of such prominent scholars as Deborah Gray White, Evelyn Brooks Higginbotham, Elsa Barkley Brown and Martha Jones, to name only a few, describe African American communities in which discourses of gender are certainly in extremely complex historical conversation with the discourses of bourgeois white society and yet remain significantly distinct from those discourses.[49] These are not mere minority variants of a normative (white bourgeois) category. They – like the categories judged normative – are evidence of the multiple and variable meanings of gender that emerge as indicators of historically specific political and cultural moments.

Like recent work in African American history, recent work in Native American history offers some promising new approaches to gender. Most early studies of Native American women, for example, were implicitly or explicitly organised according to an Anglo-European model of gender. These studies set out to assess the relative power of males and females in Native cultures (often with a view to criticising the treatment of women in Euro-American societies). Most of the work focused on the gender division of labour (Was women's work important? Did women control their own work? Did their work bring them prestige and power within the community?) and/or on the gender division of authority in community decision-making (Did women speak in council? Did women have ways of vetoing council decisions? Were women ever principal chiefs?). Related to these studies were two other streams of inquiry. One examined the roles of women as cultural mediators in early European–Native contacts. The other focused on cases where the Anglo-European category appeared to be challenged in what some scholars referred to as 'third' and 'fourth' genders: apparently male-sex persons who performed 'female' social and economic roles, or female-sexed persons who performed 'male' social and economic roles. Whatever their particular concerns, however, virtually all of these studies assumed in indigenous societies a stable sexual opposition functioning independently as a primary signifier of power – a system of gender, in other words, modelled closely on the presumed European system.[50]

Applying a twentieth-century category of gender certainly produced something recognisable to *western* eyes, but probably not much that pre-contact Native Americans would have found familiar.[51] Newer work in the field has begun to modify both the categorical assumptions and the findings of the first studies, with particular attention to the character and status of the sexual binary. In the process, these works have discovered the ways in which the analytical assumption of gender as an oppositional binary replicates the original European colonial discourse of indigenous gender.[52] As Nancy Shoemaker points out, a male/female binary certainly existed in Native American cultures, but it was not more salient than a host of other binaries, including war/peace, young/old, plant/animal and many others, and probably was not separable from them. Under some circumstances, these lined up in ways reminiscent of the modern European model – for example, 'peace' and 'female' tended to have a close 'conceptual association'. In fact, however, the field of signification they created was quite different from that predicted by the European model. For example, Cherokees described the town of Chota as a 'mother' town of 'peace' and 'refuge' – a cluster of traits that would immediately signal female domesticity and seclusion from political engagement in the modern European discourse. For the Cherokees, these qualities described 'the capital center of Cherokee politics in the mid-18th century'.[53]

This disruption of the western binary also disrupts accompanying assumptions about the kind of power signified through gender. Not signalling female inferiority, the cluster 'female/peace/refuge' also did not stably associate femaleness and vulnerability or powerlessness. The principal leaders who sat in council at Chota were males, the people they listened to were both males and females, old and young, and the power they held arose from their ability to demonstrate obedience to and respect for those people, not to dominate them. Perhaps this way of understanding gender in native cultures can move us toward a deeper understanding of 'two-spirited' people. Rather than anomalies to be somehow forced into an oppositional model by a rather mechanical reversal, we might want to consider figures of men/women and women/men as indications of the fluidity of the sexual binary – in its constant interplay with other binaries – as a signifier in Native cultures. That is to say, a 'young/active/*female*/war' cluster might not signify a gender-denominated category (in contrast to a 'young/active/*male*/ war' cluster),[54] but might instead mark a different sort of category in which *gender is subordinate* – a warrior whose powers transcend the body, for example, or whose power is made the more terrifying by the mingling of menstrual blood and the blood of battle.

Gunlög Fur makes a related argument in an essay that is at least in part directed towards historians of native America who reject gender in any form as a useful category for analysing Native American history. Indeed, Fur retains many of the assertions about gender contained in current understandings of gender as a category of analysis. But with a critical distinction: she argues that maleness and femaleness worked very differently as fields of representation in Native than in European cultures. She encourages us to look for salient bodied categories other than 'male' and 'female' in Native societies, to examine closely Native understandings of the relationships between corporeal bodies and the spirit world and to be cautious about reading the apparent absence of females from accounts as a statement about status or instrumentality.[55] For Native cultures, 'shape-shifting' – the ongoing and fluid mingling of categories – may prove a far more useful metaphor of gender than the narrower and more rigid location on a binary; a concept of power that embraces consensus, obedience, deference, silence and even invisibility may prove more useful than one limited to dominion and control.

These works, then, would seem to illuminate very different ways of defining gender – from social relations in which a male/female binary may be present and important, but not necessarily primary, to a system of gender in which multiple other axes of identity frequently modify and sometimes entirely overwhelm the binary and in which the binary, even when present, cannot be reduced to oppositionally sexed bodies. Clearly *some* sort of category of gender was present in pre- and early contact Native American cultures, but equally clearly it was not the category that so dominates current gender and women's history.

That did not make gender less significant. Among the most path-breaking insights to arise from new work on Native American history is the importance of indigenous concepts of gender in structuring and controlling early contacts with Europeans. In some respects echoing earlier studies of Native women as cultural mediators, this work is a part of the more recent emphasis on a 'middle ground' of power between Native and European cultures, with attention to the role of gender.[56] Juliana Barr, for example, argues that Native communities in the south-west borderlands were able to compel early Spanish arrivals to accept their kinship systems as principles of contact and trade.[57]

The work of beginning to theorise earlier and different models of gender requires a careful attention to historical process and to the specificity of cultural systems. However much it had in common with Britain and France, the United States was constituted from colonies. And not just any type of colonies, but *settler* colonies. Both the French in France and the British in Britain struggled with the implications of their own slave holding, but the home nations did not intermingle extensively sexually or culturally with the people they considered 'primitive'. The French in France and the Britons in Britain could with some plausibility claim that their bodies – and their cultures – were 'pure', at least in terms of African and indigenous American heritage.[58] Not so for white American settlers. They made their homes in a world recognised as 'savage' by their parent cultures and they imported hundreds of thousands of additional 'savages' to be their slaves. They traded, played, cohabited and bore children with both Native Americans and African people (even as they inflicted long regimes of brutality on both groups) and their cultures were shaped by those contacts. As the careful (if contradictory) legislating on slave descent suggests, the official delineation of cultures through bodies was of critical practical as well as symbolic importance to white Americans precisely because both their cultures and their bodies were no longer distinct from those of Native and African Americans.

This was the stuff of very complex self-fashioning, drenched in haughtiness and denial. For white Americans, the embrace of a modern trope of gender was part of a historically situated discourse that allowed them to divide the world into natural oppositions that bolstered their own brutal domination even as it redeemed them as the fulfilment of an idealised civilisation.[59] Herein may lie the answer to Lyons's question and the explanation for why the American Revolution and the founding of the republic appear to loom so large in the history of gender and sexuality in America. Much more than political independence from Britain was at stake in this act of national invention. The attempted construction of the authoritative state may have required a ritual (if not in fact effective) expunging of the assortment of gender discourses and sexualities that characterised the British North American colonies by the late eighteenth century as one of the technologies for articulating the national body and securing the hierarchies of individual bodies within the nation.

But these, or other, conclusions can become available to us only as we begin to theorise gender in early America on its own terms, and not simply as a less developed variant of a late twentieth-century American model. Of course, trying to identify a historically-grounded understanding of the meaning of relationships between the male and the female for early America will carry with it exactly the same potential snares as the use of a concept grounded in a later (and different) culture: the structural concealments, the tendency towards oversimplification and generalisation, the temptation to flatten anomalies among cultures for the sake of theoretical clarity. In addition, theorising an early modern process of gendering will require us to avoid the seductions of teleology – of assuming we know where we are going. We will need to recognise varieties of relationships that fell away entirely in the transition to the nineteenth century, as well as those that became reconfigured and/or that re-emerged in new combinations.

The 'exceptions' accumulate like the epicycles of the Ptolemaic universe, until one must ask whether we, like Ptolemy, do not need to change the framework of our assumptions. In searching the seventeenth and eighteenth centuries for roots of the nineteenth-century 'ideology of gender spheres', perhaps we have missed and/or undervalued the distinctiveness of the earlier period. Perhaps we have failed to appreciate a different structuring of the societal and discursive relationship of male and female, more diverse and more fluid, less primary as a performed organisation of power and authority. Perhaps rather than aberrations to a fixed 'gender' core, this diversity was constitutive of normative adult womanhood.

***

So let me return to Barbara Jeanne Fields, with a modest reframing of her critique. Fields complained that categories take on lives of their own. They do not really, of course; they take on the lives we give them. If the category 'gender' has supplanted the historical subjects of our work, and so narrowed and (pre)determined our findings, it is because we have let it. I want to suggest that we quit letting it.

Accomplishing that goal is harder than setting it. Especially in light of 'the largely Anglo-American history of gender as a named category', should we abandon both the category and the concept altogether?[60] Is it possible to prise any part of the concept loose for use in broader and culturally less biased ways? Can we use the term gender at all, at this point, without implying its predilection for an invidious oppositional binary?

On the other hand, have we exhausted the usefulness of asking what sorts of representational systems associated with 'male' and 'female' (if any) exist in a given time and place and the character and operation of those processes if they do exist? I am not convinced that we have. In large part because we have been so blinded by the rigidity of our category, we have yet to develop very nuanced ways to talk about systems that might include the male and the female but *not* in a fixed binary, or *not* in a primary way, or *not* in a differential relation of power. I think such a language is still analytically useful.

But we need to make certain that such an analytical language does not by definition privilege one historical manifestation of gender and thereby implicitly exclude other formations from the conversation. We need to do this, not only because such an exclusive framework leads inevitably towards ahistoricism but also because it implicitly marks any other processes of meaning as *not gender*. Formally or implicitly dividing our studies into the 'gendered' and the 'non-gendered' not only reduces our work once again to a binary, but announces the western concept of gender as the critical heart of our studies, in much the way that 'postcolonial studies' risks keeping western colonialism at the centre of the conversation.[61]

Nor am I inclined to believe that the answer to this particular problem lies in simply shifting from one all-encompassing paradigm to another – for example, from 'gender' to 'sexuality' – without confronting the problems within our current category. Terminology is important, but equally important is our willingness, *in a given historical study*, to interrogate that terminology, to ask why we are using a particular critical construct, what it means to us, from whose experience it derives and what it highlights and what it conceals in our work as historians. We need to problematise the way in which the category (any category) has been historically constructed. In the absence of that critical deliberateness – which often occurs in only the most perfunctory way in historical studies of women/gender, especially as practised in the United States and Europe – a new terminology would carry the same old limitations.

I think the first step towards achieving such deliberateness is to disinvest ourselves and our field from the claim that gender is a *category of analysis* at all, a claim originally made largely as a political statement about the importance of the field. In my view, this claim not only is *not* essential to our project, but actually hinders that work. What I am suggesting here is that we must decide just what history we want to write: the history of a particular definition of gender, treated as if it were abstract and universal, or the historically grounded histories of particular processes of gendering, resulting in distinct cultural meanings with distinct social and cultural formations – gender, that is to say, as cultural process, various and altering over time (even within the modern period and even within western culture).

Understanding that gender is not a single, named process should also enable us to examine more carefully the extent to which and the ways in which gender is a language about power in a given society. In the modern era in western European and North American culture, power has become the language through which we name the creation and maintenance of inequalities, a practice that has impoverished our capacity to name or investigate other forms of human agency, passionate connection and control.

But understanding that gender is not a fixed analytical category is only the first step. It frees us to imagine a sparer and therefore roomier concept of 'gender' – one that captures the essential elements of interest to us without predicating their relationships and meanings – but it does not automatically do the imagining for us. That is the work of our work – our 'labor of gender', to use Najmabadi's expression. That labour requires that we convert gender from a prescription to a series of questions about process, the first of which are: *were* male and female important social/cultural markers for the subjects for our work (individuals, communities or events) and, if so, how were they structured, what valences did they carry and how important were they?

Dispensing with the overarching category might encourage us to set aside the historically unproductive insistence on the primary-ness of gender and focus instead on the complex fabric of processes and meanings that constitute a social or cultural history. We know that 'gender' never exists as a self-sufficient or self-realising category. In the abstract, at least, we know that there is no social subject whose experience is solely constructed through the processes of gender (however we define gender) or whose continuing *sole* identity (experienced or attributed) is gendered. Although the complexity of social processes is seldom the main point of historical gender studies, in fact virtually all of the work on gender to date demonstrates that even an identity as male or female is in constant and inseparable interplay with other processes of status and identity.[62] The tedious ever-presence of the triad 'race, class and gender' in article and book titles and in course descriptions testifies at least to the field's awareness of the analytical limitations of distinct categories (even if its also reflects our inability to transcend these categories very fully).

I suggest that the primaryness of gender in a given situation should be one of our questions, rather than one of our assumptions. In one moment or one era or one social setting, gender may seem to rise to primacy as an expression of social position and positioning, but it is always gender as nested in, mingled with and inseparable from the cluster of other factors socially relevant in a given culture. It is never 'gender' alone. Deploying gender as a category of analysis disguises this process of reciprocal constitution and implies for gender an independent quasi-scientific causal status. I am reminded of Scott's observation on 'history's disciplinary sense of the complexity of social causation'. 'Instead of a search for single origins, we have to conceive of processes so interconnected that they cannot be disentangled . . . In anthropologist Michelle Rosaldo's formulation, we must pursue not universal, general causality but meaningful explanation'.[63] Gender is one set of historical relationships nested within a larger historical cluster of relationships from which it cannot, finally, be meaningfully disentangled.

This was the point of Elsa Barkley Brown's wonderful 1992 essay, 'What Has Happened Here', in which she criticised white feminists' alarm at the efforts of black feminists to emphasise the important racial differences in their experience of gender, comparing that fear of diversity to the classical musician's insistence on perfect order and control in the concert hall. In place of that classic politic, which Brown characterised as linear and silencing, she recommended the aesthetic of jazz – 'nonlinear ways of thinking about the world, of hearing multiple rhythms and thinking music not chaos, ways that challenge the notion that sufficient attention to diversity leads to intellectual chaos, to political vacuum, or to intellectual and political void'.[64] Brown was arguing here, specifically, for a way of conceptualising gender that could recognise its contingency and multiplicity: 'Unfortunately', she reflected, 'it seems to me, few historians are good jazz musicians; most of us write as if our training were in classic music. We require surrounding silence – or the audience, of all the instruments not singled out as the performers in this section, even often of any alternative visions of the composer's. That then makes it particularly problematic for historians when faced with trying to understand difference while holding on to an old score that has in many ways assumed that despite race, class, ethnicity, sexuality, and other differences, at core all women do have the same gender'.[65] This was a political and an analytical position that Brown rejected: 'we have still to recognize that being a woman is, in fact, not extractable from the context in which one is a woman . . . We still have to recognize that all women do not have the same gender'.[66]

As we relinquish the assumption that gender is necessarily primary, it seems to me that we must also abandon our expectation that it will always be binary, a formulation that relies upon the assumption that gender is something we can analyse in and of itself, as an analytical discrete category. Rather than assuming the binary, I suggest we let it emerge from our investigation, if it is present. One strategy here would be to follow the lead of anthropologists and ethnographers who have reframed the concept to permit the identification of 'third', 'fourth', 'fifth' genders, and so on, recognising a 'man/woman' gender or a 'woman/man' gender. Since this approach does not necessarily (or even usually) tie additional genders to reproductive body types (for example, the research on the institution of 'berdache' among Native Americans assumes male and female reproductive bodies), it does offer an opportunity to loosen the association with bodies that haunts the concept 'gender'.[67] On the other hand, the supplementary genders are generally intermediate combinations of the cultural male/female binary. Their addition makes that binary more complicated and less fixed, but does not fundamentally dislodge it.

To my mind, a more satisfactory approach to transcending the tyranny of categorical binaries emerges in recent theories of 'genderqueer-ness', a concept meant to convey a rejection of gender *categorisation* altogether. As the activist group FORGE puts it:

> There are different modes of being genderqueer, and it is an evolving concept. Some believe they are a little of both or feel they have no gender at all. Others believe that gender is a social construct, and choose not to adhere to that construct. Some genderqueers do fit into the stereotypical gender roles expected of their sex, but still reject gender as a social construct. Still other people identify as genderqueer since, though they are cisgendered [a neologism meaning 'not transgender'], they do not fit many of society's expectations for the gender in which they identify.[68]

The concept of genderqueer-ness introduces such potential variety of cultural expressions and identities as to pull hard at the tendency to reduce 'gender' to bodies and invites historians to emphasise gender as a process productive of multiple expressions sometimes associated with male and female bodies but without *necessary or presumptive* reference to those bodies for intelligibility.

For historians, the concept suggests a framework for not anticipating an association of, for example, 'strength' with 'male' or 'masculinity', or tenderness with 'female' or 'femininity' without evidence that these were the ways the specific culture under investigation understood those traits. Such a formulation permits us to recognise a boisterous, compliant, fashion-conscious bully as a gender formation without shoehorning the subject into a 'female masculine' or 'male effeminate' category – a fluidity that would surely aid us in identifying and discussing earlier and non-western gender processes and formations historically. This would not prevent historians from identifying binary gender formations where they have historically occurred, but it would give us a tool for seeing other gender formations where they have historically occurred. It would encourage us to ask first *whether* a male/female distinction is important in social relationships in this place and this time. If it seems to be, then let us ask in what ways and with what recurrence and as parts of what other processes that distinction becomes important. Perhaps most important, until we can demonstrate connections and interactions, let us ask these questions very locally, and let us try to derive our answers from and about the people and societies we want to investigate.

I suspect these shifts in perspective and practice would have several immediate and ameliorative effects. In the first place, it would force us to explain what we mean when we use the term 'gender' – the term that we claim animates the structures of power globally, but which we seem to find either too dull or too self-evident to warrant much discussion. We would require ourselves to ground the concept, as we were defining it, in place and time. Of course that would make us better historians. It might make us poorer intellectual imperialists and force us, as Dipesh Chakrabarty might put it, to provincialise gender as a category of analysis.[69]

Treating gender as a question of analysis would also encourage us to regard our sources more critically and more creatively – and more respectfully. When the framework of our findings is a foregone conclusion, the sources themselves become of minor importance, useful only for our ability to cull them for what we have already decided is present. That changes the moment we begin truly to interrogate both our category and our sources – to ask what we are seeing. Let us at least have to demonstrate, first to ourselves and then to our readers, that ours is in fact the most persuasive reading of the evidence.

In this process we may perhaps begin to square off against our strongest enemy – and I suspect our best ally: ourselves. We need to become sharply more conscious of the historian as a figured self and our field as a figured field. I agree with Elsa Barkley Brown that feminist historians have been loath to take that step, at least publicly, for fear of weakening the authority of our own truth claims. We seem to believe that, if we allow for variation in the historical relations of maleness and femaleness, we lose legitimacy to judge or intervene where those relations are vehicles of domination and subordination in the present. And so far, we seem to have accorded that anxiety higher priority than the fear that, for many societies – for many women – we might be getting it wrong historically . . . which means, of course, that we may also be getting it wrong in the present. I join Brown, then, in calling for a gender history that not only allows, in Brown's musical terms, 'riffing', but also recognises the process of riffing as the very heart of the field.

Notes

In addition to the other contributors to, and the editors of, this book and the outside reviewers, I am grateful to the following colleagues for taking the time to give me close critical feedback on various earlier incarnations of this chapter: Kathleen Brown, Nancy Cott, Lori Ginzberg, Richard Godbeer, Pernille Ipsen, Mary Kelley, Joy Newmann, Jennifer Ratner-Rosenhagen, and the members of the Gender and Woman's History Workshop at the University of Wisconsin.

1. Barbara Jeanne Fields, 'Categories of Analysis? Not in My Book', in *Viewpoints: Excerpts from the ACLS Conference on the Humanities in the 1990s*, American Council of Learned Societies Occasional Papers Series 10 (New York: ACLS, 1989), pp. 29–34.

2. I do think that historians of manhood tend to naturalise masculinity, but in much the same way that historians of women tend to naturalise womanhood.

3. 'Only by means of a break with the theoretical vision, which is experienced as a break with ordinary vision, can the observer take account, in his description of ritual practice, of the fact of participation (and consequently of his own separation from this)': Pierre Bourdieu, *The Logic of Practice*, tr. Richard Nice (Cambridge: Polity, 1990), p. 36. See also Sandra Harding, 'The Instability of the Analytical Categories of Feminist Thought', in Micheline R. Malson, Jean F. O'Barr, Sarah Westphal-Wihl and Mary Wyer (eds), *Feminist Theory in Practice and Process* (Chicago: University of Chicago Press, 1989), pp. 15–34, here p. 20; Frederick Cooper, *Colonialism in Question: Theory, Knowledge, History* (Berkeley: University of California Press, 2005), esp. pp. 8–9.

4. Joan Wallach Scott, 'Gender: A Useful Category of Historical Analysis', *American Historical Review* 91 (1986), pp. 1,056–61; Joan Wallach Scott, 'Some More Reflections on Gender and Politics', in Joan Wallach Scott *Gender and the Politics of History* (1988; rev. edn, New York: Columbia University Press, 1999), esp. pp. 199–206; Laura Lee Downs, *Writing Gender History* (London: Hodder Arnold, 2004), pp. 20–54.

5. See e.g., the classic women's history anthologies: Mary S. Hartman and Lois W. Banner (eds), *Clio's Consciousness Raised: New Perspectives on the History of Women* (New York: Harper & Row, 1974); Berenice A. Carroll (ed.), *Liberating Women's History: Theoretical and Critical Essays* (Urbana: University of Illinois Press, 1976). The term 'gender' is not used in the introduction to either collection and appears rarely in the essays.

6. Gayle Rubin, 'The Traffic in Women: Notes on the "Political Economy" of Sex', in Rayna R. Reiter (ed.), *Toward an Anthropology of Women* (New York: Monthly Review Press, 1975), pp. 157–210, here p. 165.

7. Classic work in this vein includes Joan Kelly, 'The Doubled Vision of Feminist Theory: A Postscript to the "Women and Power" Conference', *Feminist Studies* 5 (1979), pp. 216–27; Zillah R. Eisenstein (ed.), *Capitalist Patriarchy and the Case for Socialist Feminism* (New York: Monthly Review Press, 1979); Annette Kühn and AnnMarie Wolpe (eds), *Feminism and Materialism: Women and Modes of Production* (London: Routledge and Kegan Paul, 1980).

8. This work began with the advent of feminism, but the 1980s saw the publication of a host of now-classic pieces, including Angela Y. Davis, *Women, Race and Class* (New York: Random House, 1982); bell hooks, *Ain't I a Woman? Black Women and Feminism* (Boston: South End Press, 1981); Filomena Chioma Steady (ed.), *The Black Woman Cross-Culturally* (Cambridge, MA: Schenkman, 1981); Deborah Gray White, *Ar'n't I a Woman?: Female Slaves in the Plantation South* (New York: Norton, 1985); Hazel V. Carby, *Reconstructing Womanhood: The Emergence of the Afro-American Woman Novelist* (New York: Oxford University Press, 1987); Patricia Hill Collins, 'The Social Construction of Black Feminist Thought', *Signs* 14 (1989), pp. 745–73.

9. On standpoint theory, see Dorothy E. Smith, 'A Sociology of Women', in Julia Sherman and Evelyn Beck (eds), *The Prism of Sex* (Madison: University of Wisconsin Press, 1979) and the later retrospective evaluations of standpoint theory in *Signs* 22 (1997).

10. Scott, 'Gender: A Useful Category', p. 1,055.

11. Scott, 'Gender: A Useful Category', pp. 1,053, 1,055.

12. Scott, 'Gender: A Useful Category', pp. 1,058–9.

13. Scott, 'Gender: A Useful Category', pp. 1,060–61.

14. Scott, 'Gender: A Useful Category', p. 1,064.

15. Scott, 'Gender: A Useful Category', p. 1,055.

16. Scott, 'Gender: A Useful Category', p. 1,064.

17. Scott, 'Gender: A Useful Category', p. 1,067.

18. The claim to universality was in fact fairly explicitly made: passing lightly over the possibilities that her own definition of gender might be historically and culturally specific, Scott asserted the 'persistent and recurrent' primacy of gender 'in Judeo-Christian as well

as Islamic traditions' – a formulation that flattened both variety and change over time in both 'traditions'. Scott, 'Gender: A Useful Category', p. 1,069.

19. Scott, 'Gender: A Useful Category', p. 1,067.
20. Scott, 'Gender: A Useful Category', p. 1,069, referring to Bourdieu, *The Logic of Practice*.
21. Scott, 'Gender: A Useful Category', pp. 1,067–9.
22. Scott, 'Gender: A Useful Category', p. 1,069.
23. Scott, 'Some More Reflections', pp. 201, 208. See also Joan Wallach Scott, *Only Paradoxes to Offer: French Feminists and the Rights of Man* (Cambridge: Harvard University Press, 1996); Joan Wallach Scott, 'Fantasy Echo: History and the Construction of Identity, *Critical Inquiry* 27 (2001), pp. 284–304; Joan Wallach Scott, *Parité!: Sexual Equality and the Crisis of French Universalism* (Chicago: University of Chicago Press, 2005).
24. Oyèrónké Oyewùmí, 'Visualizing the Body: Western Theories and African Subjects', in Oyèrónké Oyewùmí (ed.), *African Gender Studies: A Reader* (New York: Palgrave Macmillan, 2005), p. 11. See also Oyèrónké Oyewùmí, *The Invention of Women: Making an African Sense of Western Gender Discourses* (Minneapolis: University of Minnesota Press, 1997); Bibi Bakare-Yusef, Edward Waswa Kisiang'ani, Desiree Lewis, Oyèrónké Oyewùmí and Filomena Chioma Steady, *African Gender Scholarship: Concepts, Methodologies and Paradigms* (Oxford: Oxford University Press, 2004).
25. Oyewùmí, 'Visualizing the Body', p. 13.
26. Ifi Amadiume, *Male Daughters, Female Husbands: Gender and Sex in an African Society* (London: Zed Books, 1987), pp. 31–47.
27. Barry S. Hewlett, *Intimate Fathers: The Nature and Context of Aka Pygmy Paternal Infant Care* (Ann Arbor: University of Michigan Press, 1991), p. 168. I am grateful to Hannah Nyala West for bringing this study to my attention.
28. Afsaneh Najmabadi, 'Are Gender and Sexuality Useful Categories of Historical Analysis?', *Journal of Women's History* 18 (2006), pp. 11–21, esp. pp. 11, 14; Afsaneh Najmabadi, *Women with Mustaches and Men without Beards: Gender and Sexual Anxieties of Iranian Modernity* (Berkeley: University of California Press, 2005).
29. Carroll Smith Rosenberg, 'Beauty, the Beast and the Militant Woman: A Case Study in Sex Roles and Social Stress in Jacksonian America', *American Quarterly* 23 (1971), pp. 562–84; Kathryn Kish Sklar, *Catharine Beecher: A Study in American Domesticity* (New Haven: Yale University Press, 1973).
30. Nancy F. Cott, *The Bonds of Womanhood: 'Woman's Sphere' in New England, 1780–1835* (New Haven: Yale University Press, 1977), here p. 9.
31. See e.g., Linda K. Kerber, *Women of the Republic: Intellect and Ideology in Revolutionary America* (Chapel Hill: University of North Carolina Press, 1980); Mary Beth Norton, *Liberty's Daughters: The Revolutionary Experience of American Women, 1750–1800* (Boston: Little, Brown, 1980); Laurel Thatcher Ulrich, *Good Wives: Images and Reality in the Lives of Women in Northern New England, 1650–1750* (New York: Knopf, 1982), here p. 240.
32. Linda K. Kerber, 'Separate Spheres, Female Worlds, Woman's Place: The Rhetoric of Women's History', *Journal of American History* 75 (1988), pp. 9–39, here p. 38.
33. Sarah Deutsch, *No Separate Refuge: Culture, Class, and Gender on an Anglo-Hispanic Frontier in the American Southwest, 1880–1940* (New York: Oxford University Press, 1987); Peggy Pascoe, *Relations of Rescue: The Search for Female Moral Authority in the American West, 1874–1939* (New York: Oxford University Press, 1990); Stephanie McCurry, *Masters of Small Worlds: Yeoman Households, Gender Relations, and the Political Culture of the Antebellum South Carolina Low Country* (New York: Oxford University Press, 1995).
34. See e.g., Ellen Carol DuBois, *Feminism and Suffrage: The Emergence of an Independent Women's Movement in America, 1848–1869* (Ithaca: Cornell University Press, 1978); Elisabeth Griffith, *In Her Own Right: The Life of Elizabeth Cady Stanton* (New York: Oxford University Press, 1984); Kathleen Barry, *Susan B. Anthony: A Biography of a Singular Feminist* (New York: New York University Press, 1988).

35. Rosalyn Terborg-Penn, *African American Women in the Struggle for the Vote, 1850–1920* (Bloomington and Indianapolis: Indiana University Press, 1998).

36. Lisa Marguerite Tetrault, 'The Memory of a Movement: Woman Suffrage and Reconstruction America, 1865–1890' (unpublished doctoral thesis, University of Wisconsin, 2004).

37. Nan Enstad, *Ladies of Labor, Girls of Adventure: Working Women, Popular Culture, and Labor Politics at the Turn of the Twentieth Century* (New York: Columbia University Press, 1999); George Chauncey, *Gay New York: Gender, Urban Culture, and the Making of the Gay Male World, 1890–1940* (New York: Basic Books, 1994), esp. pp. 1–29; Lisa Duggan, *The Twilight of Equality? Neoliberalism, Cultural Politics, and the Attack on Democracy* (Boston: Beacon Press, 2003), p. 50; Regina Kunzel, *Fallen Women, Problem Girls: Unmarried Mothers and the Professionalization of Social Work, 1890–1945* (New Haven: Yale University Press, 1993).

38. I am indebted for some of these examples to my co-presenters and to the audience of 'Historicizing Gender: A Roundtable', Organization of American Historians Annual Conference, Minneapolis, Minnesota, 31 March 2007. The full panel included: Richard Godbeer, 'Gender and Culture: A Multilayered Approach'; Kate Haulman, 'Bodies and Minds in Early America'; Jeanne Boydston, 'Questioning Gender' and Rodney Hessinger, 'Bringing it All Back Home: Masculinity, Femininity, and the Reintegration of Early American Gender'. See, for examples of work on these various aspects of colonial womanhood: Ulrich, *Good Wives*; Norton, *Liberty's Daughters*; Kerber, *Women of the Republic*; Cornelia Hughes Dayton, 'Turning Points and the Relevance of Colonial Legal History', *William and Mary Quarterly* 3rd series, 50 (1993), pp. 7–17; Cornelia Hughes Dayton, *Women before the Bar: Gender, Law and Society in Connecticut, 1639–1789* (Chapel Hill: University of North Carolina Press, 1995); Cynthia A. Kierner, *Beyond the Household: Women's Place in the Early South, 1700–1835* (Ithaca: Cornell University Press, 1998); Kirsten Fischer, *Suspect Relations: Sex, Race, and Resistance in Colonial North Carolina* (Ithaca and London: Cornell University Press, 2002); Kathleen M. Brown, *Good Wives, Nasty Wenches, and Anxious Patriarchs: Gender, Race, and Power in Colonial Virginia* (Chapel Hill and London: University of North Carolina Press, 1996); Sarah E. Fatherly, *Gentlewomen and Learned Ladies: Women and Elite Formation in Eighteenth-Century Philadelphia* (Bethlehem, PA: Lehigh University Press, forthcoming 2008); Jeanne Boydston, *Home and Work: Housework, Wages and the Ideology of Labor in the Early Republic* (New York: Oxford University Press, 1990).

39. Ulrich, *Good Wives*, p. 50.

40. Mary Beth Norton, *Founding Mothers and Fathers: Gendered Power and the Forming of American Society* (New York: Knopf, 1996), esp. pp. 140–80. See also, Amadiume, *Male Daughters, Female Husbands*.

41. See e.g., Dayton, 'Turning Points'; Kierner, *Beyond the Household*; Christine Leigh Heyrman, *Southern Cross: The Beginnings of the Bible Belt* (New York: Random House, 1997); Ruth H. Bloch, *Gender and Morality in Anglo-American Culture, 1650–1800* (Berkeley: University of California Press, 2003); Monica Najar, *Evangelizing the South: A Social History of Church and State in Early America* (New York: Oxford University Press, 2007); Boydston, *Home and Work*.

42. Edmund S. Morgan, 'The Puritans and Sex', *New England Quarterly* 15 (1942), pp. 591–607.

43. For discussions of sexuality in Anglo culture in early American history see e.g., Merril D. Smith (ed.), *Sex and Sexuality in Early America* (New York: New York University Press, 1998); Catherine Clinton and Michele Gillespie, *The Devil's Lane: Sex and Race in the Early South* (New York: Oxford University Press, 2002); Richard Godbeer, *Sexual Revolution in Early America* (Baltimore: Johns Hopkins University Press, 2004); Clare A. Lyons, *Sex among the Rabble: An Intimate History of Gender and Power in the Age of Revolution, Philadelphia, 1730–1830* (Chapel Hill: University of North Carolina Press, 2006). See also the forum on sexuality in *William and Mary Quarterly* 3rd series, 60 (2003), esp. the very

interesting comments by Anne G. Myles, 'Queering the Study of Early American Sexuality', pp. 199–202.

44. Lyons, *Sex among the Rabble*, here p. 3. Richard Godbeer, '"The Cry of Sodom": Discourse, Intercourse, and Desire in Colonial New England', *William and Mary Quarterly* 3rd series, 52 (1995), pp. 259–86.

45. Work in European history suggests a similar transition during this same period. See e.g., Isabel V. Hull, *Sexuality, State, and Civil Society in Germany, 1700–1815* (Ithaca: Cornell University Press, 1996).

46. Joyce Ladner, *Tomorrow's Tomorrow: The Black Women* (New York: Doubleday, 1971). See also the excerpt from this work included in Carroll (ed.), *Liberating Women's History*, pp. 179–93; Carroll with Hartman and Banner (eds), *Clio's Consciousness Raised*, which included no essays on women of colour; Gerda Lerner's important anthology, *Black Women in White America: A Documentary History* (New York: Vintage Books, 1972).

47. Jennifer L. Morgan, *Laboring Women: Reproduction and Gender in New World Slavery* (Philadelphia: University of Pennsylvania Press, 2004), esp. chapter 2, pp. 50–68. See also Gwendolyn Midlo Hall, *Slavery and African Ethnicities in the Americas: Restoring the Links* (Chapel Hill: University of North Carolina Press, 2005) for a broader framework for beginning to recognise this diversity and its implications for African American history. An important cluster of disasporic studies have identified distinct African concepts of gender and sexuality carried to the Caribbean and Latin America: e.g., Oyewùmí (ed.), *African Gender Studies*; Andrea Cornwall (ed.), *Readings in Gender in Africa* (Bloomington: Indiana University Press, 2004); Signe Arnfeld (ed.), *Re-thinking Sexualities in Africa* (Uppsala: Nordiska Afrikainstitutet, 2004); James H. Sweet, *Recreating Africa: Culture, Kinship, and Religion in the Afro-Portuguese World, 1441–1770* (Chapel Hill: University of North Carolina Press, 2006); J. Lorand Matory, *Black Atlantic Religion: Tradition, Transnationalism, and the Matriarchy in the Afro-Brazilian Candomble* (Princeton: Princeton University Press, 2005); Michele Mitchell, Sandra Gunning and Tera W. Hunter (eds), *Dialogues of Dispersal: Gender, Sexuality, and African Diasporas* (Oxford and Malden, MA: Blackwell, 2004).

48. Stephanie M.H. Camp, '*Ar'n't I a Woman?* in the Vanguard of the History of Race and Sex in the United States', *Journal of Women's History* 19 (2007), pp. 146–50, here p. 146.

49. Deborah Gray White, *Too Heavy a Load: Black Women in Defense of Themselves, 1894–1994* (New York: Norton, 1998); Evelyn Brooks Higginbotham, 'African-American Women's History and the Meta-language of Race', *Signs* 17 (1992), pp. 251–74; Evelyn Brooks Higginbotham, *Righteous Discontent: The Women's Movement in the Black Baptist Church, 1880–1920* (Cambridge: Harvard University Press, 1993); Elsa Barkley Brown, 'To Catch the Vision of Freedom: Reconstructing Southern Black Women's Political History, 1865–1880', in Ann D. Gordon with Bettye Collier-Thomas (eds), *African American Women and the Vote 1837–1965* (Amhurst: University of Massachusetts Press, 1997), pp. 66–99; Elsa Barkley Brown, 'Negotiating and Transforming the Public Sphere: African-American Political Life in the Transition from Slavery to Freedom', *Public Culture* 7 (1994): pp. 107–46; Martha S. Jones, *All Bound Up Together: The Woman Question in African American Public Culture, 1830–1900* (Chapel Hill: University of North Carolina Press, 2007).

50. See e.g., Judith E. Brown, 'Economic Organization and the Position of Women Among the Iroquois', *Ethnohistory* 17 (1970), pp. 151–67; Jacqueline Peterson, 'Women Dreaming: The Religio-Psychology of Indian-White Marriage in the Western Great Lakes Fur Trade', in Lillian Schlissel, Vicki L. Ruiz and Janice Monk (eds), *Western Women: Their Land, Their Lives* (Albuquerque: University of New Mexico Press, 1986), pp. 49–79; Patricia Albers and Beatrice Medicine, *The Hidden Half: Studies of Plains Indian Women* (Washington, DC: University Press of America, 1983); Sylvia Van Kirk, *Many Tender Ties: Women in Fur Trade Society* (Norman: University of Oklahoma Press, 1983); Susan Sleeper-Smith, 'Women, Kin, and Catholicism: New Perspectives on the Fur Trade',

Ethnohistory 47 (2000), pp. 423–52; Will Roscoe, *Changing Ones: Third and Fourth Genders in Native North America* (New York: St Martin's Press, 1998); Will Roscoe, *The Zuni Man-Woman* (Albuquerque: University of New Mexico Press, 1991); Sabine Lang, *Men as Women, Women as Men: Changing Gender in Native American Cultures*, tr. John L. Vantine (1990; Austin: University of Texas Press, 1998). An intermediate scholarship in the 1990s continued to examine Native women as a distinct group, but emphasised that gender among Native Americans was more flexible than among Europeans and that maleness and femaleness did not necessarily signify superiority and subjection: e.g., Karen Anderson, *Chain Her by One Foot: The Subjugation of Native Women in Seventeenth-Century New France* (London and New York: Routledge, 1991); Theda Perdue, *Cherokee Women: Gender and Culture Change, 1700–1835* (Lincoln: University of Nebraska Press, 1999).

51. I am obviously indebted to Chandra Talhade Mohanty for this phrasing: 'Under Western Eyes: Feminist Scholarship and Colonial Discourses', *Feminist Review* 30 (1988), pp. 61–88.

52. In addition to the works cited below, it is important to note the path-breaking contribution of Ramon Gutierrez's *When Jesus Came the Corn Mother Went Away: Marriage, Sexuality, and Power in New Mexico, 1500–1846* (Stanford: Stanford University Press, 1991) as one of the first books to analyse closely the importance of discourses of sexuality as a technology of Spanish colonisation.

53. Nancy Shoemaker, 'Categories', in Nancy Shoemaker (ed.), *Clearing a Path: Theorizing the Past in Native American Cultures* (London and New York: Routledge, 2002), pp. 51–74, here p. 59. See also Nancy Shoemaker, *A Strange Likeness: Becoming Red and White in Eighteenth-Century North America* (New York: Oxford University Press, 2004), esp. chapter 5, pp. 105–24.

54. Italics added.

55. Gunlög Fur, '"Some Women are Wiser than Some Men": Gender and Native American History', in Shoemaker (ed.), *Clearing a Path*, pp. 75–106.

56. Richard White, *The Middle Ground: Indians, Empires, and Republics in the Great Lakes Region, 1650–1815* (Cambridge: Cambridge University Press, 1991).

57. Juliana Barr, *Peace Came in the Form of a Woman: Indians and Spaniards in the Texas Borderlands* (Chapel Hill: University of North Carolina Press, 2007).

58. For recent work on anxieties of racial purity in France and Britain, see Guillaume Aubert, '"The Blood of France": Race and Purity of Blood in the French Atlantic World', *William and Mary Quarterly* 3rd series, 61 (2004), pp. 439–78; Gordon M. Sayre, *Les Sauvages Américains: Representations of Native Americans in French and English Colonial Literature* (Chapel Hill: University of North Carolina Press, 1997), pp. 248–304; Kathleen Wilson, *The Island Race: Englishness, Empire and Gender in the Eighteenth Century* (London and New York: Routledge, 2002), pp. 92–128; Deborah Wyrick, 'The Madwoman in the Hut: Scandals of Hybrid Domesticity in Early Victorian Literature from the West Indies', *Pacific Coast Philology* 33 (1998), pp. 44–57. See also Jennifer Spear's important work on the use of the law to bolster sexual binaries in French Louisiana: Jennifer M. Spear, 'Colonial Intimacies: Legislating Sex in French Louisiana', *William and Mary Quarterly* 3rd series, 60 (2003), pp. 75–98.

59. See e.g., Alexander Saxton, *The Rise and Fall of the White Republic: Class Politics and Mass Culture in Nineteenth Century America* (New York: Verso, 1990); Matthew Frye Jacobson, *Whiteness of a Different Color: European Immigrants and the Alchemy of Race* (Cambridge: Harvard University Press, 1999); David Roediger, *The Wages of Whiteness: Race and the Making of an American Working Class* (New York: Verso, 1999); Fischer, *Suspect Relations*; Brown, *Good Wives, Nasty Wenches*; Morgan, *Laboring Women*.

60. Najmabadi, 'Are Gender and Sexuality Useful Categories?', p. 11.

61. Although I am not ready to abandon the language of gender, I recognise that forty years into the life of the field, any retention of that language may hint at this kind of privileging of the west.

62. For a very useful overview of theories of intersectionality, see Leslie McCall, 'The Complexity of Intersectionality', *Signs* 30 (2005), pp. 1,771–1,800.
63. Scott, 'Gender: A Useful Category', pp. 1,055, 1,067.
64. Elsa Barkley Brown, '"What Has Happened Here": The Politics of Difference in Women's History and Feminist Politics', *Feminist Studies* 18 (1992), pp. 295–312, here pp. 296–7.
65. Brown, 'What Has Happened Here', p. 298.
66. Brown, 'What Has Happened Here', p. 300.
67. See e.g., Roscoe, *Changing Ones*; Lang, *Men as Women, Women as Men*.
68. FORGE (For Ourselves Reworking Gender Expression) website, <http://www.forge-forward.org/index.php>, Milwaukee, Wisconsin. See also Joan Nestle, Clare Howell and Riki Wilchins (eds), *GenderQueer: Voices from Beyond the Sexual Binary* (New York: Alyson Books, 2002).
69. See Dipesh Chakrabarty, *Provincializing Europe: Post Colonial Thought and Historical Difference* (Princeton: Princeton University Press, 2000).

7 Change and the Corporeal in Seventeenth- and Eighteenth-Century Gender History: Or, Can Cultural History Be Rigorous?

Dror Wahrman

Gender history, it would come as a surprise to no one, is profoundly implicated in the development of cultural history. Since the 1980s, the second wave of feminist criticism led to the expansion of feminist history to include not only women's experiences but also, more fundamentally, the historically and culturally specific constructions of gender as a mode of differentiation. Consequently gender history, with its insistent interrogation of nature versus culture, biology versus history, endurance versus change, has become one of the most productive terrains for cultural-historical thinking. The study through a gendered lens of all aspects of culture – politics, science, religion, what have you – has been one of the most successful outcomes of cultural history, and continues apace. (It is no coincidence that the intervention identified more than any other with this historiographical development, Joan Scott's 1986 essay 'Gender: A Useful Category of Historical Analysis', is without contest the most cited article in the over-century-long history of the *American Historical Review*.) In this chapter, I want to look not at the uses of gender as a category of analysis in cultural history, but rather at the reverse, more circumscribed, side of the same coin, namely the cultural history of the basic concepts in the field – gender, sex and sexuality. My point of departure is some excellent recent contributions to the history of sex and gender, and especially their preoccupation with the question of change versus continuity: a preoccupation that speaks directly to the question of periodisation in gender history that animates this volume. My purpose is to draw attention to *the limits* of such investigations, in two different senses: first, to the limitations of the *methodology* of cultural history employed therein, and to how these limits might be pushed as far as they can go (but no further); and second, to the limitations of their *presuppositions* about the cultural history of gender and sex, and how they too can be acknowledged and perhaps transcended.

Cultural historians are sometimes prone to generalisations beyond the limits of their evidence. Following in the footsteps of the social history of the 1970s and 1980s with its emphasis on 'history from below', the so-called new cultural history retains the aspiration to illuminate historical patterns that affected large numbers of actors. Indeed, whereas for social historians the understanding of large-scale collectives was typically predicated on their fundamental differentiation from other large social groups – most commonly along gender, class or race lines – the more nebulous concept of 'culture' can seduce practitioners in this field to make even bigger claims about an all-encompassing culture in a particular time and place: the cultural crisis prevailing throughout western Europe after the First World War, say. And yet the methodological safeguards that encouraged rigour in social-historical work, employing various forms of quantification to assess typicality and representativeness, are not as readily available to cultural historians. Quantification requires the equivalent weighting of whatever is being counted: but equal weighting is for the most part inadequate when dealing with meanings and significations that are the basic grist for the cultural-historical mill. This does not mean that some forms of enumeration are not possible, but they are the exceptions rather than the rule – and even then they are typically limited to one cultural form or genre, rather than extended to 'culture' as a whole. So one can group together all the novels published in the decade after the First World War, for example, as a measure of the prevailing cultural crisis, and observe that a remarkable proportion of them deal with malaise; but can they simply be tallied in this manner if some of them take malaise as their central theme, some only in passing, and some, perhaps, ironically? And could one then add Oswald Spengler's *Decline of the West* to the tally, assigning it equal weight with the novels?[1]

One fruitful response to this difficulty has been to shift focus to the careful unpacking of one particular moment, event or artefact, in order to reveal in it the traces of multiple strains of its broader context. Such a Geertzian thick description, typically more illustrative of these broader trends than positing itself as evidence for their existence, is less prone to the methodological problems of 'big picture' cultural history that is my concern in the following pages. Others, unwilling to give up on the big picture, have resorted to an alternative procedure, familiar to all readers of cultural history, which can be called the 'weak collage'.[2] The historian, identifying a seemingly similar phenomenon in several disparate cultural *loci* or forms at the same moment in time, declares it to be a pattern of historical significance. Like a child with pencil and paper, the historian connects a certain number of dots and declares 'I have an elephant'. This pattern – the elephant – is now reified as a 'thing' that has an existence independent of these dots and then extrapolated beyond them to a larger swathe of culture; perhaps even to culture as a whole – a 'Zeitgeist' event touching on everything and everyone that comes within its temporal reach. (So, in my earlier example, the argument might begin by bringing together Spengler's book, Josephine Baker's banana skirt, a new fashion of bobbed hair, a couple of especially evocative post-war diary entries and several novels – and end up with a 1920s European cultural malaise.) An even more ambitious cultural historian may then add the variable of *time*: that is, connect the dots in one particular historical moment to identify an elephant, and those of another moment to delineate a mammoth, and thus claim to uncover the temporal path of evolution.

In these projections of discrete dots into pachyderms we can perhaps see the influence of literary studies, one of the richest sources of inspiration for the cultural turn of the 1990s and beyond, since the disciplinary protocols of proof and persuasion in literary criticism are more amenable to such inductive reasoning. And yet the writing of history has its own, rather different, protocols of proof and persuasion: consequently we have all encountered examples of cultural history – that variety of 'big picture' cultural history that attempts to reach beyond the particular and the specific to broader generalisations – that are suggestive, interesting, thought-provoking, but in the end logically and methodologically indefensible. (This, *inter alia*, is a familiar critique of the historical works of Michel Foucault.) Bad cultural history, as the critics often point out, is (relatively) easy to write. An important challenge that faces this field, therefore, is to develop procedures for the construction and assessment of cultural-historical generalisations and establish yardsticks for their assessment that would be more rigorous and more persuasive.

What follows focuses on scholarship about the transformation of sex and gender from the early modern period through the long eighteenth century, primarily in Britain. This is not only because my own work has taken up this particular question and thus forced me to confront its difficulties. It is also because this field has grown to become unusually rich and theoretically informed, perhaps more so than cultural histories of sex and gender in other national contexts. And furthermore, it is because the eighteenth century has been the scene for some of the most tenacious efforts by historians of the West to engage in cultural-historical generalisations of change over time. A favourite quest of cultural historians, including the undersigned, is to track down that significant yet elusive historical transformation, the 'birth of modernity': and one of their favourite hunting grounds in this quest – or as many would have it, this wild goose chase – is the eighteenth century.

Thus, in the realm of gender history, if – as Laura Gowing, one of the main authorities on the subject, has recently written – 'the gendered body of the sixteenth and seventeenth centuries is almost unrecognisable to modern eyes',[3] then somewhere between that period and ourselves occurred that momentous change of direction into modernity that rendered the earlier past a foreign country.

The first section in what follows is a brief survey of several recent writings in this field and some of the problems and questions they raise. These will point us towards two general questions. First is the question of method: how can we write the cultural history of gender while maintaining both rigour in the enterprise and an awareness of its limits? The second question is about the nature of the enterprise itself: where might we go when these limits suddenly appear to undermine the very foundational presuppositions on which the whole cultural historical project is built?

***

The historical preoccupation with the nature and timing of the epistemic turning point in the history of sex and gender has an identifiable beginning point in one of the boldest and most widely challenged 'big picture' narratives of the new cultural history: Thomas Laqueur's *Making Sex* (1990).[4] Laqueur's book, which has been described as 'perhaps the most influential work of medical history published in the last two decades', undermined the distinction that undergirded so much of the historicist thinking about gender, namely that between gender and sex.[5] The distinction, at least heuristically, seemed crystalline: sex was biology, gender was the cultural scaffolding around the biological body. Not so, said Laqueur. The very understanding of sex – that is, of the biological basis of gender – changed over time and depended on specific historical context. In the end, everything was culture: the difference between sex and gender was one of degree not of kind.

Although Laqueur's subtitle was 'Body and Gender from the Greeks to Freud', in truth his main argument, that which exerted the greatest influence and attracted the most critical attention, was the seductively straightforward narrative leading from the pre-modern to the modern, the main turning point of which occurred in the eighteenth century. Drawing primarily on scientific and medical texts, and most memorably on highly suggestive medical illustrations, Laqueur charted a shift from a pre-modern one-sex body model, in which male and female bodies were seen as varying points along one male–female continuum which thus differed only in degree, to the modern two-sex model in which male and female were redefined as absolute opposites. 'In or about the late eighteenth [century]', Laqueur declared with the aid of Virginia Woolf's well-known turn of phrase, 'human sexual nature changed'.[6] The precise timing and cause of this transformation in the understanding of sexual bodies in Western Europe remained vague, though the Enlightenment and the age of democratic revolutions seemed to play an important part.

It does not take long to notice the disparity between the expansiveness of the claim 'in or about the late eighteenth century human sexual nature changed' and the limitations of Laqueur's body of sources put forth in support of this claim. It was as if Laqueur adopted deliberately the modus operandi of his PhD advisor, Lawrence Stone, who took pride in overstating a case in order to egg on his interlocutors to undertake further research. And egged on they were: Laqueur's boldness prodded other scholars to test his claims in other genres or cultural locations. (Although they are beyond our purview here, Laqueur's claims for the earlier periods have also been questioned: in particular by Katharine Park, who shows in a methodical intellectual genealogy of the one-sex model that it was all but unheard-of in medical sources between Galen and the beginning of the sixteenth century, and that it had a rather patchy career thereafter.)[7]

Mary Fissell, for instance, in her *Vernacular Bodies: The Politics of Reproduction in Early Modern England* (2005), takes issue with the elite nature of Laqueur's medical sources and wishes to expand the exploration of the meanings attached to sexual bodies to popular ('vernacular') understandings of medicine, which she insists do not simply trickle down from the elite's shelves. Fissell therefore focuses on cheap print, reasonably suggesting that her own sources had a wider audience than Laqueur's. Insofar as they relate to Laqueur's basic story, however, Fissell's conclusions are ones he would have endorsed and probably predicted: while her more focused lens brings to light more contestation, variety and messiness than his neat narrative, *grosso modo* her evidence supports the story of *Making Sex*. More importantly, Fissell endorses and even extends Laqueur's culturalist approach: 'bodies are local', she asserts – by which she means that understandings of sex and gender are immediate consequences of their specific, local cultural context. In particular, for Fissell, change over time in notions of gender and the body follows 'the grand events of "men's" history' (and are therefore, *ipso facto*, nation-specific).[8] Thus the impact of the English civil war and the execution of Charles I was immediately felt in a spate of popular pamphlets about the birth of headless babies. During the Restoration, on the other hand, concerns about political continuity can be found articulated in the preoccupation of medical texts with the difficulties of paternal continuity and unknowingness.

Such connections are very suggestive. But consider also the methodological problems that they pose for Fissell's argument. Tempting as it is to link a sudden cluster of pamphlets about headless babies with a headless king, the leap from these to a broader cultural context in which such anxieties supposedly prevailed remains considerable. And yet, if indeed 'bodies are local' in the sense that they are reflective of their immediate cultural environment, then it is precisely this broader environment that is presupposed (not quite demonstrated) in this analysis. What kinds of evidence would it take, then, to extend this linking with some plausibility beyond these several specific pamphlets to a broader cultural pattern?

Laura Gowing's *Common Bodies: Women, Touch and Power in Seventeenth-Century England* (2003) likewise questions the neatness of Laqueur's procedure. First, Gowing points out, the medical texts he looks at were not always as consistent as we might expect – they often advanced equally convincing evidence for contradictory views. (Although Gowing does not develop this point, it does raise an interesting question regarding the historicity of how texts work: is the expectation for logical consistency itself culturally or historically specific? A useful starting point for exploring this possibility further can be the work of Lennard Davis, a literary critic whose suggestive argument about the emergent differentiation between fact and fiction precisely during this period has not registered much among historians.)[9] Second, Gowing, like Fissell, is interested in broadening the corpus of evidence to reach a greater number of historical actors: her chosen strategy is to use legal records, which, given how litigious early modern society was (it has been estimated that one in five early modern English people was involved in legal action every year), may well allow access to wider social circles than any other single source.[10] Legal sources, moreover, take us from printed texts into social practice: surely people's notions of the body, of sex and gender, were not confined to print, but were expressed in a variety of activities.

Based, then, on a wide and often ingenious reading of the legal sources, Gowing presents us with perhaps the most comprehensive account currently available of seventeenth-century understandings of bodies, especially female bodies, as they relate to issues of sexuality and reproduction. She deftly evokes the contradictions surrounding the woman's body: as improperly bounded and inherently open, yet mysterious and unknowable; as secret, yet public; as fundamentally dichotomised between virgin and whore, and yet inherently unable to sustain this dichotomy. Importantly, Gowing's picture is largely a static one. Thus, she replaces Laqueur's narrative about the soon-to-end hegemony of the 'one-sex model' with a picture in which this model is one of several, uneasily coexisting with one another. Analogously, if historians used to assume that views of female sexuality shifted in this period from seeing female desire as natural and necessary to seeing it as disorderly and immodest, Gowing replaces this narrative of change too with a long-term picture of incompatible views coexisting in tension with each other. 'What we are left with', she writes, 'is a world in which the body is never completely comprehensible; in which a variety of models vie to provide plausible accounts of the mysteries of sexual difference, conception and pregnancy; and in which the unpredictable can never, in the end, be entirely explained away'.[11]

Recall, however, that Gowing begins her investigation by asserting (in a paragraph that owes much to Laqueur) that the early modern gendered body 'is almost unrecognizable to modern eyes'. This beginning point necessarily posits a dramatic period of change that swept this early modern world away. And yet the picture that emerges from her careful study is emphatically one of stasis and continuity within her time frame. So is it simply the case that whatever radical turning point signalled the transition from the static pre-modern to the modern, it did so not on Gowing's shift, as it were, but sometime thereafter, say in the eighteenth century? Perhaps. And yet Gowing's emphasis on the variety and mystery that 'never' go away, combined with her suggestion elsewhere that similar findings recur 'in so many other western cultures', lead one to wonder whether her reading of the evidence leaves *any* room for conceptualising when and how such epoch-shaping change could take place. In other words, once Gowing concludes that 'against the backdrop of the seventeenth century's transformations' – those social and political upheavals that provide the main engine of change in Fissell's account – 'the social life of the gendered body remained largely unchanged', she then begs the question of whether there remains a meaningful content to the assertion, in the very next paragraph, that her book has shown 'that the most apparently natural of bodily events and processes – like desire, labour or motherhood – are the product of culture'.[12] How can historians conceptualise the work of 'culture' that produces enduring, long-term continuities?

The resulting dilemma is raised suggestively by Karen Harvey's *Reading Sex in the Eighteenth Century* (2004). Harvey too extends the quest for eighteenth-century knowledge about sex, reproduction and sexual difference to a new body of sources: in her case, the genre of 'erotica', an often-neglected literary form steeped in metaphor and allusion, that Harvey carefully distinguishes from the more explicit pornography on the one hand and from the less openly sexual amatory fiction on the other. This genre's intermediate position is especially interesting in that it combined politeness and refinement with an open preoccupation with sexuality, a combination not very likely in current understandings of eighteenth-century culture. Harvey reads texts and images with remarkable sensitivity and acumen, and her book is peppered with interesting observations. Thus, for instance, she notes the complete absence of rape in erotica: this not because the genre was especially agreeable to women, but because of the implicit presence of aggression towards women in *every* sexual encounter. Harvey illustrates this observation with a neat juxtaposition of frontispieces to two related 1730s erotica poems, one depicting the extra-marital sexual submission of a servant and the other a presumably consensual aristocratic wedding night, that are nevertheless strikingly similar.

For the most part, however, the main goal of Harvey's book is to mobilise the knowledge gained from erotica to point out the limitations of current scholarship, and above all of Laqueur's sweeping narrative in *Making Sex*. She therefore mines the erotic literature for numerous counter-examples to Laqueur's claims. These, in her view, add up to a more fundamental response to Laqueur, which she describes as 'enduring synchronic diversity': every historical moment witnesses a wide variety of possible configurations – be they of understandings of sexual difference, of the body, *et cetera* – and this variety endures over long (limitless?) stretches of time. Consequently one cannot really generalise about patterns of historical change, or attach much significance to them (despite the occasional gesture towards a possible exception). Seeming patterns of change were 'short-term and insubstantial rather than long-term and transformative', Harvey writes. 'Widespread claims for linear transformation' – like Laqueur's – 'are undermined by this striking combination of short-term shifts in language combined with a range of persisting themes'.[13] To Gowing's static seventeenth century, Harvey couples an equally glacial eighteenth.

In what we may be inclined by now to call the British Continuity School we can also include Amanda Vickery, whose *The Gentleman's Daughter: Women's Lives in Georgian England* (1998) asserts, contra Laqueur, that, in the fundamental expectations from women, the eighteenth century witnessed 'no change whatsoever'. Rather, 'men and women had seen themselves as quintessentially physically different from each other for centuries. The long-standing taboos surrounding menstruation, for instance, bespeak an enduring vision of woman as the mysterious other'. *Plus ça change* ... Like Harvey, Vickery couples assertions of centuries-long continuities with 'a varied picture which allows for human diversity': an enduring diversity which some historians have misinterpreted with claims for linear transformation.[14] Always the careful social historian, Vickery acknowledges of course that, during the eighteenth century, external circumstances changed: an urban renaissance had taken place, secularisation increasingly took hold. But these, she asserts, simply provided a new bottle for the same old wine.

Distinguishing new bottles from old wine – that is, social from cultural change – may indeed be key to asserting long-term continuities during periods of obvious, radical transformations. This, in any case, is the conclusion of Alexandra Shepard in an astute overview of the history of men and masculinity from the sixteenth through the eighteenth centuries. During the long early modern period, she asserts, 'the many and varied components of masculinity remained largely unchanged'. Rather, where change took place was in men's social experiences and social status – or, more precisely, in the distribution among different men of what Shepard calls 'the dividends of patriarchy'. Thus, Shepard's *Meanings of Manhood in Early Modern England* (2003) provides an excellent social-historical analysis of patterns of change in the distribution of patriarchal dividends during the early modern period, whereby they became 'increasingly related to distinctions of social position rather than divisions of age or marital status'. Gendered access to resources, the subject matter of social history, did indeed shift as a consequence of transformations in institutions and structures: demography, economy, governance, urbanisation. So are we then encouraged simply to superimpose a picture of cultural-historical continuity – according to Shepard, after all, in the realm of representations and significations of meaning nothing much happened – on top of a picture of significant social transformation?[15]

* * *

My goal in the present chapter is not to assess the specific strengths of the argument for continuity versus change, or indeed to evaluate what validity might remain for Laqueur's original thesis. Instead, I want to push the discussion towards two meta-questions that to my mind are begged by this literature, but that are rarely given explicit consideration. The first, with which I opened a few pages ago, has to do with the methodology of cultural history – in this case, the cultural history of gender: namely, how can we develop strategies to adjudicate such contrary claims? The second, with which I shall close, involves the basic presuppositions of a cultural history of gender, and to what degree they might need revising if indeed those scholars who insist that they are observing long-term continuities are, at least in part, correct.

So, first, regarding method. Given the inevitable messiness of lived historical experience, and given the likelihood – some would say theoretical inevitability – that every cultural trend also harbours instances of its counter-trend, do we have then to accept that the best we can do is chronicle 'enduring synchronic diversity' (to quote Harvey again)? Is there a way to break through the stalemate of hurling examples and counter-examples back and forth? Should we limit the mandate of the cultural history of gender to creative localised insights, or can it still strive to make meaningful arguments on a bigger canvas about dominant patterns at particular historical moments, even if their dominance does not preclude the simultaneous existence of others?[16] If we still take the latter to be a legitimate and indeed valuable goal, then what cultural history needs are procedures for evaluating the historical significance of cultural trends: a more rigorous, self-conscious methodology for identifying a cultural pattern as dominant or residual, meaningful or adventitious, resonant or echoless.

Thus consider, for instance, from the other end of the spectrum (and from the other side of the Atlantic Ocean), Lisa Cody's evocative *Birthing the Nation: Sex, Science, and the Conception of Eighteenth-Century Britons* (2005). Cody's book is a reaffirmation of dramatic change in notions of the body, sexuality and reproduction during the eighteenth century. Cody begins with an uncontroversial transformation, that of the rise of the man-midwife as an authority on reproduction and birth, supplanting the earlier exclusive authority and access of women to other females' bodies. This is not an unfamiliar story, but Cody claims for it a much broader social and cultural significance than previously noted. First, in its effects on models of masculine comportment. The man-midwife came to hold an important middle position in developing a masculine pursuit with a peculiar understanding of women: the man-midwife – here Cody offers her own revision of the binaries framing Laqueur's narrative – demonstrated that men and women could have close affinities with each other even as they were redefined as opposites.

Second, at its broadest, the context for the rise of the man-midwife, according to Cody, was the increasing centrality of issues of reproduction to multiple domains of eighteenth-century public discourse, social, cultural and political: 'a paradigm shift occurred in the eighteenth century that placed the social significance of sex and birth centre stage in British thought'.[17] In order to show this paradigm shift, Cody takes the reader through a dizzying tour of eighteenth-century England, missing – or so it seems – very little that took place during that period and had some reproductive angle: be it the warming pan scandal (which made the spectre of trickery in birth-bed central to monarchical and religious succession after James II), the peasant woman Mary Toft who claimed in the 1720s to give birth to rabbits, contemporary embryological debates, the attacks on Lord Bute, early racial theories, satirical accounts of pregnant men, Antoni van Leeuwenhoek's bizarre drawings of humanoid sperm, the uses of birth metaphors in linguistic theory, judicial medical evidence in infanticide and abortion trials, population thinking before and after Thomas Malthus, the new poor laws. And this list is far from exhaustive.

On the one hand, therefore, Cody seems to supply a promising strategy for evaluating change versus stasis, by seeking signs of change in such a remarkable range of domains of contemporary life. Surely, if the centrality of reproduction can be shown in so many places, it must be significant, even a paradigm shift? Indeed, it is easy to argue for an advantage of such an eclectic collection of evidence over the focus on a single genre or cultural form in chronicling cultural shifts (a point to which I will return). But in this same move lies also the methodological difficulty. The multiple cultural soundings that Cody marshals forth – political events of national importance, rarefied intellectual debates, popular visual jokes, moments of undeniable and unrepeatable eccentricity – are all given in this analysis equal weight in a seamless all-encompassing view of culture. But is that really the case? How do we distinguish an odd one-off print from a repeated trend? I am of course not suggesting that the bizarre and the transient cannot be as relevant and revealing as the most important public event. But their relative weight and significance need to be evaluated, and the connections between them discussed, rather than assumed or subsumed under their simultaneity.

The basic problem, then, a problem that for the most part remains implicit and unexplored in this debate about the history of gender/sex/sexuality as in many other clusters of creative cultural-historical conversation, is how to go about evaluating the relative weight of disparate bits of cultural evidence. In contrast to intellectual history, for which individual enunciations that are especially articulate and explicit are at a premium, in the generalising, broad-canvas cultural history of the type discussed here a single enunciation or act does not, and cannot, by itself carry much weight. Rather, a key question with regard to any enunciation or practice is the extent of its *resonance*. I am thinking of resonance as a gauge of conditions of communication and transmission, one that distinguishes (along a continuous spectrum) enunciations or practices that have little echo – those that 'fall flat' – from those that get picked up to be reproduced or mirrored or objected to or bounced around again and again and that thus continue to reverberate against a mesh of other similar enunciations or practices. Elsewhere I have compared a single act or pronouncement to the plucking of the string of the violin: it is only the prior presence and depth of the adjacent sound box that turns a barely perceptible flickering movement into a resonant sound and a sequence of such movements into music.[18]

My thoughts about this problem have evolved out of difficulties I encountered in my own work on the transformations in understandings of gender during the long eighteenth century, and it may be helpful to recount briefly the strategies that I began to devise to address them.[19] In a nutshell, the story I ended up telling (and then contextualising within a broader framework of the transformations in understandings of identity and self during the eighteenth century, which need not concern us here) was about an 'ancien régime of gender' that prevailed throughout the first eight decades of the eighteenth century, at least in England, before disappearing with remarkable speed by the end of the century. In earlier decades, while understandings of sex were already grounded in the putative certitudes of biological science, gender categories were still allowed more of the fluidity and versatility of culture and were thus characterised by a remarkable degree of looseness and playfulness. Occasionally, to put it differently, a person's gender – the behavioural and cultural attributes of masculinity and femininity – was conceptually allowed to roam away from his or her sex (that is, the perception of difference in bodies), and this without causing too much concern. Then, towards the end of the eighteenth century, this relative playfulness of gender categories was replaced by apprehension and disbelief. It was no longer imaginable for an individual to escape the dictates of the sexual body through a play with gender – for a man, that is, to be able truly to inhabit femininity, or a woman, masculinity. Gender now collapsed into sex; that is, into the physicality inscribed on the body of every individual.

So how does one establish the plausibility of such a broad claim? (It bears repeating that while I ended up in this particular case in the decisive-change-over-time camp, the following discussion of method is equally applicable for an argument going the other way.) Given the weight I attribute to resonance, it is not surprising that my strategy developed around different levels of *repetition*, enfolding one another like nesting boxes. The earlier indications that I was looking at something meaningful emerged from what I called several pages ago a 'weak collage': that is to say, an apparent pattern in understandings of gender that seemed to recur in several cultural locations, and where in each one the pattern resonated often enough to appear more the rule than the exception. At this stage, the key question was whether the different phenomena observed in their disparate cultural spheres were in fact manifestations of the same underlying pattern – that pattern that can then be elevated to the status of a 'thing' by connecting the dots, even if not observed directly, and carried over into other domains. Methodologically, what increased the likelihood that the dots did indeed delineate an elephant was a certain level of repetition: it appeared possible to point to a remarkably consistent pattern of change in understandings of gender that crossed several different eighteenth-century cultural spheres. So, while the observed phenomenon could perhaps be explainable in unrelated terms in one sphere, or even in two or three, its repetition across several spheres that *were* disparate and different from each other increased the likelihood that the common denominator was indeed the pattern in question. (It is for this reason that 'big picture' arguments founded on repetition within a single cultural form, such as Laqueur's reliance on medical sources or Harvey's on the erotic genre, remain unsatisfactory. Conversely, Cody's book strives precisely for such repetition, but not always with sufficiently well-developed patterns of change in each cultural location.) With some clumsiness I call this first benchmark 'repetition in the first degree', to distinguish it from what follows: while still always a collage, the more effective the repetition, the less is the collage a 'weak' one.

Once the contours of an elephant began to emerge, it became important to determine how big it was and how far it extended. In this next step, which can be described as 'repetition in the second degree', I tried to push the hypothesised pattern to its limits by seeking the repeated occurrence of the pattern I had identified – now a describable 'thing' – across as many cultural, generic and social boundaries as possible, moving from more likely to increasingly less likely social and cultural locations for its occurrence.[20] Several cultural forms in particular provided instructive limiting test-cases for the argument: from theatre and fashion, domains characterised by playfulness, to locations characterised to the contrary by imperviousness or hostility to cultural trends – be it the milieu of learned classical translators, the technical and practical 'genre' of manuals for growing bees, or the genre of moralising jeremiad with its time-worn rigid conventions. The differentiation of varying cultural susceptibilities in different domains also raised the possibility of time lags between them, which was important for unpacking an arguably wide-ranging transformation into its components. Ideally, within each domain one could identify particular sources or behaviours that could be found abundantly and spread over time, enabling the charting of resonant reiterations as well as temporal comparisons. (Occasionally I could even indulge in crude quantification.) And again, in the best cases the evidence came from opposite sides of putative divides that typically limit such historical inquiries, such as those between discourse and practice, or between description and prescription.

I also hoped that this strategy of pushing the argument further and further would reveal its *limits*, that is to say those social, geographical, generic or other limits beyond which the proposed pattern in understandings of gender did not extend; and which, if discovered, could help explain the origins and meaning of this pattern by directing attention to whichever factor (class, genre, region) that was germane to its occurrence. Perhaps the most unexpected aspect of this exercise was how difficult it was to find such limits. It was this cumulative effect that pushed my argument close to a 'Zeitgeist' one, purporting – now, hopefully, with some evidentiary backing – to encompass almost a whole culture (albeit within the limits of the broad, primarily urban circles of literate and semi-literate society from which most of the evidence was drawn).

I could identify only two possible limits beyond which the pattern of radical change in the last two decades of the eighteenth century did not seem to take place. One, suggestive but not conclusive, seemed to be the generic boundary of pornography: in a few cases, late eighteenth-century pornographic writing retained those earlier gender-flexing cultural forms that by now were disappearing elsewhere. If these exceptions were in fact the rule, they may raise the interesting possibility that those earlier forms did not completely disappear, but could also go underground, into the very different cultural terrain of illicit homosocial humour. (If this is true, moreover, then it may raise doubts about the extent to which pornography – and perhaps also erotica, as in the case of Harvey's study – can be straightforwardly put forth as representative of wider cultural trends, without a careful consideration of this genre's quirky – and changing? – relationship to prevailing norms.) For the second boundary beyond which this late eighteenth-century pattern did not extend I had more evidence. This boundary was the Atlantic Ocean: it appeared to be the case that, whereas prior to the last quarter of the century, the Anglo-American gender regime was similar on both sides of the Atlantic, these sides diverged sharply in the wake of the American Revolution, as the nascent American republic did not follow the same path of change as its mother country. As it happened, discovering this limit directed my attention to the moment of divergence of these two formerly culturally-unified worlds – namely, the American revolutionary war – as an important component of the explanation for these late eighteenth-century developments.

This last point reminds us of an important limit of this methodological exercise itself. This analysis was phenomenological: it was concerned with how best to chart and delimit a particular cultural pattern, but not with how to explain it. The explanation itself needs to address two distinct questions: the one with which historians feel more comfortable, *why* did a particular pattern occur in a particular time and place, to be then perhaps replaced by another at a different point in time; and the one often overlooked, of dynamics of transmission – *how* was this pattern diffused across the disparate spheres in which it is observable. It is a common peril of 'Zeitgeist' arguments, with their almost mystical undertones, to mistake simultaneity for explanation: as if the moment in time has in and of itself some inherent characteristic, as well as the power – the driving power of 'the spirit of the age' – to shape all things sharing the same temporal bracket.

***

The question of explanation aside, there are obvious limitations to the strategy I have just described for evaluating the historical significance of broad cultural trends. This strategy, to recap, consisted of examining several increasing levels of repetition and resonance: beginning first within particular cultural forms, then combining several cultural forms that are different from each other ('repetition in the first degree') until a tentative broader pattern appears and finally pushing out in every direction in order to test the suggested pattern in as many and as varied cultural sites as possible ('repetition in the second degree'), moving into increasingly less likely places with the hope of encountering the limits beyond which the pattern in question did not take hold. The first problem, surely, is how to know when enough is enough: how many points does it take to delineate an elephant? For repetition in the first degree, common sense might suggest when sufficient evidence has been adduced to make a plausible argument about a repeated pattern. But for repetition in the second degree there cannot be

sufficient evidence: the best we can do is strive to make the argument increasingly compelling across a wider, though always still limited, cultural
landscape. The reader may ultimately find this relative and even arbitrary
standard for rigour in cultural history unsatisfying, though I would also
argue that the very awareness of the strengths and weaknesses of collections of evidence would already constitute an important step towards more
rigorous practice.

The second, related problem is that such a strategy balloons up quickly
to become a kind of total history with no outer limit. As such, not only
must it always remain a work-in-progress, it is simply too labour intensive
to be undertaken too often. Thus, as the critical reader quickly realises, in
The Making of the Modern Self I attempted this methodological exercise
in full only on the eighteenth-century fortunes of the category of gender,
but not on other categories of identity also discussed in the book, like race,
class, the human/animal distinction, or personal identity itself. Rather, a
compromise with the brevity of the author's working life resulted in those
latter sections remaining at the more readily attainable level that I called
here repetition in the first degree.

In passing, it is worth noting that this problem also has a perhaps unexpected technological aspect. We are entering a new age of digital access to historical evidence. Every year, huge full-text and fully-searchable
electronic databases are added to our search tools, allowing the historian
immediate access to a vastly greater range of evidence than ever before.
Among students of eighteenth-century Britain the most comprehensive is
the Eighteenth Century Collection Online, familiar to its friends as ECCO,
which offers full access and reasonably advanced and reliable searching
capabilities for a huge number – though not all – of British printed sources
from this period. On the one hand, databases like ECCO make it easier
to amass a far more comprehensive collection of cultural soundings, and
indeed to bring them together in a more systemic, serial, and quantitatively
persuasive manner than had ever been possible previously (even if in practice, satisfactory research strategies of this kind are more difficult to devise
than might first be supposed). On the other hand, databases with hundreds
of thousands of documents greatly aggravate the vertiginous ballooning
of the evidence, now ever more in danger of veering out of control. Thus,
in my own example, had ECCO been available a few years earlier, the
flood of additional materials for each one of the many cultural forms and
locations examined in my book might well have made the completion of
the project well-nigh impossible.

My own conclusion, therefore, from this experiment has been that such
a methodology would work most effectively for a better defined question
that makes more limited claims on the same broad cultural canvas; that is
to say, for such studies that retain the 'big picture' aspiration of uncovering

patterns that spread widely across many cultural locations in a given moment and place, but for whom the patterns studied are themselves more limited in scope and thus easier to track down more fully. To illustrate this, I would like to turn briefly to a recent contribution to the history of sexuality (more than the history of gender) from the pen of Thomas Laqueur himself, who thus frames conveniently the methodological developments in this field and in this chapter. For, having travelled a considerable distance since *Making Sex*, Laqueur's *Solitary Sex: A Cultural History of Masturbation* (2003) is a textbook example of a cultural history self-reflectively and methodically striving for rigour.

Laqueur's book goes back to his seemingly favourite question, the relationship between sex and modernity. Its basic claim, at first glance, suffers from the familiar weakness of cultural-historical over-reach, stretching one's credulity almost to breaking point. In or around 1712, Laqueur asserts (hello again to Virginia Woolf), modern masturbation was born, and quickly assumed a key role as the sexuality of modernity. A seductive formulation to be sure: but is it simply to be filed away with so many other announcements of the birth of modernity that cannot really be given historical substance? Not quite. Laqueur, as it turns out, goes a long way towards substantiating this claim and makes sure to show the reader the logic of his method every step of the way. The modern obsession with masturbation began with a single text, *Onania: Or, The Heinous Sin of Self Pollution, and All Its Frightful Consequences, in Both Sexes Considered...* , published in London *c*.1712, and from this text spread outward. Laqueur therefore begins by documenting the actual spread and the growing cultural resonance of this European obsession in much detail – quantitatively as well as qualitatively, moving between genres and cultural forms, crossing social, political and national lines, and even locating contemporary witnesses who were aware of what the twenty-first century historian is trying to tell us. Laqueur also attempts to demonstrate that the moral urgency about masturbation was a novel phenomenon: for many centuries of continuous moralising prior to the eighteenth century, masturbation had been a marginal, not central, problem – so whatever was happening in the eighteenth century was indeed new and different. Having thus carefully connected many dots to delineate an elephant – that is, a demonstrably far-reaching cultural pattern that can be pinpointed in time and place (though Laqueur might have done more to investigate its limits) – he then moves on to speculate on its origins and its meaning as a threshold to modernity. Laqueur identifies three aspects of masturbation – imagination, privacy/secrecy, excess – that coincided with newly pervasive freedoms and anxieties of the age, or more specifically of the new culture of the market place. Masturbation, he concludes, suddenly and forcefully became the prime locus of guilt because it was 'a reflection of the deepest problems of modern life'.[21]

It can be left for another occasion to assess the implications of Laqueur's speculations about the cultural pattern he uncovered for the understanding of the condition of the individual in modernity. I am more interested here in how Laqueur goes about documenting this pattern. Cultural history's insights, Laqueur shows, can still be applied boldly on a large canvas, by carefully and self-consciously generating procedures that can validate claims about dominant, significant and pervasive cultural patterns at specific historical moments. Such procedures will of course vary according to the specific patterns in which the historian is interested: these are examples not blueprints. But they hopefully can help persuade at least some readers that the cultural history of gender and sexuality can indeed become methodologically more rigorous.

***

On a different front, however, from the perspective of the history of sexuality/body/gender, Laqueur's argument about masturbation may in fact seem rather surprising, especially in light of his earlier work. Laqueur's later book, to borrow a well-known formulation, is a history of sexuality with the body left out. The new anxieties about masturbation were akin to those about gambling, say: the radical turning point of the eighteenth century in Laqueur's *mise-en-scène*, the proffered centrepiece of a context-specific cultural history of sex, bears little relationship to actual sexual bodies or behaviours – the fact that it was about sexuality is tangential to the argument. There is no suggestion, for instance, that eighteenth-century people actually masturbated more or enjoyed masturbation more than before; or that sexuality qua sexuality suddenly and fundamentally assumed a more central role in shaping people's 'modern' consciousness. Put differently, there is little evidence that the author of *Solitary Sex* has found much use for the supposedly fundamental eighteenth-century transformation in conceptualising sexual bodies that had been posited by the author of *Making Sex*. Instead, the advent of modernity unfolds here – rather persuasively – on top of sexual bodies, behaviours and understandings that in themselves remain constant and unchanging, and are thus written out of the narrative of cultural change.

Unexpectedly, therefore, Laqueur's recent book appears to join the thrust of most of the studies with which I began this chapter, insisting as they do on *longue durée* continuities in understandings of sex, gender and the body. This brings me to my final topic in this chapter, which has to do not with the methodology but with the presuppositions of a cultural history of gender or sex: specifically, with how these presuppositions fare when confronted with the possibility that significant components in the history of gender, sex and the body may prove to be *not* primarily shaped by culture.

Occasionally, though not often, we can find hints of such a suggestion in the pages of some of the authors discussed above. For instance, towards the end of Harvey's *Reading Sex*, in a chapter on notions of space, we read that erotica 'reveals a powerful congruity between women and enclosed spaces at the level of the corporeal'. Soft, shaded and secluded settings, Harvey writes, such as grottoes, groves and enclosed rooms, can appear as vaginal spaces – and this 'suggests a highly erotic charge to the historically powerful association between women and the "private"'.[22] What Harvey appears to propose here, then, is that the association of women and the private may well be an extra-historical one, predicated on the corporeal not the cultural, and thus applying equally well, say, to classical Greece – Harvey's other example – as to Georgian Britain.

Now to be sure, this move is not Harvey's manifest intent. On the contrary, she immediately follows it with an explicit refusal of this effect: 'However, seeing bodies only as origins for constructions of space threatens to naturalise the body, and suggests that male and female bodies are understood in the same ways in different times and places'. A threat indeed: imagine that we could not go on blaming the rise of the middle class, say, or the industrial revolution, or republican ideology, for an increasing association of women and the private at a particular time and place. Though Harvey herself is much too subtle a historian for such crude arguments, it is the assumptions behind them that she wishes to protect from the threat of a naturalised body. On the other hand, the actual historical evidence regarding the association of women and the private, as Vickery already pointed out in an influential critique fifteen years ago, does in fact defy linear narratives or an easy pinning down to a particular historical moment. Rather, Vickery warned, 'it can be found in almost any century we care to look', 'an ancient trope of western writing'. It is therefore not surprising, perhaps, that at one point in *The Gentleman's Daughter*, Vickery, too, edges to the brink of the same ahistorical precipice. Pointing to the continuities of good parenting from 1600 to the present, she concedes that such an argument 'unwittingly invoke[s] "instinct" as an historical constant, implying that the force of "nature" is immutable and inescapable – an uncomfortable suggestion for historians and feminists alike'.[23] Uncomfortable enough that, despite an apparent momentary willingness to embrace such an 'unwitting' thought, it does not in fact resurface elsewhere in Vickery's book.

Regardless of whether we find the particular explanations for the seeming transhistorical continuities that Harvey and Vickery identify in these two instances especially compelling, what I wish to draw attention to is the almost instinctive withdrawal of both historians from the possible implications of these moves even as the analyses that they have themselves undertaken suggest them. Can we think of naturalising the body as not quite the 'threatening' and 'uncomfortable' departure that Harvey and Vickery take it to be? Similarly, can we fruitfully consider Gowing's findings as a corrective to, not a simple confirmation of, the cultural historian's credo that 'the most apparently natural of bodily events and processes . . . are the product of culture'? Can one entertain the possibility that this presupposition is not *always* true, and this – importantly – without undermining the project of the cultural history of gender and sex?

In 1994, in her bold and thought-provoking *Oedipus and the Devil*, Lyndal Roper, a historian of early modern Germany, made precisely this point. 'It does not endanger the status of the historical', she stated, 'to concede that there are aspects of human nature which are enduring, just as there are aspects of human physiology which are constitutional'. Roper's book challenged the most routine procedures and presuppositions of cultural historians, especially in relation to gender and the body, by insisting that cultural history must recognise its own limits. 'It is of course true that we experience the body through mediations of various kinds', she wrote; but, 'because we want to emphasize the way notions of the body are constructed, the temptation is to write as if there were nothing *but* a historically constructed body'. This 'excessive emphasis on the cultural creation of subjectivity' rests 'on a denial of the body' as well as on an exaggerated insistence on 'the supposed gap between ourselves and the past'.[24] Culture certainly played a crucial role in any historical situation, but perhaps not always an all-encompassing one.

A decade and a half later, historians have yet seriously to pick up Roper's gauntlet. The authors discussed above, even when their materials bring them right to the brink, are only rarely and reluctantly willing to acknowledge this possibility, let alone to explore it further or incorporate it squarely into their historical analysis. (This is true of my own book as well: one of the unanswered questions in *The Making of the Modern Self* is whether the eighteenth-century *ancien régime* of gender, or of identity, was inherently unstable and in a sense doomed to collapse given some trigger or other, as indeed it did. The familiarity, however, of historical scenarios involving cycles of periods of relative playfulness followed by seemingly inevitable clampdowns should have at least raised the possibility that the dynamic in such cycles is transhistorical and extra-cultural, a possibility to which I gave no consideration at all.) In a recent study of rape in eighteenth-century America, Sharon Block displays unusual awareness of the difficulty. 'My approach', she states at the outset, 'begins from the assumption that sexual practices, desires, and ideologies are cultural constructs'. She immediately concedes, however, that 'rape seems transhistoric and transcultural'; a 'startling' realisation which causes her to admit confusion since 'as a historian, I have been trained to mark the exceptionality of an era, region, or cultural group'. Block thus concludes: 'Ultimately, I am not opposed to readers' [sic] seeing various parts of this book as transhistorical, but I also hope that they will see how sexual coercion was intricately tied to early America's specific social and cultural realities'. The admirable self-awareness underscores the uncomfortable contortions in which the historian of sex, gender and sexuality finds herself when her research pits her against the presuppositions of her chosen path as a cultural historian: Block thus assures the reader that 'I have been careful to avoid ahistoricism or essentialism'.[25]

Ahistoricism and essentialism: we all know the political as well as intellectual reasons why historians of gender are so careful to avoid them. (Indeed, we are still far from the point where essentialism is no longer put to noxious uses, even – as the recent American Historical Association report on the status of women in the historical profession makes soberingly clear – among our own ranks.)[26] And yet, as much of the work surveyed here implicitly indicates, and as Roper has already suggested explicitly, the cultural history of gender needs to develop ways to incorporate a modicum of 'ahistorical' or 'essentialist' thinking, persuasively reconceptualised and delimited, without giving away the store. In the classroom and in conferences I have sometimes provoked (or annoyed) students and colleagues by referring to this development as the 'neo-essentialist' critique. More constructively for our purposes here we can call it a 'corporeal' critique, though in other fields of cultural history it may not always be the body around which the extra-cultural domain is centred. Compelling an Archimedean point outside the cultural-historical box, this critique would push the historian to explore where the culturally constructed ends and the ahistorical and extra-cultural begins; and thus, most importantly, how they relate to each other. Unlike unreflective essentialism that presupposes that certain aspects of the human condition necessarily lie outside history and culture, and unlike unreflective constructivism that presupposes that no aspect of the human condition lies outside history and culture, the self-reflexive preoccupation of the 'corporealist' (or the 'neo-essentialist') is the un-predetermined boundary between the two.

Roper offers one way to do this, through the insights of psychoanalysis – a body of knowledge that emerged precisely from the fascination with the relationship between the physical and the psychic, the body and the imagination. In other fields of knowledge, too, fields that have made suggestive strides in understanding transformations of human behaviour – genetics, evolutionary psychology, sociobiology, neuroscience all come to mind – such braiding of nature and culture has become commonplace. And yet these bodies of knowledge typically generate considerable discomfort among scholars in the humanities, precisely because they are taken to be essentialist and ahistorical;[27] they have thus not made yet much of a dent in the historical *métier*. I would therefore like to conclude with a new book that takes on precisely this challenge. While Daniel Lord Smail's *On Deep*

History and the Brain (2008) is in the main not specifically about gender, it experiments with new ways of thinking about human culture and human nature, historical change and long-term continuities that are immediately germane to the practice of gender history. As we shall see, they even shed some unexpected light on specific eighteenth-century issues raised in the previous pages.

Smail's goal is to tell a history of humanity within a time scale that spans the divide between history and prehistory, that is to say thousands of years, and yet not such a time scale in which traditional accounts of evolution are usually framed, extending over hundreds of thousands of years, that are therefore for all intents and purposes static and ahistorical. What allows Smail to develop this finely calibrated temporal perspective, which he calls 'deep history', is the breakthroughs in biology, neurophysiology and cognitive science since the 1990s; both regarding 'micro-evolution' – that is to say, evolutionary changes that occur in historical time – and especially regarding the workings of the brain. The former enables Smail to conjecture how culture and biology interact in long-term stretches that are nonetheless not ahistorical; for instance, the evolutionary development of adult lactose tolerance in European, South Asian and Middle Eastern societies as a consequence of a cultural transformation, namely the domestication of cattle, sheep and goats and the emergence of dairy/livestock culture over the last couple of millennia. The latter – that is, neuroscience – provides Smail with the connecting thread for a deep neurohistory of humanity over the last several millennia: the main characteristic of the last 5,000 years, he conjectures, is a new regime of brain-body chemistry. (Chemistry here is meant literally, involving particular chemical agents accompanying the bodily transmission of particular feelings.) Humans during this period became more attuned to a dynamic bodily economy of particular chemicals released during mood changes, and thus to a whole range of mood-altering cultural practices; be they song, ritual, gossip (a particularly interesting example), shopping, stimulants or recreational sex. This, for Smail, is the deep historical narrative, and indeed the deep meaning, of modernity.

So how might this perspective inform our thinking about the issues discussed in the previous pages? Recall for instance Vickery's observation that there have been strong continuities in good parenting over long historical periods, which might tempt the historian 'unwittingly' to invoke 'instinct'. As it turns out, neurophysiological studies have revealed that parental caregiving is strongly associated with high levels of particular hormones (prolactin and oxytocin for males); and that species that have more parental involvement in the raising of offspring develop more brain receptors for these hormones.[28] If we go along with the conclusions of such studies, then nature and culture appear locked in a *pas de deux*: while it is not the case – as Smail wryly notes – that injecting deadbeat fathers with prolactin would turn them into model parents, since they may lack the receptors for the hormone because of cultural conditioning or personal development, it is also not the case that culture alone determines the receptivity of the brain to these hormones. Parental bonding is shaped by culture that is shaped by neurophysiology that is shaped by culture. It is thus perhaps not surprising, nor essentialist, to find good parenting – or at least parental investment in offspring (since 'good parenting' is already culturally mediated) – to be a matter of deep history.

Smail's neurohistorical narrative, in fact, can illuminate not only continuities but also – perhaps more unexpectedly – change. In his 5,000-year account of the deep history of modernity through the perspective of the brain there is one particular moment that signals faster change: the eighteenth century. (This part of the narrative is knowingly, and perhaps problematically, Eurocentric.) The European eighteenth century witnessed a significant expansion in the range of mechanisms and practices that influenced individuals' own body chemistry – what Smail calls 'autotropic' mechanisms, as distinct from those affecting the bodies of others. Eighteenth-century Europeans became prone – even mildly addicted (a new socio-cultural phenomenon) – to the chemicals released in their brains by a wide variety of stimulating practices. Some were actually stimulants available on the market in much greater quantities than before: coffee, sugar, chocolate, tobacco. Others were newly expanding cultural practices, like the excitement of shopping in an emerging market society (or speculating in an expanding financial world, an important activity that Smail does not mention), reading novels and generally reading for leisure, or consuming pornography. These activities all released particular bodily chemicals, and the desire to alter one's own body chemistry is what lay at the heart of their success. The eighteenth century, Smail concludes, had its own new 'psychotropic profile', by which he means precisely this regime or economy of body chemistry, in which formerly isolated practices came together in a new cumulative framework. Ruling elites, moreover, who had used to have greater influence on things and practices that altered the body chemistry of their subjects (a point Smail develops in some detail), responded by trying to regulate this (relatively) unfettered self-stimulation.

But now, supposing Smail is mostly right in his neurohistorical account of the eighteenth century, consider in its light Laqueur's account of the explosion of anxiety about masturbation precisely during the same period. Surely there are few practices more 'autotropic' than masturbation? The putative new psychotropic regime of the eighteenth century can account for both an increase in the actual practice of masturbation, which cannot be verified through historical sources, and for the dramatic increase in the preoccupation with it and in the cultural pressure to regulate it, which

Laqueur has documented so effectively. Putting on Smail's spectacles, then, we have a completely new context – one that now very much includes bodies – for understanding a highly significant episode in the cultural history of sexuality.

Despite these speculations, it remains to be seen what effects such a 'deep historical' perspective would actually have on the way we tell the history of gender, sex or sexuality. One perhaps insurmountable obstacle is that historians do not really have critical tools to assess the knowledge coming from these biological fields. It is thus not a bit unproblematic for an article that is preoccupied with the procedures and limits of interpretation to end with assertions about neuroscience for which neither I – nor, I believe, Smail – can offer an independent evaluation beyond asking the reader to take the statements of others, supposedly buttressed by their status as the latest 'science', at their word. So perhaps neuroscience and evolutionary biology will ultimately not materialise as the richest vein to mine in searching for that missing extra-cultural insight. But be that as it may, I hope I have convinced that a corporealist critique of the uncompromising constructivism of cultural history, far from constituting a methodological setback for or a political retreat from the cultural-historical agenda, is in fact a necessary and valuable step in making the cultural history of sex and gender more rigorous.

Notes

For comments on earlier versions of this chapter I am grateful to Donna Andrew, David Bell, Maria Bucur, Michel Chaouli, Seth Denbo, Jonathan Elmer, James Epstein, Margaret Hunt, Sarah Knott (twice!), Michael McGerr, Yael Shapira, Alexandra Shepard and Garthine Walker.

1. First published as Oswald Spengler, *Der Untergang des Abendlandes*, 2 vols (Munich: Beck, 1918–23).
2. See Dror Wahrman, *The Making of the Modern Self: Identity and Culture in Eighteenth-Century England* (New Haven: Yale University Press, 2004), p. 45 (the phonetic nod to Lévi-Strauss is mostly unintended).
3. Laura Gowing, *Common Bodies: Women, Touch and Power in Seventeenth-Century England* (New Haven: Yale University Press, 2003), p. 2.
4. Thomas Laqueur, *Making Sex: Body and Gender from the Greeks to Freud* (Cambridge: Harvard University Press, 1990).
5. Mark Jenner and Bertrand Taithe, cited in Karen Harvey, *Reading Sex in the Eighteenth Century: Bodies and Gender in English Erotic Culture* (Cambridge: Cambridge University Press, 2004), p. 5.
6. Laqueur, *Making Sex*, p. 5; Thomas Laqueur, 'Orgasm, Generation, and the Politics of Reproductive Biology', in Catherine Gallagher and Thomas Laqueur (eds), *The Making of the Modern Body* (Berkeley: California University Press, 1987), pp. 1–41.
7. Katharine Park, 'Itineraries of the "One-Sex Body": A History of an Idea', unpublished paper. I am grateful to her for the opportunity to read this important essay before publication. For correctives regarding the earlier periods see also Joan Cadden, *The Meanings of Sex Difference in the Middle Ages* (Cambridge: Cambridge University Press, 1995); Annick Jaulin, 'La fabrique du sexe, Thomas Laqueur et Aristote', *Clio: Histoire, femmes et sociétés* 14 (2001), pp. 195–205. Scholars who have engaged with Laqueur's arguments for the later

period, creatively as well as critically, include Londa Schiebinger, *Nature's Body: Gender in the Making of Modern Science* (Boston: Beacon Press, 1993); Anne C. Vila, *Enlightenment and Pathology: Sensibility in the Literature and Medicine of Eighteenth-Century France* (Baltimore: Johns Hopkins University Press, 1998), ch. 7, pp. 225–57.

8. Mary E. Fissell, *Vernacular Bodies: The Politics of Reproduction in Early Modern England* (Oxford: Oxford University Press, 2005), esp. pp. 11, 248.

9. Gowing, *Common Bodies*, p. 19. Lennard J. Davis, *Factual Fictions: The Origins of the English Novel* (1983; Philadelphia: University of Pennsylvania Press, 1996).

10. Gowing, *Common Bodies*, p. 13, citing Craig Muldrew.

11. Gowing, *Common Bodies*, pp. 19–20, 109.

12. Gowing, *Common Bodies*, pp. 2, 29, 204–5. This assertion is of course central to the project of gender history, and needs to be repeated loudly and often until the remaining bastions of ignorance are toppled. My point below is not at all that it is somehow wrong, but rather that we can still ask whether it constitutes the whole truth and nothing but the truth in each and every circumstance.

13. Harvey, *Reading Sex in the Eighteenth Century*, p. 101. Compare also the continuities noted in Julie Peakman, *Mighty Lewd Books: The Development of Pornography in Eighteenth-Century England* (Basingstoke: Palgrave, 2003).

14. Amanda Vickery, *The Gentleman's Daughter: Women's Lives in Georgian England* (New Haven: Yale University Press, 1998), pp. 93, 96. And for the parallel 'continuities evident in British masculinity over several centuries', see H. Barker, 'Soul, Purse and Family: Middling and Lower-Class Masculinity in Eighteenth-Century Manchester', *Social History* 33:1 (2008), p. 34

15. Alexandra Shepard, 'From Anxious Patriarchs to Refined Gentlemen? Manhood in Britain, circa 1500–1700', *Journal of British Studies* 44 (2005), pp. 281–95, here p. 292, which, despite its title, deals also with the eighteenth century; Alexandra Shepard, *Meanings of Manhood in Early Modern England* (Oxford: Oxford University Press, 2003), here p. 7.

16. Compare Jacques Derrida's position on this question, which is often quoted without the crucial last sentence: 'I do not believe in decisive ruptures, in an unequivocal "epistemological break", as it is called today. Breaks are always, and fatally, reinscribed in an old cloth that must continually, interminably be undone. This interminability is not an accident or contingency; it is essential, systematic, and theoretical. *And this in no way minimizes the necessity and relative importance of certain breaks, of the appearance and definition of new structure*'. Jacques Derrida, *Positions*, tr. Alan Bass (Chicago: University of Chicago Press, 1981), p. 24 (my italics).

17. Lisa Cody, *Birthing the Nation: Sex, Science, and the Conception of Eighteenth-Century Britons* (Oxford: Oxford University Press, 2005), p. 23.

18. Wahrman, *The Making of the Modern Self*, pp. xv–xvi.

19. Wahrman, *The Making of the Modern Self*. The following paragraphs rely in particular on chapters 1–2.

20. It seems to me that Peter Mandler means something similar in his call upon cultural historians to strive for 'a mental map of the *entire field of representation* in which their texts sit' in order to assess more accurately their weight or significance: see Peter Mandler, 'The Problem with Cultural History', *Cultural and Social History* 1 (2004), pp. 94–117, here p. 97, together with the judicious elaboration in Carol Watts, 'Thinking about the X Factor, or, What's the Cultural History of Cultural History?', *Cultural and Social History* 1 (2004), pp. 217–24, here pp. 219–20.

21. Thomas W. Laqueur, *Solitary Sex: A Cultural History of Masturbation* (New York: Zone Books, 2003), p. 249.

22. Harvey, *Reading Sex*, pp. 171–2.

23. Amanda Vickery, 'Golden Age to Separate Spheres? A Review of the Categories and Chronology of English Women's History', *Historical Journal* 36 (1993), p. 412; Vickery, *The Gentleman's Daughter*, pp. 6, 91.

24. Lyndal Roper, *Oedipus and the Devil: Witchcraft, Sexuality and Religion in Early Modern Europe* (London: Routledge, 1994), pp. 3, 4, 13, 17.
25. Sharon Block, *Rape and Sexual Power in Early America* (Chapel Hill: University of North Carolina Press, 2006), pp. 7, 241.
26. Elizabeth Lunbeck for the Committee on Women Historians, *The Status of Women in the Historical Profession, 2005*. See <http://www.historians.org/governance/cwh/2005Status/index.cfm>.
27. For a discussion of psychoanalytical history – including Roper's – and of this charge, see Garthine Walker, 'Psychoanalysis and History', in Stefan Berger, Heiko Feldner and Kevin Passmore (eds), *Writing History: Theory and Practice* (London: Arnold, 2003), pp. 141–60.
28. Daniel Lord Smail, *On Deep History and the Brain* (Berkeley: University of California Press, 2008), pp. 115–16.

8 Agency, Periodisation and Change in the Gender and Women's History of Colonial India

Padma Anagol

It is now widely recognised within the historical profession that measuring time and giving names to discrete periods in order to make research manageable has given rise to periodisation. Naming a period such as the Reformation, Enlightenment or Industrial Revolution has allowed historians to trace origins of change and track major transitions from one chunk of the past to another. But, as Ludmilla Jordonova has demonstrated, conventional chronologies hamper fresh thinking; naturalise particular views of history; and are often value-laden, preventing critical scrutiny of their assumptions and agendas.[1] India is no exception to this general observation with the writing of modern Indian history largely driven by the organising principle of making sense of the 300 or so years of colonial rule. Understanding the power relationship between the metropole or home country (Britain) and the periphery or colony (India) during the crucial years 1600–1947, has preoccupied historians writing on India. It has led to the adoption of a certain frame of thinking, which I term 'imperialism-nationalism'. Imperialism-nationalism refers to a mode of thinking and writing about Indian history as a contest between the British Raj and Indian nationalism. Embedded within the imperialism-nationalism frame is the central idea of a colonial and an indigenous side of Indian history wherein events, processes and phenomena that took place in India during British rule are seen, thought through and written about with the opposing principle of coloniser (dominant) and colonised (subordinate) always in mind. Over a century or so, several schools of thought have emerged, known in the historiography as imperial, Cambridge, nationalist, subaltern and postcolonial (see next section). A feature common to all the schools is that they function within the framework of imperialism-nationalism.

This chapter begins with a critique of the imperialism-nationalism periodisation and its concomitant privileging of the time unit 1885 (when the Indian National Congress was founded) to 1947 (when India achieved independence). I shall argue that the resulting fixation with the theme of the 'birth-of-the-nation', the founding of the political organ of the educated classes, namely the Indian National Congress, and the growth of nationalist consciousness, has led to the obfuscation, neglect or the complete erasure of women's agency. Further, it has resulted in many inconsistencies and unresolved issues regarding a range of topics within the broader gender and women's history of modern India. I hope to demonstrate in the first section how the use of an overarching frame has an inbuilt tendency to deny agency to certain subaltern groups like Indian women and I will call for the periodisation based upon nation and nationalism to be discarded. The second half of the chapter is devoted to making a case for enlarging the time span through the adoption of a new chronology. In the later sections of the chapter, I shall explore the way forward for the recovery of agency by proposing a new chronological time sequence and a new template for understanding agency within which scholars are sufficiently enabled to retrieve the voice-consciousness of Indian women and record change in the gender and women's history of modern India. This inquiry is conducted by interspersing the narrative with examples from the wide-ranging existing scholarship as well as my own research undertaken over several years.

Interrogating the imperialism-nationalism paradigm

As a student of gender and women's history in the late 1980s, I encountered several problems of theory and method with contemporary scholarship starting with the imperialist-nationalist historiography that every student of Indian history learns at undergraduate level. The fashioning of nationalist consciousness and the delineation of the various movements that led eventually to the birth of the nation has preoccupied historians since India and Pakistan became independent self-governing states in 1947. Scholarship, now identified as the early imperial historiography, studied the lives of British statesmen, western institutions and ideologies, and credited the British with making India into a nation.[2] The findings of the early imperial school were modified by scholars based mainly at Cambridge University (the 'Cambridge School').[3] The Cambridge school analysed imperialism as a weak force in the twentieth century, arguing that Indian collaboration was necessitated, thus allowing for the emergence of self-seeking, highly interested local factions and provincial elite groups who finally bargained effectively with the British for power and patronage. Indian nationalism in this version was explained as a selfish, rather than a heroic venture, turning the sacrifices of several generations of Indians into a base sentiment.

Reversing this metropolitan perspective, scholars belonging to the national-ist historiographical tradition studied the lives of great Indian nationalists and the movements they led, and argued that it was an idealist venture driven by indigenous forces of nationalist conscience. The point I wish to draw attention to is not the validity of one school over another, but rather the polarisation of the view regarding the core issue of 'who gets the credit for the making-of-the-nation' evident in such histories of the Indian nation. Studies continue to be governed by a dualism of people/nation ver-sus foreign/alien rule, which determines what is and is not significant in the history of India. Far from signalling a shift, some recent trends have been no more than expressions of this paradigm. For example, the subal-tern studies project should be understood as part of a postcolonial studies approach whose existence is predicated on the dualism of coloniser and colonised. Still, there have been a number of moves to escape the hold of the nationalism-imperialism paradigm.[4] More recently, Patrick McGinn has argued that, just as nationalism subsumes individual differences under a myth of the collective, nationalist historical writing renders its practi-tioners blind not only to inequalities such as class and gender, but also to important dialogues between rulers and ruled about rights and obligations which both preceded and followed the British era.[5] How the imperialism-nationalism frame marginalises women and ignores gender relationships can be demonstrated through an analysis of the main schools of thought and their preoccupations.

Since independence, practitioners of the nationalist school in India claimed that the imperialist and Cambridge schools' analyses of the In-dian national movement were based on a 'denial of the basic contradic-tion between the interests of the Indian people and of British colonial-ism'.[6] This denial was linked to the further denial that, 'the Indian national movement represented the Indian side of this contradiction, that is, it was anti-imperialist, that is, it opposed British imperialism in India'.[7] By con-centrating excessively on imperialist spokesmen and casting doubt on the intentions of Indian nationalists, the nationalist historian Bipan Chandra and his followers opined that the Cambridge school had delegitimised the national movement in order to give full credit to the Raj (that is, British rule) for preparing Indians for parliamentary democracy and thus for the creation of India. In their explanation, nationalism had thus transformed into a narrow, selfish ideology and the national movement itself was seen as a struggle for power between various groups of Indians and the foreign ruler. In turn, the focus of the nationalist school has been critiqued by the subaltern school as being equally elitist because, instead of turning the lens on viceroys and governors, these historians glorified the actions of key Indian leaders such as Mohandas Karamchand Gandhi, Jawaharlal Nehru and Muhammad Ali Jinnah. In an electrifying statement issued in 1982,

the founder member of the subaltern school, Ranajit Guha, alleged that the
writing of Indian history had been marked by an elitist bias and promised
to put the 'politics of the people [*sic*]',[8] back into history by rescuing the
marginalised groups of Indians through an 'emphasis on the primacy of
the subaltern as the subject of historical and sociological enquiry'.[9]

With the rise of the subaltern school, the picture seemed to worsen for
the Indian woman.[10] The Cambridge and nationalist schools had never
made claims for integrating gender or women, so nobody could fault them
in this regard, but the subaltern school had raised hopes by inscribing the
magic words 'oppressed', 'subordinated' and 'marginalised' in their intention sheet. However, women were totally absent from early subaltern
histories.[11] Fashioned as a tool of opposition to elite history, subaltern historians were interested in delineating the role of the autonomous peasant
as an insurgent in the national resistance movements. Using the technique
of 'reading against the grain', subaltern scholarship to some extent did recover the male peasant's mythic visions, insurgent consciousness, kinship
and community bonds but did not extend it to the woman peasant. Without
a keen interest in gender relations, the female peasant waited patiently in
the background for her role to be delineated – and in fact continues to wait
to be rescued from the condescension not of history but of subaltern historians. Further, the subaltern approach, while considering the indigenous
religious mentalities of the tribal and the peasant, denies the same attention
to groups of Indian Christian converts and their contestatory challenges to
the iniquities of the caste system. Postcolonial scholarship has followed the
Saidian axiom that Christianity in the Age of Empire can only be viewed
as an instrument of cultural imperialism.[12] This adage, too, has served to
restrict restoring subjectivities to some subaltern tribes and castes who left
the belief systems of their birth and opted for Christianity – the religion of
the rulers. Race, religion, sex and gender are not as yet rigorous categories
of analysis in subaltern studies. Ranajit Guha's original conception of what
the subaltern studies project entailed did not include the categories of religion and race.[13] Race, which includes European women's involvement
with empire, has instead been compartmentalised within the larger British
new imperial histories, and scholars with gender interests have now produced monumental works.[14] Although historians of the Subaltern Studies
Collective do consider the religious beliefs of Indian marginalised groups
such as the tribal and the peasant, the same attention is not accorded those
who chose the religion of the ruling classes. This is made evident in Guha's
original conception of who constitute the 'elite' class and here he includes
missions and missionaries as belonging to 'dominant foreign groups'.[15]
Moreover, Indian Christians are erroneously driven into the elite social
groups because Guha further defines people and subaltern classes as representing the 'demographic difference between the total Indian population

and all those whom we have described as the "elite" [*sic*]'.[16] Delineating
the histories of missions and missionaries instead has been left to church
historians in India and a small group of dedicated scholars who specialise
in empire and mission histories.[17]

In the 1970s and 1980s, there emerged a new generation of feminist historians interested in explaining either Gandhi's impact on the changing role
of Indian women or what women contributed to the Gandhian-led movements. To some extent, the picture of passive women following Gandhi
in an uncritical manner has been modified by scholarship looking at gendered constructions of the nationalist movement and by paying attention
to women's voices in the resistance struggles.[18] It does, however, beg the
question why and how thousands of Indian women suddenly lost their
age-old inhibitions and rushed outside the so-called 'private' sphere to
participate in and lead demonstrations, hoist flags, picket liquor shops and
cheerfully receive various sentences of imprisonment. Were there any continuities from an earlier period of women's assertion in India? Surely these
fiery women nationalists must have inherited, or at least benefited from, a
knowledge or experience of an earlier tradition of women's dissent. The
periodisation so far, dependent on a chronology of national liberation, has
not allowed for connected histories from the nineteenth to the twentieth
centuries to be explored. This omission needs to be rectified.

A second conundrum in retrieving women's agency is the controversy
over the term 'feminism'. A generation of scholars from the social sciences
and women's studies who had entered the brave new India of the 1970s
and early 1980s,[19] celebrated Gandhi's role in bringing Indian women
into the public by the formulation of a unique strand of Indian feminism
called Gandhian Feminism.[20] But, consistent with the inconsistencies of
the scholarship, the term 'feminism' or 'feminist' was met with great hesitancy or hostility when applied to contemporary women of India. In 1990,
Madhu Kishwar, a sterling example of a feminist who had inspired many
Indian women, including myself, rejected the term 'feminist', both for
herself and her pioneering journal *Manushi*, on the grounds that it had
an 'overclose association with the western women's movement'.[21] The
spectre of the imperialism-nationalism framework loomed large here.

The histories of feminisms in most parts of the globe have undertaken the
tasks of providing both a subject and a lineage for contemporary feminist
movements. But what about Indian feminism and feminist histories? For the
twentieth century, many varieties of Indian feminisms have been studied
and now form an impressive and rapidly developing critical system of
thought in its own right. It has ranged from the feminist nationalists[22] of
the national movement to eco-feminism[23] and a more disturbing rise of
the new woman seen through the saffron-sari-syndrome of the 1980s and
1990s. In the mid-1980s, India had witnessed the rise of Hindu militant

organisations that recruited women through the women's wing of the Hindu Right.[24] Robed in saffron-coloured saris (the deep shade of yellow is the symbol of the militant Hindu Right), these women activists led violent attacks on Muslims in the name of protecting the civic rights of Hindus. Analyses of the ideology and rhetoric of such women activists showed them to be single, independent minded and claiming to be women patriots conscious of their civic responsibilities (hence, ironically, new women) who utilised – as Geraldine Forbes puts it – 'the trappings of feminism but without commitment to a vision of gender justice and human rights'.[25] Surprisingly, and despite the growing consensus in the field of Indian gender and women's history that there has been a development of feminist thought in India over a much longer period than the modern one indicates, the terms 'feminism' and 'feminist' have been viewed with suspicion. In some ways, the legacy of the early twentieth-century women's movement has coloured and confused the perceptions of scholarship in the field, forcing historians of women into defensive positions.[26] The explanation is not too complex: from the 1920s onwards, Indian women active in the nationalist movement vehemently opposed the use of the term 'feminist' as understood in Europe and America on the grounds that it projected an anti-male ideology.[27] This helps to explain the hesitancy and ambivalence of scholars/activists working in the field of feminist and women's studies in pursuing the subject. Anything foreign is not for emulation, especially since the term 'feminist' raised the spectre of the militant suffragette.

I agree with the postcolonial scholar Mary John, who has observed sensibly that, not being like western feminists, equating the militant suffragette with a male-hater, and not wanting to be like the *memsahib*,[28] simply turns the orientalist gaze back on itself and freezes western women into essentialist categories of sensuality.[29] It is high time that contemporary Indian feminist scholarship took on the responsibility of removing such 'sanctioned ignorances' – distorted knowledges about what constitutes western feminism that have seeped from the early twentieth century.[30] Equally, the beginnings of the saffron-sari-clad new feminist, or women of the Hindu Right, can be traced to the cow protection movements of the late nineteenth century.[31] Hence, it is all the more crucial that we study women's ideology and work in the early pre-Gandhian nationalist era in the late nineteenth and early twentieth centuries. In order to understand the connections between past and present forms of feminism, one of the theoretical tasks has to be an assessment of the earlier feminist traditions, which necessitates reclaiming the terms feminist and feminism. This task can only be undertaken if we cast off the periodisation of imperialism-nationalism and find a template to define Indian women's agency.

A third problem implicit in the nationalist historiography was the widespread notion that the early twentieth-century Indian women's movement was on the brink of radicalising itself, but its marriage with the Indian nationalist movement broke its back. This association with nationalists obscured from women leaders the real issues of women's inequality and oppression. I found this interpretation a puzzle because, hidden in the explanation, was the much-bandied-about truth that there *was* an Indian women's movement which had *suddenly appeared* in the early twentieth century without its connections to an earlier era having been revealed. In a further twist, analysing the rhetoric of mainly Bengali male nationalists, the subaltern historian Partha Chatterjee argued that, even the women's question had disappeared by the early twentieth century because male nationalist discourse had successfully resolved it by relegating it to the now sanctified private sphere.[32] Utilising a deconstructionist method and based on a handful of primary sources, Chatterjee's study revealed more an astonishing ignorance of the preceding two decades of solid historical work of scholars who had analysed the links between feminism and nationalism. To illustrate this point further, Geraldine Forbes's work on the Indian women's movement conducted over twenty years of dedicated archival research makes it clear that the women's question, as configured by the main Indian women's organisations, continued to create problems for both Gandhi and other male nationalists, leading her to conclude that the women's movement and the Gandhian movement were in tension and not always harmoniously linked to each other.[33]

My question is, how do we resolve the contradictions between the findings of feminist historians and scholars of women's histories who have studied the deed, and poststructuralist historians who have concentrated exclusively on the word? I would argue that such appearances and disappearances of the women's question have occurred as a result of the periodisation of modern Indian history in which all processes, events and ideas are studied and analysed only through the nationalist framework. Further, studying history through the nationalism prism privileges the first four decades of the twentieth century, ignoring the longer chronological span of the modern era. Questions pertinent to gender relationships and women's lives, which were rapidly changing in the first half of the twentieth century, are therefore excluded from the frame of historical inquiry. Areas that need urgent attention are the changing conceptions, roles and experiences of women in the areas of sexuality, employment, motherhood and widowhood, conjugal relations, leisure and pleasure, and changes in lifestyles, dress and familial relationships. These, too, await attention from scholars strong enough to resist the paralysing frameworks of the political history of modern India and attend instead to the pressing question of retrieving women's agency in the country's social and economic historical contexts.

Assumptions about difference are present in other apparently more neutral approaches. Modernisation theory, which rose in the 1960s and 1970s, was built on the assumption of difference in which a traditional India was acted upon by forces of modernisation emanating from the west.[34] The modernisation thesis follows a distinct periodisation entailing a teleological move from traditional to modern India. In this linear approach, since modernisation was a product of westernisation, the progress of women's position too was seen as a product of modernisation and/or westernisation. In the 'western impact–Indian response' paradigm that informs much of the work on this topic, there is little room for women as agents of historical processes.[35] Meredith Borthwick, who has enriched our understanding of the changing conditions of the *bhadramahila* (respectable middle-class Bengali women) during the period 1850–1905 and pioneered empirical research based on Bengali women's writings, has utilised approaches devised to study the history of women in the west. Following the western impact–Indian response paradigm, she finds that the *bhadramahila* was emerging as a response to the *bhadralok* (middle-class Bengali men) who in turn were reacting to British rule.[36] Therefore, it is not surprising that she finds no feminist consciousness among the *bhadramahila*. In her words, 'When I began my study I was interested in locating a "feminist consciousness". The possibility still interests me, but as I understand more about the lives of women at that time, the more misguided I feel it is to expect that kind of perception then'.[37] One could argue here that the expectation was misguided, not because such a perception did not exist, but because it was already predetermined by western connotations of feminism. The hegemonic model of Bengali women as victims or as benefactors of an enlightened Bengali middle class has only recently been questioned by Tapan Ray Chaudhuri, Geraldine Forbes and Tanika Sarkar in their studies of accomplished individual women such as the first Bengali autobiographer, Rashsundari Debi,[38] and a female doctor who challenged the patriarchal social reform and medical hierarchies, Haimabati Sen.[39] However, seeking women's agency in a larger collective, studying patterns of popular participation of women in public campaigns for the betterment of women's lives, such as that for the Age of Consent, and analysing women's solidarity as expressed especially over caste and class barriers, are topics and themes that await the attention of scholars in Bengali gender studies. Certain region- and sex-specific issues have helped to reinforce stereotypes of womanhood in India. For example, the historical visibility of *sati* (burning of a widow on the funeral pyre of her husband) and the presence of *purdah* (forms of women's seclusion) in eighteenth- and nineteenth-century Bengal, or female infanticide in Rajasthan, have made the study of patriarchy more attractive to scholars than the delineation of women's agency. If women's resistance and assertion are to be emphasised, then scholarship of Bengal will have to break through the traditional grids of viewing their history in victim mode and innovate, both in method and theory.

What distinguishes the historian's craft and the practice of history from other disciplines is the ability to trace continuity and track change in historical processes. This inquiry is necessarily conducted within a time span, unlike disciplines such as sociology and literature, in which chronology can be less of an issue. In recent years, a host of scholars from other fields within the social sciences and humanities have been eager to explain how imperialism affected Indian society. This interdisciplinary approach, although welcome, has produced new dilemmas. One example is the topic of sati or a widow immolating herself on the funeral pyre of her husband.[40] Adopting post-structuralism, but still broadly functioning within the paradigm of imperialism-nationalism, Lata Mani has produced a magnificent work showing exactly how colonial knowledge about sati was produced in the early nineteenth century. She argues that the body of the Indian widow about to immolate herself was merely a site for the contest between colonial powers and Indian elites. Her assessment ends by demonstrating that the British project was not a civilising or modernising project at all, because the call to end sati was not based on humanitarian reasons but argued on the basis of scriptural sanction and non-sanction of the custom of sati.[41] In her earlier work, she was categorical about her lack of interest in the volition of the widow committing sati.[42] In a later monograph, she modified her position by incorporating the study of the widow's agency by analysing European eyewitness accounts of sati. Here, Mani argued that the dying woman's resistance and suffering is vividly recalled in the representations of the eyewitness accounts, but the widow's voice is ultimately obliterated by the urge of the spectators interested more in the horror and fascination of the spectacle itself. What we are left with, at best, are refracted voices, produced and controlled under imperial conditions and within the tight structures of the colonial discourse.[43] Mani's work, while acclaimed for its innovative theoretical insights in helping us understand how the dominant discourse erases voices of Indian widows, was also criticised for its excessive use of representation in the study of sati.[44]

In short, deconstructionist approaches do not embody successful means of recovering agency. Instead, they divert the investigator into seeking how agency is *erased* by dominant discourses of imperialism and nationalism. What began as a magnificent effort by Said and his followers to criticise Orientalist essentialism has also resulted in a paradox whereby the stereotype of the passive Indian woman has been unfortunately recycled. Chronology is also not a strong point within discourse analysis, as Mani herself admits, claiming that her reading of the debates on sati 'is not chronological but discursive'.[45] With any sense of period formations totally absent and the themes of continuity and change dispensed with, postmodern studies of sati have made events and phenomena appear as a seamless fabric in Indian history. Little wonder that post-structuralist and linguistic models have been severely critiqued by historians of India. Thus, despite the burgeoning body of literature on sati, the intentions, desires, pain and suffering of the dying widow have eluded the scholars' grasp.[46] From the metropolitan perspective, however, promising works are being released by practitioners of new imperial history. By turning the lens on British women's petitions to parliament in the protest movement against sati, Clare Midgley has countered postcolonial scholarship's contention about the agency of the colonial state. By analysing the contours of agency in a religious frame, she argues that fourteen separate groups of women petitioning were not political radicals or women's rights activists but evangelicals calling for its outlaw on the basis of humanitarian principles.[47]

Tracing the historical developments by which patriarchy emerged as the overriding form of societal order, and the ways in which it institutionalised the rights of men to control and appropriate the economic, sexual and reproductive services of women, has been a major preoccupation in the historiography of gender and women's studies in India. From within the Indian academy, feminist academics and activists, although doing excellent work in deconstructing patriarchy, have not sufficiently engaged with the idea of women as subjects of history. This is best shown in the words of the editors of *Recasting Women*, a volume which became an instant academic bestseller in the west in 1989 and which continues to dominate the field: 'This anthology has grown out of our need as academics and activists to understand the historical processes which reconstitute patriarchy in colonial India. We wish to focus primarily on the regulation and reproduction of patriarchy in the different class caste formations within civil society'.[48] Their attempts to understand how the reconstitution of patriarchy has affected present-day Indian women's problems has, predictably, resulted in the neglect of how change came about in women's lives through women's efforts during the colonial period, nor are their voices sufficiently retrieved in the process.

It is therefore not a surprise that we have reached the sixtieth anniversary of India's independence without being able to answer the following questions: did Indian women have a social reform movement that they interpreted in their own right? Did Indian women write economic critiques of imperialism? Who was India's first female cartographer and woman dramatist?[49] How did Indian women perceive the Raj? Is there a feminist lexicon in Indian languages that parallels women's experiences in other Asian and African countries? When did *hunda* (dowry) become a popular aspect of Indian material life and does *stridhan* (women's property) represent a continuum from ancient, medieval and early modern to contemporary days? We still remain more or less in a void, despite the recovery of the voices of some startlingly brilliant eighteenth- and nineteenth-century women philosophers, rulers and educationalists such as the Begums of Bhopal, Pandita Ramabai, Kashibai Kanitkar, Tarabai Shinde and Rokeya Sakhawat Hossain.[50] It is my contention here that some of these questions can be fruitfully investigated with a new chronological dimension and new ways of understanding the question of agency in order to track change in modern Indian history.

The way forward: a proposal for a new chronology

To a great extent, the periodisation of Indian history has suffered the effect of British chroniclers and textbook writers during colonial rule, such as James Mill in his much-quoted *History of India*.[51] The classificatory urges of the scientific British drove them to devise religious criteria for measuring progress in Indian history. Thus, ancient history has been approached as a Hindu period; the medieval period as Islamic; and the modern as a British (Christian) period. Although there is consensus amongst historians in the post-independent era that this classification is highly misleading, to say the least, no concerted efforts have been made to replace these three broad divisions except to add an early modern component to it.[52] Some changes have been incorporated, such as dropping the year of the birth of Christ for the more neutral BCE (Before Common Era) and substituting 'ancient India' for 'early India'.[53] Cutting-edge research has started amongst the medieval and early modern sector of the discipline, which has shifted to analyses based on new time spans that facilitate more neutral positions such as the 'seventeenth century' and the 'eighteenth century'. This approach takes inspiration from the innovative work of historians such as Irfan Habib, Muzaffar Alam and Sanjay Subrahmanyam who, along with other dynamic colleagues, have effectively questioned older assumptions such as the British-propagated 'decline theory' (that India under the late Mughals was in decline) and attended to new subjects such as military recruitment, farming and migration, trade and commerce to show continuities from earlier periods.[54] Unfortunately, however, gender and women have been sorely neglected in this zone of Indian history.[55]

Adapting the approach of early modernists in Indian history and also drawing on my own research on the modern period, I propose to adopt a new chronological time for analysing moot questions regarding gender and women for the colonial era. In the late nineteenth century, a woman-patriot called Laxmibai Dravid wrote a treatise depicting the contemporary condition of India by adopting a distinctive periodisation. In her preface, she stated that she had 'adopted three spatial and chronological periods here namely "The Past", "The Recent Past" and "The Present"'. She further justified her project thus: 'The reason for such a periodisation is that without understanding the past and recent events, it is not possible to pay attention to, or grasp the significance of the present or contemporary state of affairs'.[56] Her deployment of this innovative periodisation excited me considerably precisely because, at least initially, it appeared to suggest a radical departure from her contemporaries who followed the British historiographical tradition described above. Further, her periodisation got rid of the vexatious terms 'modern' and 'modernity' with one ingenious stroke. My enthusiasm soon dampened and instead turned into horror because, on further scrutiny, her spatial arrangement depicted a sinister schema under the innocuous-sounding period terms such as 'the past' and 'the recent past'.

Laxmibai Dravid's tract contained a highly biased agenda of glorifying the 'golden age' (the Hindu Vedic age in ancient Indian history) and damning Muslims, sending a clarion call for throwing the 'foreigners' out of the country. If one theme of her treatise is an early expression of Hindu fundamentalism, there are others that are highly significant for understanding the nineteenth-century deindustrialisation debates, and it represents a pioneering text by an Indian woman encompassing a fascinating economic critique of imperialism. I wish to suggest that the period in which Laxmibai Dravid's book is written was momentous for the formation of Indian subjectivities, with Indians interacting with the Raj and engaging actively in the cultural, social, economic and political processes of the country. Hence, I suggest that we discard the nationalist-imperialist framework which refused to treat the nineteenth century in its own right but utilised it as a mere backdrop for the development of nationalist consciousness. Working within the parameters of the widely acknowledged modern period of Indian history, I would advocate instead that we adopt the height of the colonial period as a discrete time unit in order to retrieve women's agency and understand gender relationships in the formation of modern India.

The next question to address then, is why privilege the late eighteenth and the nineteenth centuries? The establishment of British supremacy in India occurred *c*.1765 to 1877. If war and territorial conquest marked the growth of the East India Company from a trader to a ruler in the eighteenth century, the nineteenth century saw the consolidation of its political rule culminating in the handover of the administrative mantle from the Company Raj to Crown rule in 1858. The stability of the Raj by the late nineteenth century was unmistakably celebrated in the Imperial Assemblage of 1877, which, by proclaiming Queen Victoria as the Empress of India, resolved the question of sovereignty. It also proclaimed a new social order, a hierarchically arranged one which included the peasant and the Indian prince but with the viceroy at the top. India after the Mutiny (1857)[57] also saw the ideology of governance sharpened and perfected, and put in place and made famous by the Indian peasants' declaration of the notion of the *ma-bap* (paternal) government. Benevolent authoritarianism is core to our understanding of why subaltern groups such as women and peasants made use of western institutions. It represented a continuation (although obscure and ambivalent) from pre-British rulers of India, but nevertheless worked as an easily recognisable sign of sovereignty to the non- or semi-literate masses of India. Paternal authoritarian rule, however, must be acknowledged as an astute method used by the Raj to exclude direct political participation by Indian elites.[58]

By the early nineteenth century, what was secured in India was the safe-guarding of private property and the protection of the rights of the individ-ual and the rule of law to uphold the first two values. Western education in India was introduced by missionary activity from the 1750s onwards but gained much momentum from the state encouraging missionary en-terprises in indigenous education, with monetary incentives, in the early half of the nineteenth century. Christian missions in India took low-caste children – and girls besides boys – in their schools and the introduction of the printing presses by missionaries, albeit for proselytisation motives, helped Indians to garner such technology for effective use in their self-improvement programmes. The great debate on education, namely whether Indians should receive an education in indigenous languages with Indian content or a western education, was also decisively settled by Thomas Macaulay who, in 1835 leant firmly towards the creation of brown sahibs – in his words: '. . . a class of persons, Indian in blood and colour, but En-glish in taste, in opinions, in morals, and in intellect'.[59] In real terms, this translated as partially state-sponsored educational facilities for Indians; codification of law inscribing the personal laws of Islamic and Hindu sub-jects; and a bureaucracy knitted through the Indian civil service which acted as the administrative backbone of India.

So far I have drawn a picture of the momentous nineteenth century per-haps seen more from the perspectives of the ruler. If we were to view this from the eyes of Indians, although the economy of India had been opened to the forces of free trade and market competition by the Charter Acts of 1813, 1833 and 1853, this did not result in its modernisation, but rather in lengthy processes of deurbanisation and deindustrialisation. India's social economy had grown more agrarian based and traditional institutions, such as caste, had rigidified which had repercussions for women's status.[60] It should be clear from this narrative that, for better or worse, the introduction of a chain of processes had taken place as western institutions were put in place in India and these invited the new Indian subjects of the British Empire to act upon them. Indian women, too, accessed these institutions, and especially the law courts, whether for claims to inheritance, marriage, divorce and alimony, or for employment and physical mobility. Women from all classes felt the squeeze of the shrinking economy and migratory patterns affected them too. Equally, new municipal laws, forest laws and social legislation purported to interfere with their lives and livelihood. The origins of the phenomenon of 'Eve-teasing' (sexual harassment of women in public places) peculiar to contemporary Indian society can be traced to the urban modernising impulses of India's teeming cities, while the budgeting schedules of middle-class Indian women of the nineteenth century depict the pressures of the colonial economy that was impoverishing the emerging middle classes.[61] All these crucial processes were set in train in the nineteenth century, with subaltern groups such as women and low castes drawing strength from the bulwark of these institutions.

With the installation of the Indian penal code of 1860 and the criminal code in the late nineteenth century, for the first time we see the criminalisation of the body of the Indian woman over customs such as sati and infanticide. While lower-caste women suffered through the newly invented categories of 'criminal castes and tribes' in which they were increasingly re-scripted as playing accessory roles on behalf of their menfolk, upper-caste women committing infanticide were subjected to increasing surveillance through the information gathering techniques of the Raj and, if convicted, were either sentenced to death or transported to penal colonies. The politics of incarceration during the colonial period involved interesting and new configurations of power in India. For example, in the case of infanticide, a larger number of upper-caste widows jailed for killing their new-born illegitimate children had their sentences reduced to five years' imprisonment with the help of Indian middle-class elites who launched protracted agitations on their behalf. The same access to power structures was, however, not so easily available to low-caste women.[62] How women negotiated and constructed contestatory discourses in this momentous era needs greater attention. The formation of the Indian middle class is a phenomenon which scholars agree took place in the nineteenth century and it is my contention that the rise of the self and personhood of Indian middle-class women brought tremendous changes in the role and lives of Indian women during colonial rule. Whether benign or malevolent, the historical processes ingrained within colonialism were certainly acted upon by Indian women who were the harbingers of change, making the new chronology of late eighteenth and nineteenth centuries an imperative if we wish to understand how women's subjectivities took shape in modern India.

Understanding change: creating a template for defining women's agency

The concept of agency goes to the heart of understanding change in history. If Indian women experienced change and acted as the motors of change, how can one define their agency? In the last two decades, Indian gender and women's history has seen the growth of a promising literature dealing with diverse facets of Indian culture and society that have had an impact upon women's lives, such as the gendering of caste;[63] the invisibility of women (both elite and low caste);[64] and the exclusion or marginalisation of women from production processes,[65] but no concerted attempts have been made to write a template for understanding women's agency.[66]

I began by outlining how women's agency has been obscured by the functioning of dominant paradigms in modern Indian history. There are also difficulties in retrieving women's agency in India, due to the existence of complex custom-bound castes, religious groupings and tribal societies with different structures of power relationships in the domestic and public spheres. In recent years, the whole issue of 'woman as agent' has been complicated in relation to the phenomenon of sati. Postmodern interpretations of the volition of the woman burning in the flames of her husband's pyre have often been limited by a certain configuration of agency based on issues of coercion or consent. That is, the dying widow is viewed in a simplistic fashion as a victim (superslave) of Indian patriarchy or perceived as a heroine (superwoman) by eyewitnesses and spectators in history.

Significant attempts were made in the 1980s by the early subaltern school, which sought to uncover the consciousness of subordinate groups such as Indian peasants. However, their efforts were doomed from the start, due to their obsession with retrieving the independent actions of the Indian peasant. It led them to argue for a pure (autonomous) insurgent consciousness leading to a reductive notion of agency where the peasant acted independently of the structures of power. Although later subalternists have revised their position, we find that intention (in terms of human motives, aims and goals) is not adequately conceptualised in their frameworks. In other words, the transformative capacities of the human agent are not given a premium position. If the theme of change is central to the historian's task of understanding gender relations, then we cannot divorce the resister's consciousness from his or her role of acting out that intent. Is change envisaged and heralded in the many acts of women's subversion? Or, are there possibilities for transformation and a more equitable life envisaged and made possible by women? How would one define the agency of a woman's collective that deliberately excluded another group from accessing its resources, for example, the middle-class Hindu feminists of the nineteenth century who redefined their newly emerging urban middle-class roles by usurping the occupations (classical singing and dancing) of a particular caste of woman-artistes (called *Kalavantins*) and forced the latter into lesser-status occupations such as the theatre and urban prostitution?[67] Equally, and more complicated, is the agency of women who actively sought and continue to seek the collusion of patriarchal structures in their empowerment. Some of these issues can be better answered if we begin to define women's agency keeping the above constraints in mind, and also if the right kind of questions are asked about women's resistance. These lie in the context/s and conditions of their being, the role of the resister and the deliberation of their action and its impact.

Agency is construed here as conscious, goal-driven activities by women that embrace the possibility of *change*; put more simply, it is purposeful action designed to have an impact. I have found feminist philosophy especially helpful in understanding the formation of women's consciousness of subordination and oppression. In the phenomenological feminist perspective outlined by Sandra Bartky, she has argued rather persuasively that there are distinctive ways of perceiving feminist consciousness. When a woman begins to perceive the various oppressions that she and/or other women face, this awareness may lead to anger or despair. Even such an awareness, she argues, is an advance over false consciousness because it marks the beginning of an understanding of the origins of women's subordination and 'even beginning to understand this, makes it possible to *change* [*sic*]'.[68] In my study of Maharashtrian women's coming to feminism or anti-feminism, I analyse women's words and deeds as a tripartite interaction between the colonial state, Indian elites (conservatives and reformists) and women themselves.[69] This broader conception of women's agency allows for a more composite and dynamic concept that goes beyond celebratory, compensatory or 'her-story' histories. By considering women's interaction with the colonial state and indigenous men, it is understood that women's agency originates where other forms of agency are present and may coexist and/or compete with them.[70]

Further, I propose that assertion and resistance are twin aspects of women's agency. Women's will or volition to act in conscious forms to resist, strain or overturn structures of power is broadly defined as 'resistance'. 'Assertion' is defined as a form of resistance in which women use legitimised instruments of agitation, such as petitioning the state and using the law. Assertion, by its very definition, is a more positive form of resistance that allows the woman appealing to state authorities to do so through recognised forms of campaigning. In other words, it has the blessing of the state precisely because the assertive nature of women's claims draws on constitutional forms of agitation. With this conception of agency, it is possible to overcome the dead-end quest for the autonomy in which the insurgent subject of the subaltern school of Indian history seems mired.[71] A study of Indian women's agency reveals that, in a majority of cases, women started with conciliatory forms of negotiation and only when they failed did they turn to more aggressive forms of resistance. My approach to agency allows us to explore the ways in which groups of women collude with, or benefit from, consciously upheld patriarchal norms in benign, as well as confrontational, moments of resistance. It enables us, for example, to understand and explain the rise of anti-feminist, ethnocentric and racist women's agency, such as Laxmibai Dravid's text, along with the humane and liberal treatises of feminists such as Tarabai Shinde or Pandita Ramabai.[72]

In my work on Indian women, I have also made a geographic turn, that is, I have moved away from previous concentrations on Bengal and shifted the lens on to the lesser-studied region called Maharashtra or western India.[73] This shift has been necessitated by the fact that no in-depth study of Maharashtrian women exists but, more significantly, because the passivity model in Indian women's history has come from Bengal-centric studies.[74] Shifting the lens helps to challenge the idea of the universality of concepts such as *purdah* as well as sati – two topics that seem to be perennial in the study of gender and women's history of India. The nature of the study that locates agency with women has necessitated the use of new methods of inquiry and new ways of looking at known sources. Women's self-authorisation programmes and the construction of identities in non-western contexts can be traced in vernacular literature. I call into question Gayatri Spivak's argument,[75] followed by a host of post-colonial authors, that the subaltern woman's voice has been silenced by the epistemic violence of the phenomena of imperialism and the imperial archive.[76] I have instead mined vernacular texts preserved in private and public archives for such retrieval (after all, how many women wrote in the English language?). For the perceptions of women, I have concentrated basically on Marathi sources, as many women preferred to write in their mother tongue. These include autobiographies, biographies, songbooks, literature (novels, short stories, plays and tracts) and treatises on philosophical, religious or social questions. Women's journals edited by women and indisputably meant for women readers have been used to gauge the opinions of ordinary women. Letters by women to the editors of women's magazines or for important national and regional newspapers have also proved useful as an index of their awareness and dissent. I have left nothing much unturned, including book reviews, religious treatises, tracts by women on leisure and sport, letters written to editors of journals and newspapers, prefaces to sewing and knitting manuals and scrap books left by women.[77]

Perhaps not surprisingly in a male-dominated society, protest by women against men is barely recorded in historical sources, so in this sense it seems right that we should not be too hopeful of colonial records. But imperial archives used imaginatively can yield rich materials too. However, I have tried to construct a picture of resistance by women of all classes by tracing women's petitions to the government or to the judiciary over criminal and civil litigation in courts. Many of the works produced by women are no longer available, yet the proof of their publication, the extent of their circulation and brief summaries of their contents exist in the older catalogues of printed Marathi materials during this period and I have used them as important source materials in themselves. For the attitudes of the state and for indigenous male discourse, I have consulted the judicial, education and general department records of the Bombay Presidency. In addition, the opinions of leading reformers as reported in special committees on the questions of restitution of conjugal rights and the Age of Consent Bill (1891) have been helpful in the construction of male discourse. Compilations of the Marathi works of leading Maharashtrian intellectuals and newspapers and journals produced by them also provide valuable insights.

Inverting nationalist frameworks: lineages of Indian feminism

By placing the agency of Indian women as the central focus of concern in my research conducted over the last two decades, I have argued that one can track the trajectory of Indian feminism back into the nineteenth century, demonstrating that Indian women's quest for civil, political and religious rights arose straight from the belly of the momentous religious and social reform movements of the nineteenth century.[78] Within the cultural history of modern India, it has been asserted that the social reform movements had the 'position of Indian women' as their central concern that women became the beneficiaries of these movements.[79] In my work, I have overturned this framework to see instead *how* Indian women approached the great religious and social reform movements.

Indian women's subjectivities were forged within the context of colonialism, which gave them the choice of a wide array of discourses on tradition and modernity. The rise of feminism in India was made possible through a combination of factors: the presence of a colonial economy; the opportunities thrown up by the social reform movement, which allowed for a re-questioning of Hinduism and presented new choices of religion such as Christianity and the hope of forming new sects and cults; and the new web of modernising impulses, which interacted with the contending circumstances and criteria of sex, race, status, class, caste and religion. In western India, women applied gendered critiques to the older religion and some embraced conversion to other religions such as Christianity as a way of expressing their discontent with Hinduism's misogynist view of womanhood, while others remained within it. Many low-caste and high-caste Hindu widows became Christian through what is recognised as a 'coping method'[80] and a functional approach to religion, that is, recognising the ill-effects of Hinduism's harsh strictures on their behaviour and options, they decided to leave it for the religion of the rulers.[81] In western India, Christian feminists had a clean break with the Indian past by rejecting Hinduism on the basis of a gendered approach to religion. They fruitfully applied the welfare and mission rhetoric of Christianity to assert themselves, breaking traditional roles and legitimating their entry into the public world. Their refusal to belong to any one church, as well as their rejection of clerical mediation along with the funding from multi-denominational American charities, made them self-sufficient and allowed them unfettered control over the curriculum, lifestyles and managerial aspects of day-to-day administration of their schools, widows' homes and orphanages. All these factors gave them the necessary autonomy to create a unique brand of Indian feminism and Indian Christianity.

If we turn to Hindu women who wished to remain Hindus, it is noticeable that many feminists among them questioned Hindu customs and rituals but, unlike their Christian counterparts, they did not reject them. This meant working within the structures and limitations of Hindu society. Several feminist leaders overcame the hindrances of working within Hindu society through a strategy of assimilation and accommodation, which kept the larger Hindu society's criticism of their programmes to a minimal level.[82] Separate female institution-building programmes by women underpinned Hindu women's embracing of modernity and the development of the Maharashtrian women's movement. In their assertion of rights, Hindu women consciously appropriated and/or negotiated with Indian patriarchal norms especially in outward forms of behaviour such as deference to older people, style of dress, speech and mannerisms. This process is observed in the organisational work of early women's societies of Maharashtra. By the 1880s, many women's societies were set up under the umbrella of the larger social reform organisations. Women's organisations tried to combat popular prejudices against female education in Maharashtra, while simultaneously making women understand the advantages of learning. These women's networks were further strengthened by the transformation of older social events and ceremonies that predated the feminist movement, such as the women's rituals known as *halad-kunku*[83] held mainly in western and southern India, and other social gatherings such as religious discourses or *kirtans*.[84] Hindu rituals and ceremonies provided a framework, which the women's movement utilised effectively to bring their new message about the need for female education, women's rights to property and inheritance, the evils of child marriage and enforced widowhood. These expanded forums were also used further to hold readings, lectures and essay contests in order to encourage the more talented amongst women to take on leadership roles.

In western India, women ingeniously adapted and modernised many of the institutions of the private sphere in order to meet the requirements of the colonial world; indeed, if we examine the *halad-kunku* ceremonies or *kirtans* of Maharashtrian women, it becomes apparent that the private and the public are one and the same.[85] By turning the lens on what women said and did, my research has enabled me to challenge conclusively the findings of the current historiography epitomised in the volume edited by Sangari and Vaid who simply accept that Indian women in the colonial period internalised 'the offered models' of private/public sphere ideologies with 'varying degrees of conformity'.[86] Their suggestion here is that not only were models offered, but also Indian women tended to submit or conform to them. Yet, if one examines Indian women's contributions to the making of modern India in terms of their perspectives and participation in the religious and social reform movement, such a picture is shown to be highly misleading. In fact, if anything, Indian women were not only actively attempting to enter and legitimise their presence within the public sphere but, more importantly, they were blurring the divide between the two.

This period saw the establishment of the first independent women's organisation, the Arya Mahila Samaj, which specifically highlighted women's needs and aspirations and invited the displeasure of men.[87] Although the credit is given to Pandita Ramabai, a foremost feminist leader of colonial India, for its founding, she in fact simply brought existing segregated women's societies (striyancha sabhas) into a harmonious and coherent unit under the umbrella organisation of the Arya Mahila Samaj in the early 1880s.[88] Indeed, greater political capacities began to be expressed by women in the early women's organisational activities of the 1870s all over the Bombay Presidency. When Pandita Ramabai left for Britain in 1883, the work of the dynamic Arya Mahila Samaj was carried on magnificently by other feminist leaders such as Ramabai Ranade, Kashibai Kanitkar and Rakhmabai. This organisation in particular carried on a campaign to influence the Raj to address the fate of Brahmin widows found guilty of infanticide, and was successful in having sentences of death reduced to imprisonment in many cases. In the petitions of the Arya Mahila Samaj, as well as the depositions of infanticidal women, we see arguments that ranged from the injustices of the Hindu patriarchal system which disallowed remarriage to Hindu widows but allowed widowers to marry several times, sometimes, as one irate woman put it, 'before the corpse of the first wife grew cold'.[89] Certainly, the negotiating skills of late nineteenth-century Indian women were at their best when it came to using the state as a bargaining counter vis-a-vis Indian men. And it is in this process that we observe how women's agency was complicated through the different collusions it made throughout the twentieth century.

By the late nineteenth century, women's periodicals were a key instrument in the transformation and progression of the women's movement in India. Journals, such as those produced by the Women's Press in Maharashtra, conducted by and for women in the Marathi language, allowed for the development of the crucial feminist concept of *bhaginivarg* (sisterhood) within a larger women's collective.[90] I have identified ten Marathi journals run by *kartris* (female editors) that collectively encompass the Women's Press of the late nineteenth and early twentieth centuries. The periodicals were meant for an audience of women and came from different parts of Maharashtra. The most well known were *Arya Bhagini* (Indian Sisters), edited by Anandibai and Manakbai Lad from Goa and Bombay, and *Maharashtra Mahila* (Women of Maharashtra), edited by Manorama Mitra. The runs varied greatly but their lifespan began approximately in the mid-1870s and ended around 1920. The spectacular success of the Women's Press in Maharashtra, especially in raising awareness of women's issues and enabling them to participate in the popular protest campaign surrounding the Age of Consent controversy in the late 1880s and early 1890s, lay in their complete control over the organisational and managerial aspects of the business of running a medium meant for women's interests.

Even a cursory survey of the Marathi literary scene reveals the enthusiastic entry of women in appreciable numbers, many of them welcoming the 'condition of women' as a moot question posed within the social reform movement, which they adapted and wrote about. Writing gave women the opportunity to *recast themselves* as modern women, rather than being *recast by men*, thereby preparing themselves for the rapid changes brought by the colonial world. The period of the Maharashtrian women's renaissance was between 1860 and 1920, and their writing demonstrates a strong western influence, as they utilised genres such as the essay, novel and short story to disseminate their message of reform. In the area of publishing at least, women were able to assert themselves in a way that would have been unthinkable in the past.[91] The autobiography as a mode of expression is worth mentioning here, as the most damning critiques of Indian patriarchy are available in this form of writing.[92] Some of these memoirs became classics in their own time while others have been tapped, generally for their insights into women's coming to public life rather than as sources of social history.[93] It is often said about Indian social history that it is impossible to unearth popular mentalities with regard to topics such as deviant sexuality, domestic violence, rape, incest and paedophilia. But, a rich mine awaits historians in the form of women's memoirs, which remain relatively untapped for the nineteenth century. Equally noteworthy is women's eager grasp of the emerging form of writing and publishing travelogues that yield rich insights into the formation of women's subjectivities between 1850 and

1920. Although very different forms, the campaigning journalism of the Women's Press, the domestic science treatises and the school textbooks are notable, therefore, in demonstrating an increased self-confidence in building a distinct women's identity. The new forms allowed women to create resistance literature, in the form of treatises and tracts that used inversion techniques and role reversals to explore gender relations, aimed at suggesting a different, a more egalitarian world.[94]

Indian women reformers often saw nineteenth-century India as a gendered society. They also understood the creation of gender identity (expressed in the Marathi language as an opposition between *purush-jati* [men] and *stri-jati* [women])[95] not as a biological given but as a social construct. Both Christian and Hindu feminists wrote extensively about the socialisation of girls and boys in a Hindu household as shaped in difference. In the gendered critiques of Indian society and culture, Maharashtrian women resorted to a rich vocabulary in the Marathi language to express ideas that are now considered feminist terms and enriched the Indian feminist lexicon with concepts and terms such as *bhaginivarg* (sisterhood); *strihak* (women's rights); *strivarg* (womankind or womanhood); *stri-anubhav* (women's experience); *bandhivasan* (bondage); *dasyatva* (slavery); *mokaleek* (independence or freedom); *stri-jati* (female sex/women); *purush-jati* (male sex/men); *purusarth* (manliness and masculinity). The invention of this feminist lexicon reveals the nature of the advanced state of late nineteenth-century feminist thought in India.

When examining the growth of feminist consciousness in nineteenth-century Indian women's writing, it is important to have a full understanding of the nuances of the term *stri-jati*. The term was frequently used by women writers of the period, and literally means 'caste of females', although in many contexts where it was employed it would be more accurate to translate it as 'female-sex' or 'women'. Nevertheless, even when women writers utilised it in this way, the connotations of class or category remained, giving feminist writers, such as Tarabai Shinde, a powerful tool when writing her comparative study of the *stri-jati* and the *purush-jati*. In Tarabai's text, even if the category of gender is not made explicit, it is certainly evoked in the opposition between male and female sex. The various meanings that can be ascribed to it, therefore not only give it force as a description of the status of women in society in comparison to men, but also show the growth in feminist writers' awareness of their own distinct identity and speak volumes regarding the realisation of selfhood and the formation of women's subjectivities.

Interestingly, both Christian and Hindu women's critiques of gender relations in this period incorporate a similar strand of thinking on the issue of masculinity. In their discussions of the meaning of *purusarth*, it not only consisted of a narrower conception of physical traits, such as virility and prowess, but also extended to mental expressions of courage, endurance and the ability to be humane in unusual circumstances. This consensus regarding the meaning of *purusarth* can be seen in the writings of Pandita Ramabai and Tarabai Shinde who, despite their marked differences in religion, background and influences, ultimately imbued the term with the same meaning. Additionally, in a new strategy to shame Indian men, they often reserved the term 'masculinity' for British officials, with Tarabai Shinde even naming the rule of the Raj as a 'divine rule'. She expressly reserved the epithet 'Pandavas' (mythical divine heroes of the Indian epic *Mahabharata*) for the British government.[96] Support of an alien government against one's own, I would suggest, was a strategy of Indian feminists under colonial rule who colluded with the sahibdom (white man's empire) only to play off their own menfolk. There are, however, plenty of instances wherein Indian women roundly condemned the state when it retrenched Indian patriarchy, which strengthens our understanding of Indian women's backing of the Raj as a strategic move on their part and the importance of widening the remit of women's agency.

The crowning triumph of the Maharashtrian feminist movement in the nineteenth century was their support for raising the age of consent for girls from ten to twelve in 1891 against a formidable opposition of Indian male conservatives. Maharashtrian women resorted to the legal remedies provided by the colonial courts to end unhappy marriages; feminist leaders took note of the suicides and the husband-poisoning cases that wives were involved in; the writings by women of this period reveal heightened anxieties caused by dysfunctional marriages and many traced them to the institution of child marriage which caused incompatibility. It is these factors that were noted by the male intelligentsia and the press, resulting in male anxieties about the rebellion of wives in western India. Seen from the perspectives of women, it should be clear that the charges of 'effeminate masculinity' launched by the Raj against Bengali men in a bid to downplay their demands for self-rule may have worked at a rhetorical level in the game of imperial politics as Mrinalini Sinha has argued, but the everyday reality within India held genuine threats to Indian masculinity.[97] The gauntlet had been thrown down by warring Indian wives by their assertions in court either to annul marriages or demand maintenance in the case of neglect by their husbands. This, and the growing strength in the clamour of Indian feminists against child marriage practices, lay at the heart of Indian male anxieties and brought on the conservative backlash against the government over the Age of Consent controversy in the late 1880s and early 1890s.

Maharashtrian women's participation in the popular agitation over the age of consent legislation effectively locates Indian women's popular protests back in the nineteenth century,[98] contrary to the existing wisdom that women's participation in popular protests only begins with the Gandhian era.[99] The realisation that the age of consent was an issue relating to the wellbeing of the *stri-jati* united them on common ground. In India, female pressure groups gave their opinions unsolicited and tried to persuade the government by their lobbying techniques, even though the sexual politics of the colonial government prevented consultation with women. Scholarship has so far left their legacy unrecognised in providing essential support for male decision-makers in raising the age of consent.

It is only when we step outside the nationalist-imperialist paradigm that we are able to locate moments and processes of historical significance. This stepping outside frameworks also helps us appreciate the longer chronological span. The contestatory discourses and negotiatory spaces created by Indian women, as we have seen, rose out of the nineteenth-century complex web of processes set in train by Indians interacting with the structures and institutions that were put in place by the Raj. Instead of arguing that the age of consent was about nascent nationalism, my research has shown that, if anything, Indian women in the nineteenth century were engaging in historically significant ways, which had little meaning in terms of nation, nationalism or imperialism. The rights of women, and the obligations of the government and their menfolk towards the wellbeing of child-wives and mothers, underpinned their arguments against the institution of child marriage. Women were contesting nationalist male reformist and conservative discourses; they were using the colonial state for their own ends and finally aligning with their imperial sisters to improve their lives.

Conclusion

In this work, I rejected the nationalism-imperialism framework because its inbuilt assumptions about the location of historical agency effectively marginalise women. It also elevates nationalist consciousness as the dominant force at work in Indian society. Within the dominant nationalism-imperialism historiography, the assumption has been that assertive Indian women's voices would only be retrieved in the Gandhian era, which allowed for women's introduction into the public sphere. Stepping outside this paradigm and focusing on women themselves allowed for the uncovering of women's voices in a variety of contexts. Using the vernacular literature of western India and a rereading of the imperial archive serve to relocate women's agency to the nineteenth century before the rise of modern nationalism.

Women's agency has been uncovered in arenas that straddle the domestic and public spheres, as women fashioned strategies of assertion while engaging with Indian patriarchy. Women's negotiation with Hinduism and, for some, the rejection of it based on their understanding of it as a misogynist religion; their creation of a women's press; their establishment of separate female institutions; and their reworking of women's rituals and networks to facilitate access to education and professional identities are all seen as assertions of their rights as individuals. Women accessed knowledge of state procedures, such as petitioning and law courts, in order to claim their rights to property, livelihood, remarriage, mobility and custody of children and, in cases of divorce, to maintenance, thus attending to their material wants and needs. In the nineteenth century, Indian women were acting in historically significant ways that have remained invisible while the dialogue between nationalism and imperialism has been privileged in the study of Indian history. It is quite possible that the apparent lack of women's agency in other regions of India, such as northern India, has more to do with the dominance of this framework than it has with the actual historical reality. When historians step outside the confines of the nationalism-imperialism framework, a different assessment of women's agency may emerge. When we abandon the old periodisation and paradigms that have governed Indian history, only then will we see the play of real dialogues of resistance and the full engagement of women as agents of history.

Notes

1. Ludmilla Jordanova, *History in Practice* (2000; London: Hodder Arnold, 2006), p. 106.
2. For commentaries on them, see Bipan Chandra, Mridula Mukherjee, Aditya Mukherjee, K.N. Panikkar and Sucheta Mahajan, *India's Struggle for Independence* (1988; Delhi: Penguin, 1989), pp. 1–30; Ranajit Guha, 'Methodology', in Ranajit Guha and Gayatri Chakravorty Spivak (eds), *Selected Subaltern Studies* (Oxford: Oxford University Press, 1988), pp. 37–44.
3. Some schools have had names such as 'Cambridge' foisted upon them. See Sumit Sarkar, *Modern India, 1885–1947* (London: Macmillan, 1983), pp. 6–7; Sekhar Bandopadhyay, *From Plassey to Partition: A History of Modern India* (New Delhi: Orient Longman, 2004), pp. 185–7.
4. See David Washbrook, 'Law, State and Agrarian Society in Colonial India', *Modern Asian Studies* 15 (1981), pp. 649–721; Sumit Sarkar, *Beyond Nationalist Frames: Relocating Postmodernism, Hindutva, History* (New Delhi: Permanent Black, 2002).
5. Patrick McGinn, 'Beyond Nation and Empire: 1857, Resistance and the State in Nineteenth Century India' (forthcoming). I am immensely grateful to Patrick McGinn for not only loaning an early draft of his manuscript but also generously sharing his ideas on the 'imperialism-nationalism paradigm'.
6. 'Imperialist' refers to key colonial administrators, such as the viceroys and the Secretary of State for India, and their pronouncements. The 'Cambridge School' refers to J. A. Gallagher, J. H. Broomfield, Anil Seal, B. R. Tomlinson, Judith Brown and David Washbrook. See 'Introduction', in Chandra, *India's Struggle*, pp. 13–30.
7. Chandra, *India's Struggle*, p. 17.
8. Ranajit Guha, 'On Some Aspects of the Historiography of Colonial India', in Ranajit Guha (ed.), *Subaltern Studies: Writings on South Asian History and Society*, vol. 1 (Delhi: Oxford University Press, 1982), pp. 1–8, here p. 4.
9. Ranajit Guha, 'Preface', in Ranajit Guha (ed.), *Subaltern Studies: Writings on South Asian History and Society*, vol. 2 (Delhi: Oxford University Press, 1983), p. vii.
10. Twelve volumes have been printed from the subaltern project. The first ten were published by Oxford University Press, India. In 2000, Rukun Advani, who was the editor at OUP,

India opened his own publishing house, Permanent Black Press, in Delhi. The Subaltern Studies Collective transferred to Permanent Black, which produced volumes 11 and 12 and will continue to do so in the near future.

11. In the fifth year of the inauguration of the Subaltern Studies Collective, and responding to criticisms, the founder, Ranajit Guha, wrote an article that seems like a form of tokenism to the critics' demands. Ranajit Guha, 'Chandra's Death', in Ranajit Guha (ed.), *Subaltern Studies: Writings on South Asian History and Society*, vol. 5 (Delhi: Oxford University Press, 1987), pp. 135–65; occasionally, the Subaltern Studies Collective commissioned articles on gender such as the think-piece by Susie Tharu and Tejaswini Niranjana, 'Problems for a Contemporary Theory of Gender', in Shahid Amin and Dipesh Chakrabarty (eds), *Subaltern Studies: Writings on South Asian History and Society*, vol. 9 (Delhi, Oxford University Press, 1996), pp. 232–60.

12. On how postcolonial scholarship has implicated religion, especially Christian missions, in imperial agendas see Jeffrey Cox, 'Audience and Exclusion at the Margins of Imperial History', *Women's History Review* 3 (1994), pp. 501–14.

13. See Ranajit Guha, 'A Note on the Terms "Elite", "People", "Subaltern", etc. as Used Above', in 'On Some Aspects of the Historiography of Colonial India', in Guha (ed.), *Subaltern Studies*, vol. 1, pp. 1–8, here p. 8.

14. See Clare Midgley (ed.), *Gender and Imperialism* (Manchester: Manchester University Press, 1998); Philippa Levine, *Prostitution, Race and Politics: Policing Venereal Disease in the British Empire* (New York: Routledge, 2003); Mrinalini Sinha, *Specters of Mother India: The Global Restructuring of an Empire* (Durham, NC: Duke University Press, 2006); Ruth Roach Pierson and Nupur Chaudhuri (eds), *Nation, Empire, Colony: Historicizing Gender and Race* (Bloomington: Indiana University Press, 1998); Mary A. Procida, *Married to the Empire: Gender, Politics and Imperialism in India, 1883–1947* (Manchester: Manchester University Press, 2002).

15. See Guha, 'A Note on the Terms', p. 8.

16. Guha, 'A Note on the Terms', p. 8.

17. See Leslie Flemming, *Women's Work for Women: Missionaries and Social Change in Asia* (Boulder, CO: Westview, 1993); Antony Copley, *Religions in Conflict: Ideology, Cultural Contact and Conversion in Late Colonial India* (Delhi: Oxford University Press, 2000); Jeffrey Cox, *Imperial Fault Lines: Christianity and Colonial Power in India 1818–1940* (Stanford: Stanford University Press, 2002); Maina Singh Chawla, *Gender, Religion, and 'Heathen Lands': American Missionary Women in South Asia, 1860s–1940s* (London: Garland, 2000).

18. For recent studies based on vernacular sources see Suruchi Thapar-Bjorkert, *Women in the Indian Nationalist Movement: Unseen Faces and Unheard Voices, 1930–42* (Delhi: Sage, 2006); Visalakshi Menon, *Indian Women and Nationalism: The U.P. Story* (New Delhi: Har-Anand Publications, 2003).

19. Jawaharlal Nehru's period as the first prime minister of independent India heralded a new and exciting phase in addressing injustice and inequality in gender relations, as witnessed in the introduction of the Hindu Civil Code and liberalising marriage, inheritance and guardianship laws. See Lotika Sarkar, 'Jawaharlal Nehru and the Hindu Code Bill', in B. R. Nanda (ed.), *Indian Women: From Purdah to Modernity* (London: Sangam, 1990), pp. 87–98.

20. Devaki Jain, 'Gandhian Contributions Toward a Feminist Ethic', in Diane Eck and Devaki Jain (eds), *Cross-Cultural Perspectives on Women: Religion and Social Change* (Delhi: Kali, 1986), pp. 255–70.

21. Madhu Kishwar, 'Why I Am not a Feminist', *Manushi: A Journal of Women and Society* 61, (November–December 1990), p. 3.

22. A classic formulation is in Kumari Jayawardena, *Feminism and Nationalism in the Third World* (New Delhi: Kali, 1986). Beginning in the immediate post-independent India, i.e., the late 1950s, we find the trend rapidly expanding in the 1980s when scholars studied

the connections between feminism and nationalism. Key texts are Neera Desai, *Woman in Modern India* (1957; Bombay: Vora, 1977); Manmohan Kaur, *Role of Women in the Freedom Movement, 1857–1947* (Delhi: Sterling, 1967); Aparna Basu, 'The Role of Women in the Indian Struggle for Freedom', in B. R. [Bal Ram] Nanda (ed.), *Indian Women: From Purdah to Modernity* (New Delhi: Vikas, 1976), pp. 16–40; Maria Mies, 'Indian Women and Leadership', *Bulletin of Concerned Asian Scholars* 7 (1975), pp. 56–66; Gail Minault (ed.), *The Extended Family: Women and Political Participation in India and Pakistan* (Delhi: Chanakya, 1981), pp. 49–82; Geraldine Forbes, 'The Politics of Respectability: Indian Women and the Indian National Congress', in Donald Anthony Low (ed.), *The Indian National Congress: Centenary Hindsights* (Oxford: Oxford University Press, 1988), pp. 54–97.

23. Maria Mies and Vandana Shiva, *Ecofeminism* (London: Zed, 1993).

24. Tanika Sarkar, 'The Woman as Communal Subject: Rashtrasevika Samiti and Ram Janmabhoomi Movement', *Economic and Political Weekly*, 31 August 1991, pp. 2057–62.

25. Geraldine Forbes, 'Women in Independent India' in Geraldine Forbes, *Women in Modern India* (Cambridge: Cambridge University Press, 1996), p. 252.

26. Veena Oldenberg has argued that, if Indian social scientists and historians can use western theoretical models such as Marxism and post-structuralism, then why cannot Indian scholarship use the useful phrase 'feminism'? See Veena Oldenberg, 'The Roop Kanwar Case: Feminist Responses', in John S. Hawley (ed.), *Sati: The Blessing and the Curse* (New York: Oxford University Press, 1994), pp. 101–30, here pp. 102–3.

27. The stance taken by influential female leaders, such as Kamaladevi Chattopadhayaya, on the label of 'feminism' has been a theme since the 1970s. See e.g., Jayawardena, *Feminism and Nationalism in the Third World*; Barbara Ramusack, 'Catalysts or Helpers? British Feminists, Indian Women's Rights and Indian Independence', in Minault (ed.), *The Extended Family*, pp. 109–50.

28. Originally it simply meant the wife of a British official posted in India, but nineteenth-century Bengali culture caricatured her as a vacuous, lazy, luxury-loving and morally loose woman on the same lines as the literary stereotype of the sahib's wife in Kipling's works. For the Bengali caricature see Partha Chatterjee, 'The Nationalist Resolution of the Women's Question', in Kumkum Sangari and Sudesh Vaid (eds), *Recasting Women: Essays in Colonial History* (Delhi: Kali, 1989), pp. 240–47.

29. Mary John, *Discrepant Dislocations: Feminism, Theory and Postcolonial Histories* (Berkeley: University of California Press, 1996), pp. 5–68 *n*. 12.

30. Originally the stunning coinage 'sanctioned ignorance' came from Spivak, who talked about the blind spots in Foucault's brilliant analysis of the technologies of power. His conception of power, as in the birth of the prison, asylum and hospital, is also a time of imperialist exploitation and the rapacious nature of colonialism remains unexcavated in his conception of power. Gayatri Chakravorty Spivak, 'Can the Subaltern Speak?', in Cary Nelson and Lawrence Grossberg (eds), *Marxism and the Interpretation of Culture* (Basingstoke: Macmillan, 1988), pp. 271–313, here p. 291. In this context, however, I am following Mary John's suggestion that feminist scholarship in the developing world should not remain content simply with the critique of sanctioned ignorances of the west but critique our own production of prejudiced knowledges. Mary John, *Discrepant Dislocations*, p. 127 *n*. 12.

31. Padma Anagol, *Laxmibai Dravid and the Birth of the Hindu Right* (forthcoming). In 1893, communal riots between Hindus and Muslims began in North India over the issue of the sacredness of the cow for Hindus, leading to demands on a ban on cow slaughter. See John R. McLane, *Indian Nationalism and the Early Congress* (Princeton: Princeton University Press, 1977), esp. pp. 276–81, 322–5.

32. Partha Chatterjee, 'The Nationalist Resolution of the Women's Question', in Sangari and Vaid (eds), *Recasting Women*, pp. 233–54.

33. Geraldine Forbes, 'The Indian Women's Movement: A Struggle for Women's Rights or National Liberation', in Minault (ed.), *The Extended Family*, pp. 49–82; Geraldine Forbes, *Woman in Modern India* (Cambridge: Cambridge University Press, 1995).

34. C. H. Philips and Mary Doreen Wainwright (eds), *Indian Society and the Beginnings of Modernisation, c.1830–1850* (London: School of Oriental and African Studies, 1960).

35. Charles Heimsath, *Indian Nationalism and Hindu Social Reform* (Princeton: Princeton University Press, 1964). See also Nanda (ed.), *Indian Women*.

36. Meredith Borthwick, *The Changing Condition of Women in Bengal: 1850–1905* (Princeton: Princeton University Press, 1984).

37. Meredith Borthwick, 'Looking at Women's History: Nineteenth-Century Bengal', in John McGuire, Meredith Borthwick and Brij V. Lal (eds), *Problems and Methods of Enquiry in South Asian History* (Nedlands: University of Western Australia Press, 1984), pp. 17–23.

38. See Tanika Sarkar, *Words to Win: The Making of Amar Jiban, A Modern Autobiography* (New Delhi: Kali for Women, 1999).

39. Haimabati Sen, *The Memoirs of Dr. Hamiabati Sen: From Child Widow to Lady Doctor*, tr. Tapan Raychaudhuri, ed. Geraldine Forbes (New Delhi: Roli, 2000).

40. The historiography on sati is impressive. For a recent and refreshing perspective on the humanitarian aspects of the British discourse on the abolition of sati see Andrea Major, *Pious Flames: European Encounters with Sati 1500–1830* (Oxford: Oxford University Press, 2006).

41. Lata Mani, *Contentious Traditions: The Debate on Sati in Colonial India* (Berkeley: University of California Press, 1999).

42. Lata Mani, 'Contentious Traditions: The Debate on Sati in Colonial India', in Sangari and Vaid (eds), *Recasting Women*, pp. 88–126, here p. 92.

43. Mani, *Contentious Traditions: The Debate on Sati in Colonial India* (Berkeley: University of California Press, 1998), pp. 158–90.

44. See esp. Ania Loomba, 'Dead Women Tell no Tales: Issues of Female Subjectivity, Subaltern Agency and Tradition in Colonial and Post-Colonial Writings on Widow Immolation in India', *History Workshop* 36 (1993), pp. 209–27, here p. 227.

45. Mani, 'Contentious Traditions', p. 92.

46. See Werner Menski, 'Sati: A Review Article', *Bulletin of the School of Oriental and African Studies, University of London*, 61 (1998), pp. 74–81, here p. 74.

47. Clare Midgley, 'Female Emancipation in an Imperial Frame: English Women and the Campaign Against Sati (Widow-Burning) in India, 1813–30', *Women's History Review* 9 (2000), pp. 95–121.

48. Sangari and Vaid (eds), *Recasting Women*, p. 1.

49. I have made a start in this direction with my book *The Emergence of Feminism in India* (Aldershot: Ashgate, 2006), but asking such questions begs detailed micro-studies of different regions of India (especially neglected regions such as Karnataka, Orissa, Andhra Pradesh and Rajasthan) and a comparison between them before consensus can be reached amongst scholars – but this project is not in sight as yet.

50. See the recent studies of Rokeya Sakhawat Hossain, *Sultana's Dream and Padmarag: Two Feminist Utopias*, tr. and ed. Barnita Bagchi (Delhi: Penguin, 2005), see 'Introduction', pp. vi–xxvi; Meera Kosambi, *Crossing Thresholds: Feminist Essays in Social History* (Delhi: Permanent Black, 2007); Shayraryar Khan, *The Begums of Bhopal: A History of the Princely State of Bhopal* (London: I. B. Tauris, 2000); Siobhan Lambert-Hurley, *Muslim Women, Reform and Princely Patronage: Nawab Sultan Jahan Begam of Bhopal* (London: Routledge, 2006); Bharati Ray, *Early Feminists of Colonial India: Sarala Devi Chaudhurani and Rokeya Sakhawat Hossain* (New Delhi: Oxford University Press, 2002).

51. James Mill, *History of British India*, 6 vols (1817; repr. New Delhi: Associated Publishing House, 1972).

52. Hermann Kulke and Dietmar Rothermund have commented that lack of a decisive alternative has allowed the continuance of this time arrangement. See their discussion in *A History of India* (1990; London: Routledge, 1992), p. 8.

53. Some recent textbooks suggest this pattern. See Peter Robb, *A History of India* (Basingstoke: Palgrave, 2002); Burton Stein, *A History of India* (1998; Oxford: Blackwell, 2000).

54. See the collection of articles in Peter J. Marshall (ed.), *The Eighteenth Century in Indian History: Evolution or Revolution?* (New Delhi: Oxford University Press, 2003), esp. pp. 1–100; Sanjay Subrahmanyam, 'Connected Histories: Notes towards a Reconfiguration of Early Modern Eurasia', *Modern Asian Studies* 31, Special Issue: The Eurasian Context of the Early Modern History of Mainland South East Asia, 1400–1800 (1997), pp. 735–62.

55. Rosalind O'Hanlon has started research along these lines and we await eagerly a monograph from her.

56. Laxmibai Dravid, *Desh Seva Nibandha Mala: Ank Ekda* (Marathi); [*A Series of Essays in Service of the Nation: Part One*] (Poona: Vijayananda Press, 1896), p. 1. All translations are my own. I am currently engaged in bringing out a critical edition of this book. For details see note 31.

57. In May 1857, discontented high-caste sepoys (soldiers) mutinied against the Company authorities, which in turn led to some civilian revolts, and for a while it appeared that the Company troops had lost northern India to the rebels. The uprisings were quelled by mid-1858. Whether or not the events of 1857 represented civilian participation in significant numbers is still a matter of debate. For a recent discussion, see Peter Robb, 'On the Rebellion of 1857: A Brief History of an Idea', *Economic and Political Weekly* 42 (2007), pp. 1,696–702.

58. Stein, *History of India*.

59. Thomas Babington Macaulay, 'Minute on Indian Education', 2 February 1835, in Barbara Harlow and Mia Carter (eds), *Imperialism and Orientalism: A Documentary Sourcebook* (Oxford: Blackwell, 1999), p. 61.

60. David Washbrook, 'India, 1818–1860: The Two Faces of Colonialism', in *The Oxford History of the British Empire*, vol. 3: *The Nineteenth Century*, ed. Andrew Porter (Oxford: Oxford University Press, 1999), pp. 395–422.

61. See Anagol, *Emergence of Feminism in India*, ch. 4, pp. 105–40.

62. How Indian women were affected adversely by British policies is discussed in Padma Anagol, 'The Emergence of the Female Criminal in India: Infanticide and Survival under the Raj', *History Workshop Journal* 53 (2002), pp. 73–93.

63. See the excellent work of Uma Chakravarti, *Gendering Caste through a Feminist Lens* (Calcutta: Stree, 2006) in the promising series on 'Theorising Feminism', edited by Maithreyi Krishnaraj.

64. Suparna Gooptu, *Cornelia Sorabji: India's Pioneer Woman Lawyer* (Delhi: Oxford University Press, 2006); Hossain, *Sultana's Dream and Padmarag*; Gail Omvedt, *Dalit Visions* (New Delhi: Orient Longman, 2004); Sharmila Rege, *Writing Caste, Writing Gender: Narrating Dalit Women's Testimonies* (Delhi: Zubaan, 2006).

65. A solid synthesis with new materials covering the movements for women's rights from the nineteenth century to the 1990s is available in Radha Kumar, *The History of Doing* (Delhi: Kali, 1993).

66. The contours of Indian women's resistance to various oppressions and the problems attending them have been dealt in detail in Padma Anagol, 'From the Symbolic to the Open: Women's Resistance in Colonial Maharashtra', in Anindita Ghosh (ed.), *Behind the Veil: Resistance, Women and the Everyday in Colonial South Asia* (Delhi: Permanent Black, 2007), pp. 21–57.

67. See Anagol, *Emergence of Feminism in India*, ch. 4, pp. 105–40.

68. See Sandra Bartky, 'Towards a Phenomenology of Feminist Consciousness', in Nancy Tuana and Rosemarie Tong (eds), *Feminism and Philosophy: Essential Readings in Theory, Reinterpretation and Application* (Boulder, CO: Westview Press, 1995), pp. 396–406, here p. 405.

69. Anagol, *Emergence of Feminism in India*.

70. An insightful account of how and why feminist scholarship should avoid reductive conceptions of female agency is in Janaki Nair, 'On the Question of Agency in Indian Feminist Historiography', *Gender & History* 6 (1994), pp. 82–100.

71. For my disagreements and differences with Douglas Haynes and Gyan Prakash (eds), *Contesting Power: Resistance and Everyday Social Relations in South Asia* (Berkeley: University of California Press, 1991), as well as James Scott, *Weapons of the Weak: Everyday Forms of Resistance in South East Asia* (New Haven: Yale University Press, 1985); see Anagol, *Emergence of Feminism in India*, ch. 1, pp. 1–18 and Anagol, 'From Symbolic to Open', in Ghosh (ed.), *Behind the Veil*, pp. 21–8.

72. Tarabai Shinde, *A Comparison between Women and Men: Tarabai Shinde and the Critique of Gender Relations in Colonial India,* tr. and ed. Rosalind O'Hanlon (Madras: Oxford University Press, 1994); Meera Kosambi (ed.), *Pandita Ramabai through her Own Words: Selected Works* (New Delhi: Oxford University Press, 2000).

73. This region was incorporated in the administrative unit devised by the Raj called the Bombay Presidency. By 'Maharashtra' I mean the region where Marathi is the dominant spoken language.

74. Although see Malini Bhattacharya and Abhijit Sen (eds), *Talking of Power: Early Writings of Bengali Women* (Calcutta: Stree, 2003).

75. Spivak, 'Can the Subaltern Speak?', pp. 271–313; Gayatri Chakravorty Spivak, 'The Rani of Sirmur: An Essay in Reading the Archives', *History and Theory* 24 (1985), pp. 247–72.

76. A refreshing collection of articles querying these questions for British imperial history is in Antoinette Burton (ed.), *Archive Stories: Facts, Fictions and the Writing of History* (Durham: Duke University Press, 2006).

77. For a selection of such literature see Godavaribai Pandita, *Pakdarpan athava Maharashtriya Swayampakashastra [Cookery Manual or The Science of Maharashtrian Culinary]* (Pune: Dnyan Chaksu, 1893); Mainabai, *Urnavyuti athava Lonkarichi Vina [Manual on Knitting Woollen Clothes]* (Pune: Shivaji Press, 1886); Rukminibai Sanzgiri, *Sutachi Veenkam Shiknache Pustak [The Art of Crocheting]* (1891, Bombay: Gopal Narayan, 1902); Lakshmibai kom Dattatreya Bhave, *Ganapatiche Ganen va Striyanche Nashibacha Dakhala [Songs in Praise of God Ganapati and Musings on the Fate of Women]* (Pune: Siddhi Vinayak, 1895); *Ramabai Indukarin Inamdar, Striyakarita Manoranjak Ganyacha Pustak [Poetry for Women's Entertainment]* (Pune: Shivaji Press, 1884); Bhagirathibai Madgavkarin (comp.), *Muli va Striyansathin Fugadya, Kombada, Jhima, Pinga, Ithyadi Manoranjak Ganen va Khel [Fugdi, Kombada, Jhima, Pinga and Other Entertaining Songs and Games for Women and Girls]* (Bombay: Jagadishwar Press, 1885).

78. Although I track the subjectivities of mainly middle-class Indian women, I have also tried to analyse the position, roles and status of lower-class and caste women as far as the sources permit me in such retrievals.

79. Charles Heimsath, *Indian Nationalism and Hindu Social Reform* (Princeton: Princeton University Press, 1964); Kenneth W. Jones, *Arya Dharm: Hindu Consciousness in Nineteenth Century Punjab* (New Delhi: Manohar, 1976).

80. Kenneth I. Pargament, *The Psychology of Religion and Coping: Theory, Research, Practice* (New York: Guilford Press, 1997).

81. For a detailed study of Indian Christian women see Anagol, *Emergence of Feminism in India*, pp. 19–56.

82. See Anagol, *Emergence of Feminism in India*, pp. 57–104.

83. In western and southern India, *halad-kunku* rituals were performed for women-only gatherings where unmarried girls and married women gathered to exchange social pleasantries and news of the everyday happenings within their caste, family and community. At the end of the meeting, married women had their foreheads anointed with the auspicious red vermilion and yellow turmeric powders. Offerings of coconut, arecanut and fruit were also made to each other. See Anagol, *Emergence of Feminism in India*, pp. 6, 60–63, 73, 139.

84. 'Kirtans' were public gatherings consisting of both literate and illiterate people who came to listen to learned men and women deliver sermons from religious books or from ancient myths: the rendering was made lively by the accompaniment of musical instruments. Many of the *kirtankars* were women discourse-givers and, in the nineteenth century, quite a few professed reformist tendencies. See Anagol, *Emergence of Feminism in India*, pp. 6, 46, 60–66, 115, 223–8.

85. For details see Anagol, *Emergence of Feminism in India*, ch. 3, pp. 57–104.

86. Sangari and Vaid (eds), *Recasting Women*, p. 14.

87. See Pandita Ramabai, *Returning the American Gaze: Pandita Ramabai's 'The Peoples of the United States, 1889*, tr. and ed. Meera Kosambi (Delhi: Permanent Black, 2003), pp. 18, 242 *n.* 3.

88. Anagol, *Emergence of Feminism in India*, chs 3 and 5, pp. 57–104, 141–80.

89. Anandibai Lad, 'Lavkar Lagna Karnyachi Chal' ['The Custom of Early Marriage'], *Arya Bhagini* [Indian Women's Magazine], March 1886, pp. 3–6, here p. 4.

90. For the growth of the concept of *bhaginivarg* (sisterhood) and the 'Women's Press' in Maharashtra, see Anagol, *Emergence of Feminism in India*, pp. 15, 57–80, 209–25.

91. Salubai Tambwekar, *Hindustanatil Tara [Indian Princesses]* (Poona: Jagadhitechchu, 1895); Kashibai Kanitkar, *Palkicha Gonda [The Tassel at the Centre of the Palanquin]* (1913; Poona: Kanitkar and Mandali, 1928).

92. Samples are Gangutai Patwardhan, *Chakoribaher: Ek Atmakathan [Beyond the Courtyard: An Autobiography]* (Poona: Sadhana Prakashan, 1974), original date unknown but traced to mid nineteenth-century events; Yashodabai Joshi, *Amchi Jivanpravas [Our Journey Together]* (Poona: Venus, 1965).

93. An example of a woman's memoir in Maharashtra turning into a literary classic is Lakshmibai Tilak's *Smriti Chitre [Snapshots from My Life]*, tr. and ed. Josephine Inkster (Madras: Oxford University Press, 1950), written in four parts from 1934 to 1937. It has been translated thrice by Christian missionaries and also reprinted many times. For an example of a memoir utilised purely to measure a woman's progress from the private to the public sphere see Anandibai Shirke, *Sanjvat [At Dusk: A Memoir]* (Bombay: Mauj Prakashan, 1972).

94. See Anagol, *Emergence of Feminism in India*, pp. 130–40.

95. More details on the linguistic sophistication of Maharashtrian feminist ideology can be found in Anagol, *Emergence of Feminism in India*, pp. 14, 58, 90–96, 134–8, 214–23.

96. Tarabai Shinde, *Stripurushtulana athava striya va purush yant sahasi kon he spasta karun dakavinyakarita ha nibandh* (Marathi); *[Women and Men: A Comparison, or an Essay to Show who is Really Wicked]* (Pune and Buldhana: Shri Shivaji Press, 1882) p. 14.

97. 'Potent Protests: The Age of Consent Controversy, 1891' in Mrinalini Sinha, *Colonial Masculinity: The 'Manly Englishman' and the 'Effeminate Bengali' in the Late Nineteenth Century* (Manchester: Manchester University Press, 1995), pp. 138–180.

98. Anagol, *Emergence of Feminism in India*, ch. 6, pp. 181–218.

99. Jayawardena, *Feminism and Nationalism in the Third World*, pp. 1–24; for a more recent reiteration of the same position see Leela Kasturi and Vina Mazumdar (eds) *Women and Indian Nationalism* (New Delhi: Vikas, 1994), pp. 4–7.

9 The Unseamed Picture: Conflicting Narratives of Women in the Modern European Past

Lynn Abrams

> There is a need to recognise the heterogeneity of expressions of women's histori-
> cal trajectories . . . in a way that does not subordinate this task to the categories of
> mainstream history – whether this means national histories or even women's history
> itself.[1]

> The gender history of the future is one that can confidently admit the possibility of
> disparate temporalities. Rather than attempting to fit gender back into established
> chronologies and categories, its more productive outcome may be to allow dissonance
> within grand narratives.[2]

This chapter arises from a personal journey through writing the history
of women and gender in modern Europe. Other historians of Europe will
no doubt recognise my experience of being pulled in different directions,
between the general and the particular, the overarching interpretation and
the closely researched case study, because it is part and parcel of being a
'Europeanist' – someone with expertise in one part of the continent who
is then almost honour-bound to be able to write about Europe as a whole,
a task becoming increasingly difficult, maybe impossible, in view of the
changing boundaries of Europe in modern geopolitics.[3] Many historians
of women in Europe have risen to the challenge, inspired by the feminist
aim of producing alternative narratives of the past to those privileged in
mainstream histories, and informed by the belief that, despite their differences, women in western Europe at least, had more in common than the
experiences that divided them.[4] The result has been a series of histories
of European women from medieval times to the present which offer both
totalising or all-encompassing interpretations and some real challenges to
generalist histories of Europe.[5]

Both of these legitimating claims may still be heard but are increasingly subject to debate. The recognition amongst historians of women of the salience of other social categories such as race, ethnicity, sexuality, nationality and generation as well as class has unsettled narratives which privilege sex and has forced us to find ways of telling a coherent story that nevertheless encompasses heterogeneity.[6] As Kathleen Canning notes, in view of the 'extraordinary scholarly achievements' in the fields of women's and gender history over thirty years or so, and its ability to create new fields and rupture old ones, gender history must have the confidence to create its own narratives which may sit alongside, challenge or be incorporated in the overarching interpretations.[7] The alternative would merely be more synthesis and homogenisation and consequently the blunting of the critical edge of feminist writing about the European past.

The thoughts expressed here on the writing of European women's and gender history arise from a personal conflict experienced in the process of researching and writing two books concurrently. As I synthesised and narrated the story of women in nineteenth-century Europe for an all-embracing survey text, at the same time I was conducting archival and oral history research in the most northerly islands of the British Isles for an explicitly local and embedded history of women and gender in Shetland.[8] Writing the Shetland book unsettled my comfort zone with regard to the grander narratives and chronologies of change I had absorbed, presented and bolstered in my survey of European women. What is at stake here is not merely the tension between the scholarly exercise of close analysis and conceptual sophistication for the monograph study and the need to present a more general and accessible narrative for wider consumption. It is also about the kinds of stories we write, the research experiences we have, and the sense in which our mental map of the past is a crude tool for the charting of experience at the local and personal level. How can we write meaningful and recognisable histories that also contribute to the (re-)writing of the bigger picture? And what happens when the stories told about the local and the personal jar with the overarching frameworks?

I shall argue that the dissonance that exists between local or particular women's histories and general interpretations should be taken seriously; that is, the particular study that does not chime with the general framework should not be placed on the margins and regarded as peripheral to the core story. Rather, there are lessons to be learnt from historical narratives generated by women's experience embedded within the local context. Indeed, such histories born of the attempt to access women's voices and subjectivities may offer different narratives and chronologies of change, driven by female-centred sources and feminist research strategies. This chapter makes three key points. First, the analysis of a place like Shetland, which appears different or unusual, offers the historian a unique vantage point from which to form a new perspective on the general or familiar landscape of European women's history. Second, the deliberate prioritising of women's voices and interpretations in the local context provides a version of women's pasts that may jar with more familiar narratives of continuity and change. And third, this combination of strangeness and subjectivity offers the historian an authentic story with meaning for those who narrated it.

Seamless narratives, ragged edges

In the space of little more than three decades, women's and gender historians have produced an expansive corpus of work that has succeeded in creating a series of gendered narratives of the European past.[9] The story of Europe from medieval times to the present has been told from the perspective of women's experience and has been problematised using theories of gender. Yet it is precisely because of the breadth and depth of research – especially in the modern period – that any one overarching narrative is now unsustainable. Interpretations that work for national contexts seem inappropriate when applied more widely; urban-based narratives sit uncomfortably next to those emanating from places slower to industrialise and so on. The result then is a series of interpretive frameworks for telling the story of European women, which broadly run in parallel yet reflect national historiographical trajectories and material variations in different territories.

From the British perspective, the dominant framing paradigm in analyses of the period from the mid-eighteenth to the early twentieth century has been that of 'separate spheres'. The ideology that women and men were naturally predisposed to inhabit separate realms of life – the public and the private – which reached its zenith in the first half of the nineteenth century, has been a particularly powerful explanatory framework for understanding the gendered inequalities of industrialising Britain. It is, of course, a gross simplification, even a parody, of a complex and nuanced story and it has rightly been subject to sustained criticism.[10] Nonetheless, the separate spheres narrative retains a presence in accounts of modern British women and gender relations as a prescriptive discourse (though one with many competing strands) rather than a descriptive model. It is generally recognised that, notwithstanding the existence of ideological or discursive formulations that deployed separate spheres as organising concepts, public and private realms were in fact porous, the implementation and impact of discursive constructions was varied and women (and men) contested gendered constructions in their everyday lives as well as in public and organised challenges to prescriptive norms.[11] So-called 'revisionist' approaches have sought to understand women's own motivations and subjectivities and have suggested that discourses that affirmed women's relationship to the home were 'wholly against the grain of women's experiences'.[12]

Separate spheres is just one of the organising frameworks that have helped to shape analyses of European women's history, though perhaps it has had particular resonance for British-based historians where a historiographical debate on periodisation has focused on this interpretive model. It is certainly incumbent on most historians of women in modern Britain at least to engage with the concept of separate spheres even if they go on to reject it, not least because it has found its way into popular and mainstream accounts of British history and therefore exists within current discourse that, in turn, informs women's own interpretations of their pasts.[13] But in Britain and elsewhere, the chronological boundaries that separate spheres helped to create have been undermined so that narratives of continuity and change are now much more temporally fluid. Beyond Britain, the public and private framework has been less frequently deployed, notably in those places where the processes of industrialisation and urbanisation were slower and where other discourses (such as the implication of maternalism in nation-state formation) have greater relevance.[14]

Those historians who research parts of Europe outside the modern, industrialised states have expressed unease with the continued importance assigned to organising concepts based upon 'modernisation'. In 1999, Mary Nash, from the perspective of Spanish women's history, remarked that, 'A fully comprehensive view of European women's history has yet to be established . . . Meta-narratives identified as being representative of European women's history, but based on a selective reading of British or French studies, are still accepted as . . . a "European" discourse'.[15] One of the consequences of a metanarrative of modern European women's history has been a flattening or smoothing out of the complex chronologies of women's historical trajectories and experiences. Clearly, metanarratives marginalise or ignore regional and cultural difference within countries and they have a tendency to focus on those countries where change was most advanced. Thus the industrialising states of northern Europe are adopted as the blueprint for the others. The narratives of women in smaller states are subsumed into the histories of their larger neighbours and the places which seemingly lag behind economically are tacked on as interesting sideshows. Many of us would agree with Liz Stanley's view that 'rather than seeing a feminist history as the recovery of all the pieces of a jigsaw puzzle, such that we finally gain a single, complete and unseamed picture of the whole . . . there is no "whole" to piece together, but rather contiguous though clashing, and certainly not seamlessly meshing, competing histories'.[16] Competing and clashing histories are perhaps the future, especially in the light of the development of women's history in central and eastern Europe and the rather strained attempt to include these stories in existing interpretations as well as the incorporation of global and postcolonial perspectives. We need to think about how to juxtapose different narratives derived from different contexts in order to do justice to the variety of experiences we uncover.

The conceptual opportunity offered by the use of gender as a tool of analysis has widened the frame of reference and permitted a reconfiguration of the telling of European history. Whereas a determinist deployment of separate spheres, for instance, produced constraints in terms of periodisation, gender transcends traditional chronological and conceptual boundaries and has encouraged new thinking on themes such as politics and citizenship, sexuality, motherhood and the demographic transition, thus facilitating new narrative threads that may create bridges between apparently divergent experiences.[17]

As I sat in the most northerly archive in the British Isles, these issues of competing narratives and of overarching frameworks came sharply into view. I had absorbed a generation of writing about modern European women that used a series of large interpretive frames to shape the story: modernisation, emancipation, democratisation and in Britain more especially, 'separate spheres'. My feet were planted in modernising, industrialising Europe (probably somewhere in northern Germany), my perspective was metropolitan, and I had been trained in the traditional ways of the historian's craft to privilege research in the archives. But the experience of researching the story of women in Shetland disturbed my comfort. It just did not fit with the big interpretations. The stories that emanated from this place suggested new or at least different chronologies. The outcome was that I had to jettison the old tropes. The history I wrote of women in this northern archipelago marked a shift in my thinking about how we might write the history of European women, at least in the recent past. The shift encompasses two main issues: methodological, or the way we practise our historical research, and one of perspective and scale, or how we transcend particularity while providing texture and authenticity to the general narrative. If our aim is to write usable and recognisable histories of women and gender relations in the past, it is incumbent upon us to try to identify interpretive threads that span national, local and temporal differences.

Issues of historical practice

The way we practise our historical research and writing affects the kind of history we produce. One's experience in the archive and in the field should not be downplayed, since interactions with our sources – both printed and otherwise – create the environment from which we craft our stories. Living and working in a small and relatively remote place like Shetland, a collection of islands some 180 kilometres from the British mainland, brings the researcher face to face with her research subjects and one begins to traverse the line between historian and anthropologist. It should be said at the outset though, that a peripheral island community like Shetland is not especially representative or typical; indeed it was exceptional in many ways and thus may appear to be an odd choice of launch pad for rethinking the bigger picture. Yet, just as anthropologists sought out the strange to cast new perspectives on the familiar, my experience in Shetland forced me to view the traditional periodisation and explanatory frameworks through new spectacles. At the same time, Shetland was not a timeless, rural backwater, cut off from the larger forces of change. It was not a place where history stood still. As a predominantly fishing and farming community at the crossroads of northern European trade routes and characterised in the nineteenth century by high levels of migration, its inhabitants were affected by wider economic and cultural trends. The challenge for the historian of women is to integrate analysis of material conditions with women's subjectivities. My experience in attempting to do just this is my starting point.

Shetland in the twenty-first century is a place which has a keen and living sense of its past; where people harbour stories and want to tell them; where the past is very much a part of everyday life in all sorts of ways – from the remnants of ruined croft buildings that litter the landscape to the vibrancy of the Shetland dialect and the continued symbolic importance of material referents of the past: hand-knitting, peat-cutting and fishing to name a few.[18] The past is in the present in Shetland and women are at the heart of Shetlanders' own story or understanding of their past. In fact, the story of women in the past has come to dominate the way Shetlanders today – men and women – imagine and recount their history. Here is a place, then, where women's story is Shetland's history.

For the historian, being immersed in a society with a keen sense of how to tell the story of its past is a novel and exciting experience with concrete implications. To begin with, the archive was a repository of women's stories. The archival holdings of conventional printed sources such as legal records, poor law cases, kirk session minutes and employment records, are exceptionally full in Shetland, offering untold opportunities to unearth rich evidence of women's lives.[19] In addition, local family historians had transcribed reams of census data permitting the reconstruction of families and households over time. A huge collection of oral histories facilitated access to evidence of women's experience in a different form. And, as well as this source material, the archive itself attracted stories as an acknowledged repository for the past and an active facilitator of historical investigation. Visitors to the archives from the islands, but also from the Scottish mainland and overseas, brought stories with them to share. Women and men transformed the search room into a living archive, telling stories of their mothers and grandmothers, recognising names in the printed record and suggesting people to speak to – thus facilitating a dialogue between the official sources and the present. I had not counted on this interplay between the past and the present through the prism of women. I could not have imagined the tremendous power of narratives of the past in Shetland that used women and women's position in the economy and culture as the leitmotif for historical change. Undoubtedly, this interactive research experience influenced the kind of history that was eventually written. It was impossible to remain objective or distanced from the stories being told and neither was it desirable to impose on the sources a framework imported from other contexts. It soon became clear that narratives of continuity and change derived from other places were not part of the lexicon of the Shetland story.

The conversation between past and present has been extensively theorised by historians utilising oral sources. Those practising oral history are now fully aware of the implications of intersubjectivity, the relationship between individual and collective memory and the existence of what is termed the 'cultural circuit' or feedback loop between personal testimonies and external discourses.[20] Oral historians understand that memory narratives are produced within a discursive context and that the story eventually crafted by the historian cannot be free from the environment in which it was created. Recent interventions in this debate have urged that the subjective and the personal be put back into the story, arguing that subjectivity should not be reduced to a mere product of external discourses.[21] In the context of Shetland, these methodological insights are certainly relevant to the analysis of oral history and storytelling, but also they may be transferred to the research process more generally.

The interplay between past and present can be explained as follows. From the seventeenth century, Shetland was at the crossroads of fish trading routes, a transit stop for merchants, fishermen, smugglers and whalers. But it was also a relatively isolated island community dominated by farming and fishing. From the early nineteenth century, when Shetland began to be visited by writers, a female-centred narrative of Shetland's past began to be formulated. Visitors to the islands from mainland Britain invariably commented upon the centrality of women to the life of the islands. They were shocked by the public visibility of women – working in the fields, gathering peats from the hill, engaging in trade and commerce as independent actors, free from male supervision. Women's ubiquity was not surprising, for females vastly outnumbered males in these islands – in 1861, when the population of the islands numbered almost 32,000, the ratio of women to men was 143:100. Women were thus commonly engaged in outdoor work in a place where crofting, fishing and hand-knitting were the prime economic activities. By the 1880s though, it was the condition, rather than the mere presence, of women that became a benchmark for highlighting the 'backwardness' of Shetland in comparison with the British mainland. The fact of females undertaking hard, physical labour outdoors was seen by visitors as a sign of an unmodernised society and, moreover, a society which appeared to have no truck with the ideology of domesticity and of separate spheres. Sir Walter Scott, alighting on Shetland in 1903, 'greatly deprecated the invincible native habit of making the women burden-bearers'.[22] So the focus on women by visitors was a means of signifying difference.

From the early nineteenth century, islanders themselves – women and men – also used the figure of the woman to speak about their history and culture, but in a positive way that emphasised women's agency. Popular nineteenth-century interpretations of the thirteenth-century Norse sagas, reprinted and referred to in the Shetland press and in fiction, featured strong and powerful women. Popular Shetland writers too used the leitmotif of the strong, independent Shetland woman to convey a sense of place and an understanding of the past. Thus a discourse was circulated in oral and written sources of women at the heart of Shetland society. More than that, women were represented as capable of sound management and decision-making, hence legitimising a state of affairs in which they were in charge of the household and 'quite able to do the work of men'. Popular fiction and journalistic feature-writing also valorised women in their role as workers, independent of men if need be and in some cases heroic, coming to the rescue of men (in sea rescues for instance).[23] And finally, folktales and family stories too draw upon these 'myths' of Shetland womanhood.

Now one might say that this kind of representation created a caricature of Shetland womanhood that combined a romantic heroism with tragedy and resilience. But these representations would not have had such purchase and longevity if they were not at least partly grounded in material experience, and if they were not recognised as such. For instance, the fictional stories told by Jessie Saxby, Shetland's most successful writer, drew upon the women's lives she observed in her native islands, in some cases barely concealing real events and people. The film made by Jenny Brown in 1934, *The Rugged Island*, depicts the everyday lives of members of a typical Shetland crofting-fishing family centring on the loves and losses of the women. And the writings of Christina Jamieson, Shetland's foremost campaigner for women's rights, focused on the particular material poverty of women in her native Shetland.[24] All of these were (and still are) influential in helping present-day Shetlanders construct their identity and present themselves to others. So, when we turn to oral history as well as other present-day ways of representing and telling the past (museum exhibits, photographs, popular histories, community heritage presentations), we find that Shetlanders shape their stories around these public representations of history and culture. Hence the figure of 'the Shetland woman' is universally recognised in the islands as being at the heart of the community and is given greater prominence than the absent fisherman or the more contemporary oil worker.

The way in which Shetlanders use this island history was most obvious in the 1970s and 1980s, when Shetland was experiencing major economic and cultural change following the discovery of North Sea oil and the development of the oil terminal on the islands. The influx of workers to the oil and subsidiary industries from all over the United Kingdom and the growth in economic opportunities for islanders (especially women) prompted Shetlanders to emphasise their difference from the newcomers in terms of a widely accepted discourse: the gender equality they perceived to be a feature of island life, both in the past and the present.[25] At one public meeting to discuss gender roles in the late 1970s it was said that, 'Shetland society, ancient and modern, had been characterised by egalitarian sex roles, whereas Scottish society was rampant with sexism'.[26] This utterance revealed more than just some Shetlanders' sense that they enjoyed a tradition of gender equality. It also revealed a consciousness of the frameworks used to structure interpretations of gender relations elsewhere. Shetlanders consciously based their story in opposition to what they perceive as the dominant narrative beyond Shetland.

Since the 1970s, the centrality of women to Shetland's story of its past has remained strong. A good example of the way in which women's economic and cultural place in the community continues to be celebrated is the use of hand-knitting as a symbol of identity. The story of women's economic role in the Shetland hosiery production sector is well known and embedded within almost every family in the islands. Throughout the nineteenth and well into the twentieth century, knitting was the mainstay of many families, providing a meagre but reliable living and contributing to the ability of many unmarried and widowed females to survive. In recent years, the image of the female knitter has experienced a revival as traditional home production has been transformed into a revered art form. This transformation is exemplified by the work of the Shetland textile development officer whose research into the forgotten stories of innovative and entrepreneurial women hand-knitters in the inter-war years, coupled with the support for present day textile artists in the interpretation of the work of these women, demonstrates that the process of telling the story of the past through the prism of women is not static, but a fluid and creative process, reflecting changes in Shetland society.[27]

By the 1980s, the story of Shetland as a woman's place was well established. It was clear in oral testimony of those interviewed in the 1970s and 1980s that they had incorporated the discourse into their narratives of the past. I found this through using an existing oral history archive containing interviews with women and men, supplemented by a small number of face-to-face interviews with women who had been identified to me as repositories of knowledge about Shetland women in the past. In a series of unstructured interviews I found the discourse of dominant Shetland womanhood was central to the ways in which respondents narrated their histories. Indeed, the texture of the oral histories was multi-layered, drawing upon autobiography, local history, popular discourses, official sources and material referents, but common to all was the sense that women's stories, experiences and consciousness were central to an understanding of the history of this place. The narrative of Shetland was woman-centred, albeit usually nestled within a broader, more conventional socio-economic context. Unsurprisingly, female respondents placed women at the heart of their narratives, telling rich and detailed stories of mothers, grandmothers and aunts; but men too had incorporated the notion of Shetland as a female-dominated place into their memories, while acknowledging the existence of an alternative gender model. In the words of one male respondent, 'The women were in among things. That was the unusual thing. They bwirna [weren't] supposed to be'.[28]

My research was not conceived primarily as an oral history project; indeed I had started out with the aim of conducting archive-based analysis of mainly written sources. But a chance discovery of a particularly revelatory oral history interview conducted in 1982 had the effect of shifting the emphasis of the entire project. I wanted to privilege women's words and women's interpretations and versions of the Shetland past. This single interview featured the Shetland crofter, knitter and storyteller Mary Manson – who was then aged eighty-five and a typical Shetland women in many ways – whose stories conjured up an intangible past barely reachable in the printed sources.[29] Rather than merely using her testimony to illustrate a world the historian has already constructed from traditional sources, I took her narrative as a starting point, an entrée to a different interpretive world of popular belief, of community and of ritual grounded in the material circumstances of women's day-to-day life. In short, the analysis of this particular narrative aided the historian's desire to 'imagine oneself into the past', to produce a version of the past embedded in women's words and experience.[30]

Mary Manson told stories about Shetland that were drawn from her and her family's everyday experience. One story related in great detail and uninterrupted is a women-centred tale about a journey undertaken by her mother and a female cousin when, as young teenagers, they travelled across two islands in search of a wise-woman who could provide medicine for a sick relative. The journey is told as a perilous venture into the unknown, guided by hospitable strangers who provide food, directions and ferry crossings. When they finally reach the wise-woman's house, they enter deep into what sounds to the listener like a gothic fairytale as they are locked up in a dark box-bed while a potion is made over a fire. Mary described the girls' experience in great detail:

> she says you'll geng tae bed and lay you doon, I'll pit you tae bed afore I go, and the bed at she had was a boxed bed, it was a boxed bed ootbye at the partition, and this door drew close, a wooden door at drew close in the bed, I mind Mammy saying it was a fine bed at she had, she had a tattered rug and a feather bed and of course, then a days it was likely supposed tae be a wonderful bed, onywye they got aff o dem and they got intae this bed and she drew the door across the front. So you can keen what they were likely tinkin', locked in a dis black prison, didna know what was going to happen after that, so anyway, she left them in yunder and she guid out, and she was a braw while away, and at last they heard her comin in, but it had tae be kinda light, at had tae be the spring do sees at she could see, anywye, daylight coming up or something, but they heard her coming in and they heard her starting to get the fire up, it was a fire in the middle of the floor and they heard her gettin doon the peats and gettin this fire going, and a pouring a water and a rattling of pans and tins and all this, and then after a while they fan the smell o' lik dis roots, lik a strong smell of roots boiling, so Mammy said they could lie no longer for they were never fallen asleep, she got up and she tried, there was a chink in the door, and she got up and she tried tae peep and see what was going on and she said that the old wife was sitting ower the heartstane wi' all this pots and pans and a great pot hanging in the crook, boiling with this mixture. So eh, onyway she said she raise up, Mam would swear at she never made ony noise at all tae peep oot this chink and of course this old wife was sittin wi' her back til her and she never kent til she let oot a shout, lie doon an faa asleep this minute, she says, I keen ower weel at you're watching me, you're going tae deystroy the medicine.[31]

Fearful and powerless, the girls seem to become heroines in an 'other world' of magical powers, communal values and female agency.

I realised there was the potential for a deeper, or at least a richer, understanding of the place of women in Shetland society focusing not upon the content of this story but on Mary Manson's telling of the narrative. It is a story told by a woman who sees herself as a keeper of memory and a transmitter of knowledge (perhaps especially 'female knowledge'). Mary Manson is empowered both by the process of telling the story and in demonstrating her possession of knowledges that the listeners lack. She might be described as a 'memorial guardian'.[32] The narrative is not merely a tale of the imagination but a story crafted from autobiographical memory and the cultural past. Her tales (and those of other female interviewees I spoke to) are distinguished by the use of domestic detail or context, their groundedness in the specificity of the everyday life of Shetland and by their use as narratives of cultural survival. Mary Manson's narrative invokes, on the surface at least, a very different world from the one in which she (and her listeners) were materially situated in 1982. Her story is not primarily a tale of the imagination, but a conjuring up of a lost world brought to life and made 'authentic' by the use of dialogue and local detail. For the historian, this narrative offers an access point to social memory and cultural experience via a legitimate expression of a female culture. However, the telling of the story also had a purpose – to mark the passing of a culture and way of life in the islands. Mary Manson told her story in part to highlight how medical provision had changed, reflecting on the differences characterising the period in which the story is set (the late nineteenth century) and the 1980s:

> Weel, I canna mind when it would have been, but onywye I should think the difference noo, although we are never thankful enough, two nurses and two doctors here in Yell, and you just need tae feel a pain or anything, lift the phone and call the doctor and he's here afore you get the phone laid doon, at the door tae see what's wrong wi' you, and then tae think aboot the old folk, what a life they had if anything was the matter with them, aha. But that was my midder [mother] when she was a young lass, she couldna have been very old she only had tae be in her teens maybe 14 or 15, but this cousin of theirs took ill[33]

Mary Manson was using stories of heroic women in her family to narrate the historical character of Shetland culture, and through that to record the dramatic course of change. Her stories, then, help the historian to bridge the gap between generalised representations of the past and subjective memory narratives that are locally generated.

Women's oral and written narratives possess three functions in this context: the transmission of social memory, the maintenance and reification of a myth of Shetland womanhood and the validation of women's place in Shetland history (and thus, by extension, their place in the present). Another oral testimony, that of Mary Ellen Odie, a lifelong Shetland resident, active local historian and recognised enthusiast for women's history, typifies a slightly different approach to the transmission of social memory.[34] Mary Ellen's stories, told to me in 2001, were about a past that she 'knows' through her life on the island of Yell and her immersion in the history of the island. What is notable about Mary Ellen's narrative is her ability to weave together personal memories and family stories with the documented past, clearly illustrated in this conversation about the 'hungry gap' – the period of time after the previous year's grain ran out and before the new grain was harvested.

> But that hungry gap must have been such a frightener. And one thing in relation to women that I certainly know affected the people in North Yell particularly we have Palmers Evans' [local doctor] very poignant note at the end of the list of names of people, was the potato famine it happened just the second year after the Irish, and North Yell got a really bad blight. It was then that the . . . meal roads of North Yell were introduced seriously after that year. But then the meal roads had to be introduced just before when the hungry gap had really widened in the late thirties, that was a bad bad time. It comes out, I tell you where it comes out quite graphically is in the Napier Commission [1883 Royal Commission on crofting] where people

describe what it was like to be, to have your last meal and then know that after that
it was just the bare essentials. My great granny knew how to cook a starling, do you
believe that? . . . Her man was drowned and she was really left destitute, 1851. And
they caught starlings in a gun? It was just a kind of set up with a stick and a net,
when they went in the poor things it collapsed and they got the starlings. And they
cooked limpets and whelks and all that. So that was always sort of a by word when
we thought mam was being a bit mean . . . and she says I never had to eat whelks like
Granny did.[35]

Mary Ellen's authority to speak is derived from her family history and her
interest in Shetland women of the past, bolstered by researched references
to authenticating 'official' sources and legitimised by the Shetland myth
of the strong, independent woman. These are stories that serve to fix in the
memory of the listener an image of the autonomous or independent Shetland woman of the past, and they mirror the well-established discourses on
Shetland womanhood. However, at the same time these stories serve to legitimise the position of the narrator and of Shetland women in general. For
Mary Ellen Odie, social memory is a process of recovering and communi-
cating the past, but at the same time validating this version of the past as a
corrective to outsiders' image of Shetland as a masculine place and to general narratives of women's history that emphasise women's vulnerability
to patriarchy and oppression.

To a very great extent, the history of women in Shetland is now taken
broadly as the history of Shetland. This only revealed itself to me from a
close engagement with the women whose lives were under investigation.
The women who spoke to me and to whom I listened on tapes in the archive,
narrated stories conjoined by a common understanding of women's agency
in an island community where any one overarching interpretation – be it
separate spheres ideology, modernisation or emancipation – did not make
sense. Their stories did not fit the familiar interpretations of women's lives
in nineteenth- and early twentieth-century Britain. Although the historian
might identify the existence of patriarchal structures and discourses, these
women did not imagine themselves constrained by them. The same point is
made by Sally Cole in her study of women in a Portuguese fishing community. 'Life histories both allow and require us to hear women themselves
interpret their experiences and construct their identities . . . [and] remind
us that . . . women's interpretation and subjective expression of those experiences may not be easily accommodated by – may, indeed, contradict –
macro or general theories that seek to explain gender relations and women's
role in society'.[36]

Issues of scale

Prioritising women's own understanding of their past forces one to think
hard about the organising concepts with which we have become familiar

and acculturated. One advantage of a micro-study is the ability to illuminate the close-up, the minutiae of the everyday, which may in turn offer a fresh perspective on the bigger picture. Problems arise, though, when the insights of the micro-study are too inconvenient or strange for incorporation into the general. Stanley's notion of 'competing histories' goes some way to dealing with the tension between the local or particular and the general or seamless narrative, but it does not resolve the issue of how to weave these two approaches together. It is simply not the case that an accumulation of case studies that present alternative or subversive stories of gender relations will ultimately force a shift in dominant narratives.

Back in 1999, in a special issue of *Gender & History* on 'Retrospect and Prospect', Selma Leydesdorff ruminated on the possibility of oral histories to transcend the particularity of the local context. Oral histories, she argued, had been rooted in micro-histories and, although these were valuable, there needed to be a move to make oral history a 'scholarly and activist' enterprise with transcultural implications. She went on to say that she was 'convinced that the strength of life stories lies in their ability to help us analyse a kaleidoscope of cultural representations'.[37] Such an approach is reminiscent of folktale and storytelling analysis, which identifies common themes that transcend cultures, and hints at universal aspects of the human experience. Oral history, because of its base in the local or micro-context, has the potential both to change knowledge and to empower the community whence it emanates. Yet it is not clear whether, in the context of women's and gender history, it has succeeded in transcending the particular.

The key to progress here is to focus on the methodology rather than the content. Personal narratives from Shetland women are stories grounded in everyday experience. Their specificity in the local is a strength, not a weakness, for it is from the power of the personal detail that one gains a sense of female experience in this place. The testimony of Agnes Leask, a crofter on the Shetland mainland, typifies a style of personal narrative that combines autobiography with a commentary on the Shetland way of life. The details of her life experience are a testament to the centrality of women to the crofting lifestyle in the islands as this description of her own economic role in the 1950s and 1960s illustrates:

> And at that time there was practically no work in Shetland at all and Davy [her husband] sort of did odd jobs with his tractor for folks roundabout, neighbours roundabout. It wasn't a great deal of money coming in but we sort of scraped by and then of course there was a farm at the end of the road there, and there was a bigger farm further up the valley and they were always looking for casual labour, so in amongst weeding me own tatties I'd go there whenever they needed casual labour – cabbages, tatties, single turnips, or working the peats because they used to

hire in gangs of women to do the peat work. And it all helped to tide us over. When nothing else was available mother and I would go and gather winkles . . . and then in the evenings in the wintertime I'd do hand-knitting . . . I bought the knitting machine and once I got the knitting machine, got orders, firms were giving out orders because it was sort of cottage industry then. Then we were more or less financially secure, as long as I could churn out about a dozen jumpers in the week. That would put our bread on the table for the week, and then of course we had our own vegetables, our own lamb and mutton.[38]

Women in Shetland of recent decades do not doubt that they have been a very large part of the story of the islands. As Cole argues in her historical anthropology of Portuguese women in not dissimilar circumstances, these testimonies portray women with a 'sense of having a life'.[39] Indeed they do not shirk from placing themselves in the very heart of that history and, as a historian, one must honour that confidence and that sense of importance to the main story. Indeed, the well over 100 local women who participated in a conference on Shetland women in Shetland in 2007 demonstrates the vibrancy of historical engagement amongst women today with their own past.[40] Here is recognition that women's stories are valid and central to the shaping of local historical narratives.

The local context provides a fresh perspective, not just on the history of women and gender relations in Shetland but more generally. Shetland is a place that has produced its own narratives of continuity and change. Here, a story of female subordination within a wider discourse of patriarchy does not make sense. The ideology of domesticity certainly had very little relevance for the vast majority of the population and the notion of public and private spheres also fails to work as an analytical framework for understanding women's experience (although of course as a discourse it was present in all sorts of arenas). And thus these interpretive frameworks are rarely referred to in Shetland women's narratives. Women's voices expressed in printed and oral sources locally privilege a female-centred story that has its own sense of periodisation grounded in the material conditions of life in these islands. Their stories refer to change marked by the impact of environmental factors such as the weather or the presence or absence of herring in the seas and by the impact of external shocks: the two world wars, the arrival of the oil industry, the introduction of electricity. But transcending these global changes was the story of women as self-possessed and able to work with potentially transformative economic and social change. That is not to say that that there were not gender inequalities in Shetland. Rather, the story of inequality and difference is not the framework chosen by women in Shetland to interpret their own past. They acknowledge that life for many women in the islands' past was extraordinarily hard, but the lesson drawn from their experiences is one about empowerment and agency.

One might conclude that the gender relations here suggest this was a unique, even quirky place that offers a particular experience on the periphery of the European model. Maybe it suggests an alternative way of writing women's history, but not a subversive way. After all, this was a small and rather unusual place. But equally one might suggest that the transmission of memory by Shetland women offers a route into one of those contiguous, competing narratives that will strengthen and deepen the writing of women's and gender history.

Conclusions

The issue raised here concerns not merely the challenging of dominant frameworks of understanding or narratives of change, but rather it is about the way we do our history. It concerns the links we make (or fail to make) between the present and the past, the voices we hear as we sit in the archive, the voices we privilege in our stories and the theoretical frameworks we utilise. The story I told of women in Shetland was of the creation and survival of a female culture from the pre-modern era through to the twentieth century based on female networks, female knowledge and female power that stands separate from or parallel to the conventional story of female empowerment through political change and which does not conform neatly to the conventional periodisations and turning points.

What happened during the course of writing my book was a shift in my thinking about how to represent women's lives in the past. Adopting a perspective far removed geographically from the metropolitan heart of Europe and yet still very much a part of Europe, forces one to think differently about the prime motors of change and the chronology of that change. It became clear that Shetland women harboured a story that may well have a wider resonance in European consciousness – a story of female agency. And I found it was a story only accessed by listening to women's voices of the present and the past. The woman's world exposed by Shetland women reveals to the feminist scholar a different way of viewing the world and women's place within it. And this might allow us to view the all-encompassing frameworks with their periodisations and assumptions with a critical eye.

What my work in Shetland has taught me above anything else is that it is impossible to separate the past from the present, because the past is constantly reified and reconstituted in the present. In Shetland, the past is not somewhere else or something forgotten, but a vibrant, living and remembered place which is constantly evoked in local culture in order to make sense of the present. And women have a prominent place in both timescapes. This is recalled in Shetland culture as a metanarrative of women's agency vested in knowledge, economic activity and household survival. This was a *woman's world* that operated with very distinctive female rules, stories and understandings.

The juxtaposition of the micro and the macro raises some interesting dilemmas for the feminist historian who wishes to be able to tell the big story. In the process of deepening our research base and engaging in research strategies that privilege women's voices, we are creating a patchwork of contiguous and sometimes competing histories which may be resistant to overarching narratives of continuity and change. The turning points, periodisations and conceptual frameworks that may work for broad-ranging syntheses have limited applicability when one takes a microscope to a place exhibiting different tendencies. Shetland might on the surface appear to present a picture of timelessness or continuity in women's lives on account of its relatively undeveloped or unmodernised economy until the late twentieth century, offering a corrective to generalised accounts which are constrained by global patterns of industrialisation, democratisation and so on. But close analysis reveals change of a different order and a different clock. For storyteller Mary Manson, change was indicated by improvements in the health service on the islands; for Agnes Leask, it was marked by the coming of the knitting machine. For many other women on Shetland, change was contingent upon the oil industry's appearance in Shetland in the 1970s, which offered employment and new opportunities for economic independence.

Historians of women subscribing to 'universal narratives' need to avoid muting the voices of the very women we wish to hear. What might be called identity history is important to women's historians, and for me it would not have made sense to have written a history of women in Shetland that did not make sense to those women. Their history should not be subsumed within a universal European women's history narrative, because it would disappear or at the very least exist as an interesting exoticism; and that is not good enough. Weaving histories like this one (and the many other local or particular studies) into the smooth fabric of the narrative of European women's history creates more than colour and texture. It offers new and perhaps surprising points of contrast; it encourages us to look closer at the familiar stories; it disrupts narratives of continuity and change and chronologies and offers unfamiliar parallels. The experience of women in the Shetland Islands is not so unfamiliar to us; it can be found in other marginal economies, coastal communities and in other societies where men are absent.[41] The articulation of that experience in terms of the value placed on women's own interpretation of the past through the voices and memories of women is more unusual, but it does help us negotiate our way through the apparent disjuncture between the overarching interpretative frameworks and the subjectivity of women's life stories. There is another story to tell; one that emerges from an historical practice that privileges a social memory crafted around narratives of women whose sense of the past included themselves.

Notes

The author would like to thank Deborah Simonton and Perry Willson for their critical engagement with the issues raised in this chapter.

1. Mary Nash, 'Rethinking Narratives in European Women's History: Motherhood, Identities and Female Agency in Twentieth-Century Spain', in Terry Brotherstone, Deborah Simonton and Oonagh Walsh (eds), *Gendering Scottish History: An International Approach* (Glasgow: Cruithne Press, 1999), p. 113.
2. Kathleen Canning, *Gender History in Practice: Historical Perspectives on Bodies, Class and Citizenship* (Ithaca and London: Cornell University Press, 2006), p. 61.
3. A point made by Deborah Simonton in 'Writing Women into Modern Europe', in Deborah Simonton (ed.), *The Routledge History of Women in Europe since 1700* (London: Routledge, 2006), p. 2.
4. These include Rachel G. Fuchs and Victoria E. Thompson, *Women in Nineteenth Century Europe* (London: Palgrave Macmillan, 2005); Gisela Bock, *Women in European History* (Oxford: Blackwell, 2002); Bonnie G. Smith, *Changing Lives: Women in European History Since 1700* (Lexington, MA: D.C. Heath, 1989).
5. See e.g., Georges Duby and Michelle Perrot (eds), *History of Women in the West*, 5 vols (London: Belknap Press, 1992–94) and the six-volume Longman History of European Women series.
6. A point made by Marilyn J. Boxer and Jean H. Quataert in *Connecting Spheres: European Women in a Globalizing World, 1500 to the Present* (1987; 2nd edn, Oxford: Oxford University Press, 2000) where they acknowledge that the earlier sense of a 'shared woman's experience' concealed a more 'diverse and conflictual reality', p. 3.
7. Canning, *Gender History in Practice*, pp. 60–61.
8. Lynn Abrams, *The Making of Modern Woman: Europe 1789–1918* (London: Longman, 2002); Lynn Abrams, *Myth and Materiality in a Woman's World: Shetland 1800–2000* (Manchester: Manchester University Press, 2005).
9. There are too many works to mention here, but examples of studies that challenge so-called 'national' histories include: Lynn Abrams, Eleanor Gordon, Deborah Simonton and Eileen Janes Yeo (eds), *Gender in Scottish History Since 1700* (Edinburgh: Edinburgh University Press, 2005); Siân Reynolds, *France Between the Wars: Gender and Politics* (London: Routledge, 1996); Susan Kingsley Kent, *Gender and Power in Britain 1640–1990* (London: Routledge, 1999).
10. Notably Amanda J. Vickery, 'From Golden Age to Separate Spheres: A Review of the Categories and Chronology of English Women's History', *Historical Journal* 36 (1993), pp. 383–414; Eleanor Gordon and Gwyneth Nair, *Public Lives: Women, Family and Society in Victorian Britain* (New Haven and London: Yale University Press, 2003).
11. Deborah Simonton (ed.), *The Routledge History of Women in Europe Since 1700* (London: Routledge, 2006), pp. 8–9. The staying power of this organising concept is exhibited in the chapters contained in Simonton's edited volume. See also Perry Willson (ed.), *Gender, Family and Sexuality: The Private Sphere in Italy, 1860–1945* (Basingstoke: Palgrave Macmillan: 2004).
12. Kathryn Gleadle, *British Women in the Nineteenth Century* (Basingstoke: Palgrave, 2001), p. 189.
13. Leonore Davidoff and Catherine Hall, *Family Fortunes: Men and Women of the English Middle Class, 1780–1850* (1987; 2nd edn, London: Routledge, 2002) and the subsequent debate led by Vickery, 'Golden Age', and taken up by early modern historians, for

instance, Pamela Sharpe, 'Continuity and Change: Women's History and Economic History in Britain', *Economic History Review* 48 (1995), pp. 353–69.

14. Nash, 'Rethinking Narratives', p. 115.
15. Nash, 'Rethinking Narratives', p. 113.
16. Liz Stanley, 'Rescuing "Women" in History from Feminist Deconstructionism', *Women's Studies International Forum* 13 (1990), pp. 151–7, here p. 154.
17. See e.g., Mary S. Hartmann, *The Household and the Making of History: A Subversive View of the Western Past* (Cambridge: Cambridge University Press, 2004); Kathleen Canning and Sonya O. Rose, 'Gender, Citizenship and Subjectivity: Some Historical and Theoretical Considerations', *Gender & History* 13 (2001), pp. 427–43. For a comprehensive survey of these new perspectives see Canning, *Gender History in Practice*, ch. 1, pp. 3–62.
18. For the notion of symbolic referents, see Anthony P. Cohen, *Whalsay: Symbol, Segment and Boundary in a Shetland Island Community* (Manchester: Manchester University Press, 1987), pp. 115–16.
19. Shetland Archive is one of only two in Scotland (Orkney is the other) that contain devolved papers from the National Archives of Scotland.
20. For a discussion of this process see Penny Summerfield, *Reconstructing Women's Wartime Lives* (Manchester: Manchester University Press, 1998), p. 15 and Penny Summerfield, 'Culture and Composure: Creating Narratives of the Gendered Self in Oral History Interviews', *Cultural and Social History* 1 (2004), pp. 65–93.
21. See Anna Green, 'Individual Remembering and "Collective Memory": Theoretical Presuppositions and Contemporary Debates', *Oral History* 32 (2004), pp. 35–44; Michael Roper, 'Slipping out of View: Subjectivity and Emotion in Gender History', *History Workshop Journal* 59 (2005), pp. 57–72.
22. Shetland Archive (hereafter SA): D 1/135, Scrapbook, cutting from the *Scotsman*, 2 September 1903.
23. The stories of May Moar and Grace Petrie, for example, both of whom received official recognition for their acts of heroism at sea, are immortalised in publications and in museum exhibits. See Abrams, *Myth and Materiality*, pp. 28–9.
24. 'Jessie Saxby', in Elizabeth Ewan, Sue Innes, Siân Reynolds and Rose Pipes (eds), *The Biographical Dictionary of Scottish Women* (Edinburgh: Edinburgh University Press, 2005), pp. 312–13; *The Rugged Island: A Shetland Lyric* (1934), directed by Jenny Brown (Scottish Film and Television Archive); Christina Jamieson, 'The Women of Shetland', *The New Shetlander* 177, Hairst 1991, pp. 31–3; 'Christina Jamieson', in Ewan, Innes, Reynolds and Pipes (eds), *The Biographical Dictionary of Scottish Women*, pp. 182–3.
25. Cohen, *Whalsay*, p. 173.
26. Marsha E. Renwanz, 'From Crofters to Shetlanders: The Social History of a Shetland Island Community's Self Image, 1872–1978' (unpublished doctoral thesis, Stanford University, 1980), p. 291.
27. Hazel Hughson, 'Ethel and Jeanie: Twentieth Century Knitters', unpublished paper, Shetland 2007; Lynn Abrams, 'Knitting, Autonomy and Identity: The Role of Hand-Knitting in the Construction of Women's Sense of Self in an Island Community, Shetland *c*.1850 to 2000', *Textile History* 37 (2006) pp. 149–65; Anne Douglas (ed.), *How Might We Revalue Traditional Ways of Making? A Research Project Revaluing Shetland Knitting – The Maakin Lab* (CD-ROM, Aberdeen: The Robert Gordon University in collaboration with Performing Arts Laboratories, 2005).
28. SA 3 (Oral History Interviews): 1/123, John Gear.
29. 'Mary Manson', in Ewan, Innes, Reynolds and Pipes (eds), *Biographical Dictionary of Scottish Women*, p. 248. Mary was born in 1897.
30. For a more extensive discussion of this narrative, see Abrams, *Myth and Materiality*, pp. 39–44, 201–2.
31. SA: 3/1/77/2 (Mary Manson, interviewed in 1982).
32. See Janet L. Nelson, 'Gender, Memory and Social Power', *Gender & History* 12 (2000), pp. 722–34, here pp. 723–4.

33. SA: 3/1/77/2.
34. SA: 3/1/1396, interview with Mary Ellen Odie, conducted by the author, 2001.
35. SA: 3/1/1396.
36. Sally Cole, *Women of the Praia: Work and Lives in a Portuguese Coastal Community* (Princeton: Princeton University Press, 1991), p. 41.
37. Selma Leydesdorff, 'Gender and the Categories of Experienced History', *Gender & History* 11 (1999), pp. 597–611, esp. pp. 599, 604.
38. SA: 3/1/1395, Interview with Agnes Leask, conducted by the author, 2002.
39. Cole, *Women of the Praia*, p. 40.
40. 'A Woman's Island? Women in Shetland, Past, Present and Future', Shetland Museum and Archives, 20–22 April 2007.
41. See e.g., Caroline Brettell, *Men who Migrate, Women who Wait: Population and History in a Portuguese Parish* (Princeton: Princeton University Press, 1986); Allyson M. Poska, *Women and Authority in Early Modern Spain: The Peasants of Galicia* (Oxford: Oxford University Press, 2005); Marisa Rey-Henningsen, *The World of the Ploughwoman: Folklore and Reality in Matriarchal Northwest Spain* (Helsinki: Acedemia Scientiarum Fennica, 1994).

10 The Gendered Genealogy of Political Religions Theory

Kevin Passmore

In the last three decades, historians have elaborated a sophisticated understanding of the place of women and gender in fascist movements and regimes. They have shown that women occupied positions of relative, not absolute, weakness in movements that were gendered as masculine. The range of choices that they conceived and their degree of autonomy varied according to the class, political, racial, religious and other capital they possessed, and with the available knowledge of alternatives. Women used a range of discourses and practices, differentially invested with power, and exploited contradictions in fascist ideologies, to influence their own futures, and indeed those of the movements and regimes in which they participated. Their motivations were both conscious and unconscious, and they understood their actions and their own identities in a variety of ways. The consequences of their actions were both intended and unintended. A major advantage of this historiography is that it draws on the strengths of both women's and gender history, thus transcending a number of too-simple oppositions to which I shall return in my conclusion.[1] The historiography in question is also part of a wider endeavour that has illuminated the varied motivations and priorities of those who became fascists, and the complex contingencies and violence, pressures and opportunities, which made the histories of fascism.[2]

The trend in the theorisation of generic fascism is quite different. Many model-builders work at one remove from actual research into their objects of study, while those who do read historical works often see only 'empirical detail'. Yet, as Edward Thompson commented in a polemic against an earlier scholasticism, 'what a philosopher, who has only a casual acquaintance with historical practice, may glance at, and then dismiss, with a ferocious scowl, as "empiricism" may in fact be the result of arduous confrontations, pursued both in conceptual engagements . . . and also in the interstices of historical method itself'.[3] Theorists of generic fascism have been especially reluctant to engage with women's and gender history. This is even truer – if that were possible – of the recently fashionable political religions theory. This approach invests a male elite alone with meaningful agency and makes it entirely responsible for historical change. It relegates most men to passivity, effectively feminising them, and consigns women to an extra-historical limbo. In this narrative, female supporters of fascism possess little latitude to shape the nature of fascist movements and regimes, let alone resist them.

According to Emilio Gentile, who has done the most to repopularise the concept, a political religion emerges when an earthly movement or regime invests a class, nation or another entity with sacred status. A secular movement endowed with the trappings of a religion – a charismatic leader, priests, disciples, a liturgy and forms of worship – endeavours to shape the individual and the masses through an 'anthropological revolution', the creation of a 'new man'. Since it sees history as a conflict between good and evil, it brooks no resistance to its project. It is important to note that political religions theorists regard fascism as most likely to emerge in a particular *period*. The transition between tradition and modernity creates a state of anomie, of psychic disturbance. The decline of organised religion conflicts with the masses' continued desire to believe and so people seek their lost security in political religions. This periodisation connects femininity with passivity, in that women abandon tradition less easily than men do. Women are more disposed to participate in political religions because they epitomise timeless tradition.[4]

Most accounts of fascism written from the political religions perspective focus more on the male architects of the political religion than they do upon the followers, let alone female followers. A search in Historical Abstracts reveals that the journal *Totalitarian Movements and Political Religions* contains only one abstract in which the words 'women' or 'gender' appear.[5] Where contributors to that journal do discuss women, they figure as the objects of subjection or of mobilisation from above.[6] In principle, political religions theory does not rule out the study of women or gender. Indeed, the late George L. Mosse, often invoked by political religions theorists as a precursor, combined fruitfully the concepts of gender and political religion. Nevertheless, political religions theorists usually reify their concept: they make the religious drive the *core*, or the 'motor' of fascism, and thus leave no theoretical space for other perspectives.[7]

One reason for political religions theorists' neglect of women, or at least of women's agency, is that they draw upon totalitarianism theory of the 1950s and 1960s. Like political religions theory, the latter saw fascism as an attempt to remould society through the propagation of an all-encompassing, messianic, utopian project. It emphasised the diffusion of a ruling ideology, the mechanisms of control of the population and the internalisation, through ritual, of 'religious' ideologies.[8] It focused on the totalitarian regime or party and rather less upon the ruled. We may read Claudia Koonz's pioneering work on Nazi women as a critique of the totalitarian approach. She comments, 'historians have dismissed women as part of the timeless backdrop against which Nazi men made history, seeing men as active "subjects" and women as the passive "other", quoting Simone de Beauvoir's terms'.[9]

In two respects, the political religions approach differs from its precursors. It stresses the limited success of the totalitarian project in practice. This concession might have encouraged the advocates of political religions theory to investigate inconsistencies within the grand design, and the intersection between the totalitarian project and the resistance or alternative strategies of those whom it sought to control. As yet, little such work has appeared, perhaps because the apparent concession really only serves to explain away the huge body of research showing that neither fascism nor communism was totalitarian, even in intention, not least in its complex practice concerning women and the family. The second way in which political religions theory differentiates itself from totalitarianism is in the claim that political religions are both imposed from above and spontaneously generated by the masses.[10] This formulation apparently breaks with top-down history and yet Gentile insists that the political religion derives from the masses' allegedly inherent need for religious explanations in times of change – in effect, the mass is defined by its need for manipulation. We shall see that this notion has a long pedigree in social science and is inseparable from assumptions about gender, agency, periodisation and change.

In this chapter, I shall explore the persistence in political religions theory of a gendered tradition of social theory, traceable, in its academic incarnation, to the *fathers* of sociology at the turn of the nineteenth and twentieth centuries. I would not wish to claim that political religions theory is condemned by its origins – that would be to fall victim to the genetic fallacy. Neither is my method simply archaeological in the Foucauldian sense: I do not merely establish the 'conditions of possibility' of what can be said and not said, for often people do say things they ought logically not to say.[11] Any theory is dialogical in Bakhtin's sense: its author lacks control over her/his discourse in that whatever his/her intention, s/he consciously and unconsciously uses older materials and concepts, with their strengths and weaknesses. Thus political religions theory evokes anti-feminist discourses without meaning to do so. Furthermore, a given discourse anticipates objections from its intended audience, and so incorporates potentially subversive voices into itself. The canonical thinkers I shall discuss below knew that there were alternative views of women, and their thought developed in dialogue with them.[12] Similarly, scholars working today, whatever their motives, are constrained by the materials from which they fabricate their own concepts, and they must consciously choose whether or not to incorporate women and/or gender into their work. The debate between sociology and feminism represents a minor sub-theme of this chapter, but it is important to leave theoretical space for it.

My primary purpose is to show that, in spite of its claim to objectivity, the sociological tradition from which political religions theory derives did not succeed in separating itself from academic and popular prejudices about women. Political religions theory recycles these preconceptions in a seemingly gender-neutral form, and some of them find their way into a certain style of gender history too. Theorists of generic fascism could learn much from the way in which women's and gender historians have conceptualised agency, change and periodisation. That is not to argue for the superiority of history as a discipline. Historians too have used concepts taken from the tradition that I shall describe. Arguably, differences within disciplines are more important than those between them.

The gendered origins of modern sociology

The roots of political religions theory lie in the intellectual milieu of late nineteenth- and early twentieth-century Europe. I shall begin with France because, as the only democracy in Europe, and as the theatre of the Commune of 1871, the so-called problem of 'mass society' appeared unavoidable there.[13] French republicans, although they were struggling to establish a secular, democratic republic against Catholic and royalist resistance, were concerned by the problem of the masses.[14] Their gendered political and social philosophy was intended to preserve the leadership of an active, male, bourgeois elite. They held that as societies progressed from barbarism to civilisation they freed themselves from religion and embraced reason. Impressed by the prestige of contemporary science, the republicans put old prejudices on a new footing, conceiving progress in terms of biological development. Societies grew, like organisms, to maturity. Following the precepts of degeneration theory, they believed that growth depended upon the predominance in the social organism of the active element, which, predictably, they conceived in masculine terms. Men were a force for progress, just as the active sperm fertilised the passive ovum. Men were rational, but that did not mean that they lacked a spiritual self. Rather, through the process of growth, they learned to master their spirituality, allowing the ideal to guide their action in a practical direction. In the male there was a proper hierarchy of organs – the head channelled the energies of the heart. Likewise, governmental forms had to ensure the predominance of the active, male, element, so that they could guide, but also be inspired by, the implicitly feminine mass – otherwise, society would 'degenerate'.

Conventional wisdom supposed that there was no such hierarchy in the female body – science gave new force to beliefs about women that lay deep in history. The trembling of the uterus allegedly destabilised the (smaller) female brain and caused overheating and flights of fancy. By the standards of the time, these views were not entirely negative. Women could not be intellectuals, but the predominance of the lower organs made women naturally compassionate. They could care for young children, although male, bourgeois children would soon have to be separated from their mothers if they were to develop into fully rational beings. Women, though, could never achieve self-mastery. Their reproductive function defined them. Nature required reproduction, and so women were endowed with maternal instincts. Moreover, as irrational creatures, women were naturally religious; they appropriated knowledge through religious ritual and repetition, rather than through reason. Insofar as female religiosity helped develop the spirituality present in all children, this was a good thing. Yet, since women were prone to flights of fancy, they were vulnerable to manipulation by religious fanatics. French psychiatrists, who were largely anti-clericals and republicans, treated religious ecstasies as feminine delusional throwbacks to the past. Psychiatrists rarely examined the content of religious phenomena and some were more concerned to compare hysterical behaviour to the Baroque piety of the counter-reformation.[15] Women's religiosity was both a product of a timeless pathology and an atavistic relic.

There were many controversies among the social and medical scientists of this period. Yet, for most of them, organic metaphors linked individual, social and historical maturation. As male individuals and societies matured, they cast off irrational, feminine/androgynous characteristics, and the creative male element took charge. The anti-feminist polemicist, Théodore Joran, summed it up: 'routine, thy name is woman, progress, your sex is masculine'.[16] These ideas were far from uncontested in their day; on the contrary, they developed through a tetchy dialogue with feminists.[17] From our perspective, the important point is that we may glimpse some of the assumptions of political religions theory. It, too, implicitly distinguishes between the passive mass, which is epitomised by women, with its instinctive need for religion, and the active founders of that political religion.

These ideas about the passive feminised mass oblige us to take a detour into the strange discipline of collective psychology, for it, too, depended upon the gendered ideas described above. Collective psychology did not establish a presence in the universities before 1914, and is now largely forgotten. Yet, in the early twentieth century, its ability to express platitudes scientifically made it immensely popular with professionals, journalists and politicians. Collective psychology was founded by the Frenchmen Gustave Le Bon and Gabriel de Tarde, and by the Italians Scipio Sighele and Pasquale Rossi. It began as a means to study the pathological criminal mind, on the principle that segregation of mentally sick individuals would benefit the social organism (rather than the poor patient). In his classic study, *La Psychologie des foules* (The Psychology of Crowds, 1895), Gustave Le Bon extended the reach of collective psychology to crowds of all kinds. In reaction against liberal individualism, he assumed that the crowd was more than the sum of its parts. He depicted it as an organic phenomenon, possessed of a mind. However, the crowd was a primitive being, lacking proper hierarchy in its organs, dominated by the spinal cord rather than the brain. It was marked by the atavistic residue of the instincts of the primitive man.[18] The crowd was a product of the trauma caused by the breakdown of the traditional order into an atomistic mass society. Drawing upon Dr Jean-Martin Charcot's theories of unconscious hypnotic suggestion, collective psychologists argued that the crowd thought in images, and so was vulnerable to hypnosis. Whereas Charcot saw hypnosis as dangerous, Le Bon, in this respect closer to Freud, believed that it could be used for positive purposes too. He argued that socialism had become a political religion and so urged conservatives to channel the racially defined good sense of crowds in a safer nationalist direction.[19]

The parallel between views of the crowd and of women are evident. Le Bon wrote that,

> It will be remarked that among the special characteristics of crowds there are several – such as impulsiveness, irritability, incapacity to reason, the absence of judgement and of the critical spirit, the exaggeration of the sentiments, and others besides – which are almost always observed in beings belonging to inferior forms of evolution – in women, savages, and children, for instance.[20]

He added, 'The simplicity and exaggeration of the sentiments of crowds have for result that a throng knows neither doubt nor uncertainty. Like women, it goes at once to extremes'.[21] The crowd, like women, could be the source, albeit passive, of the ideal for which the male elite fought actively. One could use reason to understand the crowd, but to 'master' it a leader had to play upon its susceptibilities, to seduce it.[22]

Emile Durkheim and the crowd

Somewhat paradoxically, Emilio Gentile cites Le Bon both as a precursor of his own theory of political religions and one of the inventors of actual political religions, thus betraying his belief that crowds really are vulnerable to hypnotic suggestion.[23] Like Michael Burleigh, he also cites Durkheim's sociology as a precedent for political religions theory.[24] Durkheim had read Le Bon.

Durkheim was more reflective in terms of method than was Le Bon. His professional sociology differentiated itself from amateur social theory, including collective psychology, through its supposed detachment from the world. Durkheim set out to free sociology from determinism, grand speculation and popular prejudice. One may use Durkheim to criticise Durkheim, whereas Le Bon was disparaged even in his own day for his over-enthusiastic generalisation and haphazard use of sources. That is one reason why Durkheim founded a discipline and Le Bon did not. Yet in Durkheim's Kantian terms, objectivity was an act of will. For Durkheim, impartiality depended on the researcher's internal struggle against bias, a view that could easily be interpreted, were one so inclined, in gendered terms.

Be that as it may, according to a familiar narrative, one of Durkheim's most important contributions to sociology lay in the rejection of biological and racial determinism in favour of functionalism. Accordingly, the positions of social groups, including those of women and men, were determined by the needs of the increasingly complex division of labour, rather than by biological or sacred destiny. This sociology was not isolated from contemporary concerns. In fact, it is common knowledge that Durkheim elaborated his views as an alternative to socialism. Less well known is that functionalist sociology grew in dialogue with feminism, for Durkheim saw the family as essential to the stability of the social organism.[25] Indeed, whenever Durkheim spoke of women, he resorted to a biological determinism similar to Le Bon's. Both theorists saw society as more than the sum of its parts; both envisaged it as an organism possessed of intrinsic properties. Both believed that society's possession of a thinking brain differentiated it from the animal realm, and saw civilisation as transcendence of this organic 'being-in-itself'. They agreed too that the rise of mass society potentially led to a state of anomie, with its potential for regression.

Let us examine Durkheim's assumptions more closely. First, he posited a dichotomous periodisation – society progressed from tradition to modernity. He conceived this process as a transition from a state in which the sexes were not clearly distinct to one in which male activism predominated. Women, consequently, remained passive and traditional. In *La Division du travail* (The Division of Labour), he wrote, 'Woman is less concerned in the civilising process; she participates in it less, and draws less benefit from it. She recalls certain characteristics to be found in primitive natures'. In *Le Suicide*, he added that women were 'fundamentally traditionalist by nature, they govern their conduct by fixed beliefs and have no great intellectual needs'.[26] He believed that just as progress entailed the division of labour in the social sphere, so it differentiated male and female roles, not just between public and private, but biologically. 'As Dr Le Bon has shown', he wrote, 'with the advance of civilisation the brain of the two sexes has increasingly developed differently'. Again citing Le Bon, he opined that the weight of the brains of female Parisians was scarcely greater than that of New Caledonians.[27] For Durkheim and his contemporaries, the religious age was emotional, non-rational, and therefore feminine. In effect, as society 'grew up', it became more male, just as male children cast off their bonds with their mothers as they became men.[28]

Second, Durkheim assumed that society needed a *collective conscience*, a 'common ideology' to ensure cohesion, to provide meaning in the world and to assign individuals their place in the division of labour. As society progressed from a primitive to a civilised state, the nature of the collective conscience changed. In the former, society found its cohesion through religion; in the latter, the cult of reason became the cement of society.

Third, Durkheim believed that the manner in which people appropriated knowledge, and were integrated into the collective conscience, varied between traditional and civilised periods. In the former, people learnt passively through the repetitions and rituals of religion, whereas in modern societies knowledge was acquired actively through reason. Thus, Durkheim's *Elementary Forms of Social Life*, with its interest in the achievement of social consensus through the ritualised propagation of myths and religious beliefs, depends implicitly on the assumption that masses as a whole have an innate, 'feminine', need for religion. Moreover, since women modernised more slowly than men did, they remained vulnerable to manipulation even in a modernising society. In early twentieth-century France, politicians of the centre and the right felt that women should be denied the vote for this reason. Republicans feared that women would be manipulated by the Church, while Catholics believed that women would be exploited by socialist demagogues.

Fourth, Durkheim feared that the breakdown of the traditional collective conscience could lead to 'anomie', a sense of isolation and angst. Durkheim's fear was an intellectual banality at the time he wrote, and some conservatives argued that the preservation of tradition, in the form of religion, rurality, or corporatism was the sole means of overcoming atomisation. As a liberal, Durkheim more optimistically believed that the complex division of labour would generate a new 'cult of the individual', which meant, precisely, 'to be master of oneself'. In another respect, he agreed with the traditionalists: the rural patriarchal family with many children represented the best protection against excessive individualism, of which modern suicide was an extreme example. In the view of one critic, Durkheim's view that women were less vulnerable to suicide rested more upon received wisdom than on statistical demonstration.[29] Durkheim's views on women were more than simply casual prejudices, easily separated from the main lines of his thought. He used his study of suicide to argue against divorce by mutual consent, a major demand of feminists at the time. As a functionalist, he argued that the good of society dictated the inviolability of the family, whatever the interests of women.[30]

Le Bon's half-deserved reputation as a progenitor of fascism has obscured his liberal-conservative politics, while Durkheim's advocacy of democracy has masked his nationalism and his conservatism on the 'woman question'. Indeed, one might imagine them both voting for secular republicans, if not for the same reasons. Both sought to reconcile liberty with mass society; both were anti-socialist, even if Durkheim was more open to social reform. Durkheim was also more sanguine about the prospects for democratic individualism, yet his reputation should obscure neither the gendered nature of his sociology nor its connections with Le Bon's collective psychology and consequently its relationship to political religions theory.

Sigmund Freud's mass psychology

Freud's theory of the crowd represents another, unacknowledged, ingredient of political religions theory. It too owed much to *fin-de-siècle* collective psychology. Freud began his 1922 essay on crowds with extended quotations from Le Bon's *Psychologie des foules*, which he praised as a 'brilliantly executed picture of the group mind'. He rightly pointed out that Le Bon had given form to very old views of the crowd, but credited him especially with showing the importance of the unconscious, and with comparing the crowd mind with the mental lives of primitive peoples. Freud's own contribution was to demonstrate the importance of the libidinal ties within the crowd and between the crowd and the leader. There were some differences between Le Bon and Freud. The former assumed that trauma revealed the racial unconscious, while Freud insisted that collective pathologies were rooted in individual bio-psychology, though Freud's belief that group memories were laid down in the unconscious blurred the distinction somewhat. From my perspective, there are important convergences between Freud and his precursors.[31]

Freud did not explicitly liken crowd behaviour to that of women. Indeed, in paraphrasing a passage quoted above, in which Le Bon insisted upon the similarity between the crowd mind and the mental lives of primitive people, women and children, Freud missed out the reference to women.[32] In 1922, Freud was sensitive to feminist accusations of male chauvinism, and that may have encouraged him to embrace functionalism rather than determinism. Whatever the case, he was unrepentant. As an honest scientist, he felt obliged to ignore the feminists' displeasure 'when we point out to them the effects of a poorly developed superego upon the average feminine character'.[33] Indeed, regression to a stage prior to the development of the ego-ideal (consciousness of civilised standards of behaviour) provides a key connection between Freud's gendered psychology of individual development and his social theory.

Freud, who is sometimes seen as having destroyed the foundations of liberal rationalism, assumed the usual gendered civilising process, with its parallels between individual and social development. He wrote that 'the cultural development of mankind (some, I know, prefer to call it civilisation) has been in progress since immemorial antiquity. To this process we owe all that is best in our composition, but also much that makes for human suffering'.[34] Although Freud's psychoanalytic theory forbade him to see the origins of progress in male biology *tout court*, he did acknowledge that the greater activism of the male owed something to the vigorous nature of the sperm in relation to the reactive ovum. 'Thinking teleologically', he held that since 'accomplishment in the realm of biology has been entrusted to the aggressiveness of men and to some extent has been made independent of women's consent', then nature had placed more constraints upon the libido in women.[35]

Civilisation, like individual development, entailed 'strengthening of the intellect, which tends to master our instinctive life'. Nevertheless, stubbornly Lamarckian, Freud believed that the residues of past stages of society were laid down in the unconscious.[36] In times of upheaval, these ancient modes of behaviour might re-emerge. Sometimes they did so in masculine forms. In 'Why War', he argued that primitive man was dominated entirely by the death drive, by self-interest and by the pleasure of killing. With time, man began to measure his own behaviour against an 'ego-ideal' (the conceptual ancestor of the 'superego'). Freud hesitated between two views: first, that the superego derived from an erotic love for fellow man; second, that it arose from narcissistic channelling of the death drive into the recognition that recourse to violence harmed one's longer-term interest. Freud attributed the brutality of modern warfare to the removal of the constraints of civilisation, which were weaker in the affairs of nations than they were within societies.[37] He saw the resurgence of the death drive in war in male terms and regretted that modern warfare afforded 'no scope for acts of heroism according to the old ideals'. On the contrary, it forced men into situations that 'shame[d] their manhood'.[38]

The misleading translation of Freud's *Massenpsychologie* into English as 'group psychology' evokes images of people sitting in circles with therapists. In fact, Freud meant that social trauma could produce mass behaviour of the type described by Le Bon. Freud never abandoned the arguments of *Totem and Taboo*, (1912–1913, published in parts in a review), a work much mocked subsequently, but which advanced ideas that were taken rather seriously at the time. Freud swallowed Darwin's view that primitive societies had consisted of herds, dominated by a powerful male. The patriarch monopolised all the women, and forbade other males (or perhaps the males in the equivalent of the charismatic community) the gratification of their sex drives. In effect, only the leader was fully male, while the members of the herd, whether male or female, directed their erotic drives towards each other and towards the patriarch. Ever the Lamarckian, Freud believed that repressed memory of the primal horde was locked into the unconscious and that crowd behaviour, with its impulsiveness and predominance of affect, resulted from its release.[39] Furthermore, he contended that hypnosis 'awakens in the subject a portion of his archaic heritage'. He added that, 'what is thus awakened is the idea of a paramount and dangerous personality [that is, a leader], toward whom only a passive-masochistic attitude is possible, to whom one's will has to be surrendered'. He concluded that, 'the leader of the group [sic] is still the dreaded primal father; the group still wishes to be governed by unrestricted force; it has an extreme passion for authority; in Le Bon's phrase, it has a passion for obedience'. In Freud's terms, the crowd substituted the will of the patriarch for the ego ideal. As members of crowds, men behaved in ways that would be unacceptable to them as individuals – as Le Bon, once again, had warned. Nevertheless, Freud also saw a potential source for good in the crowd. Sublimation of sex drives into identification with fellow crowd members represented a first step on the road to civilisation, for it implied some repression of the demand for immediate gratification in order for each member to share in the leader's love.[40]

We may relate Freud's mass psychology to his theories of individual female development. Freud notoriously regarded women as suffering a sense of inferiority towards men, caused by their lack of a penis. This misfortune causes them to resent their mothers and to direct their desire towards their fathers. Yet the absence of a penis renders them immune to castration fear and prevents them from overcoming their identification with their fathers in the Oedipal stage. Accordingly, their ego ideal, their sense of justice, is stunted – like that of the crowd. In some unfortunate cases, women's repressed aggressive drives are turned inwards as masochism, which Freud saw as a largely female neurosis. In a few other cases, perhaps those in which the active instincts of the phallic stage had been especially pro-nounced, women deny their lack of a penis and develop a masculinity complex. In the happiest cases, women resolve penis envy through male penetration, childbirth and, if really fortunate, the birth of a child blessed with the missing penis. Such women abandoned active clitoral masturba-tion and transferred gratification of erotic drives to the passive sensation of vaginal penetration.[41] Thus, women rarely surmounted their need for male guidance. While Freud denied, if somewhat inconsistently, that biology alone determined women's destiny, he arrived at the conventional depiction of women as passive through his account of the interaction between female anatomy and child development.[42] The parallels between Freud's view of female/male and crowd/leader relations are striking. Like women, the crowd both demands domination and is vulnerable to hypnotic suggestion. The crowd combines passivity with sudden outbursts of emotion; it is 'impulsive, changing and irritable', capable only of simple and exaggerated behaviour. The crowd is dominated by instinct, and for Freud, instinct, the domain of the id, always entails repetitive behaviour and is contrasted with the rational action of the ego.[43]

Before we leave the period, we should note that other *fin-de-siècle* theorists are relevant to our story. One finds a similarly gendered structure in those aspects of Max Weber's theories that are used by political religions theorists. Like Le Bon (and Gaetano Mosca, Vilfredo Pareto and many others), Weber believed that all social groups were necessarily divided into leaders and led, from the family to the nation. His theories of social action applied only to the elite and he believed the masses to be incapable of rational, goal-directed activity. As such, the masses were outside the province of sociology and were to be studied by crowd psychologists such as Le Bon. Weber's concept of charismatic authority, which is so influential in fascism studies, may be understood in relation to this fundamental distinction. Weber saw charisma as the resurrection of femininity through sexual release, related to the religious experience of the Holy Spirit, counteracting the rigidities of male rationality. He saw charismatic authority as arising from outbreaks of crowd emotionalism. The bond between leader and his immediate followers – the so-called 'charismatic community' – was especially close.[44]

Weber died in 1920, three years after Durkheim. Neither witnessed the emergence of fascism. Weber at least glimpsed the possibility that progress might have a dark side, or even be reversed. Durkheim remained optimistic to the end of his life, and contributed to his country's fight for 'civilisation' against 'Germanic barbarism' in the Great War. Nevertheless, in the 1930s, Durkheim's disciples easily incorporated the notion of regression to a past age into their understanding of totalitarianism, as Marcel Mauss's comment demonstrates:

> Durkheim and the rest of us after him were, I believe, the founders of the theory of collective representation. Yet the possibility that modern societies, more or less no longer medieval, could, like a group of children, be as open to suggestion by dances and commotions as Australians were, is something that, ultimately, we had not foreseen. This return to the primitive had not been the object of our thought. We were content with a few allusions to crowds, when in fact they were much more important than that. We were content to prove that the individual could find his footing and feed his liberty and independence, his personality and his critical spirit. In the end, we did not reckon with these extraordinary new means.[45]

Freud had direct experience of Nazism. His books, as the fruits of 'Jewish science', were among the first to be burned. He attributed National Socialism to an outbreak of mass irrationality. Some years earlier he had called for government by an elite made in his own image:

> That men are divided into leaders and led is but another manifestation of their inborn and irremediable inequality. The second class constitutes the vast majority; they need a high command to make decisions for them, to which decisions they usually bow without demur ... In this context we would point out that men should be at greater pains than heretofore to form a superior class of independent thinkers, unamenable to intimidation and fervent in the quest of truth, whose function it would be to guide the masses dependent on their lead.[46]

Given Freud's views on the weakness of the female superego, we should not take his use of the term 'men' in this passage as a casual universalisation of the masculine. Aside from a few martyrs to the masculinity complex, he did not believe women to be equipped to engage in the 'quest of truth'.

Parsonian sociology and National Socialism

In 1952, the great American sociologist, Talcott Parsons, claimed that, despite there being 'several other somewhat similar formulations to be found in the literature of roughly the same period, the formulation most dramatically convergent with Freud's theory of the superego was that of the social role of moral norms made by the French sociologist Emile Durkheim – a theory which has constituted one of the cornerstones of the subsequent development of social theory'.[47]

Although not mentioned in this text, Parsons thought much of Weber's theory of authority too.[48] Parsons is important because he simultaneously elaborated some of the founding categories of western sociology and integrated them into a sophisticated reading of Nazism. He developed his view of Nazism just as he was moving from the action theory of *The Structures of Social Action* to a more structural-functionalist stage under the influence of his reading of Freud.[49] From our perspective, we may see this development as gendered: masculine action theory gave way to a view in which women played a significant role in socialisation through child-raising. As for his reading of Nazism, Parsons saw it as a contribution to the Allied programme for German re-education.[50] He had great faith in the ability of sociologists to help governments manage the inevitably destabilising consequences of modernisation. Like the collective psychologist, Scipio Sighele, he was convinced that the medical profession sustained society through the isolation of deviants. In the universities, professionals were the carriers of 'the great western rational-liberal culture'.[51]

Parsons's explanation of Nazism was far from original. Since the First World War, European and American liberals – Weber among them – had differentiated a good democratic Germany from a bad Prussian Germany. This distinction had informed the work of several American academics at the time that Parsons wrote.[52] Parsons admitted that the harshness of the Versailles treaty and the desire of business to roll back Weimar's generous welfare systems were important causes of the rise of National Socialism. Yet Nazism represented more than national or class defence: it sought to create a radically new type of society that departed from the main line of western development.[53] It was revolutionary, too, in constituting a popular mass movement 'in which large masses of the "common people" have become imbued with a highly emotional, indeed often fanatical, zeal for the cause'. Parsons continued, 'they are movements which, though their primary orientation is political, have many features in common with great religious movements in history, a fact which may serve as a guide to the sociological analysis of their origins and character'.[54] Parsons assumed that the 'common people' were most likely to participate in a secular religious movement.

'Movements of religious proselytism', Parsons explained, were most likely to develop 'in situations involving a certain type of social disorganisation, primarily that early though only roughly characterised by Durkheim as "anomie"'. He contended that anomie led to a state of vacillation, indecision and paralysis, or of 'overdetermined' hatred, devotion or enthusiasm. Often, he opined, free-floating anxiety and aggression were displaced onto scapegoats.[55] Parsons's description is not explicitly gendered, but his characterisation of mass behaviour in times of crisis does not depart radically from Le Bon's. Neither did he part company with Le Bon or Freud in insisting that anomie made one susceptible to join groups with 'vigorous *esprit de corps* with submission to some strong authority'.[56]

Parsons held that anomie was an inevitable consequence of rationalisation (modernisation), from which no society was immune. In Germany, anomie was especially pronounced because industrialisation there was unusually rapid and because the German labour movement was particularly antagonistic to tradition, not least religion. Thus, the extremist modernism of communism (itself for Parsons a product of anomie) contrasted with the atavistic persistence of feudal mentalities. Indeed, one of Parsons's major contributions to the sociological tradition under discussion was to systematise the idea, previously implicit, that different parts of society modernised at different rates.[57] In Germany, those whose modernisation had lagged behind engaged in a 'fundamentalist' reaction. They amalgamated the communists' assault on capitalism with fetishisation of tradition and linked capitalism and communism in the form of the Judeo–Bolshevik conspiracy.[58]

Parsons identified this fundamentalist traditionalism with particular groups, and here we may uncover the gendered structure of his theory.

First, the Prussian aristocracy, as a vested interest, resisted modernisation. The aristocracy defended status above all. For the aristocracy (and for the bourgeoisie which mimicked its behaviour), a person's worth in the occupational system was determined not by their functional utility, or upon the 'romanticisation of success', as it was in the US, but by their status. The same was true of aristocratic male relationships with women: status, not romantic love, governed marriage and family life, and upper-class German men regarded romantic attachment to women as 'soft and effeminate'.[59] Finding no outlet for their romantic impulses in their work or family relations, they directed romanticism outwards into nationalism and to the pursuit of unrealistic utopias. They were encouraged to do so by the strong tradition of romantic nationalism in their country and by the allegedly fatalist tendencies of Lutheranism. They also sought fulfilment of romantic needs in the companionship of all-male groups, of which the comradeship of the front was the highest form. Parsons does not explicitly gender Nazism as feminine, but he defines male affective relationships in opposition to the American family structure, based on romantic love, interaction and mutual respect between husband and wife. He detects in the sharp segregation of sexes in Germany and in the intense emotion of male friendship, 'at least an undercurrent of homosexuality'.[60] This remark may be seen in the context of the stereotypical association of homosexuality with effeminacy. That Parsons regarded Nazism as an essentially fatalist movement, the antithesis of the goal-directed activism of the liberal-democratic political group, underlines his gendering of Nazism.

If National Socialism was composed of feminised men, where did that leave women? Possibly contradicting his view that German men were effeminate, Parsons argued that German men's status consciousness made them 'authoritarian and dominating [towards women] and, conversely, to expect submissiveness on the part of their wives'. The German bourgeois woman was usually a *Hausfrau* – the antithesis of the emancipated woman. She engaged in little activity outside the home. Since romantic love had no part in bourgeois marriage, 'She tends to lack both "sex appeal" and other elements of "attractiveness". From the American point of view, she does not dress well and is more "dowdy" than is accountable for in terms of lack of financial resources'. German women married older men and there was no equality in their relationships. Women were attracted to their husbands for their status, not by emotional attachment.[61] Given Parsons's view that German women were submissive creatures, it comes as no surprise to learn that he saw them as especially open to the appeal of National Socialism, a movement that, as we have seen, he characterised as a form of religious fundamentalism with a tendency towards idealistic passivity. Parsons had no empirical evidence for women's attraction to Nazism; he simply deduced it from his theory: women, along with youth and the lower middle class, had incompletely modernised; they were therefore especially susceptible to anomie and to fundamentalist traditionalism. Furthermore, German women positively craved submission: 'from the point of view of German women, a heroic ideal could mobilize their romantic idealization of men in a pattern which adequately fitted the German segregation of sex roles, as the man in the role to which, of all roles, woman were by tradition least suited, that of fighter'.[62] Parsons arrived at the view that women hungered after male leadership and cast them as the epitome of the fascist crowd.

Parsons saw support for feminism as essential to denazification, a stance that sits ill with his reputation as conservative defender of the traditional family. Explanation for this apparent paradox casts further light on the gendering of his theory of fascism. On the one hand, Parsons regarded the separation of gender roles within the nuclear family as an integral part of the specialisation that accompanied modernisation, and conceptualised this relationship in terms of active and passive. The family was 'functional' – that is, it contributed most effectively to the stability of the social system – where it rested on a clear-cut division of labour between women's 'expressive' and men's 'instrumental' roles. A mature woman, he opined, could only love a man who 'took his full place in the masculine world, above all its occupational aspect', while a mature man could only love a woman who was a 'mother to his children' and an 'adequate "person" in her extra-familial roles'. Rather like the French republicans whom we encountered at the outset of the discussion, Parsons argued that the mother must be exclusively responsible for child-raising in the early years. Like Freud he saw the child's relationship with the mother as fundamental to early development, but placed more emphasis on her role in enforcing discipline and in making the child aware of social expectations (the superego). Female children learnt their place relatively easily, for they had merely to imitate their mothers by playing at families and weddings.[63] For the boy, it was harder. To fulfil his manly duties he had to detach himself from identification with his mother. Ideally, the father's extra-familial ties would ensure that the child did not become too dependent upon the family.[64]

On the other hand, Parsons did not see the distinction between male activism and female expressiveness as absolute. His conviction that men directed their activism positively through romantic love and secularised religion would have been quite acceptable to the aforementioned republicans too. More daring was Parsons's belief that, without abandoning their primary responsibility for the home, women should also be involved in social and associative life – this is where his 'feminism' comes in. Breaking with Durkheim, he saw the rising divorce rate in contemporary American society as a sign that people sought more emotionally satisfying relationships. The ideal family was a contractual relationship based on mutual respect and love, and the contract could be annulled if it did not provide that. In another respect, he was closer to Durkheim, for he subordinated women's right to choose their social roles to the needs of society and, through his distinction between 'expressive' and 'instrumental' roles, he evoked the old stereotypes. Like Durkheim, when speaking of women he slid from functionalist sociology into biological–constitutional assumptions. And, in spite of his insistence on the contractual nature of the family, Parsons argued that the 'leadership role' taken on by men tended to emerge naturally in all small groups, including the family – an idea he took from Weber.[65]

It follows from the above that Parsons saw male leadership in the family as essential in all societies. The German family was not dysfunctional because it was unequal, but because it was excessively so. In an essay written in 1947, Parsons explained that anomie was inevitable, even in the US, the most modern of countries. It was especially so among the young, for in them converged the parallel pressures of the transition from youth to adulthood and from tradition to modernity. Even in the US, men could regress to behaviour that Parsons characterised as both adolescent and excessively masculine. Likewise, he argued that women both resented their inferiority to men, and idealised 'precisely the extreme type of aggressive masculinity'. This in turn provoked western men to adopt behaviour patterns that stimulated female admiration.[66] Parsons betrayed his fear of the masses in democratic societies – only when speaking of Nazi Germany or, later, Communism did he idealise American society.

Parsons's view of Nazism was one instance of a general intellectual trend in understanding Nazism. In social psychology we may cite Erich Fromm's *Escape from Freedom* (1941), which blends Marx and Freud. It narrates the growth of human freedom and self-awareness from medieval to modern times. Fromm rejected Freud's libidinal theory and emphasis on instincts, which we have seen was essential to the founder of psychoanalysis' view of the crowd, and yet posited a preconscious need for community and indeed for submission. On this basis, he argued that man [sic] took refuge from the insecurities consequent upon modernisation through participation in totalitarian movements. Hitler's 'evangelism' offered a way out of crisis for the German people. Those who joined fascist movements were, for Fromm, examples of the 'authoritarian personality', contemptuous of the weak, while also submitting to those more powerful. The authoritarian family was especially common in the petty bourgeoisie. Critics accused Fromm of assuming that only capitalists acted rationally, while the petty bourgeoisie and workers acted blindly.[67]

In imaginative literature, Elias Canetti's masterpiece, *Auto-da-fé* (1935) owes much to Le Bon's understanding of crowds. Its moral is that the mass requires the guidance of an engaged and responsible elite if it is not to be exploited by the unscrupulous. In philosophy, the unorthodox Marxist Ernst Bloch wholly anticipated political religions theory. In historiography, Parsons's interpretation prefigured (probably without directly influencing) the *Sonderweg* histories of Germany produced since the 1960s by a generation of historians, starting with Fritz Fischer. This historiography studied both the intellectual roots of Nazism in the critique of modernity and participated in a broader 'social turn' in the study of fascism. Amongst other things, it examined especially the political proclivities of occupational groups, and the relationship between the NSDAP (National Socialist German Workers' Party) and the old state apparatus. Nevertheless, the idea of National Socialism as a totalitarian, traditionalist, quasi-religious reaction against modernity was integral to their assumptions. The list of those theorists for whom fascism was a form of religion is extensive. Some of those historians who rejected the totalitarian model also saw charismatic domination at the core of the regime, including the enormously influential Sir Ian Kershaw.[68]

That said, we may refrain from recounting the history of theories of fascism from the 1950s to the 1990s because – I would wish to contend – political religions theory represents a reversion to the more basic themes of collective psychology. Just as it pays scant heed to research into the complexities of female support for fascism, so it ignores years of research demonstrating that the participants in various kinds of crowds, political and social movements, cannot be distinguished from non-participants because they suffer inordinately from anomie. People may feel and behave differently in crowds, but then behaviour always varies with context. And, since the context governing behaviour cannot be reduced to where one happens to be at a given moment, then the fact of being in a crowd cannot alone determine behaviour. We cannot predict a person's behaviour in a crowd simply from the fact that they are in a crowd. Individuals do not become mad in crowds; they are not compelled to participate by collective folly and their behaviour is not usually extraordinary – when unusual things do happen, only a few members are involved.[69] From the historian's point of view, the work of Charles Tilly is particularly relevant, since he explores the repertoires of actions chosen and used by crowd members in different contexts, with different objectives in mind and with different degrees of self-knowledge.[70] This approach breaks down the opposition between the rational leader and the irrational mass, and dismisses the idea that crowds can be hypnotised. *Mutatis mutandis*, women do not necessarily join fascist movements because their feeble minds are captivated by seductive males, or by the ritual repetition of simple slogans.

Political religions theory and gender history

The advocates of political religions are unaware that they have invested the masses with characteristics once considered the preserve of women, children and 'backward' races. True, Gentile's predilection for citing the views of contemporary observers of fascism as 'proof' of the existence of political religions sometimes leads in directions he might not have chosen himself. For instance he cites the Swiss ecumenist Adolf Keller to the effect that 'the nation is a kind of personal "She", wooed and courted by innumerable lovers'.[71] Another partisan of political religions theory describes gender history as a 'tired academic fad', but his work is more indifferent to women and gender than hostile to it.[72] The gendered origins of social theory are evident rather in blindness towards women altogether, or, in research that does deal with gender, in the inability to see women as capable of meaningful social action. The avoidance of overt sexism does not obscure the fact that such authors regard women, and indeed all those men who belong to that ill-defined category, 'the mass', as both passive and prone to hysterical outbursts.

Political religions theory shares three more features with its precursors. First, it assumes that political religions arise in periods of crisis. For Gentile, they emerge in the transition from tradition to modernity; in conditions of anomie they fill the gap allegedly left by the decline of traditional religion and thus meet ordinary people's need for simple explanations of the nature of things. They began by attacking religion from a humanist and secular perspective, but they ended up creating their own political religion, 'in order to satisfy the need for faith of the masses, as well as to legitimate the power of the new chiefs'.[73] Second, in this crisis, buried religious dispositions re-emerge from the unconscious, for modern man [sic] cannot shake off 'ancient religious sentiment'. Quoting Mirceau Eliade, the historian of religion, Gentile states that man's 'formation begins with the situations assumed by his ancestors' and that the majority of men still hold to 'degenerated mythologies'. We cannot help but be reminded of Freud's Lamarckian view that residues of primitive behaviour persisted in the unconscious.[74] Third, political religions theory makes an implicit distinction between the male elite and the feminised mass, the latter never quite casting off the traditional mentality. Political religions theory relies on a distinction between those who supply and manipulate the political religion for their own ends and the followers whose agency is limited to emitting a psychological need for communion in a political religion.[75] As Freud demonstrated, the bond between leader and mass is one of mutual attraction. Thus Burleigh contends that the masses are more reluctant than the elites to abandon apocalyptic revolutionary illusions and that the 'uneducated' are vulnerable to manipulation by counter-elites.[76] By extension, political religions theorists define their own rationality in opposition to the unreason of the masses and assume that the masses really are susceptible to manipulation.

I now want to turn my attention to two (rare) historians who combine gender history with a debt to the concept of political religion. The first is Francine Muel-Dreyfus's exploration of the gendered discourse of the Vichy regime in France. The second is George L. Mosse's work on Nazism and gender.

Francine Muel-Dreyfus, *Vichy et l'éternel féminine*

In discussing *Vichy et l'éternel féminine* (Vichy and the Eternal Feminine), we may leave aside the fact that few historians, Muel-Dreyfus included, would regard the Vichy regime as fascist. This point merely highlights another difficulty with political religions theory: it is so general that it does not discriminate between fascist and other forms of extreme-right movement. Neither does it matter that Muel-Dreyfus wrote before Gentile had reinvented the theory of political religions, for we have demonstrated that the theory has long been intrinsic to studies of the far right. In fact, she quotes Yves Durand's use of the concept in 1972. Durand had argued that 'the exceptional circumstances in which the Vichy regime was obliged to live were "revealing" of some deep tendencies in contemporary French society'. Marshal Pétain's utterances connected with the feelings of the French people because they recalled child catechisms and school textbooks; Vichy 'transferred the Christian conception of personal salvation onto the collective plane'.[77]

In a similar vein, Muel-Dreyfus argues that Vichy's 'National Revolution' used the allegory of the 'eternal feminine' to restore France to a mythical state of organic purity. This myth, which has 'passed into common sense', imposes the idea of 'a "single" "eternal" female "nature" and "essence", which has always escaped and always will escape from history'.[78] Women are outside history. Like turn-of-the-century precursors, Muel-Dreyfus combines the notion of the collective unconscious with traditional–modern periodisation. Thus, the 'brutal explosion' of the ideology of the National Revolution shows that it was a repressed force that was ready to 'rise up at the right moment'. In effect, catastrophic defeat caused regression to the traditional age. Here we encounter the familiar notion of the persistence of the demand for religion and authority in both the mass and in women. Muel-Dreyfus sees Marshal Pétain as a prophet in the Weberian sense, who drew 'his authority from the correspondence between his own supply of a religious service and the public's demand for religion'. The people perceived salvation in catastrophe, and the promotion of traditional gender roles was essential to redemption, for they permitted a 'return to a golden age'.[79]

In support of her argument, Muel-Dreyfus cites Freud's idea of the 'believing expectation' – traditional gender roles persist in the unconscious, and re-emerge in times of trauma. So strong was this resurgence, that there were 'surprising conversions' on the part of those whom one might not at first sight have expected to support Vichy. Muel-Dreyfus cites the authority of neither Durkheim nor Le Bon. However, she does allude to Marc Bloch, who owed much to Durkheim. She cites Bloch's view that Vichy promoted a 'hypnosis of punishment', an expression she uses as the title for the first section of the book.[80] Interestingly, Bloch's belief that war caused the resurgence of atavistic instincts has recently been revived, along with the work of George Mosse, as a means to explore the brutality of the First World War. Some historians link this brutalisation to the emergence of political religions.[81] Finally, Muel-Dreyfus cites Pierre Bourdieu in support of the view that Pétain 'draws his legitimacy from the fact that he brings to the level of discourse representations, sentiments, and aspirations that pre-exist him, in an implicit state, semi- or unconsciously'.[82]

For Muel-Dreyfus, women internalised the simple ideas propounded by the regime. They did so because, in times of upheaval, women and men actively desired to recreate a golden age: 'the return of women to maternity and the maintenance of women in the home are part of these semiconscious aspirations, and their expectations are perpetually recharged by the Marshal's words'. Vichy ideology imposed itself through the violence of banality, the 'horribly flat' repetition of terms such as 'a woman is a woman', which Muel-Dreyfus dryly likens to the 'real-time peeling of potatoes'. She is so impressed with the repetitive power of Vichy's discourse, she fears that reading and rereading it will freeze her object of research. The 'symbolic violence of these representations of feminine "aptitudes" and "destiny" is so strongly internalised that reading them can render one mute'.[83]

Muel-Dreyfus also calls gender theory to her aid. In a Freudian reading of Joan W. Scott, she describes the defeat of France in 1940 as a cathartic moment, a 'laboratory of ideas in which one may analyse with particular clarity the process of the imposition of certain symbolic representations of the opposition between masculine and feminine, and of the manner in which these representations structure the perception and practical organisation of all social life, thus becoming an integral part of the representation and the establishment of power itself'.[84] For Muel-Dreyfus, this privileged moment enables study of the eternal binary representation of gender. At the outset of this chapter, I suggested that theorists of generic fascism could learn something from the practitioners of women's and gender history. The present example suggests that this is not necessarily so. Indeed, some forms of gender theory unwittingly reproduce the shortcomings of the political religions approach and of the social theory from which it derives. Some historians have not got beyond point two in the first subset of Scott's definition of gender, according to which ideas about gender are normally 'expressed in religious, educational, scientific, legal and political doctrines and typically take the form of a fixed binary opposition'. These schemas, Scott continues, might at particular times be contested, but one position eventually emerges as dominant and 'is stated as the only possible one'.[85] Femininity might then be expressed as the negative term of a binary opposition and women in fascist movements might be seen as imprisoned within patriarchal discourses.

Scott would not approve of this use of gender theory, for she stresses that gender is only *one* constituent element of social relations. That insight has proved fruitful for historians of fascism, especially in their explorations of the relationship between race and gender under National Socialism.[86] Furthermore, Scott insists that 'real men and women do not always or literally fulfil the terms either of their society's prescriptions or of our analytic categories'.[87] Scott may not have reconciled this quasi-Bakhtinian conception of language with the poststructuralist linguistics that she imports from Derrida and Foucault. Yet that has not prevented historians from exploring the ways in which women have negotiated their position within the fascist movements and regimes.

The tendency to interpret Scott in the manner of Muel-Dreyfus is reinforced perhaps by the fact that, in his history of the prison and in the first volume of his history of sexuality, Michel Foucault, a major influence on Scott, does not entirely break with the traditional–modern dichotomy or with conventional sociology more generally – at least before he developed the notion of 'problematisation' in his later work. It is often remarked that his vision in the earlier *Surveiller et punir* (1975) of a remorseless tendency towards rationalisation, surveillance, efficiency and control, recalls the macro-historical teleology of Weberian and Parsonian theories of rationalisation. Foucault insisted that carceral society emerges through tiny increments rather than through a grand design, and yet history moves in only one direction. We are entitled to suspect the existence of a functional mechanism.[88] In the same volume, Foucault emphasised the ways in which power relations grip the body: 'they invest it, mark it, train it, torture it, force it to carry out tasks, to perform ceremonies, to emit signs'.[89] Here is a grandchild, perhaps, of the old idea of internalisation through repetition.[90] Leaving aside the different moral gloss, Foucault's depiction of psychiatry's role in marginalising deviance represents a backhanded compliment to Parsons's and Sighele's understanding of the way in which society works.

Like many Foucauld-influenced examples of gender history, Muel-Dreyfus's book provides us with a rich and sophisticated picture of social relations as imagined by a number of elite thinkers. Yet use of political religions theory locks that perspective into the centre of her interpretation in such a way that it leaves little theoretical space for alternative perspectives. Women are reduced to vectors of the dominant ideology.

George L. Mosse and the concept of political religion

The work of George L. Mosse overcomes some of these difficulties. It is relevant because he is often cited as an inspiration by the proponents of political religions theory,[91] and yet Mosse deployed the concept more subtly than do some of his disciples. In particular, he explored the tension between political–religious drives in fascism and the desire for return to 'bourgeois' patterns of family and sexuality. This contradiction is inherent, if hitherto unexplored, in political religions theory, so may in principle be dealt with without questioning the theory itself. In fact, Mosse's work both affirmed and problematised the sociological tradition from which political religions theory issues. For instance, he accepted more or less unthinkingly that societies must 'cohere' in the Parsonian sense. In his memoirs he explained that, as a Jew and a homosexual, he first sought to attain 'bourgeois respectability' and then rejected it. He both recognised the repressiveness of bourgeois morality and realised that it was 'essential for the cohesion and functioning of society itself'.[92] Elsewhere, Mosse distinguished the study of elite ideas, to which conventional historical methods are appropriate, from the study of mass politics, in which realm 'the irrational seems to predominate', and to which anthropological methods were best suited. Effectively, he reaffirmed the old idea that the mass inhabits a non-historical time and does not engage in purposeful action. Evoking the work of Claude Lévi-Strauss, he suggested that in totalitarian movements 'conscious and unconscious wishes, desires and frustrations are manipulated in order to produce adherence to the political movement'. He was also aware that Lévi-Strauss potentially subverted the traditional–modern dichotomy.[93]

Mosse displayed a long-standing interest in religion and politics, having come to the history of fascism from the study of the Reformation. He saw fascism as a distorted form of democracy, a revolutionary movement in which a 'secular religion mediated between people and leaders'. He argued that German history possessed a strong millenarian tradition, which was 'apt to come to the fore in times of crisis'; the extreme rapidity of modernisation in Germany represented just such a crisis. The upsurge of millenarianism contained a revolutionary impulse, yet at the same time it was 'an instrument of control over the masses', channelling radicalism in appropriate directions, through the ritual repetition of religious devotion.[94] Thus, the revolutionary political religion contained a traditional element, derived from a desire for an organic community.

In terms of masculinity, this tension produced conflict between the return to the purity of the bourgeois family and the vision of fascism as an exclusively male society. At first, the rough-and-ready manly comrade-ship of some veteran Nazis challenged the ideal of respectability. Mosse interpreted this camaraderie in Freudian terms as the sublimation of ho-mosexual impulses, while his view that it protected men from the chaos of industrialisation and modernity could have been taken straight from Parsons. In the longer term, the regime's need for respectability won out. The Röhm purge in 1934 was justified as a defence against homosexuality. Mosse shows that one of the principal icons of National Socialist art was a model of traditional male beauty, invested with the values of strength, hard work, good manners and self-mastery.[95]

Mosse had rather less to say about femininity than about masculinity, and what he did say may have been said in response to feminist criticism.[96] As part of their drive for respectability, Mosse argued, the Nazis banished women from public life and emphasised chastity and the family. He noted that, while Nazi sculptures of men used the Greek nude model, the female was usually veiled, 'the modest and chaste bearer of the children of the race to be hidden from public view'.[97] Mosse accepted that, in Italy, a few women entered hitherto closed professions, but there was no equivalent movement in Germany. In the latter, some women indirectly expressed fear that the Nazi idealisation of the *Männerbund* (male society) might undermine the spiritual bond in the family. Mosse put this down to the 'confusion' that reigned in the first months of the Nazi regime and, in any case, such fears hardly contested conventional gender roles. Women as active subjects barely figure in Mosse's lengthy treatments of gender, although he does note some chafing at the lack of opportunities for women. His exploration of tensions between homoeroticism in the *Männerbund* and the regime's drive for respectability has no equivalent in his discussion of women. He assumes the passivity of women and sees signs to the contrary as 'exceptional'. Some historians have criticised him for assuming that men and women internalised stereotypes without resistance.[98]

Mosse's work half-breaches the limits of political religions theory. While he owed a sizeable debt to the sociological tradition I have described, his definition of 'tradition' is so loose that the gendered ideas he describes are not reducible to the tradition–modern schema, which is so essential to political religions theory. Indeed, his assertion that the fascist new man was constructed from bourgeois stereotypes is too much for some partisans of political religions theory. For Gentile, Mosse misunderstood the 'essence' of fascism.[99] This is an interesting observation on Gentile's part, given that he often *asserts* that political religions theory is only one way of concep-tualising fascism – if this were more than an assertion, then there would be room for Mosse's interpretation. To my mind, the *strength* of Mosse's work is precisely that he refused to identify an ahistorical 'essence' of fascism and was thus better able to historicise it. And if, as he rightly suggested, the fascist new man was constructed partly from 'bourgeois man', then we might see women's attraction to fascism less in a non-specific sense of anomie resultant upon the breakdown of traditional values, than in quite specific social and cultural tensions. In fact, if we wish to avoid a mechanical interactionism, we should go a little further than Mosse in historicising our categories. We might then understand female engagement in fascism in both the conscious and unconscious strategies pursued by historical actors in precise historical contexts and in the unforeseen consequences of those actions. Mosse points the way towards a more sophisticated understanding of the relationship between gender and fascism, in which fascism is simultaneously a gendered and contested political religion and a set of gender, class, ethnic and other relationships.

Conclusion

Either the political religions approach to fascism neglects the important role played by women in extreme-right movements and regimes, or it robs women, along with most men, of an agentive role in the history of fascism. The theory envisages fascism as a movement that seeks to heal the anomie consequent upon the transition from tradition to modernity, or of some other breakdown in traditional values, through the creation of a political religion. Women, as imperfectly modernised, irrational, emotional creatures, are especially vulnerable to the appeal of religious ideologies. They belong to an earlier, religious, period of history. Indeed, as Freud and Parsons demonstrated in different ways, women have an innate desire for masculine domination. Femininity thus stands for the need for religious, black and white explanations, that is present in the masses generally, and fascism represents a regression to a past, implicitly feminine, age. More abstractly, masculinity and femininity structure the radical distinction between elite and mass that is intrinsic to an entire sociological tradition.

I would not wish to suggest that political religions theory is intentionally or intrinsically misogynist, even though one could describe few of its practitioners as partisans of women's or gender history. Indeed, Muel-Dreyfus's book demonstrates that it can be harnessed to a particular kind of feminist history – that which emphasises the absolute powerlessness of women. Similarly, Mosse's use of political religions theory to understand National Socialism represents a pioneering work in the history of homosexuality and masculinity.

Political religions theory does not stand or fall by its political stance – which is not reducible to anti-feminism – but by its theoretical adequacy. In this respect, it falls short. It is beyond the scope of this chapter to elaborate an alternative theorisation of women and gender in fascism. I shall confine myself to suggesting that the starting point must be a less polarised view of the relationship between rulers and ruled, elite and mass. Indeed, we need to problematise and historicise these categories; we need to accept that the mass is more rational and the elite less so than some have thought. The same applies to structure and agency: we must transcend simple dichotomies. There are many relevant approaches. My personal preference is for the sociology of Anthony Giddens, which sees structure and agency as two sides of the same coin, for Bakhtin's literary theory, which sees texts as structured by an unequal dialogue, and for Toril Moi's adaptation of Simone de Beauvoir's existentialism, which breaks down the opposition between biological sex and gender.[100] Such an agenda has implications not just for theories of fascism, but for how we see the sociological canon more generally. The canon is not to be discarded: it can be read in ways other than that presented here, though not in just any way. That said, if scholars must use concepts such as elite, mass, rationalisation, modernisation, modernity, tradition, internalisation, socialisation, anomie, function and interaction, then they should handle them with care.

Notes

1. The two most important works are Victoria De Grazia, *How Fascism Ruled Women* (Berkeley: University of California Press, 1992); and Claudia Koonz, *Mothers in the Fatherland: Women, the Family, and Nazi Politics* (New York: St Martin's Press, 1987). See also Atina Grossmann, 'The Feminist Debates About Women and National Socialism', *Gender & History* 3 (1991), pp. 350–58; Ralph Leck, 'Conservative Empowerment and the Gender of Nazism: Paradigms of Power and Complicity in German Women's History', *Journal of Women's History* 12 (2000), pp. 147–69; Kevin Passmore (ed.), *Women, Gender and Fascism in Europe 1919–1945* (Manchester: Manchester University Press, 2003).

2. For an excellent critique of political religions theory from this perspective, see Neil Gregor, 'Nazism – A Political Religion?', in Neil Gregor (ed.), *Nazism, War and Genocide* (Exeter: University of Exeter Press, 2005), pp. 1–21.

3. Edward Palmer Thompson, *The Poverty of Theory and Other Essays* (London: Merlin, 1978), p. 194.

4. Emilio Gentile, 'The Sacralisation of Politics: Definitions, Interpretations and Reflections on the Question of Secular Religion and Totalitarianism', *Totalitarian Movements and Political Religions* 1 (2000), pp. 18–55; Emilio Gentile, *The Sacralization of Politics in Fascist Italy*, tr. Keith Botsford (Cambridge: Harvard University Press, 1996). For an account of the debates surrounding political religions theory, see Ulrike Ehret, 'Understanding the Popular Appeal of Fascism, National Socialism and Communism: The Revival of Totalitarianism Theory and Political Religion', *History Compass* 5 (2007), pp. 1,236–67.

5. The exception is an account of a recent conference on the relationship between mass dictatorship, a close cousin of political religions theory and gender theory. The gender historians present were sometimes sceptical of political religions theory. Not listed in Historical Abstracts is the review article, Nancy P. Nenno, 'Women, Fascism and Film', *Totalitarian Movements and Political Religions* 2 (2001), pp. 73–90.

6. Women appear in passing in Vassil Girginov, 'Totalitarian Sport: Towards an Understanding of its Logic, Practice and Legacy', *Totalitarian Movements and Political Religions* 5 (2004), pp. 25–58, esp. pp. 38, 45. The author notes simply that totalitarian regimes marginalised women's sport. Interestingly, Martin Durham, whose work on women and

fascism could not be accused of underestimating women's agency, barely alludes to women in his contribution to the journal: Martin Durham, 'The Upward Path: Palingenesis, Political Religion and the National Alliance', *Totalitarian Movements and Political Religions* 5 (2004), pp. 454–68.

7. Kevin Passmore, 'Generic Fascism and the Historians', *Erwägen Wissen Ethik* 15 (2004), pp. 403–5; Kevin Passmore, 'The Naming of Fascism', *Erwägen Wissen Ethik* 15 (2004), pp. 335–7.

8. Carl J. Friedrich and Zbigniew Brezezinski, *Totalitarian Dictatorship and Autocracy* (Cambridge: Cambridge University Press, 1956). Gentile sees the political religion as 'an essential aspect of totalitarianism': Gentile, 'The Sacralisation of Politics', p. 18.

9. Koonz, *Mothers in the Fatherland*, p. 3.

10. Gentile, 'The Sacralisation of Politics', p. 29.

11. Political religions theorists are no more lacking in agency than were women in fascist movements.

12. See e.g., the forthcoming work of Jean Pedersen on Durkheim and his critics.

13. Robert Nye, *The Anti-Democratic Sources of Elite Theory: Pareto, Mosca, Michels* (London and Beverley Hills: Sage, 1977). This brilliant book is essential reading for anyone interested in the history of the political sciences.

14. Annelise Maugue, *L'Identité masculine en crise au tournant du siècle* (Paris: Rivages, 1987); Robert Nye, *Masculinity and Male Codes of Honor in Modern France* (Berkeley: University of California Press, 1998); Kevin Passmore, *The Right in the French Third Republic* (forthcoming); Paul Seeley, '"O sainte-mère": Liberalism and the Socialisation of Catholic Men in Nineteenth-Century France', *Journal of Modern History* 70 (1998), pp. 862–91. See also Bonnie G. Smith, *The Gender of History: Men, Women and Historical Practice* (Cambridge, Mass; London: Harvard University Press, 1998) to which this chapter owes a significant intellectual debt.

15. Ruth Harris, 'The "Unconscious" and Catholicism in France', *Historical Journal* 47 (2004), pp. 331–54.

16. Théodore Joran, *Le Mensonge du féminisme* (Paris: Jouve, 1905), p. 225.

17. Including, for example, on the front page of the very conservative *La République française* of 9 July 1900. 'On s'est aperçu que la versatilité, la ruse, la complexité, n'était pas des attitudes spéciales à la femme, mais á la race humaine toute entière, sans distinction des sexes; que la différence même des sexes, sur laquelle on avait spéculé, symbolisé, esthétisé a perte de vue pendent des temps et des temps, n'étaient en réalité qu'une très petite différence, d'ailleurs essentiellement physiologique'. [We have understood that versatility, ruses and complexity are not aptitudes possessed by women alone, but by the whole human race, without distinction of sex. We have understood that sexual difference itself, on which people have endlessly speculated, symbolised and aestheticised, was in reality just a very little difference, and moreover that it was essentially physiological.]

18. Gustave Le Bon, *La Psychologie des foules* (Paris: Alcan, 1895), p. 39.

19. Craig McPhail, *Far From the Madding Crowd* (New York: Aldine de Gruyter, 1991), pp. xix–xxx; Robert Nye, *The Origins of Crowd Psychology: Gustave Le Bon and the Crisis of Mass Democracy in the Third Republic* (London and Beverley Hills: Sage, 1975), pp. 67–78; Daniel Pick, *Faces of Degeneration: A European Disorder, c.1848–c.1918* (Cambridge: Cambridge University Press, 1989).

20. Gustave Le Bon, *The Crowd* (New Brunswick and London: Transaction, 1997), p. 56.

21. Le Bon, *The Crowd*, p. 70.

22. Robert Nye, 'Introduction to the Transaction Edition', in Le Bon, *The Crowd*, pp. 14–16.

23. Emilio Gentile, 'Fascism as a Political Religion', *Journal of Contemporary History* 25 (1990), pp. 229–51, here p. 242; Gentile, 'The Sacralisation of Politics', pp. 28–9.

24. Michael Burleigh, *Earthly Powers: The Conflict Between Religion and Politics from the French Revolution to the Great War* (London: HarperPerrenial, 2006), pp. 1–17; Gentile, 'The Sacralisation of Politics', p. 28.

25. Jean Elisabeth Pedersen, 'Sexual Politics in Comte and Durkheim: Feminism, History, and the French Sociological Tradition', *Signs: Journal of Women in Culture and Society* 27 (2001), pp. 229–63.
26. Emile Durkheim, *De la division du travail social* (Paris: F. Alcan, 1893), p. 192; Emile Durkheim, *Le Suicide, étude de sociologie* (Paris: F. Alcan, 1897), pp. 99, 166; Howard I. Kushner, 'Durkheim and the Immunity of Women to Suicide', in David Lester (ed.), *Emile Durkheim*: Le Suicide *One Hundred Years Later* (Philadelphia: Charles Press, 1994), pp. 205–23, here p. 210.
27. Durkheim, *De la division du travail social*, pp. 20–21; Kushner, 'Durkheim and the Immunity of Women', pp. 211–12; Jennifer Lehmann, 'Durkheim's Response to Feminism', *Sociological Theory* 8 (1990), pp. 163–87.
28. Anthony Giddens, *Capitalism and Modern Social Theory: An Analysis of the Writings of Marx, Durkheim and Max Weber* (Cambridge: Cambridge University Press, 1971), p. 117.
29. Kushner, 'Durkheim and the Immunity of Women', pp. 205–9.
30. Pedersen, 'Sexual Politics'.
31. Sigmund Freud, *Group Psychology and the Analysis of the Ego*, tr. James Strachey (1922; London: Bantam Classic, 1960), p. 18; Paul Roazen, *Freud: Political and Social Thought* (London: Hogarth, 1969), pp. 218–32. The latter argues that Freud's theory of the crowd has nothing to do with Le Bon's because Freud's argument can only be understood in the context of Freud's whole psychoanalytic theory. I contend that Freud actually sought to show that Le Bon's valid *observations* of crowd behaviour could be *explained* by psychoanalytic methods. My argument is closer to Philip Rieff, *Freud: The Mind of the Moralist* (London: Gollancz, 1958), pp. 220–56; Philip Rieff, 'The Origins of Freud's Political Psychology', *Journal of the History of Ideas* 17 (1956), pp. 235–49.
32. Freud, *Group Psychology and the Analysis of the Ego*, p. 13.
33. Sigmund Freud, 'Femininity', in Elisabeth Young-Bruehl (ed.), *Freud on Women* (London: Vintage, 2002), pp. 342–62, here p. 357.
34. Sigmund Freud, 'Why War?', *New Commonwealth* 6 (1934), pp. 9–19, esp. pp. 17–18.
35. Freud, 'Femininity', p. 359. Frigidity in women, he added, might often be anatomical.
36. Freud, 'Why War?', p. 18.
37. Sigmund Freud, 'Thoughts for the Times on War and Death', *The Standard Edition of the Complete Psychological Works of Sigmund Freud* (London: Vintage, 1957), pp. 275–88; Freud, 'Why War?', pp. 17–18. Michael Burleigh's exploration of the Holocaust in Russia in 1941–42 owes a little to Freud's explanation: his protagonists are either sadistic, and yet personally brave men, released from the normal constraints of civilisation, whose behaviour was more typical of the dark ages, or they are Eastern Europeans driven by fanatical national hatreds. Michael Burleigh, *The Third Reich: A New History* (London: Macmillan, 2000), pp. 598–621.
38. Freud, 'Why War?', p.16. This was not the only occasion upon which Freud identified violence with genuine masculinity. He notoriously portrayed Woodrow Wilson thus: 'sickly, spectacled and shy, guarded by father, mother and sisters, Tommy Wilson never had a fist fight in his life. His emotions were satisfied in the church and the manse'. Note also the connection between religion and unmanliness. Sigmund Freud and William C. Bullitt, *Woodrow Wilson: A Psychological Study* (Piscataway, NJ: Transaction, 1998), p. 11.
39. Freud, *Group Psychology and the Analysis of the Ego*, pp. 69–71.
40. Freud, *Group Psychology and the Analysis of the Ego*, pp. 75–6.
41. Sigmund Freud, 'The Dissolution of the Oedipus Complex', *Complete Psychological Works*, pp. 173–82; Freud, 'Femininity', pp. 345, 351–62.
42. Toril Moi, 'Is Anatomy Destiny?', in Toril Moi, *What is a Woman? And Other Essays* (Oxford: Oxford University Press, 1999), pp. 369–93. Moi argues convincingly that Freud was not a biological determinist, and that he saw an interaction between family relations

and biology. Nevertheless, Freud's objections to biological determinism were rather like those who defend cultural against biological racism: he saw gender identities as formed so far in the past that they are hardly less immutable than biologically determined identities. Oddly, Moi does not cite 'Femininity'.

43. Anthony Storr, *Freud: A Very Short Introduction* (Oxford: Oxford University Press, 2001), pp. 64–5.

44. Peter Baehr, 'The "Masses" in Weber's Political Sociology', *Economy and Society* 19 (1990), pp. 242–65; Terry R. Kandal, *The Woman Question in Classical Sociology* (Miami: Florida International University Press, 1988), pp. 126–56; Arthur Mitzman, *The Iron Cage: An Historical Interpretation of Max Weber* (Piscataway, NJ: Transaction, 1985), pp. 302–4.

45. Letter of Marcel Mauss to S. Ranulf, 6 November 1926, quoted in François Chaubet, *Histoire intellectuelle de l'Entre-Deux-Guerres* (Paris: Nouveau Monde, 2006), pp. 294–5.

46. Freud, 'Why War?', p. 17. Note also that Freud regarded erotic ties, identification and suggestibility as a part of 'the normal constitution of society'. He remarked on 'how little originality and personal courage are to be found in it, of how much every individual is ruled by those attitudes of the group mind which exhibit themselves in such forms as racial characteristics, class prejudices, public opinion, etc'. Freud, *Group Psychology and the Analysis of the Ego*, pp. 62–3.

47. Talcott Parsons, 'Superego and the Theory of Social Systems', *Psychiatry* 15 (1952), pp. 15–24.

48. Talcott Parsons, 'Max Weber and the Contemporary Political Crisis', *Review of Politics* 4 (1942), pp. 61–76, 156–72.

49. Peter Hamilton, *Talcott Parsons* (Chichester: Horwood, 1983). Parsons placed less emphasis than did Freud on castration fear as a route to socialisation.

50. Uta Gerhardt, 'Introduction: Talcott Parsons's Sociology of National Socialism', in Uta Gerhardt, *Talcott Parsons on National Socialism* (New York: Aldine de Gruyter, 1993), pp. 1–77; Uta Gerhardt, *Talcott Parsons: An Intellectual Biography* (Cambridge: Cambridge University Press, 2002), pp. 58–183.

51. Talcott Parsons, 'Propaganda and Social Control', *Psychiatry* 4 (1942), pp. 551–72.

52. Gerhardt, 'Introduction', pp. 5–10.

53. Talcott Parsons, 'Democracy and Social Structure in Pre-Nazi Society', in Uta Gerhardt, *Talcott Parsons on National Socialism* (New York: Aldine de Gruyter, 1993), pp. 225–42, esp. pp. 234–5.

54. Talcott Parsons, 'Some Sociological Aspects of Fascist Movements', in Gerhardt, *Talcott Parsons on National Socialism*, pp. 203–18, here p. 204.

55. Parsons, 'Some Sociological Aspects of Fascist Movements', pp. 204–5.

56. Parsons, 'Some Sociological Aspects of Fascist Movements', p. 207.

57. Parsons, 'Some Sociological Aspects of Fascist Movements', pp. 213–14.

58. Parsons, 'Some Sociological Aspects of Fascist Movements', pp. 209–12.

59. Talcott Parsons, 'Age and Sex Structure', *American Sociological Review* 7 (1942), pp. 604–16, here p. 615.

60. Parsons, 'Democracy and Social Structure in Pre-Nazi Society', pp. 234–9.

61. Parsons, 'Democracy and Social Structure in Pre-Nazi Society', pp. 232–3.

62. Parsons, 'Democracy and Social Structure in Pre-Nazi Society', p. 240.

63. Talcott Parsons, 'Certain Primary Sources and Patterns of Aggression in the Social Structure of the Western World', in Gerhardt, *Talcott Parsons on National Socialism*, pp. 325–47, esp. pp. 332–3.

64. Talcott Parsons and Robert F. Bales, *Family, Socialization and Interaction Process* (London: Routledge and Kegan Paul, 1956), pp. 3–33.

65. Parsons and Bales, *Family Socialization*. On Weber and the structure of social groups see Parsons, 'Max Weber', p. 61.

66. Parsons, 'Certain Primary Sources and Patterns of Aggression', pp. 331–5.

67. Neil McLaughlin, 'Nazism, Nationalism, and the Sociology of Emotions: Escape from Freedom Revisited', *Sociological Theory* 14 (1996), pp. 241–61. Besides providing an accessible account of Fromm's work, this article shows the persistence of various versions of the theories that I have criticised from the 1940s into the 1990s. McLaughlin approvingly quotes Parsons's view that the appeal of Nazism owed much to 'fundamentalism', p. 258.

68. Ian Kershaw, *The Hitler Myth: Image and Reality in the Third Reich* (Oxford: Oxford University Press, 1987).

69. McPhail, *Far from the Madding Crowd*, pp. xxi–xxii, 43–60.

70. Charles Tilly, *As Sociology Meets History* (New York: Academic Press, 1981).

71. Gentile, 'The Sacralisation of Politics', p. 46.

72. Michael Burleigh, 'Dressed by Genoese, Throttled by Croats', *Sunday Independent*, 13 October 1996. Oddly, in the same sentence he expresses his aversion to the study of alchemy and witchcraft.

73. Gentile, 'Fascism as a Political Religion'; Emilio Gentile, 'Political Religion: A Concept and its Critics – A Critical Survey', *Totalitarian Movements and Political Religions* 6 (2005), pp. 19–32; Gentile, 'The Sacralisation of Politics', pp. 30–31; Gentile, *The Sacralization of Politics in Fascist Italy*; Hermann Lübbe, 'Religion and Politics in the Processes of Modernisation', *Totalitarian Movements and Political Religions* 6 (2005), pp. 53–70.

74. Gentile, 'The Sacralisation of Politics', p. 30.

75. Gentile, 'The Sacralisation of Politics', pp. 29, 45. See also Lübbe, 'Religion and Politics'.

76. Burleigh, *Earthly Powers*, pp. 1–22. See esp. pp. 5–6, in which Burleigh approvingly paraphrases Eric Voegelin's account of the 'delirious mass excitations' of the Nazi crowd.

77. Yves Durand, *Vichy 1940–1944* (Paris: Bordas, 1972), pp. 3–4, 66.

78. Francine Muel-Dreyfus, *Vichy et l'éternel féminine* (Paris: Seuil, 1996), p. 18.

79. Muel-Dreyfus, *Vichy et l'éternel féminine*, p. 12.

80. Muel-Dreyfus, *Vichy et l'éternel féminine*, pp. 11, 15.

81. Stéphane Audoin-Rouzeau and Annette Becker, *1914–1918, retrouver la guerre* (Paris: Gallimard, 2000), pp. 44–9, 65–8; André Burguière, *L'Ecole des Annales: Une histoire intellectuelle* (Paris: Odile Jacob, 2006), p. 43.

82. Muel-Dreyfus, *Vichy et l'éternel féminine*, p. 17. Were space not a constraint, I might have explored Bourdieu's ambiguous relationship with the sociological canon – particularly his notion of the pre-conscious 'habitus'.

83. Muel-Dreyfus, *Vichy et l'éternel féminine*, pp. 17–18.

84. Muel-Dreyfus, *Vichy et l'éternel féminine*, p. 10; Joan Wallach Scott, 'Gender: A Useful Category of Historical Analysis', *American Historical Review* 91 (1986), pp. 1,053–75.

85. Scott, 'Gender', pp. 1,067–8.

86. Gisela Bock, 'Equality and Difference in National Socialist Racism', in Joan Wallach Scott (ed.), *Feminism and History* (London: Routledge, 1992), pp. 267–90.

87. Scott, 'Gender', p. 1,068.

88. Lois McNay, *Foucault: A Critical Introduction* (London: Polity, 1994), pp. 92–3.

89. Michel Foucault, *Discipline and Punish* (London: Penguin, 1991), p. 25.

90. Harris, 'The "Unconscious" and Catholicism in France', p. 353.

91. Stanley G. Payne, David J Sorkin and John S. Tortorice (eds), *What History Tells: George L. Mosse and the Culture of Modern Europe* (Madison: University of Wisconsin Press, 2004); Karel Plessini, 'The Nazi as the "Ideal Bourgeois": Respectability and Nazism in the Work of George L. Mosse', *Totalitarian Movements and Political Religions* 5 (2004), pp. 226–42.

92. George L. Mosse, *Confronting History: A Memoir* (Madison: University of Wisconsin Press, 2000), p. 179. Quoted in Plessini, 'The Nazi as the "Ideal Bourgeois"', p. 228. Interestingly, Parsons also saw racial discrimination as a dangerous potential in modern society. Gerhardt, 'Introduction', pp. 58–9.

93. George L. Mosse, 'History, Anthropology, and Mass Movements', *American Historical Review* 75 (1969), pp. 447–52, esp. pp. 447–8.

94. George L. Mosse, *The Crisis of German Ideology: Intellectual Origins of the Third Reich* (London: Weidenfeld and Nicolson, 1964), pp. 2–10; George L. Mosse, *The Fascist Revolution: Toward a General Theory of Fascism* (New York: Howard Fertig, 1999).

95. Robert Nye, 'Mosse, Masculinity and the History of Sexuality', in Payne, Sorkin and Tortorice (eds), *What History Tells*, pp. 183–201, here p. 193.

96. Nye, 'Mosse, Masculinity and the History of Sexuality', p. 187.

97. Mosse, *The Fascist Revolution*, pp. 20, 51.

98. George L. Mosse, *Nationalism and Sexuality: Respectable and Abnormal Sexuality in Modern Europe* (New York: Howard Fertig, 1985), pp. 160–63, 176–8.

99. Emilio Gentile, 'A Provisional Dwelling: Origin and Development of the Concept of Fascism in Mosse's Historiography', in Payne, Sorkin and Tortorice (eds), *What History Tells*, pp. 41–109. See also Plessini, 'The Nazi as the "Ideal Bourgeois"', pp. 237–40. Nowhere are the theoretical limitations of political religions theory more evident than in the latter's artificial distinction between essence of fascism and historically contingent bourgeois respectability.

100. Anthony Giddens, *The Constitution of Society: Outline of the Theory of Structuration* (Cambridge: Polity, 1986); Toril Moi, *What is a Woman?*; M. M. Bakhtin, *The Dialogic Imagination: Four Essays* (Austin: University of Texas Press, 1981).

11 Forgetting the Past

Judith M. Bennett

When historians of women and gender gathered last summer at the 14th Berkshire Conference on the History of Women, we talked most often about contemporary history – that is, about matters so recent they are still part of living memory.[1] Nearly 700 papers were presented on a wide variety of topics and regions, but our chronological sweep was not quite so wide. At any time during the conference, roughly half the presentations focused exclusively on the twentieth and twenty-first centuries; when we took a longer view, we usually looked no farther back than 1800 (three of four papers fell into this 'last two hundred years' category); and we rarely cast our eyes far enough to consider peoples and cultures removed from us by 500 years or more.[2] A casual visitor to the conference could have reasonably concluded that, although the past is the special province of feminist history, we are at risk of forgetting most of it.

The chronological coverage of the 2008 Berkshire Conference was, in fact, relatively good, the result of concerted effort on the part of the programme committee. The effort paid off handsomely; in 2005, only 12 per cent of papers at the Berkshire Conference had treated the world before 1800, whereas 22 per cent did so in 2008. The triennial meetings of the International Federation for Research in Women's History (IFRWH) have not been so inclusive. In 2003, 20 per cent of papers considered pre-1800 topics, but in 2007 this coverage had fallen to only 15 per cent.[3] As to our professional journals, we are approaching a situation in which almost nine out of ten articles address the last two hundred years. As Table 1 shows, the three main English-language journals devoted to women's and gender history now publish little history before 1800 and even less history before 1500.

These stark figures demonstrate what many of us have observed more casually – that the field of women's and gender history has developed a contemporary bias. Our field has tilted toward the modern, not because of a lack of research on women and gender before 1800, but instead

Table 1.[4] **Chronological Coverage in Journals of Women's and Gender History, 2001–07**

Topics By Era	*Gender & History*	*Journal of Women's History*	*Women's History Review*	Totals	**Percentages**
Modern (*c*.1800–present)	138	130	187	455	**86**
Early Modern (*c*.1500–1800)	23	16	16	55	**10**
Premodern (before 1500)	9	6	4	19	**4**
Total	170	152	207	529	**100**

NOTE: This count focused on research articles. Archive reports, forums, memorials and other such miscellanea were excluded, as were articles whose chronological sweep defied categorisation. If an article spanned two eras, I placed it in the earlier one.

because of our own lack of interest in that research. Feminist investigation of classical, medieval and early modern cultures has flourished for decades and continues to flourish today. But these pre-1800 studies are now largely pursued outside the mainstream of women's and gender history. In that mainstream, as defined by our journals and conferences, 'women's and gender history' has effectively become synonymous with 'women's and gender history since 1800'. Why do we, as feminist historians, attend so poorly to the full possibilities of the past? How might we develop better practices that take fuller account of women and gender in times before 1800?

In the hope that feminist historians will discuss these questions, debate possible answers, and reach some productive solutions, I offer here my necessarily brief thoughts.[5] I can speak, of course, only from my own experience and expertise. As a US citizen trained in Canada who has spent my professional career researching English medieval history while employed at US universities, my perspectives are profoundly Anglo, in American terms, or western, in world terms. I have striven to move across these boundaries as best I can but, for better or worse, these are the intellectual traditions within which I work and from which I draw most of my observations. I look forward to seeing how colleagues will complicate and enrich these observations with ideas and experiences different from my own.

Causes

Women's history has not always focused so relentlessly on the contemporary and modern world. In the 1970s, Joan Kelly's work – and particularly her electrifying question 'Did women have a Renaissance?' – profoundly shaped the development of women's history, modern as well as premodern.[6] In the 1970s, the first journals devoted to feminist scholarship better balanced modern history with early modern, premodern and transhistorical perspectives; the first four years of *Signs: A Journal of Women in Culture and Society*, for example, offered its feminist readers fifteen articles that treated, in whole or part, topics before 1800 and twenty-three articles on the nineteenth and twentieth centuries. (*Signs* also then included a now defunct 'Archives' section, a treasure trove of primary materials that stretched as far back, in those early years, as Hippocrates). And in the 1970s, chronological coverage was also better at the earliest Berkshire Conferences, where the medievalist Jo Ann McNamara ensured that every time slot had one session devoted to medieval topics and another to ancient ones. The women's history that was launched by the second wave of feminism was by no means perfect, but one of its strengths was far-sightedness. In the decades since, we have steadily foreshortened that vision.[7] Let me briefly raise six factors – three general and three specific to feminist scholarship – that might have encouraged our new myopia.

First, it is probably not accidental that the culture of the United States – where feminist scholarship has particularly flourished in the past thirty years – encourages a denigration of 'Old Europe' and an admiration of all that is 'new' and 'modern'. The presentism of US culture stems partly from the self-evident fact that US history is mostly modern history, but partly also from a nationalistic sentiment that attention to the world before 1776 harkens back to a tradition-bound, elitist and un-American past. In such a view, any history before the revolutionary inception of US democracy can easily be dismissed as irrelevant. Henry Ford put it best, in his quintessentially US statement, 'History is more or less bunk . . . the only history that is worth a tinker's damn is the history we make today'.[8] Thus, one culprit in the present-ward tilt of women's and gender history is the present-ward tilt of the specific national culture in which our field has most taken root in the last few decades.

Second, the historical profession itself, not just in the United States but also internationally, bears part of the blame for the shallow chronological depth of women's and gender history. For members of a profession devoted to the study of the past, historians are now remarkably uninterested in most of it. As Lynn Hunt has noted, 'history' in the United States and Europe little more than a century ago was mainly *ancient* history. But in the last few decades, twentieth-century history, once 'consigned to the province of journalism', has entered the historical mainstream and taken it by storm.[9] As a result, when historians worldwide gathered in 2005 for the quinquennial meeting of the International Committee of Historical Sciences, the nineteenth and twentieth centuries dominated (75 per cent of papers), with some attention to early modern (11 per cent) and premodern (14 per cent) topics. US-based historians do much the same at the annual meetings of the American Historical Association: in 2005, for example, modern papers accounted for 75 per cent of the AHA agenda, early modern 18.5 per cent and premodern 6.5 per cent (just 38 of 592 presentations). The relentless modernity of women's and gender history reflects, in part, the relentless modernity of practices among historians more generally.

Third, classicists, medievalists and early modernists are themselves partly to blame for history's waning attention to distant pasts. Classicists long ago began to pursue their work within distinctive interdisciplinary homes; medievalists have built many similar programmes in the last half-century; and early modernists are beginning now to follow suit. These inter-disciplinary programmes offer many intellectual and pedagogical benefits, but they can also become enclaves that encourage scholars of early eras to remain apart from colleagues working in more modern times. The iso-lating effect of these time-specific interdisciplinarity encampments goes a good way towards explaining how women's and gender history in earlier eras can be flourishing but nevertheless eclipsed within the field generally: studies of ancient and medieval women are mostly shared in conferences, journals and books whose intended audiences are classicists or medieval-ists, not historians. Since classicists and medievalists have not been talking much to modernists, it is perhaps not surprising that modernists have lost sight of these past worlds.

Fourth (and I move here to factors specific to feminist scholarship), fem-inist interest in pre-1800 eras might have peaked when those eras seemed relatively golden for women and might have since waned in step with research that chipped away at this gilt veneer. When feminists began to advocate women's history in the 1970s, a lost golden age provided both in-tellectual support for a new academic field (Jakob Bachofen and Friedrich Engels were particularly credible authorities) and inspiration for feminist political work (if women were once equal, they could be equal again). It also gave ancient, medieval and early modern women integral roles in a feminist morality play that recounted how the primordial equality of the sexes was slowly undermined by private property, capitalism and moder-nity. Even today, feminists can read popular books, attend public lectures, go on package tours and buy statues that evoke a glorious matriarchal (or at least, sexually egalitarian) past. Yet academic women's history has abandoned this understanding of the past, and rightly so. In the 1990s, this golden age narrative crumbled under the weight of both empirical research and postmodernist critique. As a result, feminists now have a distant past that is more historically plausible but less positive and less self-referential: a distant past that is, simply, more distant and, therefore, more easily ig-nored.[10]

Fifth, we feminist historians probably cannot help but be influenced by the simple fact that history is now often demeaned in women's studies circles. Our feminist colleagues often see history as dull and plodding; as Jennifer Manion recently commented, 'It is no secret that cutting edge feminist scholarship is more likely found in literature and American studies than history'.[11] They can even see history as un-feminist; as Jane Newman has reported, any feminist research that reaches back before the 1960s now risks being characterised as 'antiquarian – and potentially politically incorrect – knowledge projects'.[12] And worst of all, our colleagues see history as a wretched abyss from which feminists should rightly and quickly walk away; Newman also reports that feminists in the academy – teachers as well as students – are replacing old dreams of past golden ages with its self-satisfying antithesis – a fantasy of an utterly and unremittingly horrible past from which today's feminists have luckily escaped.[13] Some feminist scholars outside history departments continue, of course, to draw on historical insights, and, of course, the turn away from history extends more broadly to general practices in cultural studies that value meaning over causation ('how' over 'why'). Nevertheless, my point here is fairly straightforward: with women's and gender history caricatured as dull, old-fashioned and possibly even politically suspicious, one good defence is to move towards the present ourselves – to render our history seemingly less dull and more relevant by focusing on more recent times.[14]

My final factor – and there could be still more that others will identify – raises the possibility that our expanding appreciation of non-western histories has encouraged a waning attention to the distant past, especially Europe's distant past. In the 1970s, 'sisterhood' tripped easily off our tongues, and virtually all women's history concerned Europe or North America. I think it is possible that the historical tunnel vision of that time made it easier for us to look farther down the tunnel – only European and North American history, to be sure, but more of it. Today, studies of women in Europe and the United States still dominate women's and gender history, but our field now extends to many more world regions than it once did. Might this expansion in spatial breadth be tied to a contraction in temporal reach? For example, *Signs* publishes today different sorts of history from what it featured in the 1970s: *less* pre-1800 western history, *less* history that crosses over several eras and *more* non-western and global history.[15] (Only the predominance of the modern west has stayed constant and, indeed, expanded a bit.) In raising this possibility of a symbiotic link between expanding geographical vision and contracting temporal depth, I do not wish to revive the 'class versus gender' debates of earlier decades in a new 'non-west versus early west' version. This is not an *either/or* situation; we need *both* more non-western history *and* more early history (and sometimes, of course, we get both at once). But for now, the steadfast dominance in feminist history of modern Europe and the United States over both earlier histories and non-western ones may be forcing us to trade off the latter two. Our vision of women's and gender history, which has long been overly focused on the modern west, is thankfully now growing somewhat more panoptic, but we may be contracting myopia.

Remedies

'Is it really the case that the recent past is more important and significant for scholarly inquiry than the more distant past?' Gerda Lerner asked us this question in 2003, when she observed that the colonial era accounts for only 6 per cent of scholarship on US women's history.[16] Kate Haulman has suggested that most feminist historians – always and already attentive to the hermeneutic powers of the past – would respond to this question with an energetic 'Of course not!' ... and then return to studies of the nineteenth and twentieth centuries.[17] We can do better than this and, if we do, we will produce not only better women's and gender history but also better feminist theory.

One fix is very simple: without abandoning our own particular historical specialities and passions, we can start talking more often across historical eras. To get this conversation going, premodernists need to speak a bit more broadly and modernists need to listen a bit more carefully. For their part, feminist classicists, medievalists and early modernists can surely reach out more often beyond our interdisciplinary enclaves, both in terms of the places in which we disseminate our work and the ways in which we pitch our findings. This outreach can break the loop (little pre-1800 coverage → fewer pre-1800 submissions → even less pre-1800 coverage) that now limits the chronological reach of feminist journals and conferences. Editors and conference organisers can help by beating the bushes for pre-1800 submissions and defining special themes in time-inclusive ways, but we feminists who work on early eras must give them the material with which to work. In so doing, we cannot expect our modern colleagues to make leaps across the centuries on their own; we must show them the way. In 2001, E. Jane Burns, who has long delighted medievalists with her wonderfully complex analyses of courtly literature, reached out to a broader audience in a *Signs* essay on 'Courtly Love: Who Needs It?' She caught the attention of *Signs* readers by linking medieval courtly love to the 1995 bestseller *The Rules: Time-Tested Secrets for Capturing the Heart of Mr Right*; she introduced her readers to the latest trends in the study of medieval romance; and she showed how feminist readings of medieval romances can help us today break apart the 'modern cage of rule-bound femininity'.[18] More work of this sort – more pre-1800 historians speaking to the interests of modern historians and contemporary audiences – is just what women's and gender history needs.

Historians of recent centuries can help this conversation by attending more closely to what classicists, medievalists and early modernists are saying. Modern women's history is persistently marred by an extensive series of myths about women in the world before 1500. There was no childhood or adolescence in the European middle ages, right? Wrong.[19] Little affection between wives and husbands? Wrong.[20] No effective birth control before 1500? Wrong.[21] No sexual identities? Wrong.[22] No advocates for women? Wrong again.[23] In all these cases (and there are many others), the distant past is mis-imagined by modern historians as the antithesis of whatever it means to be 'modern'. Silly stereotypes like these have no place in women's and gender history. The women and men who lived long before us were not profoundly 'other' in awful or admirable ways; they were like us in some ways and different from us in others. Women's and gender history is enriched when we attend to these past lives with the same attentiveness we bring to such pressing contemporary differences as class, race, religion, sexuality and world region. Yes, one of the great pleasures of the historian's craft is to see the era we study (whatever era it may be) as *ipso facto* a time of unique and earth-shattering change. Yet this is a dangerous pleasure, one that both reifies the distant past and limits our ability to understand the more recent histories on which we focus.

Most feminist historians can, in other words, reply 'Of course not!' to Lerner and return guilt-free to research on the nineteenth and twentieth centuries. But all of us need to reach out beyond the particular centuries we study to understand what was new, and not new, at that time. We will produce better, richer and wiser histories of women and gender if we attend (at least a bit) to the past histories of the past times we study. We will accomplish something else, too, for histories that take the deeper past into account will help us reinvigorate the now weakened place of history within feminist scholarship more generally. Young feminists today sometimes cavalierly reject the utility of the past, proclaiming proudly that 'we don't much remember'.[24] It is our privileged task, as feminist historians, to respond to such foolishness by working to deepen the remarkably shallow historical foundations on which feminist theory is now being built.

Feminist theory casts a wide net, from activists whose 'theory' is also 'strategy', to postcolonial and psychoanalytic theorists, to feminist theories that are so epistemologically based that they almost become, as Mary Maynard has put it, 'theory about theory'.[25] But whether strategic, middle-range, or highly intellectualised, good theory grows from temporal depth. The partnership of history and theory once relied on history-as-legacy, on history as a story that linked us with past peoples and societies from which we have supposedly descended. This assumption inspired both Bachofen in *Mother-Right* (1861) and Engels in *The Origins of the Family, Private Property and the State* (1884) to view their respective subjects from the distance provided by several thousand years of human history. History-as-legacy has less purchase now than it did in the nineteenth century, and it is especially hard to sustain in feminist scholarship, where attention to difference has rendered absurd the notion that the situation of women today somehow descends from a unitary past.

For feminist theory in the twenty-first century, a different sort of history works best. Joan Scott has judged that 'simply comparing data about women did not get us very far'.[26] I disagree. It has taken us far, and it will take us farther still, especially if we seek to build feminist theory that, in the words of Charlotte Bunch, 'grows out of and guides activism in a continuous spiraling process'. Seeking to demystify theory and root it in feminist practice, Bunch has described theory as a four-stage process: first, description of what exists; second, analysis of why it exists; third, vision of what should exist; and fourth, strategy of how to achieve that vision.[27] Feminist historians, expert in archival recovery, description and analysis, have much to contribute to the development of such grounded and strategic feminist theory.

To put this another way, we feminist historians should more confidently expect that our research – especially, if it digs a bit more deeply into the past – will help to resolve some of the central questions of feminist theory: questions about the persistence of female inequality, about the varied meanings of gender, and about differences among women. In investigating such issues, it is, of course, important for feminist theorists to undertake cross-cultural comparisons as well as temporal ones; we need to look beyond privileged world regions and people, to see, for example, how women's work has been remunerated beyond the west or among the poor or among sexual minorities. But the creation of feminist theory best takes in *both* the contemporary world in all its variety *and* past worlds, too.

We historians know that the passage of time provides new perspectives, clearer understandings and more measured analyses – this is why we pride ourselves that history is more dispassionate than journalism. In a discipline as personally fraught and politically freighted as feminist studies, the distance of the distant past is especially useful. What we cannot yet see in the twentieth century, we can sometimes see more clearly in, say, the fifteenth century. In recent years, for example, each of the three major English-language journals in women's and gender history has devoted a special issue to women and the state, but each also confined consideration of this topic to the world since 1800.[28] The authors and editors in these special issues produced fine scholarship about modern women, suffrage, citizenship and state formation, but none reached quite as far as Martha

Howell who, working on medieval cities, has posited that female access to citizenship might be linked to the extent to which citizenship was 'equivalent to access to rule'.[29] When citizenship in Howell's cities conferred little political access, women were citizens; when citizenship was equivalent to political power, women were excluded. This is a hugely important insight, one that is painful to acknowledge in our own time, but easier to see in past times. As a US citizen, I have had ample opportunity to ponder Howell's observation in the past few years: the shredding of the electoral process in Florida in December 2000; the inauguration in January 2001 of a president not elected by popular vote; and the commitment in 2003 of US soldiers to a war then opposed by the majority of US citizens. Perhaps, citizenship – such a prized achievement for US women less than ninety years ago – now has much less political meaning. This is a possibility that modern historians will have to answer, but it was raised by contemplating the distant past. For the insights that our own distance from a subject can bring, if for no other reason, the distant past has much to offer feminist theory.

***

It takes my breath away to hear young feminists reject history and embrace the supposed value of *not* remembering. As feminist historians, we know the pleasures of remembering, and we know also the importance of such memories to the achievement of a more feminist future. Feminism needs history, deep history as well as recent history. It is our special brief, as feminist historians, to ensure that history is not only ever-present (even to those feminists who prefer to ignore it) but also rich, plausible and well-informed. In so doing, all of us can benefit from reading more deeply into the past. We should not abandon the twentieth century and embrace the Middle Ages, and indeed, if all of us did so, the historical vision of women's and gender history would be limited in newly worrisome ways. But all of us can think more wisely about women's and gender history by reading across temporal divides. Let us search out the earlier histories of the specific subjects we study; let us also read eclectically, familiarising ourselves with the best, most illuminating, and even most provocative histories that each era has to offer. Feminist history requires more than the short view and so, too, does the achievement of a more feminist future.

Notes

This brief commentary borrows freely from chapter three of my *History Matters: Patriarchy and the Challenge of Feminism* (Philadelphia: University of Pennsylvania Press and Manchester: Manchester University Press, 2006). Readers will find more extended discussion there, but I have updated here my figures for journals and conferences in women's and gender history. I thank the Huntington Library in San Marino, California for a fellowship during which I wrote this chapter.

1. I use 'we' advisedly, aware that it sails over two patches of rough water: first, that all readers of *Gender & History* are not self-identified as feminist historians and second, that many diverse circumstances separate me from other feminist historians. By eliding here differences among feminist historians, women's historians and gender historians, I hope to make common cause with all readers; by using the first-person plural, I mean to evoke our shared interest in the past, not to claim any shared subjectivity.

2. The figures for the 2008 Berkshire Conference on the History of Women are as follows: 78 per cent of papers dealt with post-1800 topics (535 of 689; of these, 338 dealt with topics since 1900, usually 'living memory' topics from the 1930s to the present); 17 per cent treated the early modern era from 1500 to 1800 (117 papers); and 5 per cent discussed premodern eras before 1500 (37 papers). I am grateful to Susan Amussen for providing me with an uncorrected proof of the programme; my numbers might differ slightly from the final version. I excluded from my calculations non-research papers, roundtables for which no paper titles were provided and papers whose chronological focus could not be determined from their titles. If a paper spanned two or more eras, I placed it in the earliest possible.

3. At the 2007 meeting of the IFRWH, 85 per cent of speakers addressed the nineteenth and twentieth centuries; 7 per cent treated the early modern era; and 8 per cent considered topics before 1500. These figures are drawn from the programme published in the *IFRWH Newsletter* 42 (2007), accessed online at <http://www.ifrwh.com/> on 6 December 2007. I excluded from my calculation papers whose chronological focus could not be determined; if a paper spanned two or more eras, I placed it in the earliest possible. At the 2004 conference of the IFRWH, chronological coverage was slightly better: 80 per cent modern; 11 per cent early modern; 9 per cent premodern.

4. I have here updated figures tabulated for 2001–04 in Bennett, *History Matters*, p. 32, but the update (adding data for 2005–07) scarcely changes the overall trend. For 2001–04, 87 per cent of articles were modern; 11 per cent early modern; and 2 per cent premodern.

5. Each of these matters is discussed more fully in chapter three of *History Matters*; in chapters four to six, I offer extended examples of how a consideration of the distant past can improve both the writing of modern history and the development of feminist theory.

6. Kelly's essay on the Renaissance is now most readily available in her posthumous *Women, History and Theory* (Chicago: University of Chicago Press, 1984), pp. 19–50.

7. For a brief summary of the deficiencies of women's history in the 1970s, see Bennett, *History Matters*, p. 65.

8. Interview in *Chicago Tribune*, 25 May 1916.

9. Lynn Hunt, 'Against Presentism', *Perspectives* (newsletter of the American Historical Association), May 2002. Accessed online on 12 December 2007 at: <http://www.historians.org/perspectives/issues/2002/0205/0205pre1.cfm>.

10. For critiques of this golden age narrative, see especially: Cynthia Eller, *The Myth of Matriarchal Prehistory: Why an Invented Past Won't Give Women a Future* (Boston: Beacon Press, 2000); Lauren E. Talalay, 'A Feminist Boomerang: The Great Goddess of Greek Prehistory', *Gender & History* 6 (1994), pp. 165–83; Judith M. Bennett, 'Medieval Women, Modern Women: Across the Great Divide', in David Aers (ed.), *Culture and History 1350–1600: Essays on English Communities, Identities, and Writing* (Detroit: Wayne State University Press, 1992), pp. 147–75, and revised in Ann-Louise Shapiro (ed.), *Feminists Revision History* (New Brunswick: Rutgers University Press, 1994), pp. 47–72.

11. Jennifer Manion, 'Calling all Liberals: Connecting Feminist Theory, Activism, and History', in Jim Downs and Jennifer Manion (eds), *Taking Back the Academy! History of Activism, History as Activism* (New York: Routledge, 2004), pp. 145–59, here p. 155.

12. Jane O. Newman, 'The Present and Our Past: Simone de Beauvoir, Descartes, and Presentism in the Historiography of Feminism', in Robyn Wiegman (ed.), *Women's Studies on Its Own* (Durham, NC: Duke University Press, 2002), pp. 141–73, here p. 144. Newman's article focuses on the teaching of women's studies in the United States.

13. Newman, 'The Present and Our Past'.
14. Kate Haulman has commented on the seemingly greater political importance of more modern projects; see her 'Room in Back: Before and Beyond the Nation in Women's and Gender History', *Journal of Women's History* 15 (2003), pp. 167–71, here p. 168.
15. The comparative numbers for history articles, review essays and reports in *Signs* are as follows: (a) for 1975–78: modern west, 18; early modern west, 4; premodern west, 4; transhistorical west 5; non-western, 7 (two transhistorical, 5 modern); global, 0; (b) for 2001–04: modern west, 5; early modern west, 1; premodern west, 0; transhistorical west, 0; non-western, 2; global, 1.
16. Gerda Lerner in a forum on 'Considering the State of U.S. Women's History', *Journal of Women's History* 15 (2003), pp 145–63, here p. 147. See also her 'U.S. Women's History, Past, Present, and Future', *Journal of Women's History* 16 (2004), pp. 10–27.
17. Haulman, 'Room in Back', p. 168.
18. E. Jane Burns, 'Courtly Love: Who Needs It? Recent Feminist Work in the Medieval French Tradition', *Signs: A Journal of Women in Culture and Society* 27 (2001), pp. 23–57, here p. 50.
19. The major source for this myth is Philippe Ariès, *Centuries of Childhood: A Social History of Family Life*, tr. Robert Baldick (published in French in 1960 and New York: Vintage Books, 1962). Among the many rebuttals of this thesis, see Barbara A. Hanawalt, *Growing Up in Medieval London: The Experience of Childhood in History* (New York: Oxford University Press, 1993); James A. Schultz, *The Knowledge of Childhood in the German Middle Ages, 1100–1350* (Philadelphia: University of Pennsylvania Press, 1995).
20. See Lawrence Stone, *The Family, Sex, and Marriage in England, 1500–1800* (New York: Harper & Row, 1977) for the myth; for a summary of its many rebuttals, see Peter Fleming, *Family and Household in Medieval England* (New York: Palgrave, 2001), pp. 53–9.
21. John M. Riddle, *Contraception and Abortion from the Ancient World to the Renaissance* (Cambridge: Harvard University Press, 1992); Peter Biller, 'Birth Control in the West in the Thirteenth and Early Fourteenth Centuries', *Past & Present* 94 (1982), pp. 3–26.
22. Ruth Mazo Karras, 'Prostitution and the Question of Sexual Identity in Medieval Europe', *Journal of Women's History* 11 (1999), pp. 159–77, and responses pp. 178–98. See also Ruth Mazo Karras on chastity as a sexual identity in her *Sexuality in Medieval Europe: Doing Unto Others* (New York: Routledge, 2005), pp. 28–58.
23. Gerda Lerner, *The Creation of Feminist Consciousness: From the Middle Ages to Eighteen-Seventy* (New York: Oxford University Press, 1993); Beatrice Gottlieb, 'The Problem of Feminism in the Fifteenth Century', in Julius Kirshner and Suzanne F. Wemple (eds), *Women of the Medieval World* (Oxford: Blackwell, 1985), pp. 337–64.
24. As cited in Anne Clark Bartlett, 'Defining the Terms: Postfeminism as an Ideology of Cool', *Medieval Feminist Forum* 34 (2002), pp. 25–9, here p. 28.
25. Mary Maynard, 'Beyond the "Big Three": The Development of Feminist Theory in the 1990s', *Women's History Review* 4 (1995), pp. 259–81, here p. 273.
26. Joan Scott, 'Feminism's History', *Journal of Women's History* 16 (2004), pp. 10–29, here p. 24.
27. Charlotte Bunch, 'Not By Degrees: Feminist Theory and Education', in Charlotte Bunch and Sandra Pollack (eds), *Learning Our Way: Essays in Feminist Education* (Trumansburg, NY: Crossing Press, 1983), pp. 248–60, esp. pp. 251–3.
28. *Gender & History* 13:3 (2001); *Journal of Women's History* 13:4 (2002); *Women's History Review* 11:4 (2002) and 12:1 (2003).
29. Martha C. Howell, 'Citizenship and Gender: Women's Political Status in Northern Medieval Cities', in Mary Erler and Maryanne Kowaleski (eds), *Women and Power in the Middle Ages* (Athens: University of Georgia Press, 1988), pp. 37–60, here p. 47.

INDEX

Printed and bound by CPI Group (UK) Ltd, Croydon, CR0 4YY

13/04/2025

14656563-0004